NORTH SEA ARCHAEOL

North Sea Archaeologies:
A Maritime Biography, 10,000 BC to AD 1500

ROBERT VAN DE NOORT

OXFORD

UNIVERSITY PRESS

Great Clarendon Street, Oxford OX2 6DP

United Kingdom

Oxford University Press is a department of the University of Oxford.
It furthers the University's objective of excellence in research, scholarship,
and education by publishing worldwide. Oxford is a registered trade mark of
Oxford University Press in the UK and in certain other countries

First published 2011
First published in paperback 2012

British Library Cataloguing in Publication Data

Data available

Library of Congress Cataloging in Publication Data
Library of Congress Control Number: 2010937009

ISBN 978–0–19–956620–4
ISBN 978–0–19–965708–7 (Pbk)

Printed and bound by
CPI Group (UK) Ltd, Croydon CRO 4YY

Preface

The aim of this book is to explore how an archaeological study that is focused on a fluid maritime landscape differs from one based on a solid terrestrial landscape, and what we—as archaeologists who overwhelmingly live and work on land—can learn from such a study. From the outset, it needs emphasizing that this study does not presume that land and sea were mutually exclusive realms, or represent genuine or metaphorical opposites in the past or present. The sea itself is too dynamic, its edges are too blurred, and people's knowledge of the sea has always been far too great for such a concept to be given much validity. Nevertheless, the sea is different from the land in many different aspects: the sea is active and dynamic, often unpredictable and unreliable; it continues to be a co-constructor of landscapes; it offers a deviant place where the establishment found it difficult to exercise its powers; and it is a place where special skills and knowledge are required, not held by those unfamiliar with the sea. In these senses, the sea is an alternative space where one can explore ways in which people in the past engaged with the world they inhabited.

The selection of the North Sea as the focus for this study relates directly to my own background. Over the past three decades, I have worked as an archaeologist on the opposite sides of the North Sea. As a student, and in my early career, I participated in a number of excavations on the Dutch coast and the coastal hinterland. Later, through the work of the Humber Wetlands Project, I became familiar with England's east-coast archaeology. The discovery of a fragment of a Bronze Age sewn-plank boat on a beach in East Yorkshire by Richard Middleton in 1997, and my involvement in the publication of what we called the 'Kilnsea boat', drew my attention to the North Sea proper. Researching the literature on Bronze Age boats, I realized the wealth of the resource offered by these craft and how little endeavour had been made to place these into broader archaeological contexts. This, in turn, led to ideas on the transformative powers of the North Sea.

Some of the arguments presented here have been aired at conferences and presentations around the North Sea basin, and the debates that ensued from these are recognized for having helped to shape this book. I also wish to acknowledge the participants of the English Heritage Marine Research Framework project for their knowledge and wisdom. I am particularly grateful to the following who read and commented on draft chapters: Bryony Coles, Alan Outram, Hans Peeters, Jason Rogers, Stephen Rippon, Fraser Sturt, and Christer Westerdahl. As always, I am indebted to Jess Collins for improving on my English and to Michael Rouillard for producing the line-drawings and maps.

I wish to thank Amy Ball and Andrew Mackay at the Craven Museum and Gallery, Skipton, for access to the two small axes from the Dogger Bank, and David Field (English Heritage) for drawing my attention to these. Others, including David Campbell and Toby Heppel, I thank for making me explain things simply. Finally, I wish to thank my sons, Will and Michael, for their companionship on the trips to the Oslofjord, the Østfold and Bohuslän in 2006, the east coast of Jutland in 2007 and the Shetland and Orkney archipelagos in 2009 that completed my research around the North Sea.

Contents

List of figures

List of abbreviations

BAR   British Archaeological Reports

BROB   Berichten van de Rijksdienst voor het Oudheidkundig Bodemonderzoek

CBA   Council for British Archaeology

IJNA   International Journal of Nautical Archaeology

JAS   Journal of Archaeological Science

LBK   Linear band ceramic (Linearbandkeramik)

PPS   Proceedings of the Prehistoric Society

PSAS   Proceedings of the Society of Antiquaries of Scotland

ROB   Rijksdienst voor het Oudheidkundig Bodemonderzoek

RGZM   Römisch-Germanishes Zentralmuseum

Note to the reader

All radiocarbon dates used in this book were calibrated according to the maximum intercept method (Stuiver and Reimer 1986), using OxCal 4.0 (Bronk Ramsey 2006), and with end points rounded outwards to 10 years (Mook 1986).

For geographical names, the English version has been used where this has a general use, notably for the names of countries, major rivers and large islands, but not for the Danish island of Sjælland, to distinguish it from the Dutch province of Zeeland. Local names have been used where no English version exists or where one exists but has no common currency.

1

Introduction

the sea is 'good to think'

A 'MARITIME TURN'

The locale of nearly all archaeological research is land. Whether one studies landscapes, excavates sites such as monuments, cemeteries or settlements, or analyses material culture, the basis for study and debate comes nearly always from terrestrial contexts. Most land-locked archaeologists simply disregard the seas and the oceans, and where land is bordered by a saltwater landscape, this is all too often eagerly adopted as the convenient boundary of the study areas. Others, studying exotic material culture, are more interested in the terrestrial find spots than the maritime journeys of objects that have travelled long distances. Some archaeologists have studied the exploitation of the sea from the land, but rarely stray beyond the functional utilization of the sea and coast for food. A small number of archaeologists work on ships and waterside structures directly related to shipping activities, but this group of maritime archaeologists, with their own conferences and journals, have had very little impact on the thinking of their land-locked colleagues.

The principal reason for choosing a sea over a landmass as the geographical centre for this archaeological study is that it provides an alternative space in which to explore the ways that people related with, and connected to, the world around them. As a part of the world that is physically unmodified and unalterable by humanity (at least until very recently), the sea offers an alluring contrast to the terrestrial landscape, with its imprint of human existence visible everywhere. This inability to change and to control the sea has, and had, profound impacts on how people engage with it. Gilles Deleuze developed this concept furthest, most notably in his study of *Desert islands* (1953), in which the sea is very much seen as a different space, the 'realm of the unbound, unconstricted, and free'. The sea has since come to be seen as 'the Deleuzian Ocean' (Connery 2006: 497). One could say that this study offers a 'maritime turn' in terrestrial-dominated archaeology and, by doing so, sets out to investigate aspects of human behaviour that have been, to varying extents, disregarded, overlooked or ignored. These aspects include a range of practical matters: for example how sea-level change was understood and explained in the past, and the different ways landscapes are experienced from a boat, rather than on foot. They also include theoretical aspects of human behaviour, notably our fundamental relationship with the environment we inhabit and travel through or across, and the study of what was frequently the margin or lay outside: a place where establishment, conservatism and convention could be challenged. Sometimes, the human relationship with the sea appears to challenge the premodern–modern dichotomy, frequently invoked by archaeological and anthropological commentators alike, because many ancient beliefs, superstitions, skills and practices linked to seafaring, and engaging with the sea, have survived into the modern era. To paraphrase Claude Levis-Strauss, the sea is 'good to think'. This book, then, is in essence about human relationships with seas in the past, explored from an archaeological perspective; the North Sea is used here as a case study.

The themes that this study addresses explore aspects of the wider nature–society debate. The realization in the past three decades that nature is not something that exists and existed as an external aspect of people's lives has produced some of the more stimulating works in landscape studies in archaeology, anthropology, and geography, but this has now resulted in an increasingly dominant perception of a landscape where nature and wild(er)ness are always human constructs (e.g. Cosgrove 1984; Cosgrove and Daniels 1988), and one where 'nature' and 'culture' frequently stand in a dualistic opposition from each other, as in the concept of *domus versus agrios* in Neolithic studies (e.g. Hodder 1990; Thomas 1991). This is a position that has been challenged at the beginning of the 21st century. The central position of *Homo sapiens* in landscape studies, to the detriment of the study of the roles played by animals and plants—and increasingly also by non-living elements of the world such as climate, soils, rivers, mountains, and, indeed, the sea—is no longer considered fitting for a more ethically conscious era, where animal welfare, tree preservation, and landscape protection have become embedded in everyday life (cf. Ingold 2000; Whatmore 2000; Descola 2005). The recognition of the impact of the carbon-fuelled economy in stimulating climate change, with all its environmental consequences, also calls for a less anthropogenic-centred study of the world. This new debate has gained much currency throughout the humanities and social sciences, and the current concerns with climate change have contributed significantly to a renewed and urgent reappraisal of how people interact and interrelate with the world they inhabit (e.g. Harrison, Pile, and Thrift 2004).

In most disciplines that are concerned with aspects of the nature–society debate, recent arguments are played out overwhelmingly in terrestrial settings and this is true for anthropology, geography, history, and archaeology. Of course, exceptions exist and among the most important for archaeology are Barry Cunliffe's (2001) *Facing the ocean*, and the *World Archaeology* special on Seascapes (edited by Gabriel Cooney, 2003). Both works are presented as departures from a bias that favours the land; nevertheless, the dominant perception of the sea remains one as viewed from the land. Studies of the fuzzy boundary or blurred zone between land and sea, the coastal wetlands, have to some extent adopted aspects of the current nature–society debate (e.g. Van de Noort and O'Sullivan 2006; Peeters 2007). As a rule, postmodernists—with post-processual archaeologists embracing the universal phenomenological approach manifestly among them—have largely sought to undertake their research on the land, with the sea rarely playing a role in their considerations, even though there are some interesting exceptions to this rule (e.g. Rainbird 2007). Elsewhere in the humanities and social sciences context, the sea has played an important role in moving scholars beyond their evidence-based considerations of institutions, objects, and practices, and in unlocking the emotionally charged systems that are fundamental for understanding the past, most notably in Alain Corbin's (1994) *The lure of the sea*. The 'maritime turn' has been described as 'confronting the terrestrial character of knowledge disciplines and administrative practice' (Connery 2006, 495–8), and also as 'challenging the post-modern attempt to annihilate the ocean' (cf. Steinberg 2001), albeit that this latter expression refers not necessarily to academic discourses.

Placing a sea centre stage in an archaeological study does not make for an easy quest, and there are both physical and cognitive barriers that will need to be overcome. The principal physical barrier concerns the survival of material culture in the marine environment. Relatively little material evidence of past activities survives in the sea and along its edges. The mechanical forces of the waves, winds, and currents destroy much of what people have built on the coasts, and the metabolism of marine microbes leaves few organic remains untouched, resulting in the destruction of all but the most recent craft, unless silts and muds provide protection. Thus, by its very nature, the sea is hardly the ideal environment to preserve the ancient remains necessary for this venture, and the archaeological record shows large gaps and cracks. Furthermore, cognitive barriers are formed not only by the distance in time which all archaeologists encounter in their everyday work, but also by the very different geographical setting of this study, and the different mental attitudes that are associated with it. Even if terrestrial archaeologists do not recognize this fundamental dichotomy, those working on the sea, from fishermen to sailors, and maritime archaeologists, all agree that the landsmen cannot even begin to understand their lives (Kirby and Hinkkanen 2000: 186).

INTRODUCING THE NORTH SEA

The name for the body of water at the centre of this study has changed over time. The ancient Greeks and Romans invariably referred to it as the Northern Ocean (*Oceanus Septentrionalis* by Tacitus) or Sea, or the German Ocean or Sea (*Germanikos Okeanos* by Ptolemy, *Mare Germanicum* by Pliny the Younger), and in the early Middle Ages as the *Mare Britannicum, Frisie Mare, Fresonicus Oceanus, Magnum Mare, Occidentale Mare* and a range of translations of these terms.

Referring to seas by reference to the principal directions of the compass would have been common in the later Middle Ages (Westerdahl 1995a). The first written occurrence of the name 'North Sea', is believed to be on a map of 1526 by Jan de Beeldsnijder (*De caerte van de Oostersche See*), but the historical geographer Ferjan Ormeling (2000) has argued that this had been the popular name for the sea for the people of the Low Countries, and in particular the Frisians, for many centuries. From their perspective, there was a middle sea (*Middelzee*, now a silted-up area within the Dutch province of Friesland), an eastern sea (*Oostzee*, i.e. the Baltic), a southern sea (*Zuiderzee*, now the inland lake of the IJsselmeer), and sometimes a western sea (*Westzee* being the southern part of the North Sea basin and the English Channel) (Figure 1). The name 'North Sea' referred principally to the water body around Dogger Bank and further north. It has been argued that the predominance of the Dutch mapmakers in the advent of cartography in the 16th and 17th centuries ensured that the name 'North Sea' became commonplace, but alternatives such as the English name 'German Ocean' (after the classical *Mare Germanicum*) survived in scholarly language and on maps throughout the 19th and into the early 20th century, up to the start of World War I, by which time this name became somewhat politically inconvenient.

Just as with its name, as a geographical feature, the North Sea has never been fixed and indeed continues to change. The North Sea basin is part of the northern Atlantic Ocean and there is no logical or geographically distinctive feature that separates the North Sea from the Atlantic other than the relative shallowness of the basin between the British Isles to the west, and continental Europe to the east (Figure 2). However, for the purpose of this book, the North Sea is delimited on the west by the east coast of Britain and the Scottish archipelagos of the Orkneys and the Shetlands. On the east side, the focus of this book is delimited by the coasts of Norway south of Bergen, the Bohuslän province coast of Sweden, the shores of Denmark, the north-western coasts of Germany, as well as those of the Netherlands and Belgium, with a small part of the French coast around Dunkirk. The northern delimitation is formed by a line between the Shetland isles and the city of Bergen in Norway, and the southern delimitation by the Strait of Dover. On all sides, the concept of what

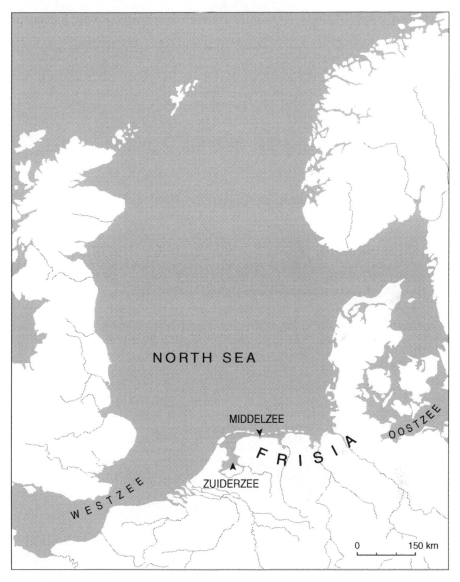

Figure 1. The North Sea: the Frisians' view of the North Sea in relation to the Westzee, Zuiderzee, Oostzee, and Middelzee

is and was the boundary has been broadly interpreted, reflecting human rather than geographical definitions of where the sea begins and where it ends.

The origin of the North Sea basin falls in the Mesozoic, when it was formed as part of the widening of the Atlantic Ocean. Among the oldest features within this basin are a probable impact crater (the Outer Silverpit, 130 km east of the Yorkshire coast; Stewart and Allen 2002), and the Norwegian

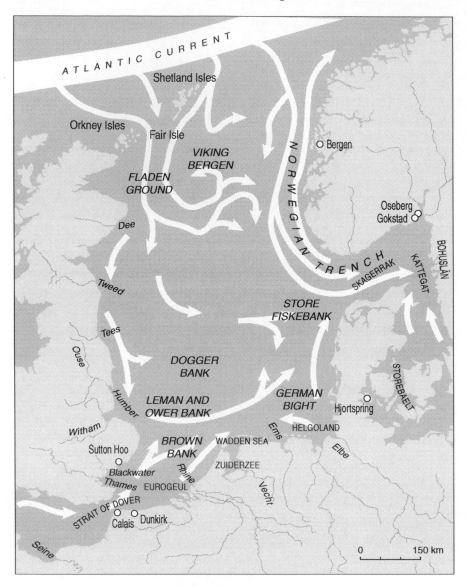

Figure 2. Places and regions mentioned in chapter 1

Trench, the only genuinely deep part of the North Sea with a depth of 250–700 m, which trails the south-west coast of Norway. The North Sea basin was given its shape in the Quaternary, during which period subsidence accelerated and sedimentary deposits filled much of the basin. In the central parts of the North Sea, Quaternary deposits are in excess of 1 km deep (Cameron et al. 1992). A number of features predate the Holocene inundation of this basin, which have been recorded through extensive marine geophysical research. The best known of these features are the extensive sandbanks of the Dogger Bank, which formed at the mouth of the Early Pleistocene River Rhine and was extensively reworked by the ice sheets (Veenstra 1965; Zuther, Brockamp, and Clauer 2000). Later features include subglacial valleys formed during the Elsterian and Saalian glaciations, originally with depths up to 400m, as well as subglacial meltwater channels or tunnel valleys (Praeg 2003), and dendritic river channels, through which major rivers carried meltwater northwards, and extensive sandbanks. Until the end of the Saalian, huge proglacial lakes existed in the North Sea basin, formed by glacial meltwater trapped between the ice front and the chalk barrier formed by the tectonic uplift of the Weald–Artois anticline (Gibbard 1995). The breaking of the barrier and the formation of the Channel had occurred by the end of the Saalian, even though some smaller-scale erosion may have occurred earlier, at the end of the Elsterian. By the end of the Devensian ice age, glacial, glaciofluvial, and fluvial activities had filled the valleys and smoothed the land surface, leaving an undulating landscape with many isolated lakes and sinuous rivers much akin to modern Jutland in Denmark, or the Holderness region in Yorkshire, England.

During the Late-glacial and early Holocene, this landscape became increasingly inundated as sea-level rose when more water was released from the ice sheets. The onset of inundation and development of the North Sea from *c.* 13,000 cal BC has been reconstructed and presented on a number of palaeogeographic maps (e.g. Shennan and Andrews 2000). The survival of 'Doggerland' as a peninsula around 8000 cal BC, and as an island until *c.* 5500 cal BC, has been well recorded. Its significance as *terra firma* within the developing North Sea lies not only in its availability as an area of human habitation into the Neolithic period (Coles 1998), but also in its specific biogeography and in the social memories of the people who travelled, traded, and lived on this submerging land. Similarly, with the northern and southern marine incursions joining around 6000 cal BC, and Britain becoming an island, a series of larger and smaller islands may have existed in the southern North Sea basin which would have enabled contacts across the North Sea to take the form, for a relatively short period, of short-distance island-hopping rather than sea crossings.

The shape of the North Sea has been strongly influenced by Post-glacial tectonic movements, also known as the glacio-isostatic uplift or Post-glacial rebound. The tectonic plates in the northern part of the North Sea had been pressed down by the sheer weight of the ice sheets, but the disappearance of the ice from the region caused the previously lowered land to rise in reaction. Thus, while the southern part of England and the French, Belgian, Dutch, German, and southern Danish coasts have all experienced relative land fall since the onset of the Post-glacial, the Scottish and northern English coasts, most of the Danish and the Swedish and Norwegian coasts have all been uplifted in the past 13,000 years (Figure 3). As a general rule,

Figure 3. First impressions of the North Sea: (A) the rocky nature of the northern North Sea coast; (B) the sandy nature of the southern North Sea coast

to the south of a line from the Humber to southern Jutland and through Funen, tectonic rise and sea-level change have augmented one another, and what was land here at the beginning of the Holocene has become sea. The picture to the north of this line is somewhat more complicated. Initially, the Post-glacial eustatic sea-level rise outpaced the isostatic rebound, resulting in relative sea-level rise, and during the early part of the Holocene extensive tracts of land were submerged. However, from *c.* 6000 cal BC onwards, eustatic sea-level rise slowed down and tectonic uplift raised the land faster than the waters rose, resulting in relative sea-level fall, reclaiming land from the sea or creating raised beaches, especially in Scotland, southern Norway, and western Sweden. Obviously, these general rules are locally and regionally counteracted by processes of sedimentation and peat growth, the depression of the North Sea basin itself through the weight of its water and sediments, the collapse of the ice sheet forebulge, and the action of people in the very recent past.

Throughout the past 13,000 years or so, the edges of the North Sea have been blurred by the development of the rivers that flow in this sea (Figure 4). With the melting of the ice sheets in the Late-glacial, many rivers in the lowlands surrounding the southern North Sea basin braided because the retreating ice sheets prevented effective drainage of the land. Once the ice sheets and any other 'nick-points' had disappeared, rivers incised often deeply where the geology comprised soft material, reflecting the contemporary sea-level of the Post-glacial at about −20 m OD. With the rising sea-level, estuaries retreated upstream, and the former river channels filled with sediments; further sea-level rise and reduced river-channel gradients caused many rivers to widen beyond the confines of the older channels, and wide floodplains developed, locally associated with extensive peatland formation. Illustrating this dynamic interaction between eustatic sea-level rise and estuary development by an example, the onset of the different phases of river development for the Humber have been estimated at *c.* 12,000 cal BC for the river braiding phase, before 10,000 cal BC for the channel incision phase, shortly after 10,000 cal BC for the channel aggradation phase, and *c.* 5000 cal BC for the floodplain aggradation phase. The earliest peatlands developed in this extended wetland from *c.* 3200 cal BC (Van de Noort 2004a: 18–29). The impact of the glacio-isostatic rebound for the Humber is considered to be minimal, as the 'spill' of the British glacio-isostatic 'seesaw' is around this estuary.

The mapping of the Post-glacial and early Holocene creation and development of the North Sea has been the subject of several modern studies, the interest in this area having developed, at least in part, as a reaction to concerns of sea-level rise as a consequence of carbon-fuelled climate change. Such work includes both North Sea-wide (Shennan and Andrews 2000) and smaller-scale work (e.g. Lotze and Reise 2005). Most recently, 3D seismic reflection data collated by the oil, gas, and aggregates industry have been utilized to produce

Figure 4. A topographic and bathymetric map of the North Sea region (Source data from the GEBCO_08 Grid, version 2009. http://www.gebco.net)

digital maps of the floor of the North Sea, which are used to protect areas of higher potential for containing archaeological sites from further development, and could potentially be used for directed archaeological research in the future (Gaffney, Thomson, and Fitch 2007; Gaffney, Fitch, and Smith 2009; Peeters, Murphy, and Flemming 2009).

STUDYING MARITIME ARCHAEOLOGIES: EXPLORING THE SOURCES

A well-informed archaeology of the North Sea is inevitably a multidisciplinary study, and this study has worked with geographical, archaeological, historical, and anthropological material ranging from sunken ships to ancient sagas, and from palaeogeographic maps to studies of fishermen in the 1950s. It is no exaggeration to say that the North Sea is one of the best-studied marine units anywhere in the world, and it is therefore a good choice for a marine-focused study of the past. In this section, the sources that underpin this study are introduced.

Geography has an increasing amount to offer to the archaeological study of the North Sea. Its contribution takes the form, principally, of an understanding of how the North Sea developed over the period since the last glacial maximum, around 18,000 BP, and how sea-level change affected the coasts and rivers flowing into the North Sea. Much of the current research is undertaken within the context of concerns over accelerated sea-level change resulting from climate change. The impact of higher global temperatures on the polar ice sheets and the resulting higher sea-levels, alongside research linked to oil and gas extraction, offshore windfarm construction and gravel extraction, are behind a number of currently funded research projects mapping future scenarios of shoreline evolution.

The pioneer in the field of North Sea development was the Dutch geologist S. Jelgersma, who, in a series of papers (e.g. 1961; 1979), mapped the advancing coastline during the late Pleistocene and early Holocene, from 19,500 to 7000 cal BC, mainly using bathymetric data of the underwater depth of the sea floor. Importantly, this was the first work to show the survival of the relatively higher grounds of Dogger Bank as an island around 8000 cal BC. More recent research, incorporating extensive coring programmes through which palaeoenvironmental macro- and microfossils could be identified and dated by the radiocarbon method, has added significant detail (e.g. Shennan and Andrews 2000; Shennan and Horton 2002). Combining bathymetric data with the dated cores offered the significant advance of being able to include the effect of the isostatic rebound on the North Sea. This allowed for a much-improved understanding of coastal developments, not simply in terms of the advancing coastline, but especially the impact of sea-level rise on the rivers and estuaries, which changed the lowlands around the North Sea ahead of the advancing coastline. In this context, it is the norm to refer to relative sea-level change, with the level of the sea measured against the local land-level which changed throughout the Holocene period because of the isostatic rebound. The project produced a series of palaeogeographic maps of the North Sea basin between 8000 cal BC and 2500 cal BC, which will be used below (see chapter 3) to describe the emerging North Sea in some detail.

A new sea-level curve for the southern North Sea produced by Karl-Ernst Behre (2007), based mainly on palaeoenvironmental samples from the German Bight and surrounding areas but including archaeological data-points, showed significant correspondence with the sea-level curve produced by British researchers, at least for the period up to 5000 cal BC (ibid. 84). However, for the more recent part of the Holocene, the Behre sea-level curve diverges from the one produced by Shennan and Andrews (2000), and whereas the latter produced a continuously rising sea-level, Behre identified seven periods of sea-level fall in the period after 3000 cal BC. In the recognition and naming of periods of sea-level fall and rise, Behre belongs to a long-standing tradition of coastal geographers on the continental side of the North Sea. Their regional work has shown aspects of the dynamics of the interaction of the sea and the land, resulting in the identification of periods of marine transgressions and regressions, notably those traditionally referred to as the Calais and Dunkirk marine transgressive deposits. However, the most recent advances in Dutch coastal geology (e.g. De Mulder et al. 2003; Weerts et al. 2005), combining geostatistics and modern computing capacity, have produced three-dimensional models of the coastal lithostratigraphy. This research has shown that alongside sea-level, regional basin topography, sediment supply and regional neotectonics are important factors controlling coastal development. Lithostratigraphic units found along the length of the North Sea coast were found not to originate in particular periods, and chronology and geogenetics have now been separated so that the entire Calais/Dunkirk classification no longer has validity.

It is worth noting that periods of marine transgressions and regressions have also been observed for the Thames estuary, signified by Tilbury transgression phases (Devoy et al. 1979). Further north, for example in the Humber Wetlands, a number of Roman sites including a small town at Adlingfleet at the confluence of the rivers Trent and Ouse, were located on marine sediments, implying that the sea had retreated or regressed for a considerable period of time before later transgression deposited new layers of clay on top of the sites (Van de Noort 2004a: 118–9). The dynamic nature of coastal change, especially after *c.* 3000 cal BC, and opportunities for human engagement with this should not be underestimated. High-resolution palaeo-geographic maps of coastlines and low-lying areas directly affected by the North Sea exist in great detail for the Netherlands (Zagwijn 1986) with a second edition of the 1:50,000 geological maps now available digitally, but these 3D-lithostratigraphical maps no longer include chronostratigraphical information (Weerts et al. 2005: 167). For the British, French, Belgian, German, and Danish coasts, palaeogeographic maps exist at considerably lower resolutions.

Only since the beginning of this millennium has it become possible to map the landscape of the North Sea proper, principally using high-resolution 3D seismic reflection data gathered in support of the exploitation of the North Sea for its natural resources. Reinterpretation of these data allow for the mapping of the main geographical features of the North Sea, such as rivers, coastlines, salt domes, and wetlands. This has now been developed success-fully by a research team of geographers and archaeologists at Birmingham University undertaking the North Sea Palaeolandscape Project (Gaffney, Thomson, and Fitch 2007; Gaffney, Fitch, and Smith 2009). The team has produced an atlas for the area of the southern North Sea basin covered by the mega-survey for the 10,000–7500 BP period. Sediment cores containing proxies of palaeoenvironmental change have been correlated with this atlas, and something of the vegetation of the landscape is emerging. To date, it has not yet been able to correlate archaeological finds with this map, or to anchor the landscape features to an absolute chronology. However, with further work, including the extension of the atlas to include the Dogger Bank area, and further collaboration with North Sea fishermen, this will only be a matter of time.

In terms of the contribution of archaeology to our understanding of the sea and human interaction, the finds from the North Sea itself are rather limited. Evidence from the edges, however, is bountiful. Fishermen working the relatively higher areas of Dogger Bank and Brown Bank have caught in their driftnets large amounts of animal bone and some human artefacts relating to the habitation of this area into the Neolithic (Louwe Kooijmans 1971; Verhart 1995; Glimmerveen et al. 2004). Bryony Coles (1998) renamed the North Sea basin 'Doggerland', drawing attention to the continued terrestrial life, and potential for human activity, on the former land surface of the North Sea before it was flooded in the Neolithic. There are a large number of studies that consider the impact of sea-level change on coastal communities, ranging from the Mesolithic in north-eastern England, through the changes in Viking Scandinavia towards the end of the first millennium AD, to studies of the Frisian islands and coasts in the early Middle Ages, which will be discussed in later chapters.

On land, much research on the edges of the North Sea has been undertaken. This includes investigations of Mesolithic-period shell middens, Neolithic fishweirs, Bronze Age salterns, Iron Age artificial mounds known as terpen, Roman forts and ports, early medieval trading settlements, and medieval ports, towns, and other settlements that flourished because of their connectedness to each other across the sea. Some of this archaeological material was marine in nature originally, but isostatic uplift or reclamation has brought it into the terrestrial realm. Most of the material, however, was always on the land, but closely linked to the sea. It is not intended to review this material extensively; rather this study will consider the role of the sea and connections across the sea in how we understand and explain this terrestrial resource.

Another aspect of archaeological research concerns interactions across the North Sea as evidenced by exotic objects, especially in the Bronze Age (e.g. Butler 1963; O'Connor 1980). There is no doubt that the submergence of the North Sea basin, and the creation of the British Isles from around 6000 cal BC, never stopped the people living on opposite sides of the North Sea and Channel from interacting with one another. The introduction of domesticates into the British Neolithic and the continued exchange of artefacts, from the earliest Neolithic through to the modern day, bear witness that interactions never ceased completely. Evidence for such activity comes from a wide range of sources: stone, pottery, metal artefacts, jewellery, and inscriptions, as well as the stories, saints' lives, and myths that have been written down in the past.

An important dataset is provided by boats and boat fragments from the North Sea basin. The oldest boats from the region are of Mesolithic date, but the first boats that can be assumed with reasonable confidence to have been employed as seagoing craft are of Early Bronze Age and younger date (as summarized in McGrail 2001). The maritime archaeology of the North Sea proper has not produced any ships that date to the time frame of this study. However, its estuaries and rivers have been more productive. The present study explores not only the craft, but also their crews and archaeological context, be it as utilized in boat burials, such as the famous ship burials at Sutton Hoo, Oseberg or Gokstad, or having been 'killed' and sacrificed, as in the case of the Hjortspring and Nydam ships. A related source of information is the growing body of work on the boats depicted on rocks and in metalwork, especially razors, in Scandinavia (e.g. Kaul 1998; Coles 2000). The significance of these iconographic representations lies in the fact that through them we can see boats in a contemporary cosmological perspective, which can offer thought-provoking insights into the ways these people understood the sea.

The introduction of commercial archaeology in the countries around the North Sea in the final years of the 20th century has resulted in a number of deep excavations in what were once the blurred edges of the sea. This is a fast-growing source of information, especially where developer-funded excavations afford the construction of cofferdams, which allow deep excavations. Although this type of excavation is still relatively rare, the first results are extremely promising in terms of offering information on how people lived around the North Sea in the Mesolithic and Neolithic (e.g. Louwe Kooijmans 2001a, 2001b; Peeters 2007).

Few archaeological studies have been undertaken with a sea as its centre of attention, but Barry Cunliffe's (2001) *Facing the ocean* probably comes closest to this. Despite the welcome innovation that this book has brought to both terrestrial and maritime archaeology, the sea (and ocean) itself remains something that is very much seen from the land, as the title of his book implies. The book also adopts something of a 'marine deterministic' slant, in the conviction that living at the land's edge must inevitably lead to aspects of behaviour and social organization that are shaped by the marine environment. Such an approach has also been adopted by Jon Henderson in his *Atlantic Iron Age* (2007). It is of course unquestionable that living by the sea created opportunities for producing salt, fishing, collecting shellfish and sometimes hunting of marine mammals, and that coastal and long-distance shipping brought coastal communities in contact with one another, and also that storms and fluctuating sea-levels altered landscapes, at times for the good of the coastal dwellers, at other times for the worse. Archaeological and historical records clearly show that these opportunities were explored and exploited during various periods in the past. But there was no predictability in this. Just as the consumption of fish varied over time and local conditions (see chapter 4), so the opportunities for exchange and contact along coasts and across the water were not always equal in the lands bordering the North Sea in the past (see chapter 7). There were no *longue durée* inevitabilities in people's relationship with the sea beyond the rather obvious ones defined by the extent of the water, and there are very few, if any, marine deterministic grand narratives to be told in this book. People's engagement with the sea was and is one of choices: to fish or not to fish, to engage in seafaring or to seek isolation, to attribute other-than-human agency to the sea or to characterize it by its natural features, to treat the sea as a fragile natural habitat that needs protection or as an oil- and gas-rich resource that can be exploited without concern for the environment. At different times, and in different places, different choices have been made.

The contribution of history to this study as a source of evidence for Roman and medieval activity in the North Sea is extensive. This should come as no surprise, since historians' interest in the sea, both as a concept and as a geographical focus of research, has an impressive record. Ever since Fernand Braudel's (1949) groundbreaking and paradigm-setting *La Méditerranée*, historians have made great strides in the development of new maritime narratives. The modern study of the diverse relationships between people and seas is exploited as a rich resource, and research themes encapsulate an enviable diversity. Alongside the well-established technological, socio-economic, and political themes of boatbuilding and navigation, trade, fishing, shipping, seafaring, and sea power, topics more recently engaged with include the changing perceptions of the sea and its social construction (e.g. Steinberg 2001), the daily lives and social identities of mariners, the role of 'maritime women' (e.g. Nadel-Klein and Davis 1988), seamen's organization and social protest (e.g. Rowe 1972), and the rise of seaside holidays and seaside resorts (e.g. Walton 1993).

Several historical studies of the North Sea are of direct relevance to this study, with John Haywood's *Dark Age naval power* (1999) and John Pullen-Appleby's *English sea power c. 871 to 1100* (2005) providing detailed historical accounts of marine activity in the North Sea in the first millennium AD, and showing that the Vikings were by no means the first pirates who used the North Sea as a deviant place. In addition, David Kirby and Merja-Liisa Hinkkanen's (2000) *The Baltic and the North Seas* is of particular relevance, even though the focus of their work is on the 14th to 19th centuries. This book is a treasure trove of information on the lives of seafarers and fishermen, their work and their boats, the social identities of the fishing communities, the economic basis for maritime trade, and the significance of specialized settlements; it provides valuable insights into the pride, hopes, and fears of the people who engaged with the North Sea on a daily basis. The reason for not extending *North Sea archaeologies* into the post-medieval period was, in no small measure, because it seemed that it would have little to offer beyond what Kirby and Hinkkanen's study provides in terms of exploring the engagement of people with the sea.

Primary sources, including Caesar, Pliny, and Strabo, are important informants on particular aspects of the engagement of people with the sea. One example is the description of British boats, made with a rawhide-covered wicker hull, mentioned by Caesar in his first-century BC *Bello civili* (1.54) and by Pliny the Elder in his first-century AD *Historia naturalis* (4.104). There is no archaeological evidence for such craft, and without the classical sources the hide-boat would exist only as a hypothesis (cf. Cunliffe 2001: 66–7).

Similarly, primary sources dated to the Middle Ages, including Beowulf, Saints' stories, and the Icelandic Sagas, illustrate perceptions of the sea not easily gained through archaeological research alone. The Icelandic Sagas especially offer unparalleled insights into seafaring activities and coastal settlement in the northern part of the North Sea basin. These sagas were written by a number of authors, Snorri Sturluson from Reykholt the most famous among them, in the late 12th to early 14th centuries recalling the history of the preceding centuries. Despite the name, the Icelandic Sagas are a treasure chest for a study of the whole North Sea, since the tales extend to include Norway, Denmark, the Shetlands, and the Orkneys, and sometimes Scotland and England as well. Occasionally, when the lead characters travel beyond these boundaries, the Sagas faithfully record exploits in other regions as well. An example of this is the voyage of Earl Rognvald of Orkney, who in 1151 set out on a pilgrimage to Jerusalem with 15 large ships, with captains and crews from Norway and the Orkney islands. Earl Rognvald completed the journey in two years, with extended spells in Narbonne, where he courted the beautiful princess Ermingard; he travelled to Galicia, where a (Christian) castle was attacked, on through the Mediterranean, where a Saracen cargo ship was taken, and to Jerusalem, Constantinople, Rome, and overland back to Norway. Alongside an appreciation of the ability of North Sea people to travel so competently over great distances, such stories can also provide insights into the importance and status of the longboats used by the elite in the northern North Sea basin: Earl Rognvald decreed that of the longships to be constructed for the journey, no other craft but his own would have more than 30 thwarts and no other boat but his was to be decorated, so as to prevent any jealousy (Muir 2005: 89–93).

The purpose of using anthropological studies in a book on North Sea archaeologies is twofold. First, anthropological studies can be valuable in archaeological research as a way of understanding the diversity of human life and ways of dealing with particular issues. Both archaeologists and anthropologists aim to gain understanding into different ways of thinking by the peoples under study, and the manner in which we interpret the evidence in hand requires the researcher to overcome this distance, albeit employing different types of analogy.

In the context of this book, the best example of such an anthropological study that can open our eyes to the great diversity of practices that involve seafaring has to be Bronislaw Malinowski's classic study *Argonauts of the western Pacific* (1922). This study of the Trobriand Islanders' activities revealed in great detail the reciprocal exchange between islands, which included *kula* valuables, used as payments in certain social contexts within the *kula* ring. The exchange of these *kula* valuables from one island to the next was prescribed, and certain objects could only be exchanged in a particular direction, while other types of objects travelled in the opposite direction. The political status of local leaders was directly related to the ownership and ceremonial display of these valuables, and as seafaring over sometimes great distances was required to partake in the exchange network, socio-political status and seafaring skills were intimately linked. Indeed, particularly valued objects such as *soulava* necklaces, of a type of reddish shell found outside the *kula* ring, required seafaring journeys of greater distance (e.g. Malinowski 1922, 507). These special objects frequently had their own biography, and ambitious leaders were the instigators of the long-distance sea journeys aimed at obtaining such high-status *kula* objects. Obtaining these objects meant the writing of a new chapter in their biography, and the inalienable nature of such valuables supported the creation of long-distance elite networks.

Whereas such principles of early political economies have been used extensively for understanding prehistoric societies, and Timothy Earle (2002) presents the Trobrianders' exchange mechanisms as an example of 'Bronze Age economics', I am not suggesting that we can import anthropological interpretations wholesale into the North Sea basin. Rather, anthropological studies are here to remind us just how different the people in the past were from us, and that in interpreting the evidence of seafaring and exchange in the North Sea, and the socio-political and ritual significance of these activities, we should consider the alternative ways of understanding trade.

Second, anthropological research on the demise of the family-based fishing industry during the second half of the 20th century around the North Sea can be valuable in this study. A good example of this is offered by Kees Slager and Paul de Schipper, who in their *Vissers verhalen; over hun leven in de delta* (Fishers' stories, on their lives in the delta of Zeeland; 1990) offer accounts of what fishing in the North Sea in the decades before and after World War II was like. The information gathered shows a way of life that is disappearing, one of 'traditional' fishing villages where nearly everybody was directly or indirectly connected to the fishing industry, as boatbuilder, net maker, shrimp peeler, door-to-door saleswoman, or fisherman with wife, parents, and children. The chapter from *Vissers verhalen* on the dangers of drowning (ibid. 139–48), is most enlightening in showing how different the current perception of the sea is compared with that of only 50 or so years ago. At the beginning of the 20th century, most Dutch fishermen were not able to swim. Despite the strong Christian beliefs within most fishing communities, it was not a reliance on God or fate that stopped young fishers from learning to swim, but a widely held belief that it was better that way. If a man should go overboard, his ability to swim would only lengthen his ordeal of a slow death in the cold water. Fishermen were not afraid of death as such, but were afraid of a slow and painful death. Here again, we cannot simply use the information uncritically to explain events of centuries or millennia earlier, but the study shows how much we have changed in the past 50 years, and that we have to guard ourselves from using our modern bodies overenthusiastically as tools in exploring the past.

Folklore can be used in a similar way. Around the North Sea, legends and myths abound on the perception of the sea. These frequently suggest either that the sea itself was perceived to be alive, or else that it housed myriad supernatural beings. Some stories relate to supernatural boats. As is the case with anthropological studies, we need to be careful not to extrapolate this information too far back into history or even prehistory. But equally we should not shy away from stories that remind us that the premodern–modern dichotomy is less than distinct when it comes to understanding the sea: too many beliefs and superstitions survive this divide, a fact illustrated, for example, by the sea legends from Orkney as recorded by Walter Traill Dennison of Sanday (1825–1881).

ORGANIZATION OF THIS BOOK

In aiming for a 'maritime turn', this book will develop a number of themed chapters that set out to develop alternative narratives of how people engaged with their environment, which have been ignored or overlooked in terrestrial-dominated archaeology. Thus, this book does not intend to offer a chronological or comprehensive overview of the archaeological information pertaining to the North Sea from *c.* 10,000 BC to AD 1500. Rather it presents a series of themes, selected to show how an archaeology focused on the sea differs from one centred on a piece of land. These themes have been organized in five parts: an introductory part (chapters 1 and 2), 'the sea' (chapters 3 and 4), 'coasts and islands' (chapters 5 and 6), 'boats' (chapters 7 to 9) and a concluding part (chapter 10).

Chapter 2, 'An archaeological theory of the sea', sets out the theoretical considerations that form the basis for subsequent discussions. It considers how concepts such as landscape and seascape can help focus our attention in investigating aspects of human behaviour that have been, to varying extents, disregarded, overlooked, or ignored in terrestrial contexts. It explores how ideas of social identities and social dynamics can be used in a maritime setting, and what the development of a maritime material culture approach can contribute to the development of an archaeological theory of the sea.

The section on the sea explores two facets. Chapter 3, 'The sea as a dynamic and hybrid landscape', describes how the North Sea developed during the Holocene period, and what the characteristics of this marine landscape were. It will consider how this development was perceived by people as a hybrid landscape, and explore past perceptions of human and other-than-human agency with respect to long-term changes (e.g. Holocene sea-level rise and the creation of the North Sea), medium-term changes (e.g. coastal change, shifting dunes), and short-term changes (e.g. storms and floods). It will review recent work on Doggerland, reconsider recent work on possible ritual depositions in the North Sea, and address other ways of exploring the complexities that characterize the relationships that people had with the living sea. In Chapter 4, 'Fish: exploring the sea as a taskscape', fishing in the North Sea from the Mesolithic through to the 15th century, and the tools and craft used for this, will be explored. Using anthropology and oral history research, the distinctive identities formed by fishing communities will be considered, and this chapter will consider whether this distinctiveness has a long heritage, or if it is of more recent date. It will, in particular, revisit recent debates on the 4000 cal BC and the AD 1000 'fish events'.

The next section concerns the edges of the North Sea. Chapter 5, 'Socializing coastal landscapes', comprises three case studies that show something of the diversity of how people in the past made the coast a familiar space. It considers the impact of disappearing monuments in the Neolithic and Bronze Age on England's east coast, and the alternative ways in which the landscape was socialized. This chapter will also consider the artificial mounds or terpen on the Dutch and German Wadden Sea coast, as an example of a specialized coastal living. It will explore the medieval transformations and reclamations of the margins of the sea, and the construction of the earliest dikes, and especially the role of ecclesiastical institutions in these activities as a form of Christianizing wilderness landscapes. Chapter 6, 'Archipelagos and islands', covers aspects of isolation and connectedness, islands as deviant spaces and the role of islands and archipelagos as island nurseries.

The section on boats comprises the next three chapters. Chapter 7, 'Moving across the North Sea', provides an introduction to the seagoing craft used in the North Sea basin. It will also provide an overview of exchange and trade for the period under study, and explores the connections created by migrants and missionaries. Chapter 8, 'The daily practice of seafaring: the ship as heterotopia par excellence' uses Michel Foucault's concept of the heterotopia as the opposite of the utopia to explore the social dynamics aboard ships. It focuses on three case studies: the sewn-plank boats of the second millennium

BC, the Bronze Age rock carvings of boats in the Scandinavian regions of the Østfold and Bohuslän, and the pirates of the first millennium AD. The three case studies show that the sea acts as a deviant space, where land-based establishment can be challenged, albeit in very different ways. Chapter 9, 'The cultural biographies of boats', revisits boat burials as liminal agents in funerary practices, the practice of killing boats and the fragmentation of boats and subsequent use.

Finally, chapter 10 offers the principal conclusions of this book, addressing five broad themes that could reshape terrestrial archaeology: the ways in which society–nature interrelationships are constructed at sea; how the study of the sea illuminates different forms of agency; the role of the sea as a deviant space; the importance of travel, skill, and the knowledge of the sea; and the creation of maritime identities in the past and the present.

Realizing a maritime turn in terrestrial-dominated archaeology is, undoubtedly, a venture fraught with danger. Consequently, I commence this book with Fernand Braudel's (1949: 19) cautionary counsel in mind, that a study centred on a stretch of water has all the charms, but undoubtedly all the dangers, of a new departure.

2

An archaeological theory of the sea

INTRODUCTION

Despite the wealth of information available on the North Sea, surprisingly few archaeologists have set out to study how people related to and connected to this sea, and other seas, in the past. In fact, we can distinguish four established traditions in archaeological research of the sea, all of which originated in the 20th century. First, many (or most) land-locked archaeologists working on any side of the North Sea have simply disregarded the sea itself, seeing it merely as the natural boundary of their study areas rather than considering its role in any significant way. At best, they are seeing the sea from the land, without genuinely engaging with it (cf. Cooney 2003: 323), although the panorama is slowly changing (e.g. cf. Bradley 1984 with Bradley 2007). Second, there are those archaeologists with an interest in long-distance exchange and exotic objects, who focused initially on the Neolithic and Bronze Age periods but have also been concerned, in more recent decades, with the early medieval period. Although these archaeologists have recognized the seas as conduits of long-distance exchange, they have rarely questioned how the practice of travel across the sea impacted on the social products of such exchange (e.g. Butler 1963, O'Connor 1980, Bradley 1984, Clarke, Cowie, and Foxon 1985, for the Neolithic and early Bronze Age; Hodges 1982, Loveluck and Tys 2006, for the early medieval period). Third, a group of archaeologists have studied the exploitation of the sea, especially for fish and salt, and the occupation and the reclamation of the edges of the sea in the Roman period and afterwards; but these studies have generally not strayed beyond the functional utilization of the sea and coast both for food and for land for food production (e.g. Clark 1961; Van den Broeke 1985; Andersen 1995, 2007; Rippon 2000; Smart 2003; Milner et al. 2004; De Kraker and Borger 2007). And fourth, maritime archaeologists' focus has been on ships and waterside structures directly relating to shipping activities, but the development of a fuller appreciation of the significance of the sea and seafaring to past societies remains something of a distant aspiration (e.g. Ellmers 1972; McGrail 2003: 1).

While this study will, to a certain extent, build on all of these four research traditions, its core objective of launching a 'maritime turn' in archaeological research is significantly different. This study is, first and foremost, an exploration through archaeological material of aspects of human behaviour in the past that have been ignored or overlooked in studies that have taken a piece of land as the focus of research. The theoretical framework to accomplish this is, to varying degrees, based on three ongoing debates, albeit that the separation into three is more for presentational reasons than a reflection of clear dividing lines in the debates themselves. The first of these debates is centred on the study of nature–culture interactions in the maritime environment, and has two components: the study of landscapes—and an ever-growing number of other 'scapes' that have been invoked to help understand past peoples' relationships with the world around them, such as seascapes, islandscapes, and spiritscapes—and the debate on hybrid geographies and other-than-human agency. The second debate focuses on social identity and social dynamics, with particular reference to the distinctiveness of the identities of seafarers, fishermen, and other coastal dwellers, and also to the social dynamics on board ships, which can be explored utilizing Michel Foucault's (1966) concept of the heterotopia. The third debate concerns material culture, in particular exotic material culture and the significance of objects from foreign countries, and introduces the importance of travel into the cultural biographies of objects, and the deliberate breakage or fragmentation of artefacts such as boats. These three debates—forming the theoretical 'toolkit' for the archaeology of the North Sea—are integrated in a concept of the world where land and sea are neither considered as opposites, nor as being indistinguishable; and where the role of the sea in the past is neither defined solely by its natural characteristics, nor is it merely the product of human imagination. In this sense, the sea is an alternative space in which to explore ways in which people in the past engaged with the world they inhabited.

MARITIME NATURE–CULTURE INTERACTIONS

Archaeological discourses on nature–culture relationships have undergone significant changes over the past few decades. The perception of nature and culture as authentic constructs, with nature understood as externalized from peoples' lives, gave way in the 1980s and 1990s to the acceptance that both nature and culture were human constructs (e.g. Cosgrove 1984). These human constructs were often placed in a dualistic opposition, such as the *domus/agrios* dualism in Neolithic studies (e.g. Hodder 1990; Thomas 1991), or the *cosmos/chaos* dualism in discussions on the significance of enclosure in later prehistory (e.g. Hill 1985). This dualism is also shown in the extensive use of the 'enculturation' concept (e.g. Tilley 1994, 2004). It explains change along an axis with 'nature' on one side, and 'culture' on the other. In archaeological practice, 'enculturation' is a process that has been observed for every period, with the outcome being a landscape that is made increasingly more cultural (e.g. Zvelebil 2003 for the Mesolithic; Tilley 1994 for the Neolithic; Steenhuisen and Fontijn 2006 for the Bronze Age). More recently, such structuralism-inspired ideas have been challenged for the simplicity of the nature–culture dialectic, and different ideas on hybrid relationships between nature and culture, or the interrelationships between people and their environment, have emerged (e.g. Ingold 2000; Whatmore 2000; Descola 2005). This section considers recent developments in the study of the sea from a landscape archaeological approach, and the benefits that the adoption of a hybrid approach can offer.

Landscapes, seascapes and other 'scapes'

The origin of the word 'landscape', takes us back to late medieval Europe. The original Dutch word *landschap* or *landscape* expresses a geopolitical idea, rather than anything to do with a view of the land as represented in a painting. The suffix -*schap* or -*scap* means skill or ability; it survives, for example, in the word *ambachtschap*, or in its English translation workmanship and craftsmanship, and in the German *Wirtschaft*, meaning economy (cf. Van de Noort and O'Sullivan 2007). Thus, the original meaning of the word 'landscape' was the perception of the ability to live in, on, and off the land.

Only during the Renaissance, with the development of scientific knowledge and the growth of the market system, did the idea of landscape come to be perceived as something that could be increasingly observed, controlled, and used for acquiring ever greater riches (e.g. Descola 2005: 91–131). The new genre of landscape paintings was produced principally for the nouveaux riche, who invested their earnings from manufacture and trade in land. It is noteworthy that the first occurrence of the word landscape in the English language, dated to 1598, relates to such paintings from Holland. These new paintings, incorporating perspective and realism, expressed a new understanding of what a landscape was, as something that can be seen, owned, and exploited (Lemaire 1970). It was this concept of the functional landscape that became the subject of academic study around the beginning of the 20th century, pioneered in the works by geographers Otto Schlütter (1872–1952) and Carl Sauer (1889–1975). In archaeological studies, this understanding of landscape was predominant for much of the 20th century. The literature reflects this acceptance of landscapes as tracts of land where societies have left their mark on nature through the functional use and exploitation of the environment—typically in the form of settlements, field systems, and roads.

Human interaction with the environment creates 'cultural landscapes' that can be deciphered through a 'reading of the landscape' (e.g. Hoskins 1955; Muir 1984).

In recent decades, post-modern studies in the English-speaking world have sought to redefine people's relationship with their environment in the pre-modern world. The outcome of this search is expressed most clearly by the influential cultural geographer Dennis Cosgrove (1984), who defines the landscape as: 'an ideological concept representing a way in which people would have signified themselves and their world through their imagined relationship with nature'. Archaeological approaches to landscapes as 'encul-tured' nature are now widespread. The landscape has come to be understood as a stage where people express their relationship with each other through the environment, characteristically (and somewhat limited in scope) in the form of monuments and ritually deposited material culture. An interpretation of these landscapes informs us about socio-political relationships in past soci-eties mainly through connections with natural features and monuments (e.g. Barrett 1994; Tilley 1994). This way of defining the landscape resonates, to a point, with what the anthropologist Tim Ingold (1993) phrased the 'task-scape', emphasizing that the way in which a landscape is experienced and perceived is closely linked to the tasks undertaken within it. In some ways, however, Ingold's paper signals the beginning of the end of the nature–culture divide in landscape studies, and the recent thoughts on hybrid geographies, discussed below, can be traced back to his development of the concept of 'embodied landscapes' and 'dwelling' in hunter-gatherer societies. In recent decades, this exploration of the socializing of nature has increasingly adopted a phenomenological approach, and the role of the body in experiencing the sights, textures, contours, and smells that make up the landscape has gained prominence (e.g. Wiley 2007).

The concept of the seascape is a more recent introduction in archaeology. While a number of important archaeological studies consider the connec-tions, trades, and exchanges made possible by the sea (e.g. Bowen 1972; Cunliffe 2001; and most papers in Cummings and Fowler 2004), the study of seascapes as socialized nature is a new departure. In his introduction to the *World Archaeology* volume on Seascapes, Gabriel Cooney (2003: 323) de-scribes the seascape loosely as 'contoured, alive, rich in ecological diversity and in cosmological and religious significance and ambiguity', and as providing 'a new perspective on how people in coastal areas actively created their identities, sense of place and histories'. In a theoretical sense, the seascape is not so different from the landscape, and the boundary between the two—where one starts and the other ends—is little more than a side issue. What matters is how people who lived on the coast or who gained their livelihood from the sea defined themselves in terms of identity, sense of place, and history. And throughout the world, it is noticeable that people who are dependent on the sea define these aspects quite differently from those who are reliant on the land. In some cases this may be because the sea lay beyond the control of the land-based powers, and the Deleuzian ocean was embraced as the realm of the unbound, the unconstricted, and the free, offering astonishing opportunities for the brave and adventurous. In other cases, this was because the sea was a place very dangerous to life and work—the labour of a lifetime could be undone by a single storm—and working on the sea brought its own restrictions, such as the tides that stopped seafarers from landing their ship and determined the working hours of fishermen.

The development of a landscape approach to the sea has not been the exclusive prerogative of terrestrial landscape archaeologists. Christer Westerdahl comes to this from a background as a maritime archaeologist, advocating an approach that goes beyond the boats and waterfront structures. Westerdahl's (1992, 1994) concept of the 'maritime cultural landscape' has evolved in a contextualized maritime archaeology where both the physical and the cognitive environment are interrelated aspects. His recent research (e.g. 2005, 2008) has focused above all on the maritime communities, the people who in their daily practice engage with the sea in roles such as fishermen, coastal traders, seafarers, and shipbuilders, and is in part based on historical and anthropological work.

His 2005 paper, 'Seal on land, elk at sea: the ritual landscape at the seaboard', considers fishermen's superstition and the systems of taboos that identify a range of land-based names, animals, objects, and certain people (e.g. women and clergymen) as bringers of bad luck, and this is linked to a corresponding system of alternative, acceptable names (so-called *noa*) which are permissible. Westerdahl understands this practice as ritual acts that aim to socialize the members of the maritime community (2005: 8). Westerdahl links the presence of taboos and *noa* as reflecting 'the world of two halves' (2005: 15–19), with the sea and the land forming opposites as a 'primary basis of categorization supported by a social archetype of two parts or contrasts as well as by gender and other classification' (ibid. 20). Crossing the liminal space between land and sea is enabled by liminal agents, such as the elk and the seal. Both species can cross the divide physically: the elk can swim and dive, and the seal can move and rest on land. The elk and the seal represent the 'other world' and provide influence precisely because of their otherness. Thus, the use of elk heads on the stem and stern of boats in Scandinavian rock carvings represents such a presentation of a powerful element from other realms, which in turn tells us something of the prehistoric cosmology. While the archaeological resource gives few additional clues about the system of taboos used by prehistoric and early historic maritime communities, the notion that schemes of ritual acts existed to create bonds, and to negotiate the different worlds of land and sea, is recognized as an important and innovative concept that is relevant to the current study.

Both Cyprian Broodbank and Paul Rainbird come to the archaeology of the sea from their research on islands which, like maritime archaeology, has become a distinctive subfield with its own conferences and journals. Their ideas on the need for a contextualized approach to islands can be related directly to the ahistorical limitations of the biogeographical origins of island archaeology, and to the realization that the land/island focus suffers from colonial overtones (Broodbank 2000: 6–35; Rainbird 2007: 26–45). The reassessment of his own world by the Melanesian anthropologist Epeli Hau'ofa puts the sea rather than the islands centre stage of the islanders' world in his influential paper 'Our sea of islands' (1993), which has been cited by archaeologists to signal that alternative stories are required. Thus, Broodbank's principal work in the Aegean, *An island archaeology of the early Cyclades* (2000), includes a critical assessment of the western study of islands. He calls for an 'archaeology of the sea' that brings together landscape and seascape research to produce 'islandscapes' which recognize the historical developments among individual islands and archipelagos. An emphasis on the continuous movements across seas replaces the previous obsession with isolation, and the work includes a study of the relationships between the islands and the surrounding mainland. This is echoed in terrestrial archaeology where isolated sites take centre stage, and an approach of places as 'time nodes', connected through continuous movement, that ensure historic liaisons in a dynamic world, has been called for (Peeters 2007, 2009).

Paul Rainbird's (2007) *The archaeology of islands* goes one step further. Building on Broodbank's archaeology of the sea and Westerdahl's focus on the maritime communities and their ritual systems, Rainbird (2007: 49) proposes a contextualized study that places the 'embodied experience at the forefront of interpretation, to show how people associated with the sea can be distinct in comparison to a wider society through different perception of the world'. The study of such an embodied experience does not involve a universal phenomenology as advocated by Chris Tilley (1994); rather it constitutes a search for local phenomenologies that are historically and culturally constructed, combining local analytical theories of experience and lived experience itself (Rainbird 2007: 57, quoting Halliburton 2002: 1126). The study of the sea therefore involves the study of perceptual experience through presence and engagement in the world (ibid. 59). A paper by Arie Boomert and Alistair Bright (2007) on the future of island archaeology also reaches very similar conclusions.

The debates on the future direction of the study of the sea as an archaeological landscape, or seascape, clearly recognize that such a study must involve both physical and cognitive aspects. They accept that people's engagement with the sea—as seafarers, fishermen, or coastal dwellers who extract sea salt or collect amber from the beach—is distinctive from that experienced by dwellers inland. As with the land, the sea is a knowable place, but never to the same extent. It is always fluid, forever changeable, frequently treacherous. On land, such treachery can occasionally be experienced, for example in earth-quakes or volcanic eruptions, but these form the exceptions to the rule. At sea, conception, perception, and experience are matters of life and death, and this trialectic of space should be the starting point for the study of the sea (Sturt 2006).

In case terrestrial archaeologists are left in any doubt as to whether the connection between people and the sea is truly that distinctive, one should bear in mind that . . .

> the inability of the landsman to comprehend the maritime world is a deep-rooted conviction among sailors. Underpinning this strong belief is the undeniable fact that to go to sea is to enter another world, unpredictable and dangerous, and that to sail the seas requires special skills and knowledge. The working world of the seaman is largely unknown to and unseen by the landsman, whose encounters with the sailors ashore are rarely conducive to mutual understanding or sympathy. (Kirby and Hinkkanen 2000: 186)

Hybrid geographies and non-human agency

While the study of the sea as an archaeological landscape has made significant advances in recent years, the structural opposition between culture and nature remains strong. Several philosophers recently have sought to redefine the 'Great Divide' between nature and culture—notably Bruno Latour (e.g. 1993)—without rejecting its importance completely. A prominent example of such an alternative approach to landscape studies is offered by Sarah Whatmore in her *Hybrid geographies* (2002). This work offers several examples of how hybridity can help us to understand the relationships between people and nature. Exploring such relationships in the Roman amphitheatre, or in the inclusion of animals as 'endangered species' under the Convention on the International Trade in Endangered Species (CITES), she describes these 'performances of wildlife' as 'relational achievements, configured within heterogeneous networks and fluid topologies' where men and beasts all play their part as active agents (ibid. 22–3). In the case of the amphitheatre, the networks involving the leopard are used as an example. Whatmore gives an idea not only of the many people involved in the capture, care, transport, and training of the leopard all the way to the performance in the amphitheatre, but also of the changes that the leopard itself undergoes in the weeks between its removal from its own world and its death in Rome. In addition, the part played by the leopard in the political, social, and economical thinking of the time is explored, including the Romans' notion of Roman Africa being the 'nursery of wild beasts' and 'very much [the] inferior portion of the habitable world' (Whatmore 2000: 23, quoting from Strabo's *Geography*). In the case of

CITES, the networks are described for the *Caiman latirostris* (broad-snouted caiman)—initially listed as an endangered species which could not be traded, but de-listed after Caiman eggs were hatched in a ranch, partly for restocking 'nature', partly for export and the fashion industry—networks through which biologists, wildlife managers, ranchers, traders, fashion leaders, and private companies and indeed *Caiman latirostris* itself have all become part of a performance of wildlife in our modern era (ibid. 26–31).

The key aspect from hybrid geographies of particular concern here is the need to understand how people's lives were interwoven with the lives of others, not in terms of linear cause and effect but in the ways in which relationships were enacted or performed. Importantly, the 'others' are not to be restricted to other humans, but must include non-humans as well; these non-humans are not merely a passive backdrop, or the subject of human actions, rather they are understood to have agency. Placed in a broader theoretical framework, this line of enquiry on human–nature relationships is a form of non-representational theory (Thrift 2007), which aims to move beyond investigating and describing—or 'representing'—social relationships towards the study of how human and non-human formations are enacted and performed. Within non-representational studies of nature–culture or nature–society relationships, the non-human elements—be they animals, trees and plants, objects, landscape features such as rivers and mountains and, of course, seas, or more intangible elements such as ancestors and gods—have been attributed 'other-than-human agency'. The networks that incorporate the human and non-human are referred to as hybrid geographies.

An example of a hybrid approach in archaeology from around the North Sea is offered by Chantal Conneller in her paper 'Becoming deer. Corporeal transformations at Star Carr' (2004). Building on work by anthropologists including Tim Ingold (2000) and in particular Viveiros de Castro (1998), she provides an alternative interpretation for the significance of the antler frontals from Star Carr, and in doing so presents a new way of understanding the role of past people in a hybrid environment. A total of 21 red deer frontals, comprising the uppermost part of the deer skull with the antlers attached, were found at Star Carr. All had two perforated holes through the frontals, and the inside had been smoothed or had protrusions removed; that these frontals had been worn as headgear or frontlets has never been disputed. In his original publication, Grahame Clark (1954) had offered two suggestions for the antler frontlets deposited at Star Carr: to disguise the hunter, or as a 'mask' in ritual dances. By doing so, Clark retained the idea that the Late-glacial hunter-gatherers at Star Carr viewed the world as being divided between nature and culture. Anthropological research has shown that the existence of such a disconnection, and a division of the environment into natural and cultural parts, lies frequently with the researcher, rather than the researched. Following Viveiros de Castro's research of Amerindians, Conneller argues that the hunter-gatherers at Star Carr may have perceived that people and (specific) animals share a common 'inner essence—a soul or spirit that is identical and immutable'. While the inner part is stable, the outer part, or the body, is 'mutable and relational' (2004: 43). The antler frontlets should in this sense be seen not as enabling a functional or symbolic change, as Clark suggested; rather the wearing of the antler frontlets produced a new hybrid form of being, with some of the animal effects transforming the bodies of the persons who put on the frontlets. The red deer had thus been understood to have other-than-human agency, and some of this agency was transferred onto the human body, creating hybridities that transgressed the dialectic nature–culture divide.

If there was no clear separation between the realms of nature and culture, or if people's perception of a blurred boundary between nature and culture existed in the case of (specific) non-human animals, can we now also consider a hybridity of landscapes and seascapes, where other-than-human agency can be attributed to non-human and even non-animal elements in the landscape, and to particular landforms? A constructive point of departure is the discussion surrounding the other-than-human agency of trees, and by extension the agency of flora in general. This debate comes mainly from cultural geography, which has focused on the way trees give shape both to the world and to the human engagement with the tree-shaped environment. As the largest living beings with which humans interact on a daily basis, trees are well suited to offering an insight into the blurred boundaries between nature and culture, and the attribution of other-than-human agency to non-humans. This blurring of boundaries has been noted for the present day. Contemporary human interactions with trees imply that trees have 'rights', and that trees shape cultural landscapes—as, for example, with the transformation of the neoclassical cemetery in Bristol into a parkland (e.g. Jones and Cloke 2002; Cloke and Pawson 2008). It has also been observed for the recent past, with historical accounts offering a range of examples where trees were attributed other-than-human agency, as in the 'tree of life' concept, or where specific trees offered people protection from prosecution (e.g. Rival 1998; Hageneder 2001).

It seems a small step from recognizing that fauna and flora can be attributed other-than-human agency, to acknowledging that other natural elements might well have possessed agency too. We should not be too surprised that people in the past attributed agency, or other-than-human agency, to large water bodies. Our historical past offers numerous examples of how seas were attributed forms of agency, either directly or indirectly as the result of a supernatural being enacting his will—most often his rage—through the medium of the seas and oceans. For example, there is the prominent passage from Herodotus' *Histories* (7. 35), where Xerxes orders his men to give the Hellespont 300 lashes and to sink a pair of shackles into the sea because it would not accommodate the crossing of his army. The Judaeo-Christian God expresses his anger at the fleeing Jonah through the raging sea, which causes the sailors to draw lots to decide who to sacrifice, with Jonah being thrown overboard and swallowed by the 'big fish' (Jonah chapter 1). In literature, it is equally not uncommon to attribute forms of agency, and also gender, to the sea, such as in Algernon Charles Swinburne's poem 'By the North Sea' (1880), where a female sea is portrayed as voracious, encouraging male Death to give her more lives of sailors and fishermen.

The attribution of other-than-human agency to the sea is not something that belongs exclusively to the premodern world. Even for sailors today, the sea is not always a predictable landscape, and the sea still 'takes' and 'gives'. Research among fishermen has shown that many of their activities remain surrounded by acts of taboos and, in the landlubbers' view, superstitions. As Christer Westerdahl has pointed out, such 'superstitions' can be found in all maritime communities around the world, and their existence is based on the firm understanding that this is a 'world of two halves', with the sea and the land forming opposites (2005: 15–19). The intertidal foreshore can serve both to diminish and to emphasize the perception of the opposition of land and sea. For example, at low tide shellfish are exposed, and the sea offers in this way its riches to people living on the land without the need for specialist knowledge or skill, thus diminishing the perceived boundary between land and sea. However, the tides themselves and the changing nature of the foreshore provide daily examples of the dynamic temperament of the sea, reinforcing the difference between the dynamic sea and the indolent land.

MARITIME SOCIAL IDENTITIES AND SOCIAL DYNAMICS

If we accept that the manner in which landscapes and seascapes are experienced is closely linked to the daily activities that are undertaken within them, then their study and the study of social identities are closely interwoven. This connection has recently been expressed by several others who have observed that landscapes, both in their natural form and as 'encultured' artefacts, are active agents in the creation of people's sense of identity (Bradley 2000; Tilley 2004). So the role of social identities and social dynamics in developing an archaeological theory of the sea is partly already encapsulated in the study of landscapes of the sea. Nevertheless, social identity theory, and ideas on understanding social dynamics, can be applied particularly well to communities engaged on a daily basis with the sea.

Social identities

Social identity theory was originally formulated by psychologists Henri Tajfel and John Turner (1979) to determine the minimum conditions for group formations in societies. The idea that group formations could be expressed in many different ways has enabled social science researchers to engage with this theory. Thus, research has clearly demonstrated that people acted, performed, behaved, ate, drank, dressed, built, inhabited, and lived in distinctive ways that constructed and negotiated social identities of class, occupation, gender, kinship, ethnicity, nationality, and age. Archaeologists' enthusiasm for identifying social identities as a way of understanding past societies is not surprising, as this concept has clear archaeologically identifiable manifestations, for example in the form of distinctive clothing, tools, food, and eating habits, rituals, houses, and settlement forms, and 'encultured' landscapes. Researching social identity in archaeology has become—principally through an analysis of material culture and the body—a means of emphasizing the ideas and knowledge that people had about their similarity to and difference from others (e.g. Meskell 2001; Frazer and Tyrrell 2000).

From more recent periods, there is extensive evidence that living by and off the sea resulted in group formations that were very powerful indeed, becoming for many fishing villages the defining characteristic of the social identity constructed within the wider (terrestrial) society. The wearing of traditional costumes (*klederdracht*) in nearly all Dutch fishing villages between the first half of the 19th century and the middle of the 20th provides an interesting case in point (cf. Slager and De Schipper 1990). The traditional costumes are principally displayed by the female population. The traditional dress was less important to the fishermen; working together on their boats, they did not need such a display of shared social identity, and wore their understated traditional dress only on Sundays when they went to church. Each village had a distinctive dress and sometimes spectacular headgear. Thus, while the Volendam women had their distinctive 'pointed' lace hats, in Yerseke the headgear was very wide and rounded; the women of Arnemuiden had close-fitting lace caps with metal (silver for those who could afford it) elaborations known as 'ear-irons'. It is clear that the traditional costumes expressed more than one social identity. Thus in nearly all fishing villages, women showed their status—whether they were unmarried, wives or widows—through their dress and headgear. Traditional costumes were not the exclusive entitlement of fishing villages, but the dress in these communities was at its most distinctive and elaborate, and survived the longest, when increasing transport and communication opportunities began to undermine local and regional social identities.

One of the tools used for the archaeology of the sea will be to discern the social identities that distinguished coastal communities and those who worked on the sea. The purpose of this is not to reiterate the point that coastal communities were distinctive from those living further inland, but to gain some understanding of how the sea, and working on the sea, played a role in defining these social identities. The active role of landscapes in forming the identity of people's everyday lives remains a relatively under-researched area in archaeology. However, several anthropological studies of the Torres Strait Islanders and groups on the northern Australian coast, collectively referred to as 'Saltwater People' after Nonie Sharp's (2002) study of that name, have offered some tantalizing insights into the ways in which people expressed their social identity through their relationship with the sea. The Saltwater People are marine specialists, who have developed specialized boats such as elaborate outrigger canoes, and specialized hunting tools such as harpoons for the killing of turtles, as well as a detailed knowledge of the sea, including an understanding of weather and tides. This knowledge extends sometimes over thousands of square kilometres of sea, and is made knowable with meaning, stories, legends, and place names. Whereas coastal aboriginal groups in southern Australia explore the sea only to the horizon, in the Torres Strait the knowable and explored seascape is much more extensive (cf. McNiven 2003: 330–1).

The Torres Strait is not simply a taskscape, but also an animated 'spirit-scape'. Ian McNiven (2003: 332) argues that for most Saltwater People the sea is 'imbued with spiritual energies, fecundity and sentience', and is the place where creator beings and 'Old People' reside. Features in the sea, such as islands, coral reefs, and sandbanks, as well as tides, currents, and sea creatures, are all attributed to the actions of creator beings during the Dreaming. Even stone-built fishweirs are attributed to such creator spirits. The names of these features and the stories of their creation help to make the sea a knowable place and, moreover, one with ongoing spiritual energies. The sea is also the place of the Old People, the spirits of the dead, who inhabit rock outcrops, caves, and islands. Thus, for a Saltwater Person, to be at sea never means to be alone. The social identity of these marine specialists is linked directly to the creator beings through totemic entities, mostly sea creatures such as rock cod or shark, but sometimes features such as protruding rocks. These totemic entities label social identities that define clans, and these provide both a sense of ownership of a particular part of the sea and a link to the spiritual beings that reside there. Archaeologically, this relation-ship with the sea and the spirit world can be demonstrated. Examples include the accumulation of the bones of dugong which played a role in hunting magic (McNiven and Feldman 2003), and the V-shaped stone arrangements in the intertidal zone, which cannot be fishweirs as they face the wrong way for this and because the stones are set too far apart to be effective, and which are understood as sites connecting people with the spirit world of the sea (McNiven 2003).

Both terrestrial and marine groups define their social identities partly in relation to their environment, but the study of the sea may offer greater insights into how landscapes and seascapes functioned as active agents in the creation of people's sense of identity. The capricious nature of the sea, and ideas about it being alive, having other-than-human agency, or being the dwelling-place of gods, ancestors, or spirits, makes for an environment very distinctive from the land.

Social dynamics

The maritime archaeologist Keith Muckelroy called, in 1978, for the study of the communities of mariners aboard ships, or shipboard societies. He recognized that these closed microcosms of society provided a rich potential, not only in terms of understanding the relationships between the crew members, but also in terms of their status in society, and the extent to which shipboard societies could inform us about societies at large. To date, very few maritime archaeologists have risen to Muckelroy's challenge, but it is clear that this theme needs to be explored by an archaeology of the sea, since dynamics aboard ships provide insights into how past societies understood the sea, and what active engagement with the sea meant for social identities and social dynamics.

Foucault's concept of the 'heterotopia' provides a useful theoretical tool for the maritime historian or archaeologist to develop an understanding of how the social networks on board ships were enacted and performed, not least because of his description of 'the ship as the heterotopia par excellence'. The term heterotopia was first presented in the lecture 'The order of things: an archaeology of the human sciences' (1966), and published as *Des espace autres* by the French journal *Architecture/Mouvement/Continuité* in October 1984. Foucault himself did not use the term heterotopia much after his 1960s lecture, but the concept has remained with us (e.g. Casarino 2002: 11). Foucault considered the heterotopia the opposite of the utopia. Thus, whereas utopias have no real place, and portray society in a perfected form, or as a 'society turned upside down', the heterotopias are real places in which society is simultaneously represented, contested, and inverted.

Foucault formulated six principles that characterize the heterotopia. First, heterotopias are found in all cultures, but take varied forms. While there is no universal form of heterotopia, Foucault distinguishes two 'classes': crisis heterotopias, which are privileged, sacred, or otherwise forbidden places that are reserved for individuals who are in some state of crisis (e.g. adolescence, menstruation, or pregnancy); and heterotopias of deviation, where individuals whose behaviour is deviant in relation to the required mean or norm belong (e.g. criminals, outlaws, and adulterers). Second, heterotopias can change their function over time. Foucault takes the example of the cemetery, describing how the meaning attributed to this 'other place' has changed over the last centuries. Third, a heterotopia is capable of juxtaposing different places that are in themselves incompatible in a single real place—illustrated, for example, in the heterotopic function of the modern theatre, garden or zoo. Fourth, particular heterotopias are time specific, and can lose their status over time. Fifth, entrance to and exit from the heterotopia are both prescribed; normally, unlike a public place, the heterotopic site is not freely accessible (e.g. Masonic lodges). Entry and exit can be compulsory or may be subject to specific rituals. Finally, heterotopias have a function in relation to all the space outside, and this unfolds between two extreme poles: the space of illusion that exposes every real space, and the space that is perfect, as in a utopia.

Foucault's heterotopia has become a powerful meme in social science. The existence of such places in the modern world cannot be doubted, and one can think of brothels, theatres, prisons, psychiatric institutions, the army, football grounds, internet-based places such as Facebook and Second Life, and possibly even archaeological excavations with their autonomous social dynamics and performances, as forms of heterotopias. In prehistory, one can imagine the ritual sites with restricted access, such as long barrows, henges, and cursûs, or hillforts, as places that functioned as heterotopias.

For the present study, the role of the ship as a heterotopia is of obvious interest and it seems best to quote Foucault at some length here:

> if we think . . . that the boat is a floating piece of place, a place without a place, that exists by itself, that is closed in on itself and at the same time is given over to the infinity of the sea and that, from port to port, from tack to tack, from brothel to brothel, it goes as far as the colonies in search of the most precious treasures they conceal in their garden, you will understand why the boat has not only been for our civilisation (. . .) the great instrument of economic development (. . .), but has been simultaneously the greatest reserve of our imagination. The ship is the heterotopia *par excellence*. In civilisations without boats, dreams dry up, espionage takes the place of adventure, and the police take the place of pirates (1966: 27).

Admittedly, Foucault only considered in this quotation ships from the 16th century onwards. However, it could be argued that seagoing ships in prehistory and in the early historic period would similarly have acted as heterotopias. After all, through explorations that connected people around the North Sea into networks, ships were the means by which, from the Neolithic onwards, dreams were kept alive and performed, seafaring was, throughout prehistory and early history, the means through which society was simultaneously represented, contested, and inverted, be it by missionaries, pirates, or conquerors from across the sea, or by the exotic goods that became so important in the material culture of the prehistoric and early historic past.

MARITIME MATERIAL CULTURE

The study of maritime material culture cannot be isolated from the maritime nature–culture interaction debate, and that concerning maritime social identities and dynamics. For example, the material culture from the sea, such as salt, engendered specialized communities on all sides of the North Sea from the Late Bronze Age onwards. Living on the coast with the weather, tides, and storms that determined the success of salt-making at these northerly latitudes produced specific taskscapes with their distinctive material culture known as *briquetage* (crude 'hand-brick' pedestals that supported the vessels containing brine placed over fires) that contributed, in turn, to the formation of distinct social identities. Amber, another product obtained from the sea, was collected from the beaches of western Jutland and the northern Netherlands throughout much of prehistory, and was exchanged to all lands bordering the North Sea and far beyond, notably to the Mediterranean. This gift from the sea was attributed 'magical' connotations because of its translucent nature (e.g. Du Gardin 1993), and this must have played a part in the formulation of the knowable sea as a landscape/seascape imbued with other-than-human agency. In terms of advancing the archaeological theory of the sea, the attention in this section focuses on two specific material culture debates that can further aid our understanding of the sea in past societies: first, the role of exotic 'prestige' goods and the significance of geographical distance, and second, the development of a biographical approach to the boats and ships that enabled seafaring and crossings of the sea.

Exotic goods and the significance of geographical distance

Nowhere has the socio-political significance of exotic goods that came from across the sea formed the focal point for discussion so markedly as in the case of the British Isles in the late Neolithic and early Bronze Age. The social, political, and economic reasons behind the material-based manifestation of elitism in late Neolithic and early Bronze Age Britain has been discussed by many reputable commentators, and there is a degree of consensus on the importance of access to, and control of, exotic or 'prestige' goods in terms of underpinning status and prestige (e.g. Shennan 1982; Bradley 1984; Barrett 1994; Harding 2000). Instead of direct control over land and subsistence as modes of production, in prehistory it was the control of people that was important in becoming powerful. The transactions involved in the reciprocal exchange of prestige goods are considered to have played a key role in socio-political order and organization—or, in other words, in the negotiation, legitimization, and reinforcement of rights over people. There is also some agreement that access to and control of prestige goods complemented and eventually replaced the social reproductive role of large monuments, such as henges and cursûs, during the third millennium BC (e.g. Barrett, Bradley, and Green 1991). Such a level of agreement does not exist for the debate on whether the significant changes observed in Britain in the late Neolithic should be associated with a new elite (e.g. as advocated by Shennan 1986), or whether they simply represent a new way in which the status of ruling groups and individuals was defined (e.g. as argued by Barrett 1994).

The common motivation for defining goods that travelled long distances as prestige goods is explained by the concept that the value of certain commodities increases with the distance to its source. Thus, the value of tin is limited in south-west Britain where it naturally occurs, but is high in the Rhineland, where it is found within richly furnished burials. Amber 'is never found in South Scandinavia after the beginning of the Bronze Age, due to its high exchange value' (Kristiansen 1987, 85). The concept of goods transported over long distances as symbols of power underpins much of our understanding of the late Neolithic and early Bronze Age (e.g. Clarke, Cowie, and Foxon 1985). Moreover, it is generally accepted that particular objects 'were imbued with an importance out of all proportion to their size', as, for example, argued by Anthony Harding (1993a: 57) for the amber spacer-plate necklaces that link the Wessex region with the Aegean and southern Germany, or for the axeheads made from Alpine jade quarried at high altitudes (Pétrequin et al. 2006). It is no surprise that these objects, often possessing reflective, translucent or transparent properties, have been considered to belong to the world of magic and the ancestors. We may postulate that such special meaning could have had its basis in the concept of keeping-while-giving, and in the recognition of the existence of very special and recognizable objects and their biographies.

Most of these exotic objects have to date been studied without reference to the journeys that brought them to the British Isles or, indeed, with only scant attention paid to the practices by which these objects became exotic and useable as 'prestige goods'. However, Mary Helms's work on travel, as expressed in her *Ulysses' sail; an ethnographic odyssey of power, knowledge, and geographical distance* (1988), has influenced the writings of a number of archaeologists who have worked with exotic goods. In her book, Helms provides a cross-cultural analysis of the importance of travel. The central argument advocated is that in premodern societies travel, in the broadest sense of the word, is in effect the only way in which communally held knowledge and understanding can be expanded. Thus, in order to gain insights into, for example, new metallurgical processes, one would either have to travel to places where these innovations are already practised, or the community would need to be visited by a peripatetic or travelling smith. In this situation the traveller obtains knowledge that is privileged, and that can be translated into various forms of authority attributed to the beholder.

Foreign knowledge can be seen as a blessing or as a threat. Helms argues that the importance given to new or exotic knowledge and objects is linked directly to the belief that, in many societies, geographical distance is meta-phorically equated with horizontal distance, or time. Thus, to travel far can be understood as visiting the ancestors, the spirit world or the gods. The medieval pilgrimage is a good example of this idea. For these reasons, travel and travellers are frequently controlled in countless ways, ranging from the exclusion of women from boats to the existence of many taboos known only to insiders. In archaeological terms these restrictions are sometimes made visible in the treatment and the context of both the boat and the exotic goods themselves. This approach to travel in prehistoric and early historic societies offers particular opportunities in a study that investigates how people en-gaged with a sea. After all, if boats and exotic goods were treated in particular ways exactly because they had travelled far, then we can start to uncover something of the perception of the space travelled across.

In the past two decades, several archaeologists have adopted Helms's thinking on the importance of travel and the significance of geographical distance (e.g. Beck and Shennan 1991; Broodbank 1993; Kristiansen 2004; Kristiansen and Larsson 2005), but few have extended this to include the practice of travel that made the long-distance exchange of artefacts possible. Stuart Needham (2000) probably comes closest. In offering an explanation for the major changes visible in the Wessex region in the late third millennium and early second millennium BC around Stonehenge, he argues that the most important ritual monuments, including the large henges, circles, and pali-saded enclosures were 'world pillars' (ibid. 189–90), which connected the current world with the other world of the ancestors. The most important or successful centres saw their influence geographically extended through pro-cesses akin to missionary activities or pilgrimage. This opened up new exchange networks and led to what Needham labels the 'cosmological acqui-sition' of new exotica. The further extension of the 'superordinate' impor-tance of exotic objects (ibid. 190) enabled individuals who acquired, possessed, or displayed these esoteric objects to become personally associated with privileged access to the other world. Needham argues that the long-term nature of the exchange between Armorica and Wessex during much of the latter part of the third and the first half of the second millennium BC indicates the possible presence of a reciprocal element in the cosmological acquisition of exotic goods. Within the context of our understanding of the importance of geographical distance, this would inevitably have played a role in the demise of the special meaning of the objects acquired over long distances. However, seafaring, with its associated dangers, real and perceived, may have provided a key in maintaining the esoteric value of objects transported over long distances. 'The acquisition process itself required great 'craft', in this case vessels for sea navigation, and navigation skills(...) These themselves would contribute to an elevated symbolic status for the objects thus procured' (ibid. 189).

Helms's ideas and Needham's application of these ideas to the archaeology of Neolithic and Bronze Age Britain constitute an important component in the theoretical toolkit of the archaeology of the sea. They link the material culture from across the sea to the social dynamics of terrestrial dwellers, and thus to their perception of the sea as both a taskscape and a spiritscape. Furthermore, given that 'cosmological acquisition' bestowed power and prestige on those individuals who obtained the exotic artefacts, these ideas also offer an archaeologically relevant context for the study of the social dynamics aboard seafaring craft. This context gives significance to the prehistoric ship as a great instrument of socio-economic development, while the ship simultaneously becomes the greatest reserve of our imagination, thus justifying the application of Foucault's concept of the heterotopia to ships predating the early modern era. And, finally, these ideas endow the 'great craft' that enabled the acquisition of exotic objects with a social and ritual significance that can be explored through their remains.

The cultural biographies of boats

The modern study of material culture is essentially about people and things, and the interrelationships between them. Following the work by Kopytoff (1986), many social science researchers now reject the notion that material culture can be externalized from people's lives; rather they understand that human and object histories inform each other. This internalization of objects into societies resonates with that of the landscape discussed earlier in this chapter. In her description of the life of the Neolithic house, Ruth Tringham (1995) has made the distinction between the use-life of objects—the description of the object as a passive and inert thing, from production or procurement through its functional use and modification to its discard—and the biography of objects, which is about the social interactions between the object and people over the object's full life. Thus, the idea or metaphor of the cultural biography of objects has been used to express the notion that objects become invested with meaning through their social interactions with people and, conversely, people become invested with meaning through their interaction with objects (Gosden and Marshall 1999: 169). The importance of contextualizing objects has become more appreciated through the work of

Appadurai (1986). The realization that, in many premodern societies, the right to display or perform certain objects is more important than ownership over them has direct implications for the archaeology of the sea. This is illustrated, for example, by revisiting the exotic objects that functioned as prestige goods in the later Neolithic and early Bronze Age. Although these exotic objects were invested with particular and possibly magical meanings, it was the remoteness of their origin—be it as gifts from the sea, such as amber, or as gifts from the land in the case of metals—and the long distances they had travelled on their journeys that produced their cultural biographies and significance. These biographies incorporated every danger and adventure encountered along the way, as well as the people engaged in the various exchanges. Exotic goods of this period included principally jewellery and weapons, both of which could be displayed or performed. The archaeological context of exotic goods is, overwhelmingly, from the graves of individuals rather than hoards, implying that the intrinsic value of the objects was not relevant, but that the right to display or perform these objects lay with particular people.

Such an approach, focusing on the cultural biography of objects, will be extended in the archaeological theory of the sea to an understanding of boats and ships (Figures 5 and 6). This is a new departure, but that is not to say that maritime archaeologists have not, to date, considered the lives of boats and

Figure 5. The cultural biography of a boat I: a second life for a faering at Brough, Yell, Shetland Islands

Figure 6. The cultural biography of a boat II: a faering abandoned on the Mainland, Shetland Islands, overlooking the Wick of Sandsayre

ships from their construction, through their use, modification and ending; however, these accounts have been use-life descriptions of boats, with the craft remaining passive and inert. Investigating the cultural biographies of boats and ships is about the interrelationships between these craft and their crew, and about the owners and recipients of objects, commodities, and people transported within them. Such an investigation requires that both craft and people are seen as active participants, invested with meaning because of their interactions. This is a highly significant aspect of the archaeological theory of the sea, and can be explored, for example, in the use of boats and ships in burial rites. In such rites, the mourners sought to 'speed up' the transfer of the deceased to the world of the gods and ancestors by using an object that could travel, and that invested the dead person with meaning, for example by stressing his achievements as a great navigator, or linking his status to distant explorations and capture of booty. Conversely, the ship used in the ritual was invested with a new meaning as an object that linked the temporal with the eternal, or a liminal agent, and as a thing that could bring people closer to their gods and ancestors (cf. Westerdahl 2008: 25). In other words, the ship was an active participant in the mortuary ritual. Its presence in the burial shows its internalized significance to the people who decided to use the craft for such a purpose, a purpose that went far beyond its functional use.

The active role attributed to boats and ships in their cultural biography also implies the attribution of other-than-human agency to the craft. In the modern world, sailors frequently attribute human-like characteristics to specific craft: we hear of boats being reliable or trustworthy (and rarely that boats had been poorly made), and it seems very likely that such a way of thinking can be traced back to the premodern era. Indeed, referring back to the discussion on the other-than-human agency attributed to trees in the modern era, and in both the recent and more distant past, it seems certainly not improbable that a form of agency passed from the trees themselves to the craft they were used to construct. Recently, Mary Helms (2009) has suggested that the manner in which the Bronze Age Dover boat was constructed implies a prolongation of the integrity and power of the parent tree, thereby enabling the tree to give the boat greater protection from the forces of—and residing within—the sea. Elsewhere in the prehistoric maritime archaeology of the North Sea, indications that other-than-human agency was attributed to boats comes in the form of eyes, or *occuli*, near the bow of the boat, such as those reconstructed for the Iron Age Hasholme logboat from the Humber estuary (Millett and McGrail 1987). Another example comes in the form of the three 'dragonheads' found in the River Scheldt, dated to the late Roman/early medieval period and believed to have been attached to the stem of the ships (Ellmers 1972: 289). In both examples, the craft were made to see and play an active role in the successful completion of journeys.

The end of the lives of boats and ships is, for archaeologists, of obvious relevance. While we know of a number of prehistoric and early historic craft from the North Sea because of the fact that they sank, others seem to have been ritually 'killed', while others again were broken up and reused in other structures. This brings us to the final part of the cultural biography of boats: their fragmentation. The study of fragmentation in archaeology was developed, principally, by John Chapman and published in his *Fragmentation in archaeology; people, places and broken objects* (2000). The concept of fragmentation is concerned with the use of objects in relationships between people, current and past, and with the use of land and the breakage of objects. Not only does the sharing of fragments from the same object symbolize social relationships, but the fragments themselves become imbued with the essence of such relationships. Fragments could also be subdivided, leading to the enchainment of individuals in a social network which extended beyond the living. Within this concept, the fragment of the object does not diminish its significance through further breakage, rather the fragment stands for the whole enchained network, a notion also applied elsewhere and known as *pars pro toto*. Chapman's ideas are of relevance to the archaeology of the North Sea because a number of boats are known from relatively small fragments, sometimes incorporated into other structures. In such cases, the boat's active part in the social enchainment continued after the end of its use as a vessel for travel, and this offers provoking insights into the perception of the sea.

CONCLUSION

Inspired by these research developments, my archaeological theory of the sea can be summarized here. Clearly, the 'maritime turn' in archaeology must start from the point of view that the sea should be investigated not in isolation, but within a contextualized study where the sea itself, its islands and archipelagos, intertidal foreshores, coastlines, and hinterlands, and the rivers and estuaries, all play a part. This is also a study that considers both the corporeal and the cognitive engagement with the sea, be it from the land or from boats, and proposes that we should approach the sea as a maritime cultural landscape, which combines taskscapes with spiritscapes in one holistic landscape. Such an approach should facilitate the critical rethinking of the central role taken by people in the development of the perceptual experience of the sea. In rethinking the anthropocentric view of the sea, and of the wider world, ideas about hybridity and the revaluing of other-than-human agency residing in animals, trees, and objects including boats, and within the landscape—especially the sea—may assist in illuminating aspects that are frequently overlooked or ignored in the archaeological study of the land. Rejecting the notion that nature and culture are merely human constructs that stand in dialectic opposition, the enculturation concept has no place in the archaeological study of the sea. It is replaced by the idea of socialization, or the familiarization of the environment through the construction of physical and cognitive constructs without reference to a nature–culture dichotomy (Descola 1994).

The sea can act as deviant space, a space that could not, until very recently, be controlled by the ruling powers. It resists, erodes and removes the kinds of monuments that play a part in the social reproduction of the authorities.

Whereas the land is 'encultured' and becomes the domain of the establish-ment, a place for the conventional and orthodox, the Deleuzian sea is living nature, offering opportunities for those who operate outside the control of the authorities. In this way, the sea becomes the edge of society, the place where social innovation can take place. As the stage for the study of social dynamics, the sea erodes the divide between the premodern and modern world. Many fishermen and seafarers in the modern period continue with practices, beliefs, and superstitions that have very long histories. More so than land, the sea has resisted modification by humanity, and modernization. The exclusion of women from seafaring craft, and indeed from the study of these craft, reverberates even today (Ransley 2005). Material culture is also affected by its interaction with the sea. It turns local produce into exotic objects, sometimes with magical connotations. Those who display such objects, and the people and the boats that played a role in such transformations, are not unaffected. Again, the sea plays an active role in the metamorphosis of people, objects, and boats.

3

The sea as a dynamic and hybrid landscape

INTRODUCTION

Since the last glacial maximum, some 22,000 years ago, the North Sea basin has undergone many transformational changes. Largely covered by ice at the beginning of the period, it became successively an arctic-like tundra, a 'park-like' landscape of extended grassland with shrubs and trees, a tundra again, and a plain with light woodland cover that was submerged eventually by the expanding North Sea (Coles 1998: 69–75). As the North Sea rose, over the last 5,000 years, to within a few metres of its current level, the interior of the sea did not alter significantly apart from changes in tidal patterns and depth. But on the periphery of the North Sea basin, the slighter sea-level changes added to the effects of marine and alluvial sedimentation and erosion and produced, regionally, periods of marine transgression—when the influence of the sea moved landwards—and marine regression, resulting in the opposite effect. The North Sea, throughout its history, has been the dynamic landscape par excellence.

The history of research into the North Sea basin goes back to the 19th century, and will be discussed further below, but it was Bryony Coles' article 'Doggerland: a speculative survey' (1998), which first raised the profile of the Late-glacial and early Holocene archaeology of the North Sea and inspired many of the current research activities, especially those relating to the southern North Sea basin (Figure 8). The renewed interest in the Mesolithic and Neolithic archaeology of the North Sea has made some significant advances, and holds the promise of even greater returns once the high-resolution reconstructions of the North Sea Plain are integrated with the archaeological finds. A series of publications has recently presented new archaeological sites. New finds from trawler fishing along the various banks in the North Sea, and from the margins (e.g. Flemming 2004; Waddington and Pedersen 2007), as well as the use of SCUBA technology (e.g. in Fisher 1995), will be discussed below.

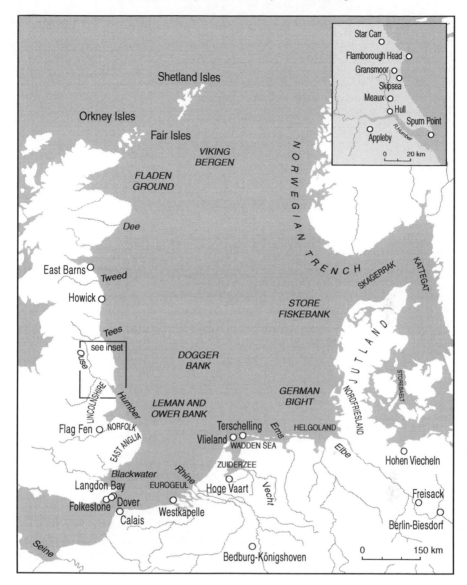

Figure 7. Places and regions mentioned in chapter 3

This chapter offers brief overviews of the history of North Sea research, the creation of the North Sea, and the archaeological evidence of human activity in the period from about 10,000 to 2000 cal BC. The archaeology of the North Sea has, to date, not progressed much beyond the operational aspects of working in the North Sea, and beyond extending the terrestrial Mesolithic seawards. Interpretative approaches to the dynamic sea remain rare. This

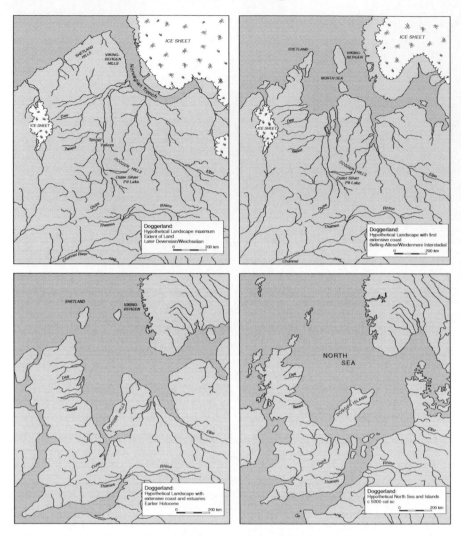

Figure 8. The reconstructed development of 'Doggerland' according to Bryony Coles (1998) from original drawings by Sue Rouillard (©The Prehistoric Society)

chapter will go beyond these accounts, and will consider the North Sea as an active agent of social identity, which can be explored through the sharing of practices such as the votive depositions of objects in and on the edges of the sea. The chapter considers principally the period during which the rate of change both of the seascape and the landscape, due to sea-level rise, was such that it would have been perceptible by individuals, especially in the form of storm surges and floods. Such changes must also have become engrained within the social memory of groups, as previously accessible regions began disappearing under the sea. This chapter, accordingly, will seek to answer the question: did rapid sea-level rise lead to the attributing of other-than-human agency to the North Sea itself?

A SHORT HISTORY OF NORTH SEA RESEARCH

The early history of research into the North Sea basin focused inevitably on Britain, where the sense of 'islandness' had long been embedded in the national psyche (Sobecki 2008). The field was broadened with the emergence of the modern science of geology towards the end of the 19th century. The concept of an unspecified landbridge existing some time in the early Holocene, connecting Britain to the Continent and facilitating the movement of animals and people, became widely acknowledged. However, it was only in the early 20th century that the idea of the North Sea Plain as a habitable and inhabited landmass was advocated. Clement Reid's book *Submerged forests* (1913) has been hailed as the first informed statement on the significance and potential of the study of landmasses submerged by the sea since the last glacial maximum (cf. Coles 1998: 47). Reid recognized the importance of sea-level change both upon the drowned landscape and on the submerged archaeology, stating that the sea may still preserve the ancient 'implements of wood, basketwork, or objects of leather' that do not survive in a terrestrial oxidizing environment (Reid 1913: 13). His map of the North Sea basin at the end of the last glacial maximum (ibid. Fig. 4), shows the major river channels flowing northwards, as well as the Dogger Bank landmass, which Reid recognized as once having survived as an island within the emerging North Sea (Figure 9). Reid's conclusions were confirmed by subsequent work by Harry and Margaret Godwin on submerged peats or 'moorlog' from North Sea coasts (1933), and by Grahame Clark, who mapped the extent of the early Mesolithic 'Maglemosian Culture' as encompassing the southern parts of the North Sea and Baltic regions. The famous find by the trawler *Colinda,* in 1931, of a Maglemose-type antler harpoon from the Leman and Ower Bank off Norfolk, provided irrefutable evidence of the North Sea Plain as an inhabited landscape (Clark 1936). The attitude towards the North Sea among archaeologists researching the Mesolithic and Neolithic since the 1930s can be described as uneven. Some more or less ignored the North Sea Plain completely as an inhabited landscape. Others, notably Leendert Louwe Kooijmans (1971) and John Wymer (1991), undertook to study the people who made the North Sea Plain their home through the many finds of animal bones and bone implements dragged up by trawling fishermen.

While archaeologists thought about the North Sea Plain as an archaeological landscape, geographers have striven to reconstruct the emergence of the

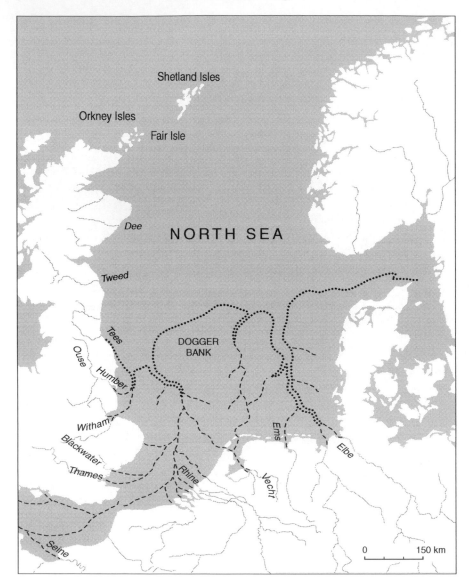

Figure 9. Redrawn version of Clement Reid's map of the North Sea with the coastline 'at the period of the lowest submerged forest' (based on Reid 1913, Fig. 4)

North Sea since the Late-glacial. Their output has come in the form of palaeogeographic maps, the most important for the North Sea being those produced by Jelgersma (1979) and Lambeck (1995). In the 1990s, a large multidisciplinary research project known as the Land-Ocean Interaction Survey focused some of its research on the east coast of Britain and the adjacent North Sea (Shennan and Andrews 2000). This was a time in which the spectre of modern rapid sea-level change brought about by carbon emission-induced climate change was increasingly recognized as a future threat. As a result the scale of research into past sea-level change was unprecedented. It is important to recognize, however, that the Land-Ocean Interaction Survey (LOIS) *modelled* the submergence of the North Sea Plain on a large scale, based on bathymetric data and extensive coring programmes, and while these models offered North Sea-wide reconstructions that gave an impression of the emergence of the North Sea, they did not offer the resolution that allows archaeological discoveries to be placed in local or landscape contexts.

The high-resolution mapping of the North Sea itself has now commenced. The work by the Birmingham University-based North Sea Palaeolandscape Project has demonstrated that it is possible to reinterpret data generated for the oil and gas industry and use this for the identification of large geographical features. In the virtual landscapes thus generated, Holocene deposits can be removed to reveal the topography of the landmass in the pre- and early Holocene, revealing salt domes, lakes, and hills, estuaries and different types of river systems alongside former coastlines, and this has allowed for the landscape characterization of the mapped area (Gaffney, Thomson, and Fitch 2007; Gaffney, Fitch, and Smith 2009). While it is not yet possible to plot archaeological finds against this landscape, due to uncertainty over the provenance of finds made by trawlers, the impact on the broader archaeological community of the new detailed understanding is difficult to overstate. From now on, the discoveries made by fishermen are no longer part of an unknowable world, a *terra incognita*; rather, this world is becoming better known and accurately mapped, thereby offering opportunities for the study of Mesolithic activity that no longer exist in terrestrial contexts.

THE CREATION OF THE NORTH SEA

The following outline description of the emerging North Sea during the Holocene is principally based on the work of the LOIS (Shennan and Andrews 2000; Shennan et al. 2000b). The models of the North Sea Plain generated by this study are based on a relative sea-level (RSL) curve (Shennan et al. 2000a: 301), which in turn is the result of an extensive coring programme which produced 'sea-level index points' (Figure 10). During the Late-glacial, around 11,000 cal BC, the RSL for the North Sea basin was some 55 m below OD. During the early Holocene, RSL rose very fast, with the RSL at 15 m below OD around 7000 cal BC, and around 5 m below OD by 5000 cal BC. After 5000 cal BC, the pace of sea-level change slowed down. The RSL curve for this period shows a 'gentle' increase, reaching OD

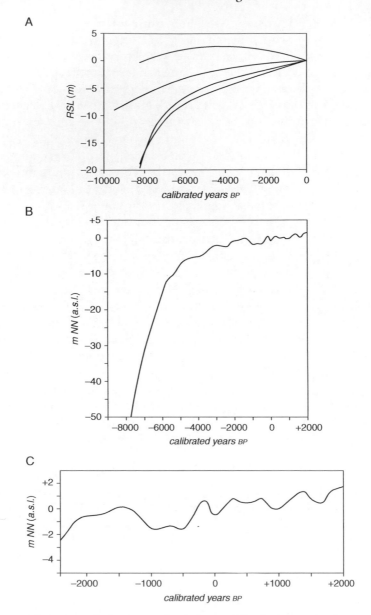

Figure 10. Variants on Holocene sea-level change: (A) relative sea-level curves for the east coast of England (based on Shennan et al. 2000a: 295); (B) sea-level change in the southern North Sea (based on Behre 2007: 84); (C) sea-level change in the southern North Sea from 2400 cal BC (based on Behre 2007: 91)

in the current era, but we must recognize that this is a statistical regression curve, based on the accumulation of sediments, which cannot demonstrate shorter-term dynamics such as shorter periods of sea-level fall or stand-still in the sea-level; neither can we use the curve to identify the effects of marine transgressions and regressions that have been observed at local and regional level. Nevertheless, the work of the LOIS offers an unparalleled impression of the geographical changes that have taken place in the North Sea basin over the past 10,000 years. The following descriptions are enhanced with reference to Coles (1998) and Glimmerveen et al. (2004), especially those relating to the very early prehistory of the North Sea, to river systems on the North Sea Plain and to the evidence of flora and fauna.

Starting with the Late-glacial, around 17,000–12,700 cal BC (16–13 ka BP), the whole of the North Sea was an extended plain, with only the Norwegian Trench existing as an area of open water. Much of Scandinavia, and the Scottish Highlands, were still covered by ice. Three great river systems had emerged by this time. The river system based on the River Elbe, and a second on the Great Ouse, which included the Rivers Humber, Tees, Tweed, and Dee, flowed northwards to the Norwegian Trench; the third river system flowed southwards, combining the Rivers Rhine, Thames, and Seine to form the 'Channel River'. The watershed between the northerly and southerly systems was formed by areas of windblown sand between Norfolk and Holland (Coles 1998: 58–60). The character of these rivers, taking vast amounts of meltwater, was of a deep incising nature. There is very little evidence of life on the North Sea Plain during this period. However, during the subsequent Bølling-Allerød/Windermere interstadial (12,700–10,900 cal BC) the North Sea Plain is likely to have been the home for a broad range of animals, including mammoth, Irish elk, red deer, aurochs, bison, horse, and woolly rhinoceros, as well as bear, wolf, hyena, beaver, and walrus (Van Kolfschoten and Van Essen 2004, 78–9).

The millennium leading up to 9500 cal BC was the Younger Dryas/Loch Lomond stadial, a colder period with tundra conditions and with reindeer the dominant mammal species (Coles 1998: 62). Around 9500 cal BC (the 10 ka BP palaeogeography in Shennan et al. 2000b) the North Sea was largely a lowland plain, bordered to the north and north-east by the deep waters of the Norwegian Trench, which includes the Skagerrak, and on the north-west by a large embayment on Scotland's and England's east coast extending as far south as Flamborough Head in North Yorkshire (Figure 11). What were to become the Shetland and Orkney archipelagos were large islands, separated from one another by narrow straits. In the south, the coastline is modelled at some 100 m west of the Calais-Dover channel.

Significant changes occurred in the following millennium (up to *c.* 8250 cal BC; 9 ka BP) as a consequence of warming and a rapidly rising sea-level. The

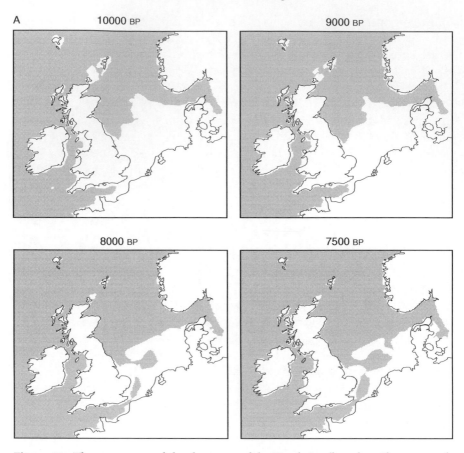

Figure 11. The reconstructed development of the North Sea (based on Shennan et al. 2000b: 310–1)

north-western embayment had extended further southward to Spurn Point in Yorkshire and the coastline of eastern Scotland and north-east England had come to resemble the current coast. As part of the extension of this embay-ment, a shallow estuary south of Dogger Bank had formed. A number of individual islands within the Shetland and Orkney archipelagos were identi-fiable at this time. To the south, estuarine activity characterized the Strait of Dover and a tidal embayment extended northwards to the east of East Anglia. Birch woodland, with some alder, hazel, juniper, and pine, colonized the Plain from refuges in sheltered locations where trees survived the Younger Dryas/ Loch Lomond stadial. In the centuries to follow, hazel became the dominant tree species. In terms of fauna, the reindeer was no longer the dominant species, and horse, aurochs, red and roe deer, wild pig, otter, and beaver inhabited the North Sea Plain (Coles 1998: 65). Waterfowl were abundant, and fish were plentiful along the North Sea coast.

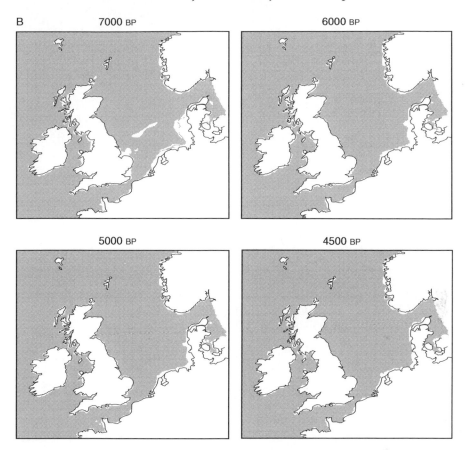

B   7000 BP   6000 BP

5000 BP   4500 BP

By 7000 cal BC (8 ka BP), a narrow strait connected the North Sea and the Channel. The date of the connection between the North Sea and the Channel in the LOIS model concurs with earlier suggestions (e.g. Jelgersma 1979). The northern embayment south of Dogger Bank was by now fully marine, and extended tidal areas stretched off eastwards, leaving Dogger Bank connected by a landbridge to the land west of southern Jutland/north-west of Nordfriesland. The embayment off the coast of East Anglia was by this time also fully marine. The Shetlands and Orkneys were becoming archipelagos.

By 6400 cal BC (7.5 ka BP) the two marine embayments had expanded further, but extended estuarine flatlands survived to the north of East Anglia, to the west and north of the Netherlands, and alongside the full length of an extended Jutland. Dogger Bank had become an island only connected to the mainland during low tides. Another 500 years later (6000 cal BC; 7 ka BP), Dogger Bank itself had become inundated and was only exposed at low tide. Other islands, such as the later Brown Bank, may also have survived above the elevated seawater levels. Saltmarsh peats developed at this time in the Humber estuary and along the coast of Lincolnshire and Norfolk.

By 5000 cal BC (6 ka BP), Dogger Bank was no longer above sea-level, although a 'Dogger Island' at this time has been suggested as a hypothetical possibility by Bryony Coles (1998: 68). The North Sea looked, at this scale, very much as it does today, but with wide intertidal areas surviving in the area of the later Wadden Sea, as well as off the Dutch/German/Danish coast and within the estuaries of the River Thames and the Humber, and off the East Anglian fens.

The period after 5000 cal BC sees the sea-level rise more slowly, and on the margins of the North Sea a range of coastal changes can be observed. In the southern North Sea basin, these include the formation of dunes and coastal barriers, and extensive growth of peat in coastal areas protected from direct marine influence. These changes in the landscapes are closely linked to the decelerated sea-level rise and the build-up of marine and riverine sediments, and to the growth of peat, all of which outpace the rise of the surface level of the North Sea. During the past three decades, geographers and archaeologists have come to realize that phases of transgression and regression are essentially regionally determined, especially once the rate of sea-level change slowed down. Alongside sea-level change, the behaviour of individual river systems, marine sedimentation patterns, dune formation, peat growth, and glacio-tectonic movements all contribute to local and regional phases of transgression and regression. Thus, we are warned against the uncritical use of the North Sea-wide transgression/regression schemes developed during the 20th century.

Within this broad picture of sea-level change in the North Sea in the past 18,000 years, we should be mindful that short-term natural events had an important impact on coastal developments. For example, three tsunamis are known to have taken place in the North Sea, leaving their traces sometimes far inland. The best known of these is the Storegga Slide tsunami, which hit the east coast of Scotland one day around 7070 cal BC. In the Shetland Islands, this tsunami left marine deposits including marine diatoms in coastal lakes and on peaty hillslopes to a height of 9.2 m above the present high-tide mark. Considering that the sea-level at 7070 cal BC was about 15 m below OD, the height of the tsunami wave and the run-up of deposited material onto hillslopes must have exceeded 20 m. This tsunami was triggered by an enormous landslide on the Norwegian continental plate. It has been recently suggested that the Storegga Slide tsunami would have resulted in the catastrophic flooding of Doggerland, with devastating consequences for any inhabitants (Weninger et al. 2008), but no lithostratigraphic evidence for this is currently available. The impact of this tsunami in the southern North Sea is not well recorded and may have been weak. Two further tsunamis are dated to 4350 cal BC, with a run-up of more than 10 m, and around cal AD

550–600, with a run-up 5–6 m above present high tide (Bondevik et al. 2005). Recent archaeological research has suggested a lacuna in the evidence for human presence on Scotland's east coast around the time of the Storegga Slide tsunami, and a direct causation has been suggested (e.g. Dawson, Smith, and Long 1990).

Historical sources also tell us of less dramatic periods of increased rainfall and storminess, which had disproportionate effects on low-lying regions along the North Sea coast. For example, the formation of the Zuiderzee from a complex of contiguous freshwater lakes into a saltwater sea is attributed to storms in AD 1170 and 1196 (Van der Vleuten and Disco 2004: 293). Another example is provided by the chronicles of the monastery of Meaux in the Hull valley of the Humber Wetlands. The chronicles testify to a great flood in 1253 (Bond 1866), and recount the desertion of villages and townships in the Hull valley, along with the reduction of local taxes, during the century that followed (Sheppard 1958). Other recorded floods, notably the St Elisabeth flood of 1421, and the 'Watersnoodramp' of 1953, have also impacted strongly on people's lives and their perception of the North Sea. We should be mindful that such events would have occurred throughout the later prehistoric and early historic periods as well.

EARLY EVIDENCE FOR ENGAGEMENTS WITH THE NORTH SEA

This section considers the archaeological evidence for people's engagement with the rapidly expanding North Sea in the Late-glacial and early to mid Holocene. It will thus provide the building blocks for the following section, which will consider whether the North Sea itself was an active agent of social identity, and whether it was attributed other-than-human agency. For practical reasons, this section considers first the finds from the North Sea and second the archaeological evidence from the coastal margins. Archaeological evidence of early fishing activities, and the role of fishing in the shaping of distinct social identities, has been largely reserved for the next chapter.

Finds from the North Sea

In the phase between the retreat of the ice and the submergence of the North Sea Plain, this area was a hunting ground. The archaeological evidence suggests that people tracked the retreating ice from as early as the 12th millennium cal BC in pursuit of large mammals such as the reindeer, which had been their staple food source for the preceding millennia. The evidence

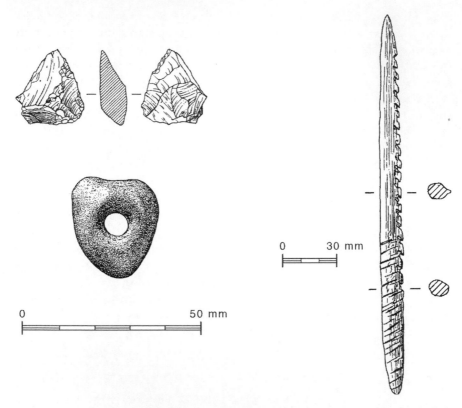

Figure 12. Archaeological finds from Viking-Bergen (left top), Store Fiskebank (left bottom), and the Leman and Ower Bank (right)

for such a move northwards from the North Sea Plain itself is rather sparse, and the earliest evidence for people hunting and living on the Plain comes in the form of the Maglemose-type antler point trawled by the *Colinda* from the Leman and Ower Bank, north-east of Norfolk, and dated to 11,950–11,300 cal BC, falling in the Bølling-Allerød/Windermere interstadial (Clark 1936; Housley 1991) (Figure 12). Additional evidence comes in the form of a single worked flint from Viking-Bergen. This has been placed, hypothetically, in the first half of the Bølling-Allerød/Windermere interstadial as it has been argued that this area of higher ground had become submerged by 12,000 cal BC, and any human activity must therefore predate this. However, independent dating evidence is lacking and it is not unlikely that Viking-Bergen survived for some time thereafter as an island (Long, Wickham-Jones, and Ruckley 1986; cf. Coles 1998: 60). A drilled stone, obviously a human-made artefact, was fished up from the Store Fiskebank north of Dogger Bank in 1985, but this object remains undated (Louwe Kooijmans 1985).

As we have already noted, the oldest Holocene artefact from the North Sea is the Maglemose-type antler point from the Leman and Ower Bank. Early Mesolithic antler (and bone) barbed points are also known as single finds or in small concentrations from all sides of the southern North Sea basin and further east, to present-day northern Poland and Lithuania (Clark 1936; Louwe Kooijmans 1971: 64–5). Much larger concentrations have been excavated at Star Carr and Friesack in northern Germany (Gramsch and Kloss 1989). Dredging work in Europoort, west of Rotterdam, has produced over 500 fragments of barbed antler and bone points, dated by radiocarbon assay of the artefacts to between 9450 and 7050 cal BC (Verhart 1995). These points are interpreted as being either of harpoons or part of leisters (two-pronged spearheads), used most effectively for fishing and catching eels. While isolated finds of these barbed points have been attributed to accidental loss during hunting, large concentrations of such points are considered by some archaeologists to have been deliberately deposited (Conneller and Shadla-Hall 2003: 102). If this is true, then the Europoort barbed points may be a case where local wetlands and the emerging sea had been selected for the deliberate deposition of barbed points, and this may indicate how hunter-gatherers constructed their identity in connection to water and the sea.

Evidence of Mesolithic-period human presence in the southern North Sea from the Eurogeul includes four instances of human remains: two mandibles and two cranial bones, with radiocarbon dates ranging from 9660–9220 cal BC to 7600–7100 cal BC (Glimmerveen et al. 2004: 50). Around this time, red deer, aurochs, moose, horse, and boar were hunted on the North Sea Plain, and evidence of butchery is particularly strong for boar (Post 2000). From the same area come three perforated axes made from red deer antlers; one of these was dated to 7180–6820 cal BC (Glimmerveen, Mol, and Van der Plicht 2006). The largest collection of artefacts from the North Sea Plain comes from the Brown Bank, a north–south orientated ridge halfway between the coasts of Norfolk and Holland, possibly a submerged beach barrier, spit or barrier island, surrounded by freshwater clays of Early Devensian age. These finds, described by Leendert Louwe Kooijmans (1971), consist of nine worked bones or implements: eight axes, adzes, and a shaft-hole pick of aurochs bone, and one implement of red deer bone (Figure 13). They have never been dated independently, but were estimated to be of late Pre-boreal or early Boreal age, around 8000 cal BC, on the basis of Jelgersma's (1961: 35) curve of relative sea-level; the Mesolithic date of these finds have, to date, not been called into question (Glimmerveen et al. 2004: 50). Similar finds are known from both sides of the southern North Sea, from present-day Belgium and the Netherlands (Louwe Kooijmans 1971: 64–5), and from a lake at Skipsea in Holderness, England (Smith 1911; Van de Noort 2004a: 35; see also Fletcher and Van de Noort 2007). The lack of contextual data means that we do not know whether the Brown Bank bone axes and adzes were deposited as a group or

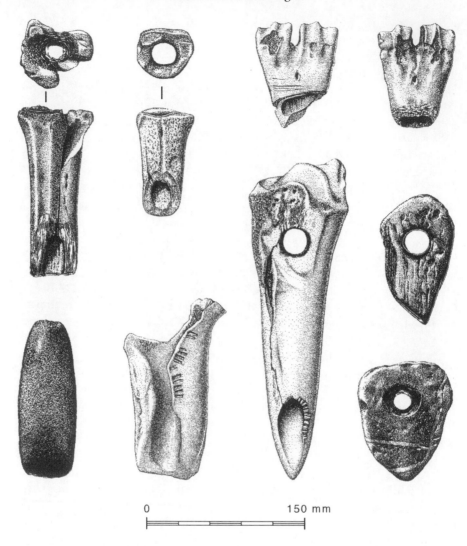

0   150 mm

Figure 13. Archaeological finds from the Brown Bank (based on Louwe Kooijmans 1985: 14)

lost over an extended area, but the Holderness find at least appears to form a cache, deliberately deposited in a wetland context. The final Mesolithic find, an antler or bone artefact trawled from the Dogger Bank, was recently dated to *c.* 6050 cal BC (Coles 1999: 57).

Neolithic material from the North Sea is rather sparse. At the Brown Bank, two early Neolithic polished axes have been found by trawlermen. Both are typologically part of the Michelsberg culture and dated to *c.* 4300–3700 cal BC (Maarleveld 1984). From the Dogger Bank come two small polished axes, both

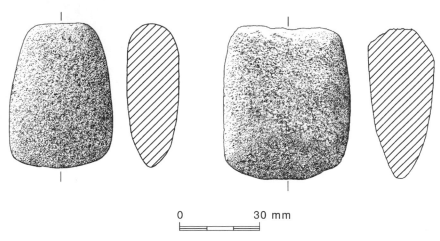

0   30 mm

Figure 14. Two small axes from Dogger Bank (held in Craven Museum and Gallery, Skipton)

of volcanic tuff. These had been acquired by J. F. N. Dufty and loaned to Craven Museum in Skipton on the 27th August 1934 (Figure 14). No additional information is available on the origin of these two axes. However, Mr Dufty, master of Ermysted's Grammar School in Skipton and recorder of the newly founded museum, was a collector of local renown, and alongside the axes from the Dogger Bank he loaned to Craven Museum a number of other artefacts from well-known archaeological sites in Yorkshire. We have no reason to suspect that the Dogger Bank entry is in error, and it seems not improbable that he had acquired the axes from fishermen based on Yorkshire's east coast. According to the RSL curve for the North Sea as developed by the LOIS project, the Dogger and Brown banks were, at the time of the deposition of these axes around 4000 cal BC, long since submerged and only the very highest points may have been visible at periods of low tides as small islands (see also chapter 5).

As yet, no archaeological excavations have been being undertaken at the Brown Bank, Dogger Bank or Viking-Bergen, principally because this would as yet be too much like looking for a needle in a very large haystack. However, with ongoing recording of finds from trawler nets, the diving activity related to the gas and oil industry, and the growing activity of recreational divers in the North Sea, linked to the ongoing mapping of the early Holocene seabed, it is only a matter of time before such a project provides value for the significant amounts of money associated with underwater archaeology. However, such research is already being undertaken in southern Scandinavia. The region lends itself particularly well to research into the Mesolithic period, since in northern Denmark and southern Sweden parts of the early Holocene North Sea are now above sea-level due to post-glacial rebound; in southern Denmark, the early Holocene coast, though submerged, is found offshore close to the land.

The survey of the Danish seabed has resulted in the discovery of many, often well-preserved, settlements ranging from the early Mesolithic Maglemose complex to the late Mesolithic Ertebølle type of sites. Anders Fisher (1995) attributed the success of the seabed survey to the use of a topographical model. The basis for the model came from northern Denmark where former coastal sites had 'rebounded' into inland positions and could be found by traditional terrestrial survey methods. This showed that late Mesolithic sites were most likely to be found in what were contemporary locations on the coast, notably at narrow inlets of larger water bodies that were best suited for coastal fishing using stationary structures. The results of the underwater survey were impressive, especially for the late Mesolithic Kongemose and Ertebølle sites, with 80 per cent of predicted locations producing remains of Mesolithic settlement. Within the context of the European Mesolithic, the coastal settlements suggest a greater degree of social complexity than can be argued for the terrestrial sites (Fisher 1995: 382). The investigations also revealed that many sites had become submerged quickly, reflecting the rapid marine transgression taking place at this period or alternatively storm surges and related floods. Research in northern Denmark and southern Sweden, where late Mesolithic sites are now to be found above the shoreline, has confirmed these findings. Here, in the absence of the fish fences, which do not survive, research has focused more on middens, and has added significant detail to our understanding of the marine resources exploited. The middens (*køkkenmøddinger*) contained the remains of a diversity of fish species, with a dominance of eels, shellfish including oysters, cockles, mussels, and periwinkles. The remains of sea mammals were dominated by the grey seal, with ringed seal, harp seal, porpoise, killer whale, and bottle-nosed and white-beaked dolphin also present, alongside the bones of a great diversity of sea birds, especially duck and swan (Andersen 1995).

Apart from such finds as the polished axes from the Brown Bank and Dogger Bank, the Neolithic period is not well represented either within or along the coastal margins of the North Sea. The apparent shift from hunter-gatherer-fishers—who were largely non-sedentary and whose itinerant lives included periods on the North Sea coast—to agriculturalists who adopted sedentary lifestyles which did not include periods on the coast, produced a significant shift in the consumption of fish. In recent archaeological discourse, this has been referred to as the '4000 cal BC fish event', and this debate will be discussed in chapter 4.

A final group of archaeological finds from the North Sea which requires attention at this juncture are the bronze tools, weapons, and implements found in the North Sea. Until recently, such finds would have been rationalized as loss associated with the wrecking of ships, and in such contexts this aspect of material culture would have little to say about how people in the past perceived the North Sea. However, in a recent provocative paper, Alice Samson (2006) has argued that the wrecking of ships does not account for all aspects of the material culture in question. Instead, she offers the alternative explanation that at least some of the offshore bronze finds could be attributed to structured or selective deposition of carefully selected objects in the North Sea as a watery 'natural place' (cf. Bradley 2000). Samson lists a total of 18 bronze finds from the Channel and the North Sea. Seven finds come from the North Sea:

- a middle Bronze Age axe from the strait between Terschelling and Vlieland in the Wadden Sea
- a middle Bronze Age axe found 500 m off the present coast of Westkapelle in Zeeland
- the famous Langdon Bay 'cargo', found 500 m off the coast not far from Dover harbour, comprising 182 swords, rapiers, dirks, knives, and hilts, 48 palstave axes, 79 other axes and axe fragments, seven chisels, and 40 other objects dated to *c.* 1300–1150 cal BC
- a late Bronze Age sword found 37 m offshore from Folkestone in Kent
- a late Bronze Age sword found in the sea off Whitstable in Kent
- a late Bronze Age axe from the Alexandra Dock in Hull, East Yorkshire.

Samson argues that in terms of material selected, especially the distant origin and deliberate damaging of many of the weapons, these deposits are very similar to the votive depositions in wet places, reinforcing the idea that the North Sea acted here as a recipient of votive deposits (cf. Bradley 1990).

In all these cases of trawled or dredged finds from the seabed, our confidence in attributing the presence of such finds to specific events or actions—such as a shipwreck or the deliberate deposition of artefacts within the sea margins—and thus to the way in which people actively constructed their social identity in relation to the sea, is undermined by poor contextual data as a result of the method of discovery. For example, we do not know for sure that the Europoort collection of barbed points was deposited in concentration(s), and we can do little more than speculate on the contexts of these finds until the mapping of the North Sea has progressed further. Similarly, we do not know whether the polished axes found on the Brown Bank came from its submerging margins or from a settlement on the dry part of the Bank. Future high-resolution mapping of the Late-glacial and Holocene seabed may provide us with a greater insight into the contexts of these finds.

Evidence from the coastal margins

The evidence for the early northwards migration of people from the northern part of the North Sea basin, where isostatic uplift has brought former North Sea Plain surfaces within easy reach of archaeologists, is much more extensive than that from the present North Sea. On the east side of the Norwegian Trench, on the Galta peninsula in present-day south-west Norway, flint points of the Ahrensburg complex have been discovered in redeposited beach sediments. The beach sediments are dated to between 11,200 and 9250 cal BC, and the Ahrensburg flint tanged points are possibly slightly older (Prøsch-Danielsen and Høgestøl 1995). This complex has led to the suggestion that the region of south-west Norway was suited for reindeer hunting at the end of the Younger Dryas stadial or very early Holocene. It seems that much of the Norwegian North Sea coast was inhabited soon after 9500 cal BC, as evidenced by flints from the Fosna complex. Hein Bjartmann Bjerck (1995: 140–2) has argued that this rapid settling of the coast, when compared to inland areas, points at adaptation of the hunting strategies which, alongside the ongoing hunting of large mammals, and reindeer in particular, also included marine resources and would logically have been undertaken from boats.

The earliest evidence for using the North Sea as a source of food comes from the Hensbacka-phase complex sites in western Sweden which, despite their current location between 50 and 55 metres above sea-level, were coastal locations around 8500 cal BC. In the Late-glacial, this region was a peninsula connected to present-day Denmark by a landbridge but otherwise surrounded by water: to the west by the North Sea, which extended, by 9200 cal BC, through the Norwegian Trench into the Skagerrak and Storebaelt; and to the north, east and south by the Yoldia Sea, the meltwater lake, south of the Scandinavian land ice, which covered most of the Baltic Sea basin and present-day Sweden. Excavations of the Hensbacka sites, in particular the Almeö site, have produced palaeozoological evidence of elk, aurochs, and beaver alongside wild boar, red deer, roe deer, bear, fox, and wolf. Importantly, 30 per cent of the bone assemblage comprised fish bones (Kindgren 1995: 177).

On the British side of the North Sea, the earliest evidence for Late-glacial and early Holocene human activity comes from Star Carr, in East Yorkshire, and other early Holocene sites around Lake Pickering. Since its excavation from 1949 to 1951 by Grahame Clark (1954), and its initial identification as a winter base camp on the edge of Lake Pickering, followed by its subsequent reinterpretation as a spring/early summer hunting camp (Legge and Rowley-Conwy 1988), Star Carr has now lost its role as an early Mesolithic representative site. Its exceptional material culture, including its 192 barbed points of antler and bone and its 21 perforated red deer antler frontlets, have led to recent reinterpretation that this was an exceptional possible ritual site at a significant locale where Lake Pickering joined with the River Derwent (e.g. Conneller and Shadla-Hall 2003). The early date and prolonged use of this site, for a period of 120 years around 10,600 cal BC (Day and Mellars 1994: 421), remains nevertheless highly significant to our understanding of the early move northwards following the retreat of the ice. Recent research has only reinforced the notion that Star Carr and the other early Mesolithic sites around Lake Pickering were essentially terrestrial sites, with little or no evidence for the use of marine resources (Mellars and Dark 1998).

Recent excavations at Howick in Northumberland have provided the earliest—albeit rather thin—direct evidence for the use of marine resources from the British side of the North Sea. At Howick, archaeologists revealed a timber-framed hut built directly on the coast, dated to *c.* 7800 cal BC. Detailed radiocarbon dating of the three distinct phases of the hut indicated that this locality was lived in, permanently or intermittently, for a period of 150–200 years. The excavation retrieved over 13,000 lithics, burnt bone of pig, fox, dog, a gull, and a grey seal, alongside some fragmentary evidence of shellfish (Waddington et al. 2003; Waddington 2007: 105–6). At East Barns, in East Lothian, a structure of similar type and date was recently discovered and excavated (Gooder 2007: 52). Despite relatively poor preservation, a single piece of burnt seal bone was identified, suggesting that the nearby North Sea was being used as a source of food.

As well as the late Mesolithic Kongemose and Ertebølle sites from the Danish waters, sites have also been found on land, especially in the northern parts of Jutland where the isostatic rebound has outpaced the RSL and where the former coastline can be researched with terrestrial survey techniques. When compared with their underwater counterparts, these terrestrial sites disappoint somewhat in terms of offering new insights because of the limited range of material culture that survives in oxidized environments. In the southern North Sea basin, excavations of late Mesolithic Swifterbant sites have produced both inorganic and organic material culture. The Swifterbant complex has been extensively researched for over four decades, aided in recent years by developer-funded research that has allowed for deep excavations that were previously unaffordable (for the Rhine-Meuse delta: Louwe Kooijmans 2001a, 2001b; Louwe Kooijmans and Jongste 2006; for the IJssel-Vecht delta: Raemaekers 1999; Peeters, Hogestijn, and Holleman 2004). The hunter-gatherer-fisher traditions survived on the edges of the first farming communities for a period of about 1000 years after the first LBK settlements materialized in the southernmost parts of the Netherlands, with the earliest evidence for small-scale arable cultivation in the wetlands dated to *c.* 4300–4100 cal BC (Cappers and Raemaekers 2008). The discarded material shows something of the attractiveness of living in wetlands (an intra-coastal plain), with the bones of duck, swan, beaver, otter, wild boar, and red deer all represented in this broad-spectrum economy.

The middle and late Mesolithic on the British side of the North Sea also shows significant changes. In northern Scotland, a number of shell middens have been found, with the oldest dating to the sixth millennium cal BC (Guttmann 2005; Wickham-Jones 2007: 87). The oldest shell midden deposits on the Orkney and Shetland archipelagos are of late Mesolithic date, having been laid down towards the end of the fifth millennium cal BC (e.g. Melton and Nicholson 2004). A number of the Scottish middens remained in use for extended periods, and apart from the famous Neolithic settlement of Skara Brae on Orkney, which was set within a midden, purportedly to provide insulation from the unrelenting winds, midden deposits of Bronze Age, Iron Age, and medieval date have been recorded for much of Scotland's coast. It is thought that the known middens represent only a fraction of those originally accumulated, as the calcareous and nutrient-rich midden deposits were used as a fertilizer for Scotland's acidic soils from as early as the Neolithic. Ard marks can sometimes be identified because of the distinctive soil colour and vegetation, and this may be the reason for the longevity of midden formation (Bell 2007: 316).

In contrast to the Neolithic ground and polished stone axes from the Dogger and Brown banks, the contexts of the deposition of stone axes from the edges of the North Sea have been extensively studied. From the expanding wetland margins of lowland rivers around the southern North Sea basin, a large number of structured depositions of axes, pottery, and human remains have been recorded. For example, ritual depositions at the Swifterbant site Hoge Vaart, *c.* 4700 cal BC, included caches of flint, aurochs skulls, and the lower mandibles of pigs from which the tusks had been removed (Peeters 2007: 201–5). Clusters of polished axes including rare Scandinavian imports and other exotic types are known from the floodplain of the River Thames; maceheads and pottery also found their way into the river (Edmonds 1995: 133). Research in the Humber Wetlands has recorded, in the Ancholme valley, the deposition of 44 stone and flint axes, including 18 ground and polished examples, even though it is not always clear whether the axes were placed in the water or in the alder woodlands on the margins of the wetlands (Van de Noort 2004a: 95). In Denmark, the earliest examples of structured deposition in watery contexts are dated to the early Neolithic, *c.* 3950–2900 cal BC, where whole Funnel Beakers, stone axes, and animal skulls were placed in shallow water, some distance from the nearest dry land; many are closely associated with human remains (Koch 1998; 1999). Here, the transgressive nature of the wetlands would overwhelm the depositions and incorporate them into the developing mires.

For the Bronze Age, sites along England's east coast reveal this pattern even more clearly. In the Humber Wetlands, for example, at least 50 metal artefacts, including axes, chisels, spearheads, rapiers, dirks, shields, bowls, and a golden torc, could be provenanced to the margins of transgressive wetlands (Van de Noort 2004a: 95). In the fenlands of East Anglia, this picture extends to a wider range of artefacts. In the Wissey embayment area, Frances Healy (1996) reassessed the finds made in this area since the 1960s, and noted a strong link between marine transgressions and the deposition of flint, worked bone, antler, and wood, skeletal material, pottery, and metalwork, ranging in date from the late Mesolithic through to the Bronze Age. The excavated and contextualized bronze artefacts at Flag Fen in the East Anglian fens provide the clearest example of how some of these objects—weapons and tools—were carefully placed on the edge of the wetlands, which subsequently transgressed landwards and enveloped them (Pryor 2001). It has been suggested that the deposition of human skulls along particular stretches of the Thames were in the same way votive depositions (Bradley and Gordon 1988).

THE NORTH SEA AS AN ACTIVE AGENT
OF SOCIAL IDENTITY

In view of the evidence of the human engagements with the encroaching North Sea, it is not surprising that nearly all archaeologists stress the role of food procurement as the key to understanding why people lived near the sea. While there is no denying that the sea was the ultimate larder, this focus on the functional and economical has meant that the debate on these people has barely stretched beyond a discussion of subsistence strategies. Only in recent years has this debate moved tentatively to consider alternative issues, and now includes contributions on the other-than-exploitative relationships between people and the environment they inhabit, including exploring social identities in the early Mesolithic (e.g. Warren 2003).

In theorizing the evidence of early human engagement with the North Sea, the study of social identities offers a way in which to understand the connectedness with the sea. We are reminded by Christopher Tilley (2004: 222) that places and things are active agents of identity, and if the North Sea was a significant aspect of how people in the Late-glacial and Holocene constructed their social identities, we may expect this to be reflected in the archaeological record. In turn, the North Sea as an active agent of social identity connects closely to whether past people attributed other-than-human agency to the sea—especially such a dynamic and rapidly expanding sea, and also to whether forms of hybridity can be noted in the relationships that people had with the sea.

From a geological point of view, the sea has no agency. The way it changes its shape as a landscape feature is controlled by climate change, including the alternating glacial and interglacial phases which determine the amount of seawater available; other controlling factors include the sediments brought into the sea by the rivers, in addition to the combinations of lunar and stellar gravity, atmospheric pressure, and wind, which determine the tides and storminess of the sea. However, from the reading of ancient and not-so-ancient texts, it is evident that seas were believed, for most of our past, to have agency. This agency existed either in a direct form, in the sense that the sea was perceived to be some form of creature, or indirectly through the operation of deities or spirits. Thus, the tides could be understood as the 'breathing' of a living being, while storms were interpreted as a mood such as anger. Alternatively such phenomena were explained through the medium of a god such as Neptune or the Christian God. In some religions, such as Shinto, and in the beliefs of the Saami of northern Scandinavia, the sea and all other natural features were thought to have their own spirits and did indeed have agency (Bradley 2000). This belief is recognized as an important starting point: if we are to understand the social networks of early sailors, fishermen, and those who lived from and alongside the sea, it is the notion that the sea had direct or indirect other-than-human agency that would have determined how it was engaged with, and what role this 'living landscape' played within their networks.

The previous chapter introduced Chantal Conneller's paper *Becoming Deer* (2004), in which she argues for a blurring of the boundaries between human and non-human animals. Conneller's reinterpretation of the red deer antler frontlets from Star Carr, and how these renegotiated the boundaries of the human body, is not restricted to this site or these objects. She has linked the frontlets from Star Carr with similar perforated antler frontlets from three sites in northern Germany: Berlin-Biesdorf (Reinbacher 1956), Hohen Viecheln (Schuldt 1961), and Bedburg-Königshoven (Street 1991). Her research implies a North Sea-wide perception of the environment in the Late-glacial and early Holocene that simply does not conform to our modern separation of nature and culture. The same could be stated for the barbed points. The link between the red deer antlers and the red deer barbed points at Star Carr is a direct one: many of the antlers used as headgear had been made lighter by the removal of antler material, which could have been used for the making of barbed points. Star Carr shares the very large barbed points assemblage with only four other places around the North Sea basin. Hohen Viecheln and Bedburg-Königshoven are both sites that included perforated antler frontlets. Friesack, also in northern Germany (Gramsch 1987), and Europoort (Verhart 1995) are the other two sites, although the finds here come from reworked deposits. Within their geographical regions, these four sites do not conform to what would be characterized as base or hunting camps. The accumulation, over long periods of time, of large numbers of antler and bone barbed points in watery contexts at these sites suggests some kind of structured deposition rather than loss. These deposits may, therefore, reflect something of the agency attributed to the animals, and the parts of the animal reworked by people.

The perforated antler frontlets were all deposited in 'aquatic contexts' (Conneller 2004: 51), as were the assemblages of large numbers of (unfinished) barbed points at Star Carr, Friesack, Hohen Viecheln, Bedburg-Königshoven, and Europoort. In the rare cases where barbed points are excavated *in situ*, such as the one stuck in a log of wood at the bottom of the small but steep-sided kettle hole at Gransmoor in East Yorkshire (Sheldrick, Lowe, and Reynier 1997), we may suspect that this was not the result of a hunter's misjudgement when throwing a harpoon, since at the time, 11,300 cal BC, there were no fish in such lakes (cf. Wheeler 1978). Depositions in water in early Mesolithic Scandinavia included human skeletons, isolated bone, and the carcasses of elk and aurochs (Strassburg 2000; mentioned in Conneller 2004: 51). Although the axes and adzes of perforated aurochs bone from the Brown Bank are without specific context, the only other recognized assemblage of such axes, from a shallow lake at Skipsea, East Yorkshire, is considered to be the result of structured deposition (Louwe Kooijmans 1971; Fletcher and Van de Noort 2007).

So the question is, can the attribution of other-than-human agency be extended to the sea itself? That sea-level rise was experienced as part of social memory, as paths and routes trodden by previous generations were no longer accessible, or else within the memory of individuals who experienced the effects of storm surges or tsunamis—or, less dramatically, when landscapes were inundated as nearby nickpoints were eroded or overtopped—is in little doubt. The people who resided on the Brown Bank, and made the axes and adzes from aurochs bone, and those at Europoort who manufactured the barbed points, must have been aware of the impact of the rapid sea-level rise on the lowlands surrounding them (Mithen 2003: 151; Leary 2009). If 'the landscape is the main locus for social memory, with both myth and history inscribed on the landscape', as argued by Chris Gosden and Garry Lock (1998: 5), how would social memory be altered when a landscape was changed dramatically, by the action of the sea? It does not seem far-fetched to assume that the North Sea itself became an actor in the myths and histories that were inscribed in the landscape. Indeed, attributing some sort of agency to the sea in such a situation seems a convincing way of dealing with extraordinary environmental change.

The barbed points from Europoort are possibly the earliest example of structured deposition in the North Sea itself, but they are by no means the only one. How are we, then, to understand the practice of votive, ritual or structured deposition? How were certain locales selected to receive the material culture deposited? Deliberate depositions, be they in the form of offerings, hoards, dedications, or other forms of votive deposition, have been ignored by many archaeologists for a very long time (Osborne 2004), and it was only with the publication of Richard Bradley's (1990) *The passage of arms: an archaeological analysis of prehistoric hoards and votive deposits* that this aspect of the archaeological record was given some prominence and attention. The disposal of valuable objects such as axes or bronze tools and weapons, especially during the Neolithic and Bronze Age, has been described as the placing of offerings, in the form of 'gifts to the gods' (e.g. Bradley 1990; Edmonds 1995). According to this concept—developed by Gregory (1980) to distinguish from the Maussian gift that creates reciprocal obligations—a gift to the gods cannot be returned and has been understood as giving status to the giver, who acts as the intermediary between the community and the gods, spirits, or ancestors. More recently, Johanna Brück (1995; 1999; 2001) has taken the deliberate depositions concept further, arguing that during the middle and late Bronze Age, the emphasis in deposition practices appears to focus increasingly on concepts involving the idioms of transformation and regeneration, which were 'central cultural metaphors through which people conceptualized the passage of time, the production of food and other categories of material culture, and the creation of social agents' (Brück 2001, 158). Archaeologically, this phenomenon is shown in the return of artefacts, including bronzes, food, and human and animal remains into the ground in the form of ritual or structured depositions, but also in the reuse of pottery fragments as temper in the next generations of pots. The concept of deliberate deposition is now widely recognized for later periods as well, and material that was previously approached as 'ordinary' rubbish and refuse which offered insights into daily lives, is now reanalysed and reinterpreted within the context of structural depositions (e.g. Hill 1995).

In all this, the reasons why specific places were selected for deliberate depositions, and how this relates to the social identities of the people who were involved in the depositions, has been largely under-explored, with the notable exception of Bradley's (2000) *The archaeology of natural places.* Aquatic/watery/wet places were originally thought to have been chosen for deliberate depositions as it was thought that these contexts ensured the sacrificed goods could not be retrieved. However, a detailed review of the context of such material suggests otherwise.

Possibly the best indication that these depositions were undertaken in clearly defined ways comes from studies of material found along England's east coast. The evidence here would suggest that the processes involved in deliberate deposition related directly to coastal and riverine wetlands which, because of sea-level rise, had transgressed onto the terrestrial realm. For example, in the case of the Appleby Hoard, from the River Ancholme in the Humber Wetlands, the eight rapiers, three or four spearheads, and the one cast-hilted sword had not merely been thrown into the river, but had been carefully placed, on the very margins of the expanding wetlands (Davey and Knowles 1972). Several of the Appleby items had also been deliberately broken before deposition. The impression given is one where the transgressing wetlands or the expanding rivers are invited to take possession of the gifts (Van de Noort 2004a: 168). Research at Flag Fen has suggested that deliberate depositions, ranging in date from the Neolithic to the beginning of the Iron Age, adhered to specific rules including clear separation into wet and dry depositions, where 'wet finds represent a final rite of passage and those from drier grounds something more transitory, such as the completion of apprenticeship' (Pryor 2001: 427). It has also been suggested that the materials deposited here had been earmarked from an early stage for deposition: many of the metal depositions showed little or no wear, and some of the swords had casting flaws; the querns had never been used, or had been used only very lightly. Nearly all objects have evidence of deliberate breakage or damage before deposition. The Flag Fen material includes fragments that appear to have been thrown into the water, and others that had been placed on the ground; missing fragments may lie, as yet undiscovered, in the landscape that was submerged at the time of deposition. In all this, it is apparent that the ritual depositions at Flag Fen adhered not only to conventions on selection and treatment of the material culture, but also to rules involving the landscape and especially the wet–dry separation of that landscape.

The refocusing brought about by *The passage of arms*, with its argument that votive depositions of metal objects in 'wet places' were gifts to the gods, has resulted in an extensive literature following this line of argument. As a consequence, the environmental component in the practice has been under-played. It is important to recognize that the 'god' in the 'gifts to the gods' phrase is a metaphorical one—it simply means that the gift was intended to be irretrievable and non-reciprocal. From the Neolithic and Bronze Age evidence reviewed here, it is apparent that the type of wet place selected for deliberate depositions had been carefully chosen. The North Sea was the ultimate 'wet place'—more specifically, a dynamic, living sea, manifest on its margins as wetlands that changed recognizably over the lifespan of the individual or the community. Sea-level rise meant that previously dry and accessible land was submerged by floods, or overwhelmed by marine or freshwater sedimentation. Objects deposited on the margins of these wet-lands, especially where tides were evident, could be understood as offerings or sacrifices to the encroaching sea, or to the expanding wetlands, with the sea or wetlands being attributed other-than-human agency. This may explain, to an extent, the dearth of votive depositions at the edge of the sea where the Post-glacial rebound outpaced sea-level change. People lived with the North Sea in a hybrid interrelationship, with both parties exercising agency.

Sometime after *c.* 1000 cal BC onwards, the structured deposition shifted away from the North Sea and the estuaries and wetlands on its margins that had transgressed under the pressure of sea-level rise. Instead, deposition focused increasingly on other wet contexts, such as raised mires and rivers (e.g. Roymans 1991). That the timing of this shift coincides broadly with the North Sea reaching levels not far below those of the present day, and with the wetlands reaching their maximum extent, is more than coincidence. I would argue that the perception of the North Sea as a living landscape, or one with apparent other-than-human agency, diminished in importance around *c.* 1000 cal BC. The fact that other wet places such as raised mires and certain rivers were visibly changing the landscape meant that they were accorded agency and thus became the principal recipients of deliberate depositions.

CONCLUSION

This chapter has outlined how the North Sea has developed since the last glacial period. Initially, this was a rapidly expanding sea creating islands such as Dogger Bank and Brown Bank, and submerging the North Sea Plain. In the past 3,000 years, with sea-level rise slowing down significantly, the impact of the sea was felt principally along the coastline in the southern North Sea basin, in a series of regional and local marine transgressions and regressions, while the coasts in the northern North Sea basin generally experienced uplift because of the glacial rebound that outpaced sea-level rise. The chapter has also shown that, from as early as the Late-glacial, people inhabited the North Sea coast, and that the exploitation of marine resources dates back to the ninth millennium BC. It has argued for the structured deposition of artefacts from the early Mesolithic through to the Bronze Age on the transgressive margins of the North Sea. More controversially, it has argued that the North Sea was perceived as being alive, and was attributed other-than-human agency. People would have expressed their connection with the North Sea not as one where nature and culture were separated entities, but as one where both people and the sea shared the same hybrid geography.

While the archaeological evidence for a living North Sea after *c*. 1000 cal BC is not evident, the perception of the sea as having direct or indirect agency in some form continues for a considerable time, and extends into the modern period. For example, in the 19th century, Walter Traill Dennison recorded local stories and myths from the rural people of the island of Sanday (Muir 1995). Many of the stories relate to the relationship between land (or the islands) and the sea, and provide 'premodern' local explanations for natural phenomena. The case of the Mither of the Sea, a benign and calming female creature who resides in the sea, where she had a calming influence, and her battles with the 'black-hearted' male rival Teran, who caused the storms at sea, provides an Orcadian version of the attribution of other-than-human agency to the sea stories, albeit in a dualistic form which is considered typical for the northern traditional myths (Muir 1995: 20–1). Dennison's ethnographic collection contains many more examples where myths about sea creatures are created to explain its changing nature, and Nuckelavee, Sea Trows, and Fin Folk are just a few examples of this, and which may have had their counterparts in other places around the North Sea.

By exploring the living nature of the sea, and the attribution to it of forms of agency, the intention has been to develop a different way of exploring the hybrid nature of the relationship between humans and the environment they inhabit. When one perceives the sea to be alive, then the way in which one engages with it is very different from a landscape that has no agency. This engagement goes beyond simple sacrifices, offerings, or 'enculturation'. Living landscapes have their own motivations, and the many different relationships that individuals and societies have with the sea must be constantly negotiated, as shown in this case by the many centuries of structured deposition of selected artefacts, or by the rituals that surround every journey across the sea.

4

Fish: exploring the sea as a taskscape

INTRODUCTION

Food and social identities are closely connected. The idea that 'to be Mesolithic is to be a fisher', with all the connotations that differentiate the Mesolithic fisher from the Neolithic farmer, characterizes some of the debates that are ongoing (e.g. Thomas 2003). Food and social identities are connected, especially in the case of societies of fishermen, for example in the wearing of distinctive national dress by the female relatives of fishermen in the Netherlands in the 19th and first half of the 20th centuries (see chapter 2). However, we should not forget that fishing as a full-time occupation appears in the North Sea only around the 15th century AD, and that before that date fishing was only ever a part of people's occupation and social identity (Kirby and Hinkkanen 2000; Fox 2001).

Nevertheless, to be a successful fisher required skill, tools and knowledge of the tides and the movement of fish. All these created distinctive taskscapes where people's daily engagement with the sea followed the rhythm of the tides, rather than that of the sun. This chapter considers the North Sea as a taskscape, focusing on the long history of fishing and fish consumption, and the current debates on the importance of fishing in our prehistoric and historic past. It presents a short overview of the role of fishing in the North Sea from the Mesolithic through to the 15th century AD, and the tools and craft used for this. Using anthropology and oral history research, the distinctive identities formed by fishing communities will be considered, and the chapter will ask whether this distinctiveness has a long heritage, or is of more recent date.

THE NORTH SEA AS A SOURCE OF FOOD: A CHRONOLOGICAL OVERVIEW

Late Palaeolithic and Mesolithic

The earliest indirect evidence for the use of marine resources in the North Sea basin goes, possibly, back to the tenth millennium cal BC. The zoo-archaeological evidence from the Galta peninsula in present-day south-west Norway, where flint points of the Ahrensburg complex have been discovered in redeposited beach sediments, has already been introduced (chapter 3; Prøsch-Danielsen and Høgestøl 1995). This evidence has been invoked to argue that south-west Norway was suited to reindeer hunting at the end of the Younger Dryas stadial, or very early Holocene. Lou Schmitt (1995) has gone one step further and argued that the presence of Ahrensburg-type flints should be understood as a specialized or seasonal exploitation of marine resources, including seals for their fat, by hunters whose base camps were found further south, in north-east Germany or north-west Poland. There is, as yet, no zoological evidence corroborating this argument.

When the ice retreated from Norway and the large mammals migrated further northwards, humans followed in pursuit of these animals that had formed their staple food for thousands of years. As is the case for the Galta peninsula, the clear preference for coastal locations of the Hensbacka/Fosne sites in the second half of the tenth millennium BC may indicate that, alongside reindeer, the use of marine resources formed part of the subsistence strategies, even though direct palaeozoological evidence is lacking here too (Bjerck 1995: 140–2, 2007: 17). The location of tenth- and ninth-millennia sites in the outermost part of the archipelagos off the coast of southern Norway has been interpreted to mean that seal hunting must have been a central part of the hunting strategies of the time. If this was indeed the case, the use of boats from which these animals could be most successfully hunted was required, unless the seals were hunted when they come on land to pup (Bjerck 2007: 19). The argument for marine food consumption has been made convincingly for the Hensbacka-phase complex sites in western Sweden, dated to around 8500 cal BC. Here the palaeozoological data from the Almeö site provides direct evidence for early use of marine resources. The bone assemblage comprises 70 per cent terrestrial mammals and 30 per cent fish bones, especially from pike and perch (Kindgren 1995: 177). To date, this represents the earliest direct evidence for the use of marine wildlife in the North Sea basin. In the two millennia after 8500 cal BC, the utilization of marine food sources appears to have become less specialized. The majority of coastal sites are understood as seasonal camps, with the marine mammal and fish bones existing as relatively small components in well-preserved palaeozoological assemblages (Bjerck 2007: 22).

On the other side of the North Sea in east Scotland and north-east England, a picture of early Mesolithic activity is emerging that resembles that from southern Scandinavia. Star Carr in the Vale of Pickering remains the earliest well-studied site, with dates for its use around 10,600 cal BC, but the site did not produce evidence of marine or freshwater fish exploitation. The absence of North Sea fish is unsurprising, as the marine extension southwards along Scotland's and England's east coast is of a somewhat younger age (see chapter 3),

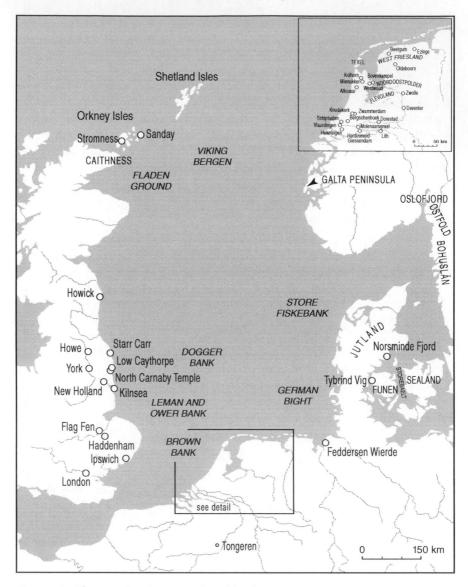

Figure 15. Places and regions mentioned in chapter 4

and the absence of freshwater fish is explained by the observation that fish had not colonized the Derwent headwaters at this early date, with the Malton gorge proving a barrier for pike and its prey species (Wheeler 1978). The eighth millennium cal BC coastal settlement site at Howick in Northumberland, comprising traces of a timber-framed hut, included bone of grey seal and some fragmentary evidence of shellfish (Waddington et al. 2003;

Waddington 2007: 105–6), providing the earliest palaeozoological evidence for the consumption of marine foods on the British side of the North Sea.

Coastal settlement in the middle and late Mesolithic in the northern North Sea basin is dominated by middens. Middens have now been recorded in southern Norway, notably the Oslofjord area, and in the Østfold, in Sweden's Bohuslän district, as well as in northern Jutland, on Funen and Sealand, and in Scotland from the Firth of Forth in the south to the Shetlands in the north (Figure 16). The Kongemose and Ertebølle traditions in Denmark are the most extensively studied. As already noted, these middens contained the bones of a range of fish species, dominated by eel and shellfish. Also included in the middens were the remains of sea mammals, dominated by the grey seal, together with the bones of sea birds, especially duck and swan (Andersen 1995). The oldest shell midden in Denmark dates to *c.* 5600 cal BC—the late Kongemose. The majority of sites are dated to 4600–4400 cal BC, but many middens continued to accumulate shells, fish, and mammal remains, and middens of Neolithic date 'are also very common' (Andersen 2007: 33). The impression gained from the Mesolithic sites around the North Sea is of an increased importance of marine foods in diets towards the end of this period. For example, at the early Kongemose site of Tågerup, a promontory on the edge of the Öresund on the coast in western Scania, isotope analysis of human remains are indicative of a diet of mainly terrestrial foods, but at the middle and later Kongemose sites of Bloksbjerg and Carstensminde in Denmark, and Segebro in Scania, diets had become markedly 'marine' (Karsten and Knarr-ström 2003: 54).

Extensive survey on the Baltic side of Denmark, including terrestrial and marine survey, showed that late Mesolithic sites were most likely to be found in what were contemporary locations on the coast best suited for coastal fishing using stationary structures, such as at narrow inlets of larger water bodies (Fisher 1995). The research has also shown that a 'typical' late Meso-lithic coastal settlement site consisted of a habitation area with hearths immediately above the shore, with refuse and the odd damaged logboat on the water front, and wicker fences with basketry fish traps running out from the shoreline. Where human burials were part of the settlement, these were located beneath the higher part of the habitation area or further up the slope. Research on Ertebølle sites has also provided unparalleled information on the fishing techniques used in the North Sea basin in the period between 5600 and 3700 cal BC. These include the use of stationary fishweirs and traps of woven basketry, fishing lines with bone hooks, fishing nets made of plant fibres, with further archaeological evidence of wooden net floats and stone net weights or sinkers, and leisters used for eel fishing. Barbed red deer antler or whale bone points and harpoons were used for seasonal seal and whale hunting (Andersen 1995: 54–62).

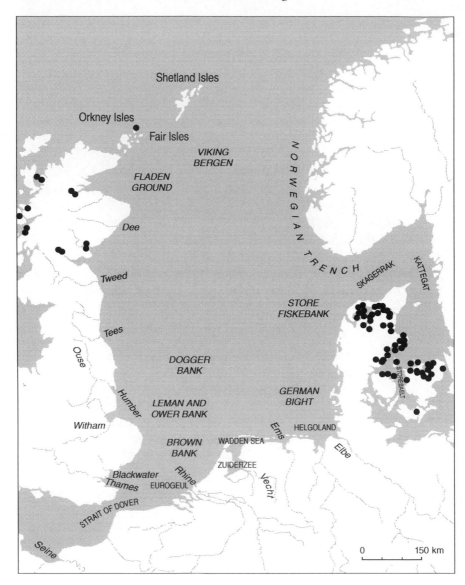

Figure 16. The distribution of middens in the North Sea basin (based on Andersen 2007: 32 and Wickham-Jones 2007: 86)

Albeit located in the Baltic rather than the North Sea, the excavations of the Ertebølle site of Tybrind Vig, off the island of Funen, have provided further evidence of engagement with the sea. This submerged site comprises a set of fish fences of hazel stakes, middens, a grave of a woman and child, three linden logboats, and 10–15 fragments of paddles (Malm 1995). The paddles were decorated with incised notches, forming interrupted lines and 'wavy' forms (Andersen 1987). The excavations of the Ertebølle site of Smakkerup Huse on Sjælland (5000–3800 cal BC) also revealed a community that lived in part off the sea. The excavations revealed a submerged midden and an *in situ* fishing and boat-landing area. The midden showed that fish, including marine, brackish, and freshwater species, and oysters were eaten alongside terrestrial foods. Evidence also included fish traps and fishhooks, and fishing spears with bone awl tips (Price and Gebauer 2005).

Early coastal activity in the southern North Sea basin is to be found, principally, at some depth under water, but evidence for late Mesolithic–Neolithic activity is reasonably well known from the Netherlands. The palaeozoological assemblages are suggestive of a broad-spectrum economy, with fish forming part of the diet. For example, excavations at Bergschenhoek in South Holland provided details of a winter hunting camp that included a fish trap of dogwood, dated to *c.* 4200 cal BC (Louwe Kooijmans 1986). No evidence for cereal cultivation or domesticated animals, other than dogs, was encountered. The Swifterbant-type hunter-gatherer-fisher traditions survived on the coast for a period of about 1,500 years after the first LBK settlements materialized in Limburg, and the consumption of fish continued throughout this period (e.g. Louwe Kooijmans 1993: 82).

Studies of the Mesolithic in coastal and marine contexts elsewhere in north-western Europe have shown the importance of understanding seasonality when using archaeological evidence in the reconstruction of prehistoric life. Martin Bell (2007) has suggested that the main areas of activity in the Severn estuary on the west coast of Britain fell in the autumn, with shorter periods of habitation occurring in the early spring, and during the summer and winter months. This implies a dynamic utilization of coastal resources at several points in the year, and he argues for the careful examination of the complete archaeological record before assigning activity all too readily to a single period. This research has also indicated the widespread occurrence of burning events, where woodland vegetation was deliberately fired as part of a strategy by Mesolithic hunter-gatherer-fishers to modify the landscape to their advantage. Interestingly, Bell argues that the location of Neolithic sites on the coast were, to some extent, determined by the preceding Mesolithic, and that the vegetation created by the burning of woods and the making of paths produced extended timescales. This, he states, could be understood as 'a principle which might be called the structuration of landscape by antecedent conditions' (Bell 2007: p. xliii). Finally, analysis of middens on the British coast of the Irish Sea have shown here, too, the importance of fishing, particularly of eels, in the Mesolithic, with a shift to shellfish as a staple food in the late Mesolithic and early Neolithic, *c.* 4500–3400 cal BC (e.g. Mellars 2004). We should recognize that in this respect, the hunter-gatherer-fishers of the North Sea formed part of a much wider tradition.

Neolithic

Recent evaluations of the importance of marine resources at the beginning of the Neolithic in the North Sea basin, around 4000 cal BC, suggest a remarkably rapid shift from a diet that included ample marine resources to one with very little food from the sea. The basis for this conclusion is provided by the isotopic analysis of human remains of Mesolithic and Neolithic date from Britain and Denmark. Diets that include a significant marine component are shown up in skeletal material with elevated $\delta^{13}C$ levels, in the order of $-12‰$ $\delta^{13}C$, whereas diets without such a marine component result in depleted $\delta^{13}C$ levels, in the order of $-20‰$ $\delta^{13}C$ (Tauber 1981; Richards and Hedges 1999; Richards, Schulting, and Hedges 2003). In a nutshell, the isotope analysis implies that around 4000 cal BC, with the first adaptation of the Neolithic way of life, people in Britain and Denmark turned their back on the sea as a source of food. This appears to be the case for people living both near to and remote from the coast, with very similar $\delta^{13}C$ levels observed in the skeletal material of those living within 10 km of the coast, and those living beyond this limit. Tauber (1981) examined human skeletons from shell middens, while Richards, Schulting, and Hedges (2003) found no difference in the $\delta^{13}C$ measurements of 68 coastal and 99 inland skeletons, but it should be noted that none of the coastal skeletons came from the North Sea coast. What is so remarkable about this transition is not so much that fish, shellfish, and marine mammals became less important in the Neolithic period, but that the change took place so swiftly and over such a vast geographical extent.

The results of the isotopic analyses have not been wholeheartedly accepted by all. In particular, based on the zoo-archaeological evidence from the shell middens of the Ertebølle complex, the counter argument has been made that the speed of change has been overstated. In addition, if marine food comprised less than 20 per cent of the total intake within particular diets, such as those involving cereals, it would be difficult, it has been argued, to trace the marine component through the analysis of isotopes (Milner et al. 2004). Defending both the stable isotope methodology and the statistical presentation, the original authors have maintained that the method was robust, and that the observed change was both rapid and geographically extensive (Hedges 2004; Richards and Schulting 2006). Among other things, they have pointed out that while shellfish remains are archaeologically very visible, in the form of shell middens, they deliver relatively little nutritional value to people. For example, Geoff Bailey (1978: 39) estimated that a single red deer carcass equals approximately 52,000 oysters, 157,000 cockles or 31,000 limpets in terms of calorific value.

Re-examination of Tauber's (1981) analysis of Danish skeletal remains from middens, allowing for the radiocarbon marine reservoir effect, has produced dates for his skeletons that are younger by between 200 and 400 years, shifting some of these from the late Mesolithic into the early Neolithic. When this has been combined with the determination of $\delta^{13}C$ of skeletal material from contexts other than middens, it has been observed that in the early Neolithic of Denmark, both marine and terrestrial diets were present (Price and Gebauer 2005: 153).

The rapid dietary shift based on $\delta^{13}C$ measurements has not been observed in the Netherlands either. For example, the superbly preserved palaeozoological remains from the late Swifterbant site of Schipluiden in South Holland (3600–3400 cal BC), where domesticated cattle and pig dominated, has shown that a significant part of the diet of the people living here was still derived from marine resources and estuarine and freshwater fish, including the marine grey mullet, bass, roker, estuarine sturgeon, eel, salmon, and flounder, and the freshwater bream, carp, perch, and fish of the pike family (Brinkhuizen 2006). Isotope analysis on human remains from the site corroborated the palaeozoological conclusions that fish continued to form part of the diet. The high $\delta^{15}N$ measurements and elevated $\delta^{13}C$ measurements of 36 samples revealed a reservoir effect normally associated with consumption of marine resources (Smits and Louwe Kooijmans 2006: 102).

Beyond the isotope debate, there is plentiful archaeological evidence for the continued importance of fishing for local groups on the North Sea coast and on its estuaries and rivers. Indeed, there is evidence to suggest that the successful fisher may have held some status. In post-Ertebølle Denmark, the archaeological support for fishing activities—albeit entirely from the Baltic coast—comes principally in the form of wicker fish traps or stationary fish structures. Excavated stationary fishweirs, each comprising V-shaped 'wings' (or a single 'wing') of woven hurdles placed vertically in the shallow water, forming a funnel leading to a wicker or woven fish trap, date to as late as 2600–2500 cal BC, the Funnel Beaker 'culture' (Pedersen 1995: 83). The same types of weirs and traps were in use into the 20th century. The main catch was eel, with the ten-year-olds migrating from the Baltic through the Danish Belt to the Sargasso Sea to spawn. This migration occurred in the late summer and through the autumn, and eel fishing would have been a seasonal activity.

Detailed analysis of many of the shell middens has also noted ongoing accumulation of debris after 4000 cal BC, although a sharp decrease in this accumulation process is dated to c. 3500 cal BC, as is the case, for example, with the middens of the Norsminde Fjord in Jutland (Andersen 2007: 42). Danish shell middens have been dated as late as c. 2500 cal BC; after this date 'shellfish remains are only found as small piles on the settlements' (ibid. 33). A second period of accumulation of shell middens in this region was dated to the first millennium BC and the first millennium AD.

Further south, fishweirs and woven fish baskets used as traps, and fish bones in deposits near settlements form the majority of the evidence. In the

Flevoland Polder, once part of the Zuiderzee, the remains of three fishweirs with their associated baskets were found in a gully of the River Eem and dated to 4300–4200 cal BC. Similar baskets are known from the Dutch Neolithic (Peeters et al. 2002: 101). From the excavations at Vlaardingen (phases 1b and 2b: *c.* 3100–2500 cal BC) and Hekelingen come large number of fish bones, with a wide variety of fish represented, but dominated by the remains of the sturgeon. This fish is probably over-represented, since its bone plates preserve relatively well compared to those of most fish, but its presence in the deposits shows that fish was on the menu for coastal dwellers deep into the Neolithic. Sturgeon would have been caught mainly in May, June, and July when they swam up the rivers to spawn. The remains of a woven fish trap of dogwood, similar in design to the examples from Bergschenhoek, and net sinkers made of pottery shards rolled in birch bark, imply that for these communities fishing was both well-practised and seen as an important component to the diet (Van Gijn and Bakker 2005: 296).

From the British side of the North Sea, very few fish remains are present on Neolithic sites. This may be explained in part by the rapid change in fish consumption as advocated by the isotopic evidence. Occasionally, for example at the Grooved Ware-type sites of North Carnaby Temple and Low Caythorpe on Yorkshire's coast, discoveries of marine molluscs have been relatively abundant. At the former site an incised depiction of a fish on a pig bone was also noted (Manby 1974: 62 and 110). At Tofts Ness and Pool on the island of Sanday in the Orkney archipelago, fish bones were found dating from the Neolithic through to the Viking period, and the evidence led the specialist to conclude that, even in the Neolithic, fishing activity was not necessarily restricted to coastal activity but may have been undertaken in open water (Nicholson 1998).

Bronze and Iron Ages

Evidence for fishing and the broader utilization of marine animals as food becomes somewhat limited in the Bronze Age, in part because the ongoing glacial rebound puts all sites of this date in the northern part of the North Sea basin well above current sea-levels and, consequently, very little organic material survives on sites of this date. However, we have some intriguing evidence of fishing from the rock carvings at Kville, Askum, and Snenneby in Bohuslän. The depicted scenes show people fishing; in the latter example, two people fish with line and hook, and possibly using rods, from a small boat which is anchored on the seabed (Figure 17). However, the depiction of fish on rock carvings in Bohuslän and the Østvold is rare, especially when compared to the very large numbers of boats and ships shown on the rocks (Hygen and Bengtsson 2000: 73; Coles 2005: 60).

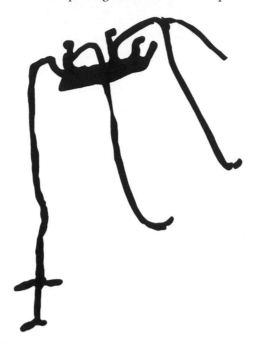

Figure 17. Reproduced image of the rock engraving of fishermen at Kville, Bohuslän (based on Coles 2005: 32)

For the Danish Bronze Age (*c.* 1700–500 cal BC), evidence for some use of marine resources is present at nearly all settlement sites, with mussels dominating the marine component of the palaeozoological assemblages. Alongside the shellfish remains, fish bone analysis indicates a preference for large species such as cod, which, almost certainly, were caught with line and hook from boats in open water (Andersen 2007: 39). The stable isotope analysis of individuals from the Danish coast showed that half the population had consumed significant amounts of marine food (Berntsson 2005: 120; cited in Andersen 2007: 40).

Further south, from the Dutch coast, the evidence is more complete. In the West Friesland area of the province of North Holland, early Beaker-period settlements such as Kolhorn include refuse deposits containing large amounts of mussel and oyster shells, alongside a range of fish bones (Van der Waals 1989; Fokkens 2005: 407). It has been argued that during this period, between *c.* 2600 and 2400 cal BC, fishing may have been undertaken from specialized seasonal camps. This certainly appears to be the case for the small campsite of Mienakker near Hoogwoud in the West Friesland region. Here, abundant remains of haddock, cod, and whiting were found, but the heads and tails of the larger specimens made up the majority of the bones, implying that the catch was not consumed here but transported, possible after drying, salting, or smoking, to the larger settlements for consumption at a later date (Hogestijn 2005: 429). At Molenaarsgraaf in the lower delta of the Rhine and Meuse, a grave dated to 2500–2000 cal BC included three bone fishhooks as grave goods, alongside an antler hook that was interpreted as an implement for lifting fish traps, and flint scrapers that had been used for removing fish scales (Louwe Kooijmans 1974: 248; Drenth and Lohof 2005: 434). A grave of a teenager nearby included part of a fin of a pike at his throat, and it has been suggested that this may have caused his death.

For much of the Bronze Age, fish remained of importance for coastal settlements, but further inland, freshwater fish were caught as well. At the early Bronze Age site P14, currently in the Noordoostpolder but originally situated in the delta of the River Vecht, freshwater fish such as carp and pike, alongside migratory species such as eel, amounted to 82 per cent of the animal bone assemblage, while at the settlement site of Oldeboorn in the River Boorne in Friesland, pike was the most common fish species, representing 84 per cent of all fish remains. Here, too, fish heads dominated the assemblage, suggesting that fish was caught and prepared or preserved for transport and for consumption elsewhere (Kasteleijn 1982; Van Wijngaarden-Bakker and Brinkkemper 2005: 492–3). Fish bones were also found at the middle and late Bronze Age settlement sites of Westwoud and Bovenkarspel-Het Valkje in West Friesland, in the province of North Holland in the Netherlands. Eel was the favourite fish at these sites, but the zoo-archaeological analysis established that bream, perch, pike, and stickleback had also been caught and eaten (IJzereef 1981; Buurman 1998–9: 134). Nevertheless, Leendert Louwe Kooijmans (2005: 705) has noted the surprising lack of interest among early farmers in such a readily accessible source of foods—notably fish but also fowl—from the middle Bronze Age onwards. This is apparent even among those who lived in the wettest parts of the landscape.

An overview of animal remains from the western Netherlands in the late Bronze and Iron Age (IJzereef, Laarman, and Lauwerier 1989: 16) mentions that sturgeon remains had been found on ten sites, seven of these located within the floodplains of the major lowland rivers Rhine, Meuse, and Oer. Furthermore, grey mullet and perch were found on two Iron Age sites. Other fish species represented in deposits of this period are cod, pike, and bream; further inland, the consumption of freshwater fish has also been noted, such as at Lith in the province of Noord Brabant on the River Meuse, where pike and carp were caught and eaten (Van Wijngaarden-Bakker and Brinkkemper 2005: 494). From excavation of coastal settlements, remains of a whale, a grey seal, a bottle-nosed dolphin, and a porpoise are mentioned, but the overall impression is that, with the exception of sturgeon, fish and sea mammals were not extensively caught and eaten in the Iron Age on the coast of the Netherlands. The contribution of marine foods to the Iron Age diet is, considering their potential contribution, remarkably low. The same applies to the terpen and wierden in the Dutch and German parts of the Wadden Sea. Excavations on these artificially heightened mounds in areas that were inundated during spring tides, such as Feddersen Wierde (Haarnagel 1979) or Ezinge (Boersma 2005: 569–70), have illustrated the mixed agricultural economy of these settlements in the Iron Age, with fishing and hunting being of a negligible order.

On the British side of the North Sea, evidence for fishing and fish consumption is limited. An exception to the dearth of information is offered by a conical fishtrap, made of hazel withies and radiocarbon dated to *c.* 1720 cal BC, from New Holland in the Humber estuary. The trap was found in a small palaeo-creek, at right angles to the Humber (Fenwick et al. 2001: 103–5). On the opposite side of the Humber estuary, a large number of Bronze Age wooden structures have been discovered, and while none of these can be presented as offering direct evidence for fishing in the Bronze Age, it is possible that they were used for fishing and fowling (Van de Noort 2004a: 45–8).

The North Sea has produced very little in the form of positive evidence of the use of marine resources in the Iron Age, and the singular reference in Barry Cunliffe's (2005: 442–3) overview of the Iron Age in Britain is telling in this respect. This reference concerns north-western Scotland and the Northern Isles, where the abundance of shellfish and fish is presented as underpinning food-producing strategies. Excavations of the Iron Age-period settlement at Howe on Stromness in the Orkneys has produced the best evidence to date of fishing and fish consumption. The settlement has three major phases: a roundhouse of fourth/third century BC date, and two brochs, one of which was constructed and lived in during the second and first centuries BC. The assemblage includes limpets, winkles, and whelks, which would have been collected from Stromness's rocky shores, and the bones of cod, saithe, polling, whiting, and plaice which could indicate that at least some of the fishing was done from boats in the open water, as well as an abundance of seabirds (Ballin-Smith et al. 1994). Further south, in the English Fenlands, the extended excavations at Flag Fen did not illuminate the use of fish during the Bronze Age, but from Iron Age contexts, fish bones were recovered representing pike, tench, bream, and carp (French 2001: 403). However, at the nearby enclosed Iron Age settlement of Haddenham, no fish remains were found, rather the bones of beaver and waterfowl dominated the bone assemblages (Evans and Serjeantson 1988).

Roman period

The Romans' delight in preparing their meals with various types of fish sauce is well known and clearly demonstrated in the archaeological record of the Roman period. But the evidence for eating fish, either from the North Sea or imported from the Mediterranean, is rare. The evidence for the use of fish sauce comes mainly from amphorae imported from the Mediterranean. Heinrich Dressel himself had already recognized that amphorae were used for shipping fish products. On the basis of painted inscriptions in Rome, a range of Latin names for different fish sauces is known to us, including *muria, scomber, garum, hallec,* and the ubiquitous fish sauce *liquamen* (Peacock 1975). A particular illustrative example from Flavian deposits in Southwark, London, was found to contain fish bones, probably of mackerel, while the amphora itself had a painted inscription on the neck which described the contents as *liquamen* from Antibes (Hassall and Tomlin 1984: 344). A distinctive type of amphora, grouped as Dressel 7–11 'salazon' amphorae or as type Pelichet 46, was produced in the south of Spain principally for the transport of fish sauce. The distribution of this type is widespread in the northern provinces of the Roman Empire, including Britannia, Germania Inferior, and Gallia.

The remains of fish bones have been found on a number of Roman-period sites around the North Sea, but usually in rather small quantities. For the military, we know from ancient texts and inscriptions that legionaries and auxiliaries ate fish and shellfish as part of a broad-ranging diet. Shellfish, particularly oysters, have been found at a large number of military sites (Davies 1971: 128–9). Archaeological excavations of military sites around the North Sea seem to confirm that, apart from the ubiquitous fish sauce, fish remains tend to be scarce. At the military Roman fort of Ribchester in Lancashire, for example, excavations included an extensive sieving programme with the recovery of only a very few fish bones. Species present at Ribchester included salmon, eel, smelt, plaice, flounder, and thick-lipped grey mullet, all of which are thought to have been caught locally (Nicholson 1993).

Evidence of fish consumption from civilian settlements comes in various forms. From the settlement at Zwammerdam, South Holland, graffiti on sherds of an unidentified-type amphora could be interpreted as PI(sces) ACIDI SI(ngulares): best of fish in vinegar (De Raaf 1957–8: 46). In Belgium, from Roman towns such as Tongeren, the remains of marine fish include Spanish mackerel (*Scomber japonicus*), which represents imported saltfish, or *slasamenta*; however, no North Sea species have been found, with the exception of small fish from the Scheldt estuary used in the production of local *garum* (Van Neer and Ervynck 2007: 47). From excavations at Guy's Hospital in the London borough of Southwark comes evidence of second-century AD wooden structures in the marshes of the River Thames, interpreted as the remains of a possible fishweir (Taylor-Wilson and Kendall 2002). In York, a late Roman deposit of fish bones at St Mary Bishophill Junior has been interpreted as a place where fish sauce was made. However, to put this into context, the very large-scale excavations at the Tanner Row site in York produced a huge number of animal bones, dominated by cattle, pig, and lamb but including house mouse, black rat, and garden dormouse, the latter an undoubted delicacy. Yet fish bones, or the remains of other marine mammals, were conspicuous only by their absence (O'Connor 1988). Finally, at Kilnsea, Yorkshire, in the Humber Wetlands, a concentration of Roman domestic pottery was found during field walking on the north edge of the estuary. The pottery came from an area that stood out in the landscape because of the high concentration of oyster shells. The deposits had been ploughed out from their original context, but the evidence was interpreted as a sort of Roman midden, where oysters had been collected and consumed (Head et al. 1995: 290). No military presence is known from this area.

Fishing is also recorded, to the north of the Roman *limes*, in written records. In his *Naturalis historia* (XVI, 2–4), Pliny famously described the Chauci, living on terpen in the eastern part of the Wadden Sea, eking out a meagre existence from the fish they caught in small nets in the gulleys at low tide. However, the archaeological evidence suggests that the Chauci, and their neighbours the Frisii, were first and foremost stockbreeders; their three-aisled farms, such as those excavated at Feddersen Wierde, were built to house cattle during the winter months, and the terpen provided dry ground during the twice-daily tides (Haarnagel 1979; see chapter 5). Another piece of evidence comes in the form of a votive altar from the terp village of Beetgum, Friesland. Dated on the basis of the inscription to the end of the first century AD, the altar was dedicated to Hlundada, and erected for Q. Valerius Secundus by the tenants who held the local fishing rights. It has been argued that this altar shows that professional fishermen, presumably living within the *limes*, occupied some sort of trading station on the coast for trade with the Roman Empire, but Van Es (1965/6) has suggested that the altar could have been moved at some point in antiquity, and that the idea of professional fishermen on the Wadden Sea may be in error.

In Denmark, a period of renewed interest in marine foods is demonstrated by large numbers of shell middens, mainly dated to 500 cal BC to cal AD 400, found principally on the Baltic Sea side but also on the North Sea coast of south-western Jutland (Andersen 2007: 40). Species present in the assemblages are mussels, cockles, periwinkles, and oysters, and the middens have been interpreted as specialized coastal sites for shellfish collection and processing, by cooking or smoking. Shellfish remains have been found up to 6 km from the coast, providing a clear measure of the coastal contact zone.

Middle Ages

Unlike the preceding archaeological periods, research into the importance of fishing and fish consumption in the Middle Ages has been the subject of systematic research, mainly by James Barrett and associates. In a recent article, which includes the results of the analysis of 127 fish bone assemblages from England from AD 600 to 1600, Barrett, Locker, and Roberts (2004a; 2004b) come to the conclusion that in the centuries before AD 1000, freshwater fish such as pike and members of the carp family, alongside migratory species including eel, salmon, trout, smelt, and flatfish, dominated these assemblages. After AD 1000, the fish bone assemblages change in composition, and the marine taxa cod and herring become dominant. Importantly, the assemblages used for analysis come mainly from proto-urban and urban sites, rather than coastal settlements. The authors assert that this demonstrates a significant increase in the importance of the trade in staple goods over the prestige goods economy during the decades around the year AD 1000, and is referred to as 'the AD 1000 fish event horizon'.

The provenance of the fish itself cannot tell us whether the trade in fish was of a regional or a long-distance nature, but with the practice of drying and salting of marine fish recorded as an established practice in the 12th century, it is possible that this practice of conserving fish was in place around AD 1000. If this is the case then the long-distance trade in fish would have been possible. Barrett and colleagues conclude that it was exactly the rise of the town and the market that created the demand for staple foods in the first place, and it is therefore not surprising that the pre-urban *wics* and urban conurbations were the places where the earliest consumption of large amounts of marine fish, relative to their hinterlands, has been noted. The growing numbers of fish-weirs of Late Saxon date, known in particular from the coasts of Essex and Suffolk, may have provided the proto-urban settlements, and possibly monastic houses too, with fish in the final phase of the first millennium AD. Suggestions that climatic changes or Christian beliefs were responsible for increased fishing activity are considered to be without clear evidence. The introduction of drift nets as the reason for increased marine fish consumption is also rejected; this technique would have been unsuccessful in the catching of cod, and this species was caught using hook and line throughout the Middle Ages (Robinson 2000).

Alongside marine fish, sea mammals also became more highly valued in medieval England. Mark Gardiner (1998) has shown that between AD 1000 and 1300, bones of cetaceans are mainly to be found on high-status sites and, in the 11th century, stranded whales were claimed by the king as 'royal fish'. Gardiner makes the point that the consumption of whale meat became a way of expressing social status and aspiration, and that this, rather than a developing taste for whale meat, created the restrictions on their consumption.

This picture of fishing and fish consumption in England appears to be, by and large, replicated elsewhere on the Continent. Evidence from Flanders, northern France, and the Baltic countries all seem to concur with the shift from freshwater to marine fish around AD 1000. In the Netherlands, this pattern is also evident. An overview of the state of environmental archaeology in the Middle Ages from 1990 confirms that cod and herring became frequently occurring fish in the early urban settlements of Deventer, Zwolle, and Alkmaar, in the final part of the first millennium AD, but show up in castle assemblages only from the 12th century onwards (Groenman-van Waateringe and Van Wijngaarden-Bakker 1990). In Belgium, the shift from coastal catches of flatfish (*Pleuronectidae* sp.) to larger marine species especially cod, haddock, and whiting, around AD 1000, is attributed to the urbanization process and to the development of sea fishing (Van Neer and Ervynck 2007: 49).

Comparison of the weights found in the extensive excavations at Dorestad with those from the Koudekerk settlement on the River Rhine has provided some fascinating insights into the fishing practices used here in the early Middle Ages. Henk Kars (1982) concluded that the stone weights from Dorestad were significantly heavier than those from Koudekerk, and that the weights from the former settlement were loomweights, but those from the latter were net-sinkers, and used for fishing using seine-nets. This technique, for use in rivers with low gradients, utilized net floaters on the top of the nets, and required net-sinkers with just the right mass which held the net in place without pulling it to the bottom. This fishing method was probably already practised in the Roman period, and may account for the majority of freshwater and migratory fish caught inland.

In Viking Scandinavia, marine foods appear to have become more important from *c.* cal AD 850, with a renewed period of shell midden formation that lasted until *c.* cal AD 1050. Corroborating evidence exists in the appearance of new fishing tools such as the iron leister and stable isotope analysis of human bones from the coastal zone, both of which indicate an increased consumption of marine foods at this time. In the Orkney Islands, where evidence of fishing dates back to the Neolithic, the fish bone assemblages from shortly after the Viking colonization suggest that fishing became more specialized, with fewer species present and a greater predominance of cod and herring. This is not to suggest, however, that commercial fishing was taking place (Nicholson 1998). Instead, Barrett, Locker, and Roberts (2004a; 2004b) have linked the change to the significance of fishing within Viking communities, comparing the relatively low proportion of fish in the pre-Viking Pictish diet in Scotland to the much larger contribution made by marine taxa once the Vikings settled in the Northern Isles and northern Scotland. Recent research combining the fish bone evidence with stable isotope analysis from the Orkney Islands supports the theory of a terrestrial diet for the Picts and the introduction of a marine diet with the coming of the Vikings around cal AD 850–950. An upsurge in the consumption of marine food appears to have taken place from the 11th century, until its decline in the 14th and 15th centuries (Barrett and Richards 2004). It appears that fish of the cod family was caught in the northern half of the North Sea region and dried for consumption in the towns in the southern half from the 11th century onwards; analysis of the fish bone evidence from the joint Norse earldoms of the Orkneys and Caithness raises this as a likelihood (Barrett 1997). Further north, in the archipelagos of the Lofoten and Vesterålen in Arctic Norway, commercial fishing of cod developed in the 13th century AD, from a long-established tradition of local fishing going back to 3000 cal BC, and gave rise to the commercial fishing stations known as *fiskevaer* (Simpson et al. 2000). As such, the evidence from the northern part of the North Sea corresponds with that from the southern part, in that large-scale commercial fishing in the north only took off with the growth of towns in the south after AD 1000.

In addition to the use of hook and line from fishing boats, fish were here also caught using coastal and estuarine fish traps and weirs. In the Blackwater Estuary in Essex, a number of intertidal weirs have been dated to the seventh to the ninth centuries AD (Gilman 1998). The fish traps were of considerable size, with some of the alignments of the V-shaped weirs over 1 km in length. Where fragments of the wooden hurdles survived, these were shown to have been made of birch, oak, and willow from managed woodland, and the fish baskets from hazel (Murphy 1995). The first documentary records on intertidal fisheries are to be found in the Domesday Book of 1086, which shows that these were both extensive and still in use in the 11th century AD. It is interesting to note the early date of the fishweirs on the east coast of England, predating the fish event horizon of AD 1000 by several centuries. It has been argued that in the 'long eighth century' regional variations included the development of trading places or *wics* such as Ipswich and London, and early demand for commodities such as fish may have grown with these trading settlements (cf. Rippon forthcoming). On the other side of the North Sea, for example at the early trading settlement of Dorestad, herring did form part of the bone assemblage, despite being situated over 30 km from the nearest marine environment, the Zuiderzee. Thus, the seeds for a specialized fishing industry that served the urban conurbations from AD 1000 may have been sown as far back as the eighth century.

Whereas the fish bone evidence defines the 'fish event horizon' at around AD 1000, the development of distinctive and specialized fishing communities largely engaged in deep-sea fishing is more difficult to ascertain. Research in the Lofoten and Vesterålen in Arctic Norway, has indicated that the *fiskevaer*, dated to around AD 1300, possibly represent the earliest specialized fishing settlements (Simpson et al. 2000). On the basis of historical analysis, Kirby and Hinkkanen (2000) argue that the occurrence of North Sea villages specializing in fishing, and in the preserving of fish through drying, salting or smoking, is a phenomenon of the early modern era. Before the 15th century, most fishing was undertaken by farmers with fishing boats; in the

Shetland archipelago alone would one find fishermen with plots of land to farm. Professional fishers, it is argued, are characteristic only of the post-medieval era. Harold Fox (2001), in his study of the fishing villages of Devon in south-west England, came to a similar conclusion for this region: that the transition from coastal 'cellar' settlements where a smallholder-craftsman class engaged in fishing, to specialized fishing communities, only occurred in the later 15th century. Longshore fishing voyages before this date were undertaken by ships based in urban ports. The development of fishing communities in the North Sea basin can be illustrated by the example of Texel, the easternmost island in the Wadden Sea. It appears that by the beginning of the 16th century about one-third of the population of Texel was wholly or partly professional fishermen: according to the *Informacie,* which included a count of hearths for taxing purposes, 500 men took to the sea out of a population of 648 households, salted fish would have been taken from Texel to the Hanseatic cities (Woltering 1996/7: 194).

THE NORTH SEA TASKSCAPE AND THE SOCIAL IDENTITIES OF FISHERS

In this section, the impact of the North Sea taskscape on the social identities of the people who lived and worked here is considered. The role of fish and sea mammals is clearly important in the way that people engaged with the sea, but from the evidence presented in this chronological overview, it is clear that North Sea fish and sea mammals were valued as sources of food at certain times more than others. Two distinct 'fish event horizons' have been noted: a decline in marine foods consumption around 4000 cal BC, and a resurgence around AD 1000. The latter event is not the subject of significant controversy, insofar that the data from many countries around the North Sea all point to the same broad conclusion: the growth of towns caused a rise in the demand for staple food, with fish as a principal component. This resurgence was preceded on a smaller scale by developments in pre-urban *wics* including London, Ipswich, and Dorestad, while in Viking Scandinavia an increase in marine food consumption, as represented by the shell middens, is dated to cal AD 850–1050.

The debate on the 4000 cal BC shift in marine foods consumption event is, however, ongoing. The scientific evidence is not in the dock: few, if any, archaeologists would argue today that the isotope analysis of human bones was in itself flawed or biased. However, agreement on the interpretation of the data is another matter. For example, in accepting the accuracy of the isotope analysis, Julian Thomas (2003) argues that the rejection of fish around 4000 cal BC could be understood as a marker of social identity, in this case of 'being

Neolithic', just as the consumption of domesticated food was a positive aspect of this social identity. Thus, people seeing themselves as 'being Neolithic' created a new social taboo: 'touch not the fish' (ibid. 69). Thomas is well known as a proponent of the idea that the 'Neolithic revolution' was primarily a cultural phenomenon, but that the transformation from a Mesolithic to a Neolithic subsistence strategy was a gradual process extending over centuries (1999). This attempt to argue that a rapid shift in fish consumption should be understood as a cultural phenomenon and not one of subsistence is, at the very least, paradoxical (Figure 18). It also appears to contradict the archaeological evidence.

The evidence from coastal sites throughout the Neolithic and Bronze Age, including fish bone assemblages, fish traps, middens of shellfish, occasional Bronze Age rock carvings from the Bohuslän area of people fishing with line and hook from boats, and the grave goods such as the three fishhooks from the Early Bronze Age grave at Molenaarsgraaf, demonstrates the continued consumption of fish. It does not suggest that fish or shellfish were no longer eaten as a matter of taboo or principle. In addition, new isotope analysis from Denmark and the Netherlands has shown that fish still formed a significant part of the diet by the mid fourth millennium BC date. So how are we to square these contradictions?

There is little doubt that fishing and fish consumption declined in importance around 4000 cal BC, but for coastal communities fish remained an important component of the diet. A number of potential explanations are available as to why the isotope analysis of human remains has failed to identify this continued activity. First of all, the debate on the 4000 cal BC

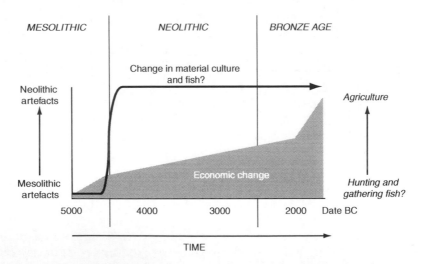

Figure 18. Julian Thomas's (1999) graph of the Mesolithic/Neolithic transition—but is fishing an aspect of economic change or of a change in material culture?

fish event has not, as yet, considered the validity of the 10 km boundary from the coast used in the isotope analysis to distinguish between coastal and non-coastal dwellers. This boundary may have defined 'coastal' too generously, and included the populations from settlements only a few kilometres from the coast that were nevertheless wholly reliant on terrestrial sources of food. The concentration of shellfish waste in coastal middens in Denmark and Scotland, and the absence of shellfish remains from sites only a few kilometres from the coast, could be considered as evidence that marine foods were not transported inland over any great distance, but were consumed where caught or gathered. The earliest archaeological evidence for the preparation of fish for transport and consumption elsewhere is the Early Bronze Age campsite of Mienakker in West Friesland (*c.* 2600–2400 cal BC), where the heads and tails of marine species such as haddock, cod, and whiting were found to dominate the fish bone assemblages. From Iron Age Denmark we know that the maximum extent of the marine contact zone in that period was 6 km. For the Neolithic, there is no archaeological evidence for such specialized practices, and it may be that fish was consumed very close to where it had been caught. Thus, a more restrictive definition of coastal communities, for example as settlements located directly on the coast, may have resulted in a different outcome in the isotope analysis of human remains.

Second, there appears to have been a shift from marine to freshwater fish consumption, including migratory species such as eel and sturgeon. This would not have shown up as elevated $\delta^{13}C$, but as elevated $\delta^{15}N$ measurements in the human skeletal remains. In more recent research in the Netherlands, Denmark, and Sweden, where $\delta^{15}N$ measurements were included in the isotope analysis of human remains, the consumption of freshwater fish in the Neolithic, alongside variable levels of marine fish, has been proven beyond any doubt (Richards, Price, and Koch 2003; Price and Gebauer 2005; Smits and Van der Plicht 2009). Furthermore, there is ample archaeological evidence in the form of fishweirs and fish traps on rivers some distance from the coast, especially in the lowlands of the Netherlands, sug-gesting that freshwater fish may have grown in importance in subsistence strategies, relative to marine fish. The fish bone assemblages from several Neolithic and later-period settlements in the Netherlands away from the coast show that freshwater fish such as carp and pike were the main species eaten. The previously mentioned evidence from the Neolithic settlement site of Swifterbant corroborates this further, with the isotope analysis of its popula-tions indicating that fish remained an important part of the diet.

Third, fishing may have become a seasonal activity, with fish consumption as a year-round practice diminishing in importance and therefore becoming less noticeable in the results of isotope analysis. The key evidence for this possible explanation comes from the Danish coast, where the orientation of the fixed V-shaped fishweirs has been interpreted as a specialized adaptation for eel fishing. Since the migration of the ten-year-old eels to the spawning grounds in the Sargasso Sea occurs in late summer and autumn only, fishing may well have been an important activity for part of the year only, not producing the significant marker in terms of isotopic distinctiveness.

Fourth, fishing on the North Sea coast may have retained much of its importance in the Neolithic, whereas on England's south coast and in Wales, the location of all coastal skeletal material used for the British analysis, fish lost its significance. There are good reasons behind this idea. The south coast of England and the coast of Wales are dominated by hard and soft rock cliffs and smaller beaches, environments in the main unsuited for logboats and, unsurprisingly, no logboats are known from here dated to before the Bronze Age (Lanting 1997/8; see also chapter 7). However, successful fishers required the use of boats on a daily basis, for example to empty their fishweirs and baskets, or for line-fishing, and communities that did not use boats could not have maintained a substantial fishing industry. In contrast, much of the North Sea coast of the Netherlands and Denmark was dominated by extensive wetlands and archipelagos, environments ideally suited for logboats, and the oldest evidence for logboats can be found here (Lanting 1997/8). Thus, it appears that the continued practice of fishing and fish consumption in the Neolithic was determined by the importance of the daily use of boats.

During the later Mesolithic and early Neolithic periods we should expect to find regional diversity in marine and freshwater fish consumption, principally based on the types of coastal landscapes and the local significance assigned to boats. Lidén et al. (2004) arrive at a similar conclusion for the Mesolithic–Neolithic of southern Sweden, and Smits and Van der Plicht (2009) for the Dutch coast. To catch and eat fish was a matter of choice, not marine determinism.

Returning to Julian Thomas's 'touch not the fish' argument (2003), we can only conclude that the 4000 cal BC fish event horizon was not one that can be explained by the widespread rejection of a 'being Mesolithic' social identity in favour of one of 'being Neolithic' that excluded the consumption of fish; there is simply too much archaeological evidence to show that people who were farming continued to catch and to consume fish, albeit on a diminishing scale, to argue that there was a taboo on fish. It seems much more likely that fish continued to be consumed, possibly seasonally, by coastal communities, as evidenced by the shell middens and fishweirs from the northern part of the North Sea basin and the fish bone assemblages from the southern part. Fish was not, however, transported to and consumed by people living in settlements even a few kilometres from the coast. As shown earlier, there is no evidence predating the Early Bronze Age for specialized camps where fish were prepared for consumption elsewhere.

The idea of a great divide between Mesolithic and Neolithic identities is, of course, of our own making, and while we can observe significant changes in the material culture around 4000 cal BC, we need to recontextualize this information. The role of landscapes as active agents in the creation of people's sense of identity has recently gained recognition (Bradley 2000; Tilley 2004), and we can apply this concept to the people for whom the North Sea was a significant provider, and for whom the coast was their taskscape. The identity of people living on the shores of the North Sea in the Mesolithic has been, to date, closely linked to fishing. 'To be Mesolithic is to be a fisher', is a statement that seems to characterize current thinking. The successful fisher required specialist tools and skills, which would undoubtedly have given the coastal dwellers identities distinct from those who did not share these tools and skills. However, the evidence before us does not suggest that fishing and fish consumption were key aspects in defining the social identity of groups that lived on the coast. Fishing in the Ertebølle and Swifterbant complexes was never the only source of food, and there is ample evidence of early adoption of artefacts and, indeed, food from nearby farming communities. It appears that the identity of people living alongside the North Sea in the Mesolithic was determined less by fishing than by the use of logboats.

Boats were important not only for hunting and fishing on the North Sea coast and in its estuaries. The significance of using a logboat as a way of moving through the landscape and seascape has not really been recognized. When travelling in logboats rather than walking, moving through the landscape becomes a very different activity and experience. Tracks and paths no longer define the landscape; instead natural rivers and streams determine the direction of travel. In this regard, it is worth remembering the significance attributed by archaeologists to tracks and paths as primary human artefacts that 'encultured' landscapes (e.g. Tilley 1994: 206–7). To walk through a wild(er)ness is, through the creation of tracks, an act of enculturation, but to travel in a logboat leaves no mark on the natural landscape. Thus, the shared mental map of a coastal region is not made up of paths and trackways, but of rivers and creeks. An intimate knowledge of tides, currents, and winds, essential for navigating through the landscape, would have distinguished these 'logboat-people' from the 'walking-people'. The social identities of people living on the edge of the North Sea, where dynamic landscape change was the order of the day and where the taskscape was one of fluidity, may well have been primarily defined by their boats. These craft were not only by far the largest artefacts created by the coastal dwellers, but also defined the way in which food was procured, the landscape experienced, where one could settle, what a family could accumulate and transport from one camp to the next—about ten times as much as a family moving through the landscape on foot—and even the size of the family itself. 'Nautical dwelling' would have constituted a way of life that was wholly different from 'dwelling on foot', and is much more likely to have defined the social identities of Ertebølle,

Swifterbant, and similar but unspecified British complexes than any taboo on the consumption of fish.

The physical evidence associated with such a 'nautical dwelling' concept comprises the handful of logboats of Mesolithic date and those associated with the Ertebølle and Swifterbant complexes (see chapter 7), and is seen also in the long-term use of clearances alongside rivers. The Ertebølle and Swifterbant sites have produced a number of long logboats that could have carried families, including three from the Ertebølle site of Tybrind Vig, one from the Swifterbant-type site of Bergschenhoek and two more from Hardinxveld-Giessendam. All were made of lime, a tree that is relatively easy to work and the species of choice for boatbuilders using stone axes. Two of the Tybrind Vig craft had fireplaces towards the stern of the boats, which have been interpreted as a way of attracting eels during night fishing. Alternatively, these hearths may have been used to carry embers from one settlement site to the next (Pedersen 1995). The site locations in the Dutch Delta clearly suggest that islands within the wetlands and estuaries were preferred over edge-of-dryland locations, for reasons of safety, accessibility, or isolation. This confirms the essential role of logboats in how these people travelled through the landscape. Many of these islands, which shrank over time as sea-levels rose, were visited over long periods, and as the 'logboat-people' returned again and again to the same locations, their distinctive social identities were confirmed and reconfirmed.

Research in the Humber Wetlands has also indicated that people travelled by boat rather than by foot through this landscape; all 80 flint scatters including artefacts or debitage that could diagnostically be attributed to the Mesolithic were found at water-edge locations (Van de Noort 2004a: 36). We do not know whether these sites were primarily used for hunting of animals that came to the waterside for drinking, or for fishing activities, such as the regular clearing of fish traps. But it was noted that nearly half of these scatters also included flints that could be positively attributed to the Neolithic, implying the existence of a hybrid Mesolithic–Neolithic set of subsistence activities in this North Sea-bordering region, which presumably resembled aspects of the Swifterbant complex sites on the Dutch coast on the other side of the sea. However, it should also be noted that in the Fenland region, further south on England's east coast, Mesolithic flint was notably absent from the islands within the wetlands (Hall and Coles 1994: 34), and we should not assume that all people living on the edge of the North Sea followed similar hybrid developmental trajectories.

In terms of the role of fish consumption in determining social identities, it has been argued that this is not a case of 'you are what you eat' in the sense that eating fish was a defining part of the social identity of Mesolithic or Neolithic communities. Fish consumption only ever appears to have formed part of a broader diet, which included hunted mammals and birds alongside the fish, as in the case of the Swifterbant complex. Fishing may also have been a seasonal activity, as has been suggested in the case of the Scandinavian Ertebølle. Conversely, fish evidently did not become a taboo food in the Neolithic, and to continue this argument is to deny the existence of an extensive body of archaeological evidence for the consumption of both freshwater and saltwater fish and shellfish in the Neolithic and Bronze Age. However, the practice of fishing was closely connected with the use of log-boats, essential for reaching fishweirs and nets, and it has been argued here that it was the daily practice of moving through the landscape in boats which set fishers apart from their non-fish-eating contemporaries.

In the Bronze and Iron Ages, fishing and fish consumption continued. The Bronze Age rock carvings from the Bohuslän region in Sweden, the early Bronze Age grave from Molenaarsgraaf with its three fishhooks, and the appearance in the early Bronze Age of the specialist fishing camp of Mienakker in West Friesland, could all be understood as representing a shift towards fishing as a specialist activity. The sea had become the taskscape for the 'specialist' fishers. The rock carvings in Bohuslän and the Østfold gener-ally do not include scenes of the everyday lives of the people living here, and the fishing scenes have been understood as representing 'mythological fishing expeditions' (Hygen and Bengtsson 2000: 73). The three fishhooks in the Molenaarsgraaf grave are unusual as grave goods, and may be understood as an expression of the social identity of fishers with explicit reference to their specialist skills. The sea was by this time no longer the place where everybody could supplement their diet by engaging in fishing.

Roman sources treat the North Sea with a degree of disdain and are dismis-sive about its value as a source of food and other goods, and bones of marine fish rarely occur in Roman settlements in the countries around the North Sea south of the *limes*. Pliny's description of the Chauci in the Wadden Sea region as living off fish caught at low tides is contradicted by the archaeological evidence, which shows that even in this tidal landscape, stockbreeding rather that fishing was the main occupation of the people living here. We can understand Pliny's words as ascribing negative social identities to the barbarians north of the Roman *limes* through his reference to 'fish eaters'.

For the Middle Ages, there is clear evidence of renewed interest in the North Sea as a taskscape with which coastal people engaged on a daily basis. The earliest evidence for renewed marine fishing and fish consumption dates to the sixth century AD onwards, and during the 'long eighth century' the development of the *wics* in eastern England is temporally and spatially closely associated with the establishment of fishweirs and the consumption of fish in these proto-urban settlements. The use of fishweirs produced completely different taskscapes, where the fishers' daily lives were defined by the tides, rather than the sun, and where the boat became the most important tool (O'Sullivan 2001). The fish event horizon of AD 1000 has been attributed to the urbanization around the North Sea, and the fish bone assemblages of towns all include greater proportions of marine fish. The development of specialized fishing villages began in the latter part of the Middle Ages. The strong sense of identity linked to fishing—as opposed to fish consumption— appears to originate only at this time.

CONCLUSION

This exploration of the North Sea as a taskscape has shown an oscillating pattern of the importance of marine foods from the Late-glacial through to the Middle Ages. Where archaeological evidence is present, in the form of marine mollusc, fish, and marine mammal bone remains, this pattern shows relatively high levels of marine food consumption in the Mesolithic, followed by a rapid reduction in Neolithic communities that have no immediate connection with the coast, but a continued consumption of marine products for coastal Neolithic communities, such as those of Ertebølle sites in Denmark or the Swifterbant sites in the Netherlands. Marine fishing involved fishweirs and specialized equipment, with eel being favoured. Freshwater fish species also continued to be caught and consumed. In the Bronze Age, the favoured marine food was larger fish species, such as cod, which must have been caught with line and hook in open water. The earliest evidence of specialized fish preparation dates to the Bronze Age in the Netherlands, and to the Iron Age in Denmark for shellfish. Where the evidence has been systematically analysed, it would appear that marine foods were transported only relatively short distances from the coast, with the Danish evidence suggesting 6 km as being the upper limit. Despite the predilection for cooking with fish sauce in the Roman Empire, fish eating was not favoured, and few Roman sites include fish bones of any significant quantity. North of the Roman *limes*, fish continued to be con- sumed, and when Scandinavians settled on the northern Isles, a significant increase in fish consumption seems to have occurred. In the Middle Ages, increased fish consumption has been noted from the eighth century on- wards, within proto-urban settings, but the main fish horizon event is dated to AD 1000, a time of intensive urbanization around the North Sea basin which gave rise to a ready market for marine fish.

The nutrient-rich freshwater that is discharged by the main rivers into the North Sea creates an environment where a broad range of fish can flourish. The northern part of the North Sea additionally benefits from phytoplank- ton-rich currents of the North Atlantic Drift, the extension of the Gulf Stream, which has a direct impact on the North Sea fish stock (Turrell 1992). There is little actual evidence for fluctuations in the influence of the

North Atlantic Drift on North Sea currents and fish stock over the past ten millennia, but it is clear that in the past four decades, significant changes have taken place and that these have had a direct impact on fish stocks. Similarly, fluctuation in seawater salinity, especially on Denmark's Baltic coast, has been invoked as an important factor in the abundance of marine molluscs during the Holocene (Andersen 2007: 42). Nevertheless, the long-term view of fishing and fish consumption around the North Sea appears not to have been determined by the availability of fish and shellfish, but by choices made to eat, or not eat, fish and shellfish. The fish event horizons of 4000 cal BC and AD 1000 illustrate this point.

Social identities were not defined through the consumption of fish or shellfish. The archaeological evidence presented here has dismissed the argument of the Neolithic fish taboo (Thomas 2003), and has shown that fish continued to be consumed throughout the Neolithic and Bronze Age, although this consumption was restricted to those who lived, permanently or seasonally, close to the sea, or to the estuaries and rivers. The study of fishing in our prehistoric past blurs the distinct boundary between the subsistence economy of the Mesolithic hunter-gatherers and that of Neolithic farmers (Bailey and Milner 2002), but does not offer those who understand ideology as the prime mover of change in this period much solace either (cf. Rowley-Conwy 2004). Instead, fishing as an activity may have been a factor defining the social identity of the first specialists in the Bronze Age, as illustrated by the three fishhooks in the Molenaarsgraaf grave. More important, however, was the engagement with the sea as a taskscape through the medium of the boat which would have distinguished coastal dwellers from their terrestrial counterparts.

5

Socializing coastal landscapes

INTRODUCTION

For many decades, archaeologists have studied the ways in which past people have made the landscapes they inhabited their own, through the construction of paths and roads, monuments, settlements, and field systems, leading to what has been termed 'cultural landscapes'. Such approaches have great validity on land. Archaeologists' interest in constructed monuments, for example, enables the analysis of social structures and social changes over centuries, and nowhere is this approach more vigorously pursued than for the monument-rich Wessex region in the Neolithic and Bronze Age (e.g. Renfrew 1973; Barrett 1997). In order to achieve such a social analysis of monuments, understanding the sequences of construction, alteration, modification, and sometimes conversion is a long-standing theme in archaeological landscape research (e.g. Bradley 1998). The notion that 'one type of monument could only be read and understood in relation to the others' (Tilley 1994: 203) is broadly accepted. Most archaeologists have taken it for granted that man-made features and monuments survive for centuries, and much human activity in the landscape, including the construction of new monuments, is believed to have been guided by the presence of these monuments of the ancestors. A century is a short time in the lifespan of a monument. On the coast, however, few constructed monuments survive for so long.

A recent example may help to illustrate the short-lived nature of monuments in coastal settings. On the North Sea coast of Jutland, between the villages of Lønstrop and Nørre Rubjerg, stands the Rubjerg Kunde lighthouse (Figure 20). Inaugurated in 1900, this 23 m-high lighthouse was taken out of commission in 1968, but the outbuildings were converted into a cafeteria and a museum. These were abandoned in 2002 as the sand dunes covered the outhouses, leaving only the upper part of the lighthouse prey to the dunes. Some of the nearby dunes stand higher than the top of the lighthouse. The site now attracts unprecedented numbers of visitors, who come to see the interplay between human creation and natural forces at work. On the coast, the

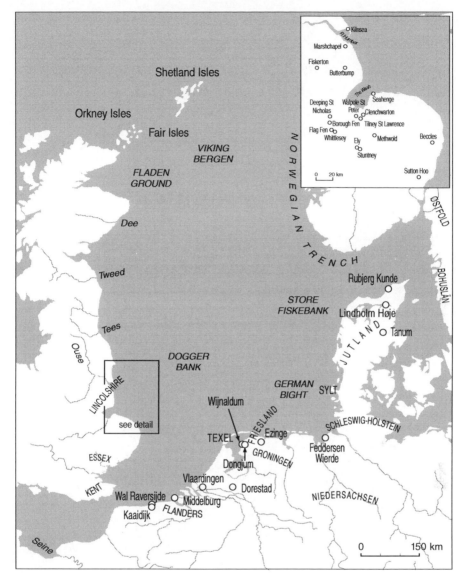

Figure 19. Places and regions mentioned in chapter 5

landscape is changing constantly. At the smallest scale, the sea erodes rocky coasts at an only just observable pace and the wind moves individual sand grains. With time, these barely perceptible actions result in the reconfiguration of coastlines and the formation and movement of dune systems. The impact of the dynamic nature of the sea in shaping landscapes can be observed nowhere better than in the coastal zone.

Figure 20. Rubjerg Kunde lighthouse, Jutland.

Socializing coastal landscapes is a challenge. Through the forces of the sea, the coast is a place where people are not the sole actors in the creation of landscapes. The sea is an actor too. Constructed monuments are subject to marine erosion, burial by dunes or clay, or peat growth that has its ontogeny in sea-level rise and resultant higher groundwater tables in coastal flatlands. In this sense, coastal landscapes appear to resist attempts to socially reproduce the established order through the construction of monuments, and as such we can recognize something of the Deleuzian Ocean on the North Sea coast.

However, there are opportunities and choices involved in how one makes the coastal landscape a familiar place. For example, it could be argued that the deliberate accumulation of shellfish remains and other rubbish to create pronounced mounds or middens in the coastal landscapes of Denmark or Scotland are deliberate actions anchoring the human story into the landscape. The role of middens as locales for feastings is known anthropologically (cf. Bailey and Milner 2002: 6). Similarly, the Iron Age and Roman-period saltern mounds in the landscape of eastern England, made up of briquetage and domestic rubbish, could be understood as a way of socializing the intertidal zone. This was an especially important process as the production of salt was a seasonal activity, and the man-made saltern mounds offered a semblance of continuity in landscape use (cf. Van de Noort 2004a: 74). In different places and at different times, coastal landscapes have been socialized in various other ways. Examples include the construction of fishweirs, such as those from Neolithic Denmark or early medieval eastern England, or the rock carvings overlooking marine inlets in Bronze Age Østfold and Bohuslän. The positioning of early medieval burials using boats is another case of the socialization of the landscape; examples are those at Sutton Hoo, with its views over the Deben valley in Suffolk, and the Viking-age boat-shaped stone settings at Lindholm Høje overlooking the Limfjord in northern Jutland which gave direct access to the North Sea and the Skagerrak. In such ways, and undoubtedly through myths and story-telling as well, the sea and the coast became knowable places.

This chapter presents, in some detail, three case studies to illustrate the diversity of ways in which coastal landscapes were socialized. In each case the role of the sea as a co-actor in the creation of the landscape is acknowledged. The case studies should not be understood as representative for their period, as at any one time the ways in which coastal landscapes were socialized showed remarkable variety. The first study considers how the interplay between the sea and the land removed the monuments constructed by people, and what this meant for the way in which people in the Neolithic and Bronze Age reproduced social structures and identities. The second study concerns a particular group of coastal dwellers, that is the inhabitants of the terpen in the Wadden Sea region who lived, throughout the Iron Age, Roman period and early Middle Ages, with the rhythm of the daily tides. The third study considers the 'greatest gift of the sea', namely reclaimed land, and explores how coastal dwellers in the Middle Ages made their lives on land that really belonged to the sea.

MONUMENTS ON THE NORTH SEA COAST

The coastline of the North Sea is hugely varied. Fundamentally, though, it consists of two distinct parts. In the northern part of the North Sea, the effect of the postglacial isostatic rebound has been to lift up former coasts. As a result, most of the prehistoric and in some places early historic coasts of Norway, western Sweden, north Denmark, Scotland, and north-east England have been elevated to different extents above the current sea-level. As a consequence, the coast here is characterized by pre-Quaternary hard rock cliffs, and includes many steep-sided geomorphological features where the glacial and glaciofluvial activity scoured the surface of the landscape. As a result of the isostatic rebound, many of the former marine inlets have become terrestrialized, for example in Sweden's Bohuslän province where prehistoric marine inlets are now prime agricultural lands. Holocene sea-level change has affected northerly coasts as well and flooded some of the steep-sided glacial valleys to form fjords, or to create the archipelagos of the relatively low-lying Shetlands and Orkneys, which, before *c.* 8250 cal BC, were unified islands.

In the southern part of the North Sea, the combined effects of Holocene sea-level rise, and the relative fall of the land as counterpart to the postglacial isostatic rebound, resulted in the drowning and submergence of extensive Pleistocene and early Holocene coastal landscapes. The interplay between the transgressing sea, the coast, the wind, and the rivers that flow into the North Sea has produced new low-lying landscapes characterized by deep drift cover. These include dune formations that bring about the sandy beaches of western Jutland, the German North Sea coast, the west coast of the Netherlands and the north-east of England's North Sea coast. With some dunes reaching an impressive height of up to 30 m, these landscapes can be awe-inspiring, but drift geology is susceptible to rapid erosion and the dunes are constantly changing. The islands in the southern North Sea basin are essentially sand banks, barriers or dunes that have been elevated above the contemporary sea-level. Few are stable, and the islands of the southern part of the Wadden Sea famously 'wander' slowly south-eastwards as their north-western part is eroded and the sandbanks to the south-east of the islands aggrade. Much of England's east coast is formed by soft rock formations of Pleistocene glacial till. This material withstands marine erosion somewhat better then the sandy deposits, but the speed of erosion was and is sufficiently rapid to be noted within the lifespan of individuals (e.g. Valentin 1957).

This broad division between the northern and southern parts of the North Sea can also be recognized in the presence of monuments. Coastal landscapes in the northern North Sea include a large number of constructed monuments on hard rock coasts, and the interplay between the natural and the cultural spheres is frequently played out by locating these monuments in such a way that they are visible from, or look out onto, the sea. Monuments may have been located to aid navigation, as argued for example by Tim Phillips (2003) for the Orcadian Neolithic chambered cairns, the placing of which stands in direct contrast to the emphatically terrestrial location of tombs elsewhere in northern Scotland. The Bronze Age cairns in the Bohuslän region of Sweden frequently overlook the marine inlets, with some of them standing above carved rock panels, such as at the site of Tanum, where the rock carvings include a large number of boats (Hygen and Bengtsson 2000: 42). Nevertheless, constructed monuments are often dwarfed by the natural monuments such as steep cliffs, natural arches, and stacks.

In the coastal landscapes of the southern North Sea, constructed monuments of Neolithic and Bronze Age date are much rarer, and consequently harder to place within large geographical contexts that allow for the comparison of broad swathes of coastal and inland landscapes (e.g. Van Es, Sarfatij, and Woltering 1988: 73, 77, 79). There is no doubt that such illustrations are biased in various ways, for example where dune formation, peat development, or marine and riverine alluviation mask prehistoric landscapes, but the evidence points unmistakably to a genuine phenomenon. Two plausible explanations for this relative dearth of monument construction in Neolithic and Bronze Age coastal landscapes in the southern North Sea are first that the absence of hard rock formations dissuaded people from constructing monuments, and second that the absence from view of earlier monuments discouraged the construction of new ones. In view of recent debates on the significance of monuments in their relationship to the landscape and specific landscape features, and also in their connection to already existing monuments, it cannot be surprising that coastal landscapes contain few Neolithic and Bronze Age monuments.

Research on the east coast of England has revealed several clusters of Neolithic and Bronze Age monuments close to the contemporary coastline, such as the small Neolithic circular monument and group of Bronze Age barrows at Kilnsea in East Yorkshire, the barrow cemetery at Butterbump in Lincolnshire (Van de Noort 2004a: 103), or the barrow cemeteries in the Fenlands at Deeping St Nicholas, the Crowland peninsula, in Borough Fen and on an 'island' east of Whittlesey (Hall and Coles 1994: 73–5). In nearly all these cases, no natural features such as rock outcrops were present in the landscape to which the monuments could have related, and instead the majority of monuments can be found near rivers or on promontories surrounded by the flatlands which were most prone to waterlogging, mire development or marine transgression.

The way in which the landscape was socialized in the context of an advancing sea can be studied in detail in the Fenlands of East Anglia, which has a long tradition of archaeological research. This 'flat uncompromising wilderness' (Hall and Coles 994: 1) around the Wash was formed by the rising and transgressing North Sea from *c.* 6000 cal BC, and by the impact of this on the groundwater table which led to the formation of extensive mire development. Beneath the silts and peats, which are in places over 26 m deep (Sturt 2006: 122), was an undulating landscape which had been shaped by glacial, glaciofluvial, and fluvial activity, and which offered 'islands' of higher grounds for human settlement. Many of these higher grounds were submerged by the sea, buried beneath silts and clay or covered by peat during the Neolithic and Bronze Age.

The barrow at Little Duke Farm, Deeping St Nicholas, in the Fenlands of England, provides an example of a monument that was submerged by sedimentation related to sea-level rise. The reconstructed sequence of events is complex. Initially a Neolithic settlement site, in the Early Bronze Age the site was used for the burial of a child in a wooden coffin, marked by two posts and eight concentric rings of stakes. Some 20 or 30 years after the child's burial the construction of a ditched burial mound revetted with gravel took place; this mound was later surrounded by a ring of posts. The body of an adult was placed in a pit dug into the mound, and the burial of a second adult in a pit dug into the mound followed. The mound was enlarged to a diameter of 35 m with a ring ditch some time later, and four cremations were inserted into the barrow. The final act included the burial of another six cremations in a small pit outside the barrow edge, before the whole complex was buried by peat as the level of groundwater rose following marine transgressions (French 1999; Hall and Coles 1994: 73–4). Such sequences of activity surrounding pre-existing monuments is not without parallel elsewhere, but the question that needs to be asked here is: what happens to communities when the places that symbolize their ties with the past, and where the social order is reproduced, disappear?

In response to the disappearing monuments of the ancestors, local communities may have created new monuments on higher grounds which lay outside the influence of the transgressing sea, and the archaeology of the Fenlands indeed shows a significant number of Bronze Age barrows and barrow fields situated on 'islands' and the higher skirtlands, above and beyond the influence of the sea, some nearby but others without pre-existing monuments in their surrounding areas (Hall and Coles 1994: 65–91). Rather than retaining a visual link between old and new monuments within the landscape, such relationships could only have been part of the social memory. But while some communities appear to have put their effort into socializing their remaining higher grounds by the construction of new ancestral monuments, not all people retreated from the lowlands, and in the Fenlands two alternative ways in which the coastal landscape were socialized can be identified.

The first was an extension of the practice of votive deposition of artefacts. As already discussed (chapter 3), artefacts such as polished stone axes and bronze tools and weapons were deliberately placed on the very edge of the landscapes where marine transgression was noted, and where the expanding wetlands could take possession of these votive objects. In eastern England, this practice originated in the Neolithic. By the end of the early part of the Bronze Age, *c.* 1900 cal BC, human burials seem to have been deliberately placed, on a number of occasions, in similar environmental situations. Evidence for these burials was uncovered at a time when the agriculture of the Fenlands was not fully mechanized; farm workers like Frank Curtis noted fragile human remains in the bottom of drainage ditches. These included the skeleton of a possible young adult female with a bracelet of eight barrel-shaped jet beads on a bed of sedges, as well as the graves of an adult and two children, and the articulated bones of an adult woman 'lying on a regular setting of parallel pieces of wood' in the parish of Methwold, Norfolk (Healy 1996: 30–6). All appear to have been found near the bottom of the peat, and could have been placed at the very edge of the transgressing wetlands. The same appears to be true for a number of whole pots found in the same area, most notably some middle- and late-style Beakers, some of which contained human remains, which might also have been ritual deposits. This group, deliberately placed on the edge-of-wetlands, predates the well-known practice from the middle Bronze Age onwards of the deposition of human remains in close association with metal-work in wetlands (e.g. Bradley and Gordon 1988). Frances Healy (1996: 181) notes that these human interments in the Fenlands 'correspond to the peak of local post-fen clay occupation but are unusually early for bog or river burials in Britain'. In other words, in the aftermath of marine incursions, represented geologically by the fen clay, local communities socialized their landscape not through relating their dead to pre-existing monuments, but through direct association with the transgressive wetlands, and thus indirectly with the sea.

The second way in which Fenlanders socialized their landscape, in places where ancient monuments had been taken by the sea, was through the construction of new types of monuments which were organic and transient in nature. The best known of these are the Bronze Age timber circle at Holme-next-the-Sea, Norfolk, better known as 'Seahenge', and the Bronze Age post alignments and platform at Flag Fen near Peterborough. The 'Seahenge' site is not a henge but an elliptical space measuring *c.* 7 m from north to south and just over 5 m from east to west, enclosed mainly by split oak trunks, and with a very large inverted oak placed within the enclosed space (Figure 21). The trees were felled in 2049 BC, and detailed analysis of the axe facets on the wood shows that 51 different axes were employed in their felling and modification, implying that at least this number of people partook in its communal construction. All bar one of the timbers showed bark to the outside; this would have produced an external texture to the monument akin to that of a very large tree. The timber structure had been built on a saltmarsh, close to the point of the highest spring tides. Nearby, a second structure that appeared to be a timber circle, named Holme II, was identified; this structure may have been a barrow, of which the central burial and the timber revetment partially survived. This second site was dated to 2400–2030 cal BC (Brennand and Taylor 2003). The function of 'Seahenge' remains somewhat unclear, in the sense that it cannot with any great confidence be ascribed a funerary function, since no human remains were uncovered. Nevertheless, Mark Brennand and Maisie Taylor hypothesize that the importance of the monument lies in the

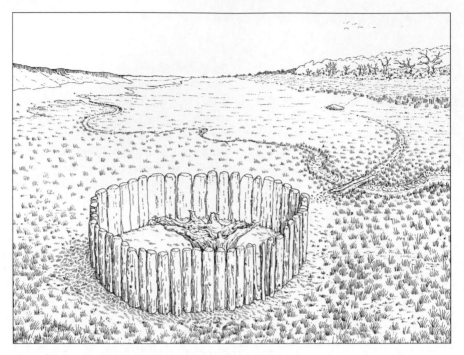

Figure 21. Reconstruction of 'Seahenge'. Original drawing by David Dobson (in Brennand and Taylor 2003: 67 ©The Prehistoric Society)

creation of a significant space, and that the act of construction was what mattered, commemorating or celebrating a central event, such as a death or a festival, in a liminal area between the land and the sea (ibid. 71).

In essence, the Flag Fen site comprises a complex of timber alignments and a platform constructed in the first half of the 13th century BC. Modifications and alterations, divisible into three phases, took place until shortly after 924 BC. The alignment was made up, at its fullest extent, of five rows of posts: these can be divided both axially and transversely. Axially, the middle row (no. 3) formed a wall; the posts in the rows north of this wall (nos. 4 and 5) appear to have formed a defensive palisade, while the rows to the south (nos. 1 and 2) functioned as a walkway (Figure 22). Transversely, the alignment seems to have been segmented into sections of 5–6 m in length; this is understood to reflect the way in which the structure was organized ritually, rather than the actions of groups of workers. Over the four centuries of use, significant changes were made to the construction of the post alignment. In phase 1 the structure comprised timbers in two rows only (nos. 1 and 3); it was extended to the full five rows in phase 3, and in phase 3-final, row 4 resembled a *chevaux de frise*, and the wattle revetment in row 5 disappeared. Different wood species were used, with alder dominating the early phase of

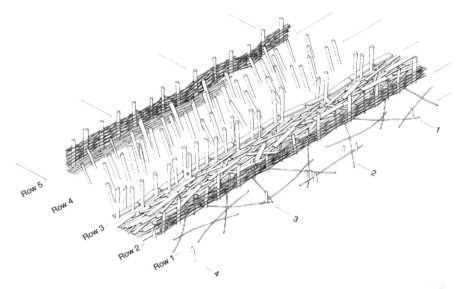

Row 5
Row 4
Row 3
Row 2
Row 1

1
2
3
4

Figure 22. Reconstruction drawing of Flag Fen, Phase 3, middle stage. Original drawing by Colin Irons (in Pryor 2001: 424 ©English Heritage)

construction, and oak the later modifications. Ritual depositions took place to the south of the structure. It is evident that certain segments were given over to ritual depositions of metalwork, but also of dogs and quern stones, most notably in the poolside area where in phase 1 a 'portal' was identified. Deliberate deposition continued at this locale throughout phases 2 and 3, with a final (closing?) deposit of a finely decorated Le Tène II sword scabbard plate. The votive deposition of metalwork extends beyond the tenth century BC, and the latest objects suggest that votive deposition in the water was practised here perhaps as late as the Early Roman period. The Flag Fen platform, believed originally to be sufficiently robust to support a settlement, is now understood as an 'island' of diverse ritual importance, which possibly held pools and waterbodies that played particular roles in these rituals (Pryor 2001: 421–7).

Excavator Francis Pryor recognizes a clear association between the Flag Fen site and the North Sea, in the sense that 'the principal local stimulus for its construction can be seen in the steadily rising waters of the Fens to the north-east. The posts can, indeed, be seen as a symbolic weir or dam against their inexorable rise' (ibid. 431). Rising sea-levels and the resulting higher ground-water tables had submerged part of the older field system and droveways, and would have created significant pressures on the intensive agricultural practices in this low-lying region, and ensuing social tensions may have given rise to a different means of socializing the landscape.

The timber structure at Holme-next-the-Sea, and the Flag Fen alignments and platform, are both representative of how communities socialized the landscapes that they inhabited in ways relating directly or indirectly to the sea, in particular the transgressing sea and the resultant expansion of wetlands. For 'Seahenge', socialization is achieved through the use of the liminal space between the land and sea as the chosen locale for a small monument; at Flag Fen the essence of the monument is related directly to the threatening sea. Coastal communities elsewhere appear to have responded in ways analogous to that adopted by the Flag Fen community. Three more timber alignments with evidence of associated ritual deposition—between Fordey and Little Thetford near Ely; between Ely and Stuntney, with the Stuntney hoard of 80 bronzes packed in a wooden tub found next to the causeway; and at Lingley Fen—are known from the Fenlands (ibid. 432–3). Other sites in eastern England include Beccles on the Norfolk/Suffolk border (William Fletcher, personal communication), the Whitham valley in Lincolnshire, where evidence of ritual deposition is associated with ten causeways across the floodplain (Stocker and Everson 2003), and the published site of Fiskerton (Field and Parker Pearson 2003).

While both Seahenge and Flag Fen could be read and understood with reference to other and pre-existing monuments, the central role of nature, especially the sea, in comprehending these monuments is striking. For Seahenge, the excavators use the sea to explain the locale, while at Flag Fen the principal local stimulus is the sea itself. Without the sea, these monuments would have lacked social context. The prior existence of early Bronze Age burials on the edge-of-wetlands in the Fenlands must have reinforced the position of the sea as a monument in its own right. This cannot be a surprise. After all, with the landscape as the main locus of social memory, and with the loss taking place of ancient monuments that inscribed history on the landscape, the new history was inscribed, principally, through the perceptions and experiences of the dynamic and living sea (cf. Gosden and Lock 1998: 5; Sturt 2006).

SOCIALIZING THE WADDEN SEA

The Wadden Sea is the part of the North Sea bordering the very south of Jutland, the German North Sea coast, the coast of Groningen and Friesland, and the top of North Holland. It is an idiosyncratic part of the North Sea, dynamic and ever changing; the Wadden Sea is now a World Heritage Site in its own right. Its creation was the result of the combined impact of Holocene sea-level rise, a significant drop of the land surface—formerly raised as part of the forebulge of the Scandinavian icesheet during the Weichselien glacial—and sedimentation processes. The socialization of this coastal landscape was undertaken over a period of *c.* 1,500 years, from 500 cal BC to AD 1000. It involved the construction of artificial islands along the coasts of Friesland, Groningen, Niedersachsen, and Schleswig-Holstein, known in Dutch as terpen or wierden and in German as *Wierden, Wurten,* or *Warften,* and hereafter referred to as 'terpen'.

The earliest marine incursions in this area have been noted in the deepest Pleistocene palaeochannels around 8000 BP, for example in the Lauwerszee area. At this time, sea-level rise outpaced local sedimentation processes, but by 6500 BP, the aggradations of sediments and sea-level rise become more balanced, resulting in the creation of extensive saltmarshes on the landward side of the coastal barrier islands (Vos and Van Kesteren 2000). The formation of the barrier islands are dated to *c.* 6000–5000 BP, or possibly somewhat earlier (e.g. Flemming 2002). The gaps in the coastal barrier correspond to the location of Pleistocene river valleys; these gaps ensured continued marine influence in the Wadden Sea throughout the Holocene. The coastal island barriers themselves migrated landwards, in response to continued sea-level rise—possibly by as much as 10 km over the past five millennia—and much of the Wadden Sea expanded to cover dry land. From around 5000 BP, the rate of sediment accumulation exceeded the rise in sea-level and the area between the coastal barrier islands and the dry land to the east and south created an intertidal saltmarsh landscape which became less frequently inundated by the tides. Increases in the tidal energies resulted in the deposition of amounts of sands which over time created undulations in the saltmarsh landscape of the Wadden Sea. Extensive saltmarshes developed from *c.* 1000 cal BC, and these later became the focus of settlement. Towards the dry lands, freshwater drainage became gradually impeded, resulting in the development of progressively larger peatlands. The landscape of the Wadden Sea was constantly changing, and the tides, sea-level fluctuation and sedimentation patterns created a dynamic interplay between the sea, the land, and the muddy banks that were neither land nor sea. With the construction of embanking dikes from the tenth century AD onwards, both the landward and seaward landscapes of the Wadden Sea have changed.

The evidence for the socialization of this dynamic landscape, in the form of terpen, comes overwhelmingly from the area which is now protected from the influence of the sea by the dikes, but which in the later prehistoric and early historic periods was intertidal. Outside the embanked area, evidence for human activity is largely restricted to the islands at the extremes, such as Texel in the west and Sylt in the north. Pleistocene land surfaces form the core of these islands (Woltering 1975; 1979); other islands are essentially sand barriers, which have all migrated or wandered over the past millennium and have largely lost the evidence for early human activity.

Towards the end of the sixth century BC, people living on the higher and drier Pleistocene grounds started to use the saltmarshes as grazing grounds for cattle, possibly in a transhumant form using the saltmarshes in the summer. The earliest terpen were of middle Iron Age date, *c.* 500–250 cal BC, and it seems probable that the mounds were initially simple house 'podia' which over time were connected to other podia to form the distinctive terp settlements (Bazelmans 2009). The terpen in the Wadden Sea region provide an example of an extremely distinct form of socializing coastal landscapes, and this distinctiveness is closely linked to the specific landscape of the Wadden Sea. Here, extensive tracts of land were submerged during high tides on a daily basis, and all the land but the terpen themselves were submerged during spring high tides. The terpen provided access to the saltmarshes, which provided individuals and communities with rich grazing for their animals.

Archaeologically, the best known of these terpen is the Feddersen Wierde in Land Wursten in the state of Niedersachsen (Haarnagel 1979), which was extensively excavated between 1955 and 1963, and gives us an understanding of the dynamics of a coastal terpen community. This settlement, on the low-lying marshland on the right bank of the River Weser, was established on a shore ridge in the second half of the first century BC (Siedlungshorizont phase 1a) and consisted of five houses, later extended to ten, with the same dimensions: 20.0 × 5.5 m. The presence of a granary with every house was taken to mean that each house represented an independent economic unit, with storage organized at that level. Each house comprised living quarters in the east half of each house, centred on a single hearth, and stables in the west half. The construction of the terp commenced in phase 2, attributed to the end of the first or beginning of the second century AD. The houses were laid out radially with the highest point of the terp forming the central village square. The village grew to contain 14 houses each with its own granary, but included a house without stalls for cattle and without an accompanying granary, and two workshops. A house without stalls is understood to have been a labourer's house, which implies that social differentiation had occurred by this time. In phase 3, in the first half of the second century AD, the settlement grew further to include 17 houses, four labourers' houses, two workshops, and one hall, that is a nearly full-sized house without any cattle stalls but with two hearths. The hall was given prominence by a wide ditch and fence which surrounded a complex of buildings, and cattle may have been kept in one of the other buildings within this enclosed space. The presumed presence of a village 'head' in phase 3 may have its origin in the wealthier family that occupied house 12 in phase 2.

In phase 4 (second–third century AD), a new hall (no. 35) was surrounded by a woven fence, and the entrance to the enclosure was marked by a horse burial (Figure 23). This is considered to imply that either the horse had a special status and was buried by the owner of this hall, or else the burial was a ritual act, and the owner of the hall held priestly functions. Excavator Werner Haarnagel noted that the power and wealth of the village was concentrated in the radial section of the village that included the hall, coinciding with the concentration of Roman imports. During phase 5, third century AD, the

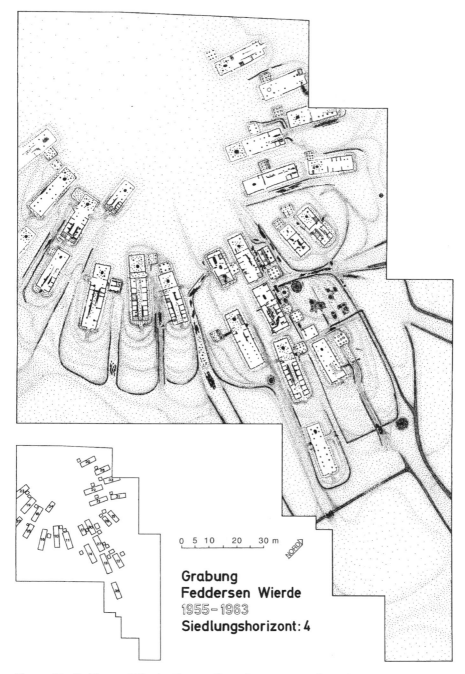

Grabung
Feddersen Wierde
1955-1963
Siedlungshorizont: 4

Figure 23. Feddersen Wierde Phase 4 (based on Haarnagel 1979)

village grew to include 25 houses; evidence for phase 6 was badly damaged; but phase 7, fourth century AD, shows a rapid decline in the fortune of the Feddersen Wierde. A final phase 8, fourth–fifth centuries AD, shows the village in rapid decline. Only two houses comparable to the large buildings in phases 1–6 are present, alongside some 20 smaller buildings. The area of the two halls is represented in this phase by several buildings and one of the two remaining granaries.

The economic basis for the inhabitants of Feddersen Wierde, and for those living on terpen elsewhere in the Wadden Sea, was farming. Despite what Pliny says in his *Natural history* (XVI, 2–4) about the Chauci who lived on terpen in the eastern part of the Wadden Sea, the evidence points overwhelmingly to a community of farmers who, rather than eking out a meager existence from the

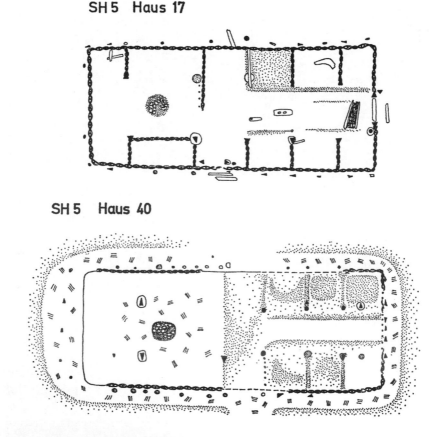

Figure 24. Feddersen Wierde—layout of two houses in Phase 5 (based on Haarnagel 1979)

fish they caught in small nets in the gulleys at low tide, were preoccupied mainly with the raising of cattle, as evidenced archaeologically by the cattle stalls (Figure 24). The saltmarshes were used for grazing, and the higher ground, including the terpen themselves, for growing crops, as signified by the granaries. Certainly fish were caught, but the bones from hunted and caught animals combined constituted only 0.5 per cent of the total bone assemblage (Haarnagel 1979: 272). Even accounting for preservational bias, it seems reasonable to argue that the people living on the terpen did so for good economic reasons. The inhabitants at Feddersen Wierde were connected to local markets where their surplus goods, such as the cattle, dried meat, animal fats, and hides, were exchanged. Haarnagel identified the nearby ringwall settlement of Heidenschanze as the most likely regional central place—the market where the produce from marsh and Geest (the Pleistocene soils to the east) could be sold. Among the imports were many goods from within the Roman Empire, including Samian ware, pearls, glass, and especially basalt quern stones from the Mayen region. Haarnagel notes that the volume of trade resulting in Roman imports increased significantly in the second century AD (ibid. 312). The same observation can be made for other terpen, even though none have been as thoroughly excavated as Feddersen Wierde.

The end of the Feddersen Wierde settlement coincides with the abandonment of many other terpen in the Wadden Sea region, at least as far as archaeological research suggests, and settlements on the pre-Holocene lands nearby similarly show a discontinuation of occupation (e.g. Meier 2004 for Schleswig-Holstein; Halbertsma 1963 for Friesland). This begs the vexed question whether the abandonment of the wider Wadden Sea region and the Anglo-Saxon migration to England are linked phenomena.

From the end of the sixth century AD, people returned to the Wadden Sea, in some cases reoccupying the earlier terpen such as at Ezinge in modern Friesland, but frequently constructing new mounds, avoiding the raised mires that had spread over the inner saltmarshes (e.g. Meier 2004: 63). This phase of habitation of the Wadden Sea is traditionally associated with the Frisians, who are known to us historically especially through the writing of the Franks, for example the *Lex Frisionum* of *c.* AD 802/3, who had incorporated the majority of the Frisian lands into the Carolingian Empire by AD 734. The nature of the social and territorial structure of the Frisians remains a much debated issue. Anthony Heidinga has summed this up by stating that there were people who considered themselves Frisians who remained beyond the reach of Carolingian authority, especially to the north of the River Weser, and that there is ample evidence too for the presence of non-Frisians in parts within Frisia, especially to the south of the River Rhine. However, the Franks had to deal with a 'strong Frisian' political military power, which suggests political coherence in the greater part of the Frisian realm at least (Heidinga 1999: 6). The kind of political structure envisaged is one of leader and retinue (or *Gefolgschaft*), with the king being a successful military leader of a group of followers with whom he had personal relationships, and who received gifts from the king in return for their willingness to fight. Such a system depends on the availability of high-value goods, which can only be obtained with trade or exchange with distant lands. The terp at Wijnaldum in Friesland's Westergo was selected for excavation in the 1990s as the potential seat of a Frisian king, this terp being the location of an early-20th-century find of a gold cloisonné brooch, which resembles in various respects the cloisonné brooch from ship burial 1 at Sutton Hoo. In shape a Scandinavian object, in its use of Christian and non-Christian themes it is thought to be a product from Kent or Suffolk, but with possible influence from southern Germany (Schoneveld and Zijlstra 1999: 200). The excavations revealed ample evidence for metalworking at Wijnaldum, and it is not inconceivable that the goldsmith who made the brooch was based here (Nijboer and Van Reekum 1999: 214). While no additional evidence was found for royal activity at Wijnaldum, the importance of the terpen as locations for wealthy and powerful individuals, who were connected to both the broader Frisian region and to other powerful individuals across the North Sea, is undoubted.

The exchange of goods in the early Middle Ages changed in the late seventh century from one focused on prestige goods for the maintenance of gift-giving to one where commodities were exchanged in a market system, although the role of kings as protectors of the *emporia*, such as the Frisian trading settlement Dorestad, remained strong (Heidinga 1999: 9). The success of the Frisians as traders whose influence was felt around the North Sea and the Baltic, has been attributed directly to the watery landscape which they inhabited. The terpen region provided the Frisians with an environment where stockbreeding produced a marketable surplus, while their familiarity with moving across their landscape in ships facilitated the ready progression to the development of long-distance traders. In addition, the comparative isolation of the terpen safeguarded the homesteads from attack by pirates or foreign armies, who did not share an intricate knowledge of the landscape with the Frisians (but see chapter 9 on Viking piracy in Frisia).

The construction of terpen in the period from *c.* 500 cal BC through to the end of the first millennium AD provides us with a remarkable example of how the Wadden Sea was socialized as people made the landscape their own. This landscape was only ever modified by people, accepting the role played by the sea as a co-constructor of the landscape, but never transformed (cf. Rippon 2000). The active role played by the sea in the process of landscape formation remains an important element in the development of the terpen. This is shown in two ways: the seaward direction of the establishment of new terp settlements in order to be close to the lower and richest saltmarshes when peat formed on the higher saltmarshes, and the periodic heightening of the terpen. The heightening and extension of the terpen has generally been understood as being connected to relative sea-levels (e.g. Van Es 1965/6). While this remains an important aspect in the growth of the terpen and their occasional submergence, it is becoming increasingly clear, with the greater use of radiocarbon essays to date the extensions, that local rather than regional causes should be considered (e.g. Boersma 2005: 558). Nevertheless, the establishment of the earliest settlements on the saltmarshes, from around the middle of the first millennium BC, coincided broadly with a period during which sedimentation outpaced the rising sea-level. The resulting 'flat' settlements sought out the natural higher grounds such as saltmarsh ridges or former river levees. Subsequent phases of enlargement and heightening of the terpen can no longer be assigned to broad transgression–regression models (Vos 1999: 65), but the availability of saltmarsh for stockbreeding, alongside local fluctuations in sea-levels and the occurrence of storm floods, as well as socio-political and economic choices to enlarge the terp to increase the size of the village and arable land, all played their role in the evolution of the terpen.

The settlements themselves were not distinct. Excavations at Midlum and Holßel on the Geest showed that the beginnings of these settlements in the first century BC, and their ends in the fourth century AD, were very similar to those of Feddersen Wierde. Haarnagel had already noted that the type of house and size of settlement of the Feddersen Wierde compares readily with the settlements on the *Geest* (1979: 173). Similarly, the architecture of the terpen in the Middle Ages, such as the sod houses, long houses, and sunken huts on Wijnaldum, are also present elsewhere in the landscape (Gerrets and De Koning 1999). What made the terp settlements distinct, and what gave the inhabitants their distinctive social identity, was the setting in the landscape. The terpen occupied a wild(er)ness that was neither land nor sea, rather it was a hybrid world created by the interplay of a slowing rate of Holocene sea-level change and increased sedimentation that had been augmented through the action of the people who lived there and in the hinterland. It was a landscape where the tides and storm floods determined the daily work patterns of those who dwelt in the isolated houses and villages, and where boats could be used only when their crews had a familiarity with the landscape and the tides. From *c.* AD 1000, this way of life was eroded with the construction of the dikes, which separated the land from the sea (Meier 2004: 65).

TAKING LAND FROM THE SEA: COASTAL TRANSFORMATION AND RECLAMATIONS

The construction of dikes is the subject of the third case study showing the diversity of how the North Sea coast was socialized. Taking land from the sea constitutes the ultimate socialization of the sea: that which was natural is made cultural through artifices such as dikes. Saltmarshes are well suited for stockbreeding, as we have already seen in the case study of the terpen. Through frequent flooding, saltmarshes are nutrient-rich, producing vegetation that can be grazed or cropped, as well as helping to prevent foot rot and liver fluke in sheep; due to the influence of the relatively warmer sea in winter saltmarshes also have longer growing seasons (Dinnin and Van de Noort 1999; Gerrets 1999). However, in times of demographic pressure, and especially when the price for arable produce is high, there are good economic reasons for embanking parts of the sea. Even though a number of experiments have shown that it is possible to grow arable crops on the higher salt marshes (e.g. Van Zeist 1974; Van Zeist et al. 1976), arable agriculture within tidal reach is a high-risk activity, and few farmers in the past would have used the intertidal landscape for arable use. While the artificial mounds in the Wadden Sea already supported arable activity, this was principally subsistence for those living on the terpen. The use of dikes, to exclude the tidal seawater from the land, offered the only possibility of larger-scale arable activity on the North Sea coast.

In his book, *The transformation of coastal wetlands* (2000), Stephen Rippon develops a model for coastal wetland exploitation and modification which can help to contextualize the use of dikes (Figure 25). The model has three strategies of coastal landscape use: exploitation, where the natural resources are used without changing the natural landscape to any great extent; modification, where minor changes are made to the landscape such as the digging of ditches to drain the higher parts of the saltmarsh more effectively after high tides; and transformation, where the coastal wetlands are reclaimed through the construction of dikes, and the sea is permanently excluded. Thus, while fishing and the use of saltmarshes for grazing cattle are forms of exploitation, and the terpen are a form of coastal landscape modification, the construction of dikes and reclamation of the coastal marshes are transformations of the natural landscape. It is something of a new departure in the North Sea basin. No longer is the sea a collaborator, but an adversary, to be kept out of the cultural landscape.

Diking occurred mainly in the second millennium AD, and only in the southern part of the North Sea basin. It is true that forms of embankment in coastal situations are known from the later Iron Age, as at Vlaardingen in South Holland, for example, where a complex of seven dams and five sluice gates was uncovered during the construction of new sea defences (De Ridder 1999), and in Friesland where the remains of sod walls believed to have been early dikes were found beneath the terpen of Wijnaldum and Donjum (Bazelmans, Gerrets, and Vos 1988). Roman dikes facing the sea are also known, such as the one recently found in Walraversijde, West Flanders (Durnez 2006), but there are no known extensive coastal areas reclaimed with the aid of sea dikes. There are also historical charters referring to embankments on the

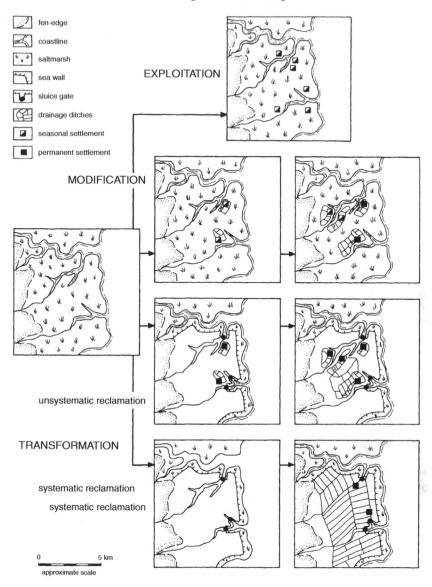

Figure 25. Schematic model illustrating the range of potential strategies for the exploitation, modification and transformation of an area of coastal saltmarsh (based on Rippon 2000: 53)

Thames in north Kent in the early ninth century AD, but no settlement was protected by it (Rippon 2000: 168).

In parts of the coastal fens in Norfolk, the sea wall at Tilney St Lawrence and Walpole St Peter overlay material of middle Saxon date, and the excavated Sea Bank at Clenchwarton incorporated pottery of the 11th century (Hall and

Coles 1994: 127; Crowson et al. 2000: 225). Palaeoecological analysis of land behind the Sea Bank shows that the transition from an environment under marine influence to a landscape without direct marine influence can be dated to the transition from middle to late Saxon period, traditionally dated on the basis of pottery types to *c*. AD 850. Analysis of foraminifers, ostracods, other crustacean, and molluscs shows that the Sea Bank at Clenchwarton was constructed in short sections during low tides, and comprised a ditch to intercept marsh drainage, and a bank seaward of it (Murphy 2005: 261). By the 10th century, the embankment of the East Anglian Fenland was complete. On the continental side of the southern North Sea basin, the first embankments are of similar age. In Flanders, the Kaaidijk is 11th century (Tys 1997; cf. Rippon 2000: 178). In Zeeland, the earliest dikes are thought to be 11th century, in South Holland 12th century, and in North Holland also 12th century, although some smaller-scale embankments date to the 9th and 10th centuries (Besteman 1990; Van den Broeke and Van Londen 1995; Vos and Van Heeringen 1997; Rippon 2000: 185). Embankments in the Dutch part of the Wadden Sea area date back to the 10th or 11th century, with raised roads linking the terpen possibly functioning as prototype dikes (Rippon 2000: 183–5). In the German part of the Wadden Sea, the first dikes constructed for the purpose of keeping out the sea were the so-called ring dikes, which safeguarded fields from spring and summer floods, but were not designed to offer year-round protection. In Niedersachsen, such ring dikes date from the end of the 11th century. From the 13th century onwards, ring dikes were connected to form continuous sea defences which were capable of resisting even the highest tides and floods (Behre 2003: 49).

The early dikes were, in general terms, not high enough or strong enough to resist the worst winter storms. Embankment of the coast also meant that storms were denied the space to dissipate their energy, with ensuing higher water levels during storms, and amplified tidal ranges. This resulted in occasional breaches and flooding of the reclaimed lands and it is, in this respect, unsurprising that the historical charters of landholdings in newly reclaimed land frequently describe the land use as pasture, rather than arable (Rippon 2000: 167–85). Another consequence of the continuous embankment of the coast was that, during storms and high tides, the waters rose against the dikes, increasing both the tidal reach and the tidal range up the estuaries and rivers that discharged into the North Sea. This caused extensive flooding in the deltas and floodplains once the rivers' levees were overtopped, as was the case for the Ems, Weser, and Elbe in the German Bight. The Dollart Bay, on the modern Dutch–German border, was created in the later 13th century when the natural levees of the River Ems were breached, flooding the backswamp area, which had in previous centuries been used from the many terpen that are known from this area (Behre 2003: 49–50). Dike construction also resulted in large-scale habitat transformation and, effectively, the replacement of a continuum that included marine, brackish, freshwater, and diverse terrestrial habitats by a separation of the marine and terrestrial worlds. This resulted in a simplification and homogenization of the food web structure, and a reduction of the biodiversity of the coastal landscape. While more recent changes such as pollution and eutrophication have played their role in this process, the habitat loss that commenced with the construction of the dikes is recognized as one of the two main causes—over-fishing being the other—of reduced biodiversity in coastal areas. In the case of the Wadden Sea, about 20 per cent of the macrobiota (144 species) became extinct or severely depleted during the second millennium AD (Lotze et al. 2005).

On England's east coast, the majority of the coastal marshes of Kent and Essex had been embanked before the middle of the 13th century. Historical records after AD 1230 for the coast of Kent concern the maintenance rather than the construction of sea walls, and the Isle of Foulness, the easternmost part of the Essex marshes, had been reclaimed by AD 1235 and sea walls are mentioned in AD 1270–71 (Rippon 2000: 199–207). The saltmarshes that developed in front of the existing sea wall of the Fenlands were reclaimed in a piecemeal fashion and embanked in the 12th and 13th centuries, although it should be noted that the reclamation of the lower-lying back-marshes received much greater attention (Hallam 1965; cf. Rippon 2000: 208–11). In Lincolnshire, the first continuous sea wall must post-date Domesday, as a late Saxon salt-production site was excavated at Marshchapel to the west of the wall; it was probably in place by AD 1200 (Fenwick 2001: 239). In the Humber estuary, the piecemeal reclamation of saltmarsh undertaken in the 11th-century was followed by a major programme of reclamation in the 12th (Sheppard 1966).

On the continental side of the North Sea, the 12th and 13th centuries saw the completion of the sea dikes. In Flanders, the 11th-century embankments were extended and enlarged, resulting in a closed sea wall before the end of the 12th century (Tys 1997). In Zeeland, extensive floods in AD 1134 appear to have provided the impetus for the construction of a continuous sea wall, which was completed before the end of the 12th century (Lambert 1971). The coast of South and North Holland was generally well protected by extensive dunes, but the enclosure of the West Friesland district of North Holland, bordering the Wadden Sea to the north and the Zuiderzee to the east, was completed by the middle of the 13th century (TeBrake 2002). The coastal marshes of Friesland and Groningen were completely embanked by the 12th century and in adjacent Niedersachsen, the process of connecting ring dikes with a continuous sea wall was completed in the 13th century (Behre 2003: 49). In Schleswig-Holstein, dike construction began in the 11th and 12th centuries, but frequent storms caused breaches and extensive flooding, and the house mounds (known here as *Wurten* or *Warften*) continued to be extended and heightened into the 14th century, for example, the *Wurt* Hundorf (Meier 2004: 66). Completing the sea walls afforded the subsequent reclamation of the extensive back-swamps and coastal peatlands, both in England and on the Continent.

The role of ecclesiastical institutions in the reclamation of coastal wetlands is well known from both sides of the North Sea. In a review of the widely held perception that the Church and monastic orders, as major landowners, were indeed the driving force behind the reclamation of coastal wetlands (e.g. Duby 1968: 69), Stephen Rippon warns against the oversimplification of a complex situation (2000: 246–59). It is not doubted that monastic orders, the Cistercians foremost among them, played a major role in the reclamation of coastal wetlands, but Rippon argues that the initial stages of drainage and embankment had already commenced before ecclesiastical institutions entered the fray. He argues further that the monastic orders were major movers in the reclamations of the back-swamps and peatlands that could only be drained once the influence of the sea had been excluded, and this process could only commence once the sea walls were completed. The skills to achieve the permanent exclusion of the sea on coastal landscapes were developed during the 'long eighth century' (Rippon 2009). Only in Friesland does Rippon find evidence for a monastic role in the construction of new sea walls, but not in the case of the first sea wall (2000: 252). Though the role of the Cistercians is not doubted, the Order was only founded in AD 1098, and could not therefore have played a significant role in the initial stages of coastal wetland reclamation. Other, non-monastic, ecclesiastical involvement in reclamation is well attested. The Bishops of Hamburg and Bremen, for example, took the lead in the reclamation of their coastal lands, famously employing Dutch settlers. The perception is, in part, the result of the bias of the historical records, which favour the literate church over an illiterate laity. There are ample archaeological and historical examples where non-ecclesiastical institutions and freemen took the initiative, such as the Counts of Holland who organized the 'cope' reclamation in South Holland (Lambert 1971), or the freemen who reclaimed the peatlands of North Holland (Besteman 1990), or the independent, land-owning occupants of the terpen who built the sea walls in Schleswig-Holstein (Meier 2004: 65).

From the beginning of the 12th century, the church began to take a dominant role in the reclamation of coastal wetlands. The economic motivation for land reclamation at a time of demographic growth, with 'the emergence of a dominant subsistence paradigm focused on crop raising' (TeBrake 2002: 481), is undoubted, and the ecclesiastical institutions certainly grew very rich over the following centuries on the profits from their reclaimed lands. However, in recent years, a reconsideration of the economic basis as the sole incentive for reclamation has been called for, and this debate is leading to the construction of a hybrid geography of coastal landscapes in the Middle Ages.

The Dutch philosopher Hub Zwart (2003) explores this idea in what he refers to as 'a moral geography of the landscape', that is the interpretation of 'anthropogenic modifications as forms of moral criticism directed towards the values, choices, and achievements of *previous* generations' (ibid. 108). The conversion to Christianity of the Dutch coastal dwellers in the first millennium AD represents a turning point in Zwart's moral geography. Before the conversion of the Frisians, coastal habitation in the form of terpen, where the tides and storms determined the rhythm of daily life, had already received scorn from Pliny, and Zwart argues that the terpen embodied a moral attitude of *Gelassenheit* (detachment, or 'releasement'). In other words, the Frisians lived with the sea, utilizing its particular resources such as the saltmarshes without feeling a need for change. Christianity came to Frisia shortly before the eighth century, but was only adopted by the Frisian elite following the conquest of the northern Netherlands by the Franks during the eighth century. The large-scale transformation of the coastal landscape occurred in the centuries following the conversion to Christianity. Zwart argues that 'Christianity, as an ideology, rendered the erection of dikes and the reclamation of wetlands morally legitimate, or even obligatory' (ibid. 111). In a moral geography, the transformations made to the coastal landscape signify not only a disparagement of previous pagan generations but also the creation of Christianized landscapes through the process of reclamation. By reducing the powers of the sea, and of the uncultivable wetlands, nature as a wild(er)ness and the abode of pagan gods was demystified. Zwart highlights the actions of the Church, for example the reclamations made by monastic orders such as the Cistercians, or the reclamation of the Elbe marshes by the Bishop of Bremen, mentioned in AD 1103, but also fully recognizes that the initial stages of coastal landscape transformation were undertaken by lay Christian Frisians.

The idea that reclamation of wetlands should be understood as incorporating both economic and symbolic perceptions, especially in contexts where the Christian ideology was dominant, has gained support in recent years (e.g. Clarke 2008; Rippon 2009). Hybrid geography would suggest that the Frisians, the ecclesiastical institutions, along with the anthropogenic constructs such as the terpen and the dikes, and the natural world including the sea, the backswamps, the wild and domesticated animals and the crops utilized by people, were all intertwined in a network, with agency not restricted to humans alone. The way in which the North Sea reacted to being embanked, producing more devastating floods and extending its influence further up the rivers through greater tidal reaches and increased tidal ranges, could have been perceived as the response from a natural feature that had other-than-human agency. In Zwart's explanation, this agency was attributed indirectly to the sea through the proxy of Christian and non-Christian deities, but the attribution of some form of agency to the sea by the people living on the North Sea coast throughout this period is not in doubt. Thus, the role of the Church in the reclamation movement was not just one of optimizing the economic value of the land it was gifted. Indeed, reclamation was as necessary and important as the conversion of pagans themselves. Reclaiming land, and creating *polders* (a word that first appears in AD 1219 in a charter of the Cistercian monastery of Middleburg) was as much an act 'to the glory of God' as was the construction of a church or cathedral. One is reminded of the Benedictine motto *ora et labora* (pray and work): in many ecclesiastical institutions, to work was as important as to pray. I like to think that in Christian ideology the expression 'the devil makes work for idle *hands*' has its landscape equivalent in 'the devil makes work for idle *lands*'.

The dikes themselves were also more than simple constructs underpinning economic expansion. The argument has already been made that, in lowlands, dikes are as impressive and visible as any other man-made structure or monument (Van der Vleuten and Disco 2004: 293), and that their impact on the landscape was as visually and symbolically significant as, for example, Neolithic monuments, Roman roads, or any field system defining ownership. Furthermore, the construction of a dike would have represented the largest artefact produced through communal cooperation, and in this way dikes actively defined local social identities, and also passively, since the livelihoods of those living off the proceeds of the reclaimed lands were reliant on the strength of the sea wall. The large-scale communal effort needed for the construction of coastal sea walls contrasts with the family- or village-sized effort required to construct a terp. A unifying ideology, that is Christianity and its perception of wild(er)ness as being essentially un-Christian, may have played an important role in rallying large groups of people in expelling the sea from the land. It seems likely that dikes would have been attributed forms of other-than-human agency. Unfortunately, very little archaeological research into the early dikes has been undertaken to date, as many form the core of extant, much enlarged, embankments or function as elevated roads. There is therefore no archaeological evidence for ritual depositions associated with dike construction.

However, Theodor Storm's well-known novella *Der Schimmelreiter* (1888) offers a literary example of ritual deposition in a dike construction, and an insight into the attribution of human-like characteristics to dikes in the modern period. The story, set on the east Frisian coast of Schleswig-Holstein around 1800, concerns a progressively thinking autodidact, Hauke Haien, who has taught himself to read Dutch and who, as a young man, observed over many nights the action of the breaking waves, testing ideas by making model banks of clay to see whether the traditional method of (steep) dike building could be improved upon. Hauke, son of an unassuming land surveyor and smallholder, becomes, against expectations, the new *Deichgraf* and therefore assumes responsibility for the upkeep of the sea dikes, much against the wish of his arch enemy, Ole Peters. When after several years in the job a dike is required for a new *Koog* (polder), the opportunity arises to test the ideas from his youth. The local farmers and labourers want to include 'something living' within the body of the embankment. While in the distant past gypsy children were buried alive on such occasions, the workers have selected a dog for this event, but the dog is saved by Hauke from being used as a ritual sacrifice. The final acts of this story describes how, when years later a storm threatens to breach the old dike, Ole Peters organizes the breaching of Hauke's new dike, which is distrusted by the older farmers and held responsible for the problems they face, to alleviate the pressure on the old one, and Hauke sacrifices himself with his white horse by jumping into the breach made into his dike.

CONCLUSIONS

Whereas terrestrial landscape archaeology has progressed continuously from a consideration of natural to increasingly 'encultured' or cultured landscapes as the norm, the three case studies presented here on the socialization of coastal landscapes provide somewhat different insights. In the case of the construction of monuments, a twofold picture has emerged. In the northern North Sea basin, monuments of the Neolithic and Bronze Age survive on the coast. A number of these faced the sea and may have played a role in navigation. Just as on the land, the constructed monuments on the North Sea coast relate to other monuments, both natural and constructed, albeit that the cairns and barrows were frequently dwarfed by the monuments created by the sea, such as the natural arches and stacks. In the southern North Sea basin, coastal monuments of Neolithic and Bronze Age date are relatively scarce, and many were submerged by the transgressing sea; others again may have been destroyed. The disappearance of ancient monuments which had inscribed history onto the landscape and played a role in the social reproduction of society, led to the adoption of new practices that related directly to the sea. In the case of the Fenlands of eastern England this included laying the dead on the very edge of the transgressing coastal wetlands, where the sea could embrace the deceased, as well as the conception of new types of monuments, such as 'Seahenge' or Flag Fen, which related directly to the North Sea and enabled a new social memory to be inscribed on the coastal landscape.

In the case of the terpen in the Wadden Sea, the sense of co-construction of the landscape is particularly strong. The terpen themselves must have increased in height naturally over the long periods during which they were in use, as sea-level continued to rise, but alongside environmental factors a broader range of explanations for their enlargement, including socio-polit-ical and economic reasons, is now considered more appropriate. While the terpen themselves were distinctive elements in the landscape, a distinct social identity was expressed not in the houses or the husbandry, but rather through the taskscape of the saltmarshes, which determined the rhythm of daily life.

The dike construction and transformation of the landscape of the southern North Sea basin can be understood as an attempt to annihilate the sea as a co-constructer of the landscape. There are good economic reasons for constructing sea walls that exclude the influence of the sea, but the embankment process also has strong visual, symbolic, and ritual expressions. Christianity is identified as an ideology that encouraged the replacement of a wild(er)ness— where the marine, brackish, freshwater, and terrestrial elements formed continuous and dynamic landscapes which merged at the border between land and sea—with a binary division between cultural/Christian and natural/ pagan landscapes. The embankment led to increased storminess, flooding and extended tidal reaches and ranges, and these effects may well have been perceived as the sea exercising other-than-human agency, either directly or indirectly through the work of deities.

In summary, the socialization of the coastal landscape differs from the process in terrestrial settings in the sense that nature, in the form of the North Sea, remains through time an active agent of landscape creation, or a co-creator of the landscape. This co-construction of landscape blurs the distinction between what is natural and cultural, and the ways in which coastal landscapes are socialized at any one time around the North Sea shows a remarkable degree of diversity. Only with the construction of the dikes, which changes the balance of the relationship into one in which the sea becomes the adversary in a starkly divided landscape, can we recognize large-scale similarities in the socialization of coastal landscapes around the North Sea. The sea socialized the coastal dwellers as much as the people socialized the sea; and as such, the active role of nature in the creation of social identities is nowhere more evident than on the margins of the sea.

6

Archipelagos and islands

INTRODUCTION

The North Sea is not renowned for its islands, and much of the modern land–sea interface is sharp, especially along the coasts of Jutland, North and South Holland and much of England. Nevertheless, the North Sea does contain a surprisingly large number of islands and archipelagos, which can be presented with reference to a clear north–south divide. In the northern half of the North Sea, most islands are of hard rock with shallow soils, and their islandness is the result of ongoing glacio-isostatic uplift of previously drowned lands and sea-level rise. With the exception of the Shetland and Orkney archipelagos, few of these islands are found at a great distance from the mainland, and the majority of the countless islands, islets, and rock outcrops off the North Sea coasts of Norway, Sweden, Scotland, and north-east England can be found within a few miles of the mainland. In the southern half of the North Sea, the islands are mainly made up of sand and clay and, in their history if not today, were frequently sandbanks formed by the sea utilizing both marine and riverine sediments. Most of the islands of the Wadden Sea in Denmark, Germany, and Holland are sandbanks elevated by aeolian-formed sand dunes. Further south, the core of the large islands of Zeeland is principally formed of riverine sands and marine clays intercalated with peat, reflecting coastal wetland conditions at various times in the Post-glacial and Holocene (Vos and Van Heeringen 1997). As with Zeeland, the islands on the English side of the North Sea, such as Mersey Island in the Blackwater estuary and Foulness Island in Essex, have now been incorporated into the mainland. Only a few islands cannot be so simply classified: Helgoland in the German Bight, a Sherwood Sandstone stack of Triassic date, is the best known example.

Island archaeology, as we have seen (chapter 2), has for many decades approached islands as environments that were relatively isolated from the wider world. Paul Rainbird (2007: 26–39) among others has pointed out that the study of islands as isolated environments, or microcosms, can be traced back to the impact of Charles Darwin's study in 1835 of the fauna of the Galápagos Islands—in particular of the finches, which appeared to have evolved in response to the specific environments on the individual islands. The perceived potential of islands for offering answers to research questions, precisely because of their isolation, has engendered island-specific ways of thinking in biogeographical, anthropological, and archaeological studies, as advocated for example by John Evans's (1973) paper 'Islands as laboratories of the cultural process'. More recent research, however, has critiqued this presumption, and new ideas on island archaeology recognize that island communities in the past were often closely connected across the seas, and that developmental pathways were the result of human choices and decisions, not environmentally determined in an island-specific way. Nevertheless, islands are worthy of study, if for no other reason than that they have acted on the minds of the people under investigation in this study: the bits of land in the North Sea helped to make the sea a knowable place.

This chapter seeks to explore four aspects of the islands in the North Sea. First, it will consider the isolation and connectedness of islands. To what degree did the islands in the North Sea develop in isolation, and to what extent did the 'sea of islands' create communities engaged in many aspects of the wider world? How are these aspects expressed in the social identities and material cultures of the islands in question? Second, navigation in the wild will be explored, in conjunction with the role that islands and archipelagos might have played as sailing nurseries—a concept first developed by Geoff Irwin (1992). The basic question in this section is whether or not the existence of archipelagos and islands within the North Sea encouraged early seafarers to range further than they would otherwise have done. Third, the chapter examines islands as deviant places within a Deleuzian ocean. Islands gave shelter to individuals and communities that chose not to live on the mainland, and the diverse reasons behind this preference will be considered. Finally, the memory of lost islands will be investigated, in particular with reference to the polished axes fished up from the Dogger and Brown banks.

ISOLATION AND CONNECTEDNESS

The essence of island archaeology for most of the 20th century, taking the lead from biogeographical research, concerned the relatively isolated nature of island communities, and how it was possible to study these communities with only limited external interference. This claim of insularity of human island communities has now been challenged, as exemplified in the shift from the study of individual islands to that of inter-island and island–mainland relations, and a consideration of 'islandscapes' and 'seas of islands' (cf. Broodbank 2000). Unlike in the Mediterranean, a *longue durée* study of the isolation and connectedness of islands in the North Sea is very much

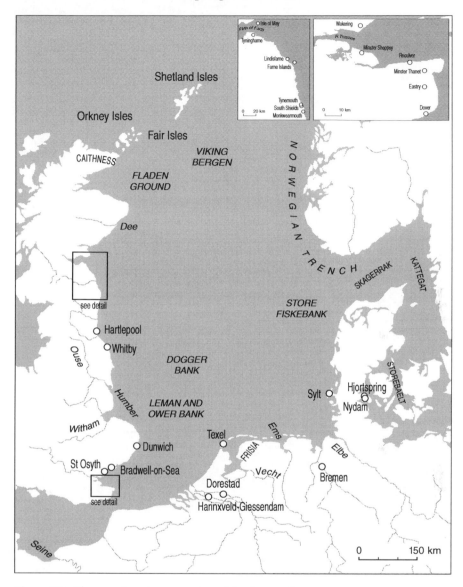

Figure 26. Places and regions mentioned in chapter 6

hampered by their histories. For example, the islands of Zeeland only formed as a consequence of the gradual widening of the lowland rivers caused by Holocene sea-level rise, while the islands in the Wadden Sea were created only when sea-level rise and the aggradations of sediments became balanced, after *c.* 5500 cal BC (Vos and Van Kesteren 2000; see also chapter 5). The islands

continued to 'wander', and no evidence for their occupation predates the
later part of the Roman period (Van Es, Sarfatij, and Woltering 1988). Two
exceptions are Texel, the westernmost of the Wadden Sea islands, and Sylt,
Germany's northernmost island in the Wadden Sea, both of which contain
a pre-Holocene core. However, the Upper Palaeolithic and Mesolithic finds
from Texel, and the Neolithic finds from Sylt, belong to periods that predate
these areas becoming islands (Kossack et al. 1980). The island of Helgoland is
hampered by a very different history: as the location of German anti-aircraft
guns, it was heavily shelled during World War II, and subsequently used as a
bombing range by the Royal Air Force until 1952, leaving little material for
archaeological research.

The best place to study colonization and continuity of habitation is offered
by the Orkney and Shetland archipelagos (Figure 27). These islands have
existed from about the ninth millennium cal BC, are hard-rock based, and do
not 'wander', and they have also been extensively researched. The Orkney
and Shetland archipelagos were colonized by the end of the Mesolithic. The
20-plus sites with Mesolithic-period flint tools from the Orkney islands imply
that this archipelago was either frequently visited or else permanently settled
by the end of this period (Wickham-Jones 2006: 24), while the Shetlands have
recently produced incontrovertible evidence of human habitation in the late
fifth millennium BC, or late Mesolithic period (Melton 2008). Following their
initial colonization, the Shetland and Orkney archipelagos were never isolated

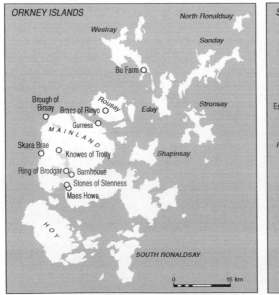

Figure 27. The Orkney and Shetland Isles

for any great length of time. Thus, the Neolithic monuments on the Mainland of the Orkney archipelago have remarkable antecedents or parallels in Neolithic monuments elsewhere. For example, certain aspects of the Maeshowe burial tomb, especially the alignment of the long passage with the midwinter solstice sun, are strikingly similar to aspects of the tomb of Newgrange in the Boune valley in Ireland (MacKie 1998; Wickham-Jones 2006, 63–4). The monuments on the adjacent Brodgar Peninsula have been interpreted in the light of recent research in Wessex, with the Stones of Stenness viewed as the ceremonial ring of the living, as is the case with Durrington Walls, and the Ring of Brodgar as the circle for the ancestors, like Stonehenge (Parker Pearson 2000). It is clearly implied that at least from the Neolithic, if not earlier, the islands and archipelagos in the North Sea were fully integrated into broader cosmologies that can also be found on the Continent and in the British Isles.

In a recent paper on Orcadian island identity, Colin Renfrew (2000) presents the concept of 'epitopic analogy', by which archaeologists can compare certain aspects of life from different times within the same place (ibid. 3). He refers, in particular, to the medieval and early modern Lammas Fair or Market as an epitopic analogy for how people in the Neolithic came to Orkney from distant places for a combination of commercial and ritual reasons. In the case of the Lammas Fair, people came from as far afield as the Shetlands, Caithness, the Hebrides and possibly Ireland, and something similar may have happened in the Neolithic. Such get-togethers, combining the practical need to exchange goods, animals, and marriage partners with ritual desires (or pilgrimages), may have provided the motive for the construction of such 'over-sized' ritual monuments as the Ring of Brodgar and the Stones of Stenness. Connectedness with other islands and nearby mainlands was both necessary and desirable.

Connectedness was maintained through the later Neolithic and Bronze Age. The distribution of Beaker-type pottery—epitomizing the elite networks of this period—extends to include the Orkneys, for example at the Braes of Rinyo on Rousay, and fragments of AOC Beakers have been found in Shetland (Clarke 1970, 557). This suggests either that these islands were connected to the elite networks that developed around the North Sea in this period, or that social enchainment involving Beaker pottery extended as far as the Shetland Isles (Chapman 2000; see also chapter 8). Alongside the Beaker pottery, other finds corroborate the notion that the elite groups of the Northern Isles, if not the broader population, were connected at the time of the early Bronze Age. The cist from one of the 12 barrows at the Knowes of Trotty on Orkney's Mainland, containing a cremation with four gold discs and amber pennants and beads, offers the most ornate example of this (Petrie 1862; cf. Wickham-Jones 2006, 94–6). The discovery of late Bronze Age baked clay casting moulds for socketed axes, swords, and other objects at Jarlshof on Shetland's Mainland (Hamilton 1956; Cunliffe 2001: 278) shows that with the increased availability of bronze tools, weapons, and scrap in the period, even the remotest archipelago in the North Sea had acquired the skills, by this time, to develop a regional style.

Connectedness in the Iron Age is still clearly visible today in the shape of the broch, or circular dry-stone tower-like house, examples of which survive on many of the Orcadian and Shetland islands, and along the coasts in northern Scotland and the Hebridean islands. Discussions on their origin and function are ongoing, and the degree to which the brochs were intended to be defensive structures, or merely imposing dwellings, remains unresolved (e.g. Armit 2003; Sharples and Parker Pearson 1997). However, the distribution of this innovative construction implies a degree of connectedness between the Northern and Western Isles and the mainland of Scotland, and a similarity in the socio-political changes that can be observed outside the Roman-controlled part of the British Isles. Roman imports, though rare, are not unknown—for example the Roman amphorae unearthed from the Orcadian Broch of Gurness (Wickham-Jones 2006: 103).

By the fourth century AD, the Pictish political configuration appears in northern Scotland, and this includes the archipelagos of the Shetlands and Orkneys. Pictish customs include the frequent depiction of persons and distinctive symbols on carved stones, for example the Mail Stone, from the graveyard at Mail, Cunningsburgh, on the Mainland of Shetland, which shows a dog-headed man carrying an axe (Turner 1994). The Picts adopted Christianity as their overarching cosmology in the second half of the sixth century AD, with St Columba credited for this, and a modified version of the symbols on carved stones, alongside the remains of stone altars and shrines, are known from the Shetlands and the Orkneys. Connectedness in the middle of the first millennium AD may have been redirected towards Ireland, as the spiritual homeland of the new-found Christian belief.

Around the beginning of the ninth century AD, the Norse conquest of the Shetlands and Orkneys created a very different kind of connectedness. We know little about the nature of the Norse conquest and early settlement, but the archaeological evidence suggests that the most important Pictish sites were used by the Norse early in the ninth century AD, implying an aggressive rather than a peaceful coming together of the two groups of people. The architecture and setting of new settlements on Shetland's northernmost island, Unst, closely resemble those of contemporary settlements in Norway, although evidence of acculturation remains archaeologically undetectable. According to the Orkneyinga Saga and the *Heimskringla*, the settlement at Brough of Birsay on the Mainland of Orkney, the Pictish 'centre of power', became one of the more important Viking settlements, eventually becoming the seat and burial place of Jarl Thorfinn the Mighty in the middle of the 11th century AD. Thorfinn extended his territory to include parts of Scotland, the Hebrides and Ireland and, for a short period, was put in charge of Norway following the expulsion of King Olaf by King Knut the Mighty of Denmark and England, thus creating new connectivities between the Northern Isles and the mainlands of the northern North Sea (Muir 2005: 43–54).

The Northern Isles stayed in Norse or Danish hands until the late 15th century, although the proximity of Scotland meant that their daily business became increasingly Scottish, especially after the signing of the Treaty of Perth in AD 1266, when the Norse retreated from Scotland's mainland. In 1468, Orkney was given to the Scottish Crown as part of the marriage agreement between James III and Margaret, daughter of Christian I of Denmark. Shetland was added in the next year (Mitchison 1970: 76).

Having noted aspects of connectedness, we should now identify aspects of distinctiveness that arose from the relative isolation of island life on the Orkney and Shetland Isles. The northerly latitudes of these archipelagos, and their exposure to the winds from across the Atlantic, creates a natural environment not conducive to extensive tree growth. The possible lack of suitable home-grown timber for the construction of domestic and ritual structures, alongside the availability of readily worked Old Red Sandstone on Orkney, produced a highly distinctive vernacular architecture. Examples of the use of stone architecture include the Neolithic settlements of Skara Brae and Barnhouse, as well as Maeshowe, the Stones of Stenness, the Ring of Brodgar, and many other sites from the archipelago (Figure 28). The use of large flagstones in both domestic and ritual monuments is widely held to mean that the world of the living, in the view of the Neolithic Orcadians, was

Figure 28. The Old Red Sandstone architecture on Orkney: the Ring of Brodgar

very similar to the world of the dead, and in this way, architectural distinctiveness was reinforced.

The Shetland archipelago, apart from its southernmost parts, is not endowed to the same extent with stone that is easily transformed into usable
flagstones. Smaller flagstones, however, produced a distinctive dry-stone-
walling architecture, seen most impressively in Bronze Age houses such as
those at Clickhimin on the Mainland (Hamilton 1968), or the Iron Age broch
on Mousa. Timber suitable for building was even scarcer in the Shetlands than
in the Orkneys, and driftwood must have been a welcome sight. Indeed,
archaeological research has revealed some interesting cases where driftwood
was used on these northerly isles. The most notable example has to be the
Stanydale hall, or 'temple', on Shetland's West Mainland. This structure has
been dated to the late Neolithic or early Bronze Age on the basis of its pottery
(including 'Beaker-types') and tools (Calder 1950). The hall is, in plan, not
dissimilar to houses from this era: oval-shaped with a concave entrance façade
and alcoves built into the thick stone walls. But its dimensions are more than
double those of any other house. The hall was roofed, and the two very large
central posts were of spruce, a tree that did not grow at that time on the
Shetlands; it has been argued that this was a rare and valuable material used
for a special construction (Fojut 1993: 22). Driftwood was also present in
Bronze Age burial cairns at Bu Farm, Rapness on Orkney's Westray (Barber,
Duffy, and O'Sullivan 1996), and was used in the Viking-period settlement at
Underhoull on Unst (Small 1966).

Isolation was expressed too in other aspects of material culture, and the
discoidal or oval knives of blue-grey felsite from the Shetland Isles provide
probably the best example. Stashes of these knives have been found in wet
places, such as the 11 'Pict's knives' from Esheness, Northmavine (Munro
1906), but none has been found outside the Shetland archipelago. Isolation
also played a role in the survival of oral histories and traditions, such as the
Orkney folklore and sea legends collected by Walter Traill Dennison in the
19th century from the rural people of the island of Sanday (Muir 1995). Many
of Traill Dennison's retellings of these oral histories are preceded by state-
ments in which he deliberately disassociates himself, as an educated collector
of stories and myths, from the uneducated indigenous people of Sanday, in
the same way that a colonial anthropologist or missionary might distinguish
himself from 'his' tribe. Connectedness was the preserve of the elite; isolation
was the rule for the majority of the Orcadians.

This short exploration of the isolation and connectedness of North Sea
island communities, based on the case of the Orkney and Shetland archipelagos, brings to the fore some new aspects of living with the sea. First,
islands were visited and inhabited very early on, towards the end of the
Mesolithic: this should not be surprising, considering the importance attributed to marine food resources during that period (see chapters 3 and 4), and

the fact that islands and archipelagos were the most advantageous geographies for utilizing the edge of the sea. Second, island communities throughout the prehistoric and historic past were without doubt connected to other island and mainland communities, as illustrated by the presence of exotic artefacts, such as Beaker fragments, or the gold discs from the Knowes of Trotty. However, this connectedness was not experienced equally throughout island communities, and while the island elite was connected to—or socially enchained within—networks that extended across the sea, no evidence exists for such connectedness across the whole community: it may, indeed, have been the exclusive privilege of the elite. The disparaging way in which the stories of the inhabitants of Sanday are described by the educated Walter Traill Dennison reflects, in the modern era, a long tradition of island-dwelling elite and non-elite being respectively connected to, and isolated from, the wider world. Third, islands became what could be called 'landscapes of familiarity'. Island settlers brought with them domesticated animals such as cows, sheep, and pigs (and possibly deer in the case of the Orkney islands), domesticated crops, and concepts and ideas that found their expression in the architecture of ritual monuments and vernacular buildings. This resulted in the creation of socialized landscapes similar to those on the mainland. The recent debates on island research, arguing for a shift from the study of island isolation to one of island connectedness, and recognizing that islands are often more connected than mainland bodies, clearly resonate with the story of the islands and archipelagos of the North Sea (cf. Noble 2006).

ISLANDS AS DEVIANT SPACES

In an ardent paper on why islands, and 'islandness', are worthwhile of study, Andrew Fleming (2008) presents a short overview of islands in literature, showing how islands have been the focus for the imaginary tales of some of the greatest authors: Thomas More's (1516) *Utopia*, Charles Kingsley's (1863) *The water babies*, and William Golding's (1954) *Lord of the flies* are just three examples from a much longer register. What strikes Fleming as remarkable is how frequently islands become the location for the imagination of different kinds of worlds. These different kinds of island worlds include populations that are progressive, tolerant, and enlightened, such as in *Utopia*, or where darker forces are at work, as in *Lord of the flies*. In this sense, the imagined islands are deviant spaces, contradicting the conventions of the mainlands, undermining the power of the establishment, and providing refuge to the defeated, the defiled, and the dead.

Interment of the dead on islands has been a long-standing theme in archaeological research. Stephen Mithen (2003: 168–77) recalls the discovery, excavations, and various interpretations of the Oleneostrovski Mogilnik, an island in Lake Onega in north-west Russia. This island was known as the 'Island of the dead' because of the many skeletal remains that were found here in the first half of the 20th century. The cemetery contained some 500 burials, dated to the second half of the seventh millennium BC. Grave goods included bone points, harpoons, slate knives, daggers, beads made of beaver teeth and pendants of elk, beaver, and bear teeth. Interpretations on the level of social complexity and stratification differ, but the idea that an island was used as the final resting place of the dead because of a belief—held by the Saami well into the modern era—that spirits cannot travel across water, has been widely accepted.

Nearer to the North Sea, Chris Scarre (2002) has studied the landscape context of the settings of Neolithic monuments in Brittany, a region which at this time experienced sea-level change through the submergence of the lowland coast, creating islands and archipelagos such as the Molène archipelago off the north-west coast of Brittany. The rate of relative sea-level rise was such that it must have been observable by individuals living in this area. Scarre argues that the location of burials and tombs on the islands should be understood in the context of the 'transformative nature of the sea/land boundary and the character of the landscape as a world populated by spirits' (ibid. 36). Added to this was an undersea world full of sea creatures, the idea of the sea as a liminal space—and a perception of off-shore islands as being surrounded by this liminal space—all combining to produce a shoreline charged with cosmological significance.

There are no 'islands of the dead' in the North Sea, but interments on islands are well known. For example, the islands or *donken* in the Dutch delta were not infrequently places where the dead were buried during the late Mesolithic and early Neolithic, although as has been determined in the case of the sites at Hardinxveld-Giessendam Polderweg and De Bruin, burials coincided here with habitation (Louwe Kooijmans 2001a; 2001b). The formal burial of dogs at the Polderweg site shows that dogs were seen as non-human persons, with other-than-human agency attributed to them. The same argument could be made for one of the deserted logboats at the De Bruin site, which was not damaged in any way, but had come to the end of its life, possibly because its maker or owner had died (Louwe Kooijmans 2001a: 526). Orkney provides another example of islands with burials. Whereas it has been argued that the distribution of Neolithic passage graves reflects the focus of human endeavour, which throughout time had been on the shore (e.g. Fraser 1983), others have sought to explain the location of the tombs, on the shore or on cliffs overlooking the sea, from a visual perspective, arguing that the tombs were intended to be seen from the sea for navigational, territorial, and symbolic purposes (e.g. Phillips 2003). However, there is no suggestion that the Orkney islands were islands of the dead. Finally, Richard Bradley (2000) has suggested for Bohuslän that the correlation between boat carvings and hills with burial cairns can be understood through the idea that the boats on the rocks symbolized water. As a consequence of the postglacial rebound, much of the Bronze Age coast of Bohuslän became terrestrialized, with islands turning into hills surrounded by land rather than water. The carvings may have been intended to put water between the realm of the living and that of the dead, thus isolating the spirits on the 'islands'. It is the nearest we come to islands of the dead in the North Sea.

Other forms of deviant islands can found in the North Sea. For example, when the King of the Frisians, Radbod, was defeated by the Franks in AD 697, he fled to the island of Helgoland, as we are reliably informed by Charlemagne's favourite scholar, Alcuin of York, in his *Life of Willibrord*. Elsewhere, the Orkneyinga Saga provides many examples of how the Earls of Orkney collaborated with, or conspired against, the Kings of Denmark, Norway, and Scotland, using their seafaring prowess to best Machiavellian effect. Even in the modern period islands have been used as deviant places. The small volcanic island of Inchkeith in the Firth of Forth was used as a place of quarantine for 'glandgare' sufferers in the late 15th century AD and for plague victims in the 16th (Haswell-Smith 2004).

During the centuries when Christianity was introduced into the lands bordering the North Sea, islands in the North Sea acted as deviant places in the form of religious retreats and outposts. In their *Maritime Ireland*, Aidan O'Sullivan and Colin Breen (2007: 124–6) argue that the sea in the early Christian imagination was a frontier zone between this world and the abyss of hell, a space where 'monks battled the forces of evil' (ibid. 125). Islands offered the early missionaries both practical and symbolic separation from the heathens who lived on the mainland, but also functioned spiritually as places at the forefront of the fight against the devil. The earliest Christian missionaries to the North Sea region, St Columba and St Aidan among the more successful, belonged to the Celtic Church and came from Ireland. Their earliest establishments were located on islands, with the Columban monastery on the Isle of May providing an example. Situated 8 km from the Scottish mainland in the outer Firth of Forth, this monastery was in existence from the sixth through to the ninth century AD, with the cemetery containing predominantly male burials being taken as clear archaeological evidence of this documented site (Yeoman n.d., cf. Carver 2004: 23). A church was built here in the ninth century, and by the twelfth century it had become a place of pilgrimage. Its reputation was such that the monastery was raided by the Orcadian chieftain Svein Asleifsson (Muir 2005: 107–9).

The most important missionary island in the North Sea is Lindisfarne or Holy Island, linked to the Northumbrian mainland by a causeway which is traversable during low tides. The monastery was founded in AD 634 by St Aidan, at the invitation of the Northumbrian King Oswald, as a base from which the north-east of England could be converted. This was accomplished following the defeat of the Mercian King Penda in AD 655 and the subsequent conversion of the Mercians. The most famous monk was St Cuthbert, who came to Lindisfarne from Melrose with St Aidan's pupil Eata. Cuthbert became bishop of Lindisfarne in AD 685. His elevation to sainthood was based on his miracles, prophecies, angelic visitations, missions, and his reputed close connections to birds and animals (Wormald 1991a: 79–82). Cuthbert sought further isolation on the Farne Islands, located some 19 km south-east of Lindisfarne and the perfect place for a hermitage, where he died in AD 687. Lindisfarne's deviant history does not end with the establishment of the monastery and the conversion of the English heathens. The island was famously attacked by the Vikings in AD 793, and this attack heralded a new era of piracy on the North Sea. Following further Viking incursions, the monks left Lindisfarne in AD 875, taking the relics of St Cuthbert with them. They settled in AD 883 at Chester-le-Street, and following a renewed phase of Viking attacks on the Northumbrian coast, at Durham in AD 995.

Evidently, not all early Christian monasteries were located on islands, but many early ecclesiastical foundations, dated to before AD 850, were situated on the coast. Among these, on the English North Sea coast, are Tyningham, Tynemouth, and Monkwearmouth, as well as South Shields, Hartlepool, Whitby, Dunwich, St Osyth, Bradwell-on-Sea, Wakering, Minster Sheppey (at this time still an island in the outer Thames estuary), Reculver, Minster Thanet, Eastry, and Dover (Wormald 1991a: 71). The evangelization of the continental heathens was endorsed by the ruling powers, notably the Christian Franks, and a correlation between the coast and the location of early monastic outposts in the heathen lands of the Frisians has been observed here too (see chapter 5).

SAILING NURSERIES AND NAVIGATION IN THE WILD

The sea can be a daunting environment, and the idea of engaging with it from a small boat does not come naturally to many people. The presence of islands within view of the mainland could offer encouragement and motivation to develop the skills and tools needed to explore the sea. After all, islands hold the promise of finding new or different things; they offer 'stepping stones' for longer journeys, and present safe havens from dangers and enemies on the mainland. The idea of the 'sailing nursery', originally developed for islands in the Pacific Ocean (Irwin 1992), is based on the premise that the incentives offered by islands and archipelagos contributed to the development of craft and seafaring skills. More recent studies have seen variations of this concept applied to the Cyclades and Malta in the Mediterranean (Broodbank 2000; Rainbird 2007).

The earliest 'sailing nurseries' in the North Sea basin are presumably of late Mesolithic and early Neolithic date, and are to be sought on the islands in the Storebaelt and in the delta formed by the rivers Rhine, Meuse, IJssel, and Vecht in the Netherlands. Both areas could be described as 'islandscapes' in the sense that human habitation was based along the islands' coasts, and interconnectivity between the islands—or in the case of the Dutch delta, between the *donken*—is attested by the presence of material culture from other islands or the mainland. The hybrid Mesolithic–Neolithic mode of subsistence in both areas is of particular importance (see chapter 4). Both the Ertebølle complex in the Storebaelt and the Swifterbant complex in the Dutch delta have been shown to have made optimal use of the marine resources available, with fish, seabirds, and sea mammals providing a substantial component of the daily meals. Boats would have been essential for the day-by-day emptying of fishtraps, for travelling to places where mammals that came to watering places could be hunted, for travel between the islands and for occasional journeys of a greater distance—to obtain flint nodules for tool fabrication, for example. The point has been made earlier that hunter-gatherer-fisher societies who experienced landscapes by boat had distinct advantages over their contemporaries who had to walk everywhere and carry everything (see chapter 4). These advantages could only be fully realized if boat handling (and boatbuilding) were skills readily available within a community. It can come as no surprise that the archaeological evidence for early boats from the islandscapes of both the Ertebølle and Swifterbant complexes is well known, and some of the oldest logboats from Europe come from these two areas. The Storebaelt and the Dutch delta have been identified as core areas where the logboat originated, and from where the logboat as a concept spread to other parts of Europe (Lanting 1997/8; see also chapter 7).

A number of innovative boat or ship designs appear to have evolved over the millennia in the islandscape of the Storebaelt-Skagerrak area, home to the Ertebølle complex. The Iron Age sewn-plank Hjortspring warship is one example; another is the Nordic clinker-built ship that brought the Vikings their success, although the oldest example of a clinker-built boat comes from a bog at Nydam, in southern Jutland (Rieck 1994; see also chapter 7). It seems likely that other archipelagos, notably Zeeland's islands and the Orkneys and Shetlands, similarly witnessed the emergence of boats and seafaring skills: the archaeological record has produced evidence for exotic goods and sea-fishing in all these locations, but in the absence of any craft it is difficult to ascertain the extent to which skills and innovations were acquired from the traffic between the islands, and between the islands and the mainland, and which were indigenous developments.

For the early medieval period, two further candidates for sailing nurseries emerge in the North Sea: the Frisian islands, together with the island-like terpen, during the sixth to ninth centuries AD, and the Danish islands in the Storebaelt in the late eighth through to the eleventh centuries AD. The rise to prominence of the Frisian traders in the early Middle Ages has been attributed to the economic basis of the coastal habitation, rooted principally in a pastoral-dominant agriculture where surpluses were generated as a result of the extensive and bountiful saltmarshes (e.g. Slicher van Bath 1965; see also chapter 5). Stockbreeding is comparatively labour-extensive, and any free time could have been channelled towards the development of trading activities, building on existing skills in boatbuilding and travelling by boat between the islands and terpen. The use of sails and the development of sailing skills in the sixth or seventh century AD may have been an important factor here but, unfortunately, no craft of this period survive from Frisia to illuminate what types of boats or ships were used. Initially, the Frisian trade was one of middlemen who focused their attention on the acquisition of exotic or luxury goods necessary for the gift exchange between the patron and his clients or retinue, allies, and gods, but this type of trade was replaced by a commercial trade system of commodities in the later seventh or early eighth century (Heidinga 1999: 9). The emergence of Dorestad as a proto-urban settlement at the centre of craft production and commodities exchange in the third quarter of the seventh century should be understood in this context (Van Es 1990).

The development of the Nordic clinker-built boat in the Storebaelt-Skagerrak area in the eighth to eleventh centuries AD is much better known to us in the form of the the Viking boats. The socio-economic and environmental reasons that lay behind the emergence of the Viking activity of raiding and piracy remain a matter for debate. Population pressure in the Scandinavian homeland, resulting in a 'bulge' of young males in need of bride-wealth for a decreasing number of available brides, an increasingly competitive socio-political system, and a prevailing warrior ideology have all been noted as contributing reasons (see chapter 8 for a fuller discussion). The development of the clinker-built boat and its associated skills, notably rowing from the fourth century AD and sailing in the eighth century AD, would have been made easier in the context of island communities for whom communication and fishing by boat had a long history.

Apart from the development of craft that could successfully undertake intended journeys, and the skills to master the boat or ship in a range of conditions, seamen also had to develop navigational skills. Essentially, the navigator needs to be able to answer the question 'Where am I?' at any point in time, so that the craft can be steered towards the destination. Although the sea's surface has three dimensions, a minimum of two one-dimensional constraints are normally required for position fixing: this is normally done by dead reckoning—that is, deciding the boat's position in relation to two or more landmarks. Once the landmarks have disappeared over the horizon, the limited field of vision prevents the positioning of the boat through dead reckoning. Such a situation is encountered usually only a few nautical miles from the coast. For example, a navigator standing in a hide-covered boat or logboat with his eyes at 1.5 m above the surface of the sea, will see the horizon at 2.6 nautical miles distance only; a navigator on the deck of a ship 5 m above the water can see the horizon at 4.7 nautical miles, and even from the top of the mast of the Bremen cog, 21 m above the sea (Sauer 2003: 23), the horizon is still only at 9.7 nautical miles. It is therefore not surprising that many maritime archaeologists presuppose that most seafaring in the period under study was coastal in nature, crossing the North Sea only in the Channel.

Edwin Hutchins, in his study *Cognition in the wild* (1995: 66–93) recalls research on the navigational abilities of Micronesian seafarers. Even though only 0.2 per cent of the Pacific's surface in Micronesia is land, experienced navigators steer their outrigger canoes directly to islands up to 150 miles away. These navigators use dead reckoning when possible, but in addition use environmental navigation, such as the colour of the sea as affected by deep reefs, swell patterns, and seabirds' behaviour as guides. Above all, the Micronesians observe the stars, using the star paths or linear constellation to guide their canoes through the night. In the Micronesian archipelago, only a handful of individuals had the extensive knowledge to accomplish long-distance journeys. Of course, it is not possible to project navigational abilities from modern Micronesia to the prehistoric North Sea, but Hutchins (1995: 95) argues that the early European tradition of navigation has diverged only in relatively recent times from one relying wholly on naturally observable phenomena, such as practised in Micronesia. He notes, as an example of early navigation in the west, that Homer has Odysseus using the stars to travel home. Columbus, much later, observed the flight of seabirds: similarly we can imagine that the position of islands such as Helgoland, which cannot be seen from the mainland but was populated by the Bronze Age, could have been detected by observing the seabirds that nested on its cliffs.

The many great rivers that end in the North Sea also add recognizable detail to the texture of the sea, enabling environmental navigation. From satellite images, the sediment plumes emanating from the rivers can be seen to stretch deep into the North Sea, and especially after rainstorms on land no parts of the sea remain unaffected and uncoloured. While riverine sediment plumes are more apparent in the North Sea in the present day than they were in the past, due to the soil-erosive nature of modern agriculture, the extent of the plumes remains largely unchanged, and the individual rivers would have coloured the North Sea in more subtle ways. The behaviour of fish, sea mammals, and birds was, and still is, affected by these relatively mineral-rich outpourings of rivers into the North Sea. For the experienced navigator, these would have provided important information in determining the boat's position.

The currents and tides in the North Sea offer additional clues as to where one is (Figure 29). These have known preponderances, generated principally by the tide wave from the Atlantic. While there is no conclusive evidence that

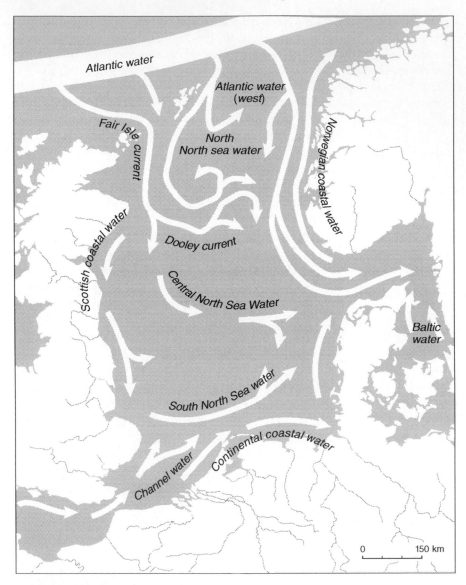

Figure 29. Present-day currents in the North Sea

modern currents have ancient ancestries, and while we know that changes in
the behaviour of currents coincide with fluctuating salinity levels in the North
Atlantic, past currents will have had broad characteristics comparable with
those of the present day (e.g. Turrell 1992). The behaviour of 20th-century
currents in the North Sea has been attributed to the effect of the Atlantic tide
wave, which produces three currents. The first is the Fair Isle Current, which
enters the North Sea between the Orkney and the Shetland archipelagos. This

current flows broadly anticlockwise around the North Sea, producing a predominantly north–south direction along the coasts of eastern Scotland and England before it turns east and north, where it is known as the South North Sea water. The second current emanating from the Atlantic tide wave produces an anticlockwise current over Witch and Fladon Grounds, and is known as the North North Sea water. An offshoot of this (the Central North Sea water) flows towards the top of Jutland. The third current, named the Atlantic Water West, flows through the Norwegian Trench. Additional flows come through the Channel, augmenting the South North Sea water to produce a predominantly south–north current along the North Sea coasts of France, Belgium, Holland, and Denmark. For small shallow-draft boats, surface currents generated by the wind, which in the North Sea is predominantly westerly, and by on-shore and off-shore breezes in the mornings and evenings, add further detail to the texture of the sea.

Islandscapes offered environments in which the acquisition of skills of boatbuilding, seafaring and navigation would have been an essential part of daily life, and these scapes provided platforms for extending embedded experiences into the open sea. When crossing the North Sea, the principal technique used for much of the period under study was probably 'latitude sailing', achieved by maintaining the altitude of the North Star, or by using the sun for guidance. The journey from Norway to the Shetlands, some 170 nautical miles due west, was certainly accomplished on a regular basis in the Viking period relying on this method, and the successful landfalls indicate that the navigators must have had significant knowledge of the currents to avoid drifting off course. The use of the magnetic compass represents the first widespread deviation from reliance on natural phenomena for navigation in the North Sea. The oldest reference to a compass in Europe dates to the very end of the 12th century AD, and in Norway the 'lodestone' is mentioned around AD 1225. On the basis of the orientation of 12th-century churches in Denmark, where a significant number are rotated between 5 and 15 per cent clockwise, coinciding with a declination of the magnetic field between AD 1000 and 1600, Abrahamsen (1992) has concluded that the magnetic compass was in extensive use by this date. Steering by compass would have allowed for journeys to be undertaken on cloudy nights, and would have enabled directional travel to all points of the compass.

In the archaeological record, the navigator in the North Sea first appears in the Bronze Age, principally in the form of enlarged figures in the sterns of the boats carved on the rocks in the Østfold and Bohuslän regions, assuming that the helmsman knew where he was steering the boat to (cf. Ellmers 1995; Coles 2005; see also chapter 8). As was the case of the Micronesians, navigators were likely to have been specialists who possessed the accumulated knowledge of foreign lands, stars, currents, weather, and winds, and of the North Sea itself. Navigators guarded this knowledge, not just because it was the basis of their power and status, but because this was sacred knowledge, linked to the cosmology of the age (cf. Kaul 1998). Our navigators, then, were part of social networks that included other individuals who shared this sacred knowledge, and who spoke a language full of terms—such as kenning or in the offing, or in modern times knots or nautical miles—that were unusable or meaningless on land. In a hybrid world, these networks also included the crews, the currents and winds, foreign lands and islands, the boats themselves, and the sea.

THE MEMORY OF ISLANDS

Many islands in the North Sea are of a temporary nature, with their existence largely dependent on the tides. Today, temporary islands or tidal sands exist principally in the southern half of the North Sea basin, for example in the form of Maplin Sands, off Essex on the northern banks of the Thames, or the 16-km-long Goodwin Sands, off Deal in Kent, which have been responsible for the foundering of hundreds of ships over the centuries. On the continental side of the North Sea, Noorderhaaks is a very large tidal sand between the mainland of North Holland and the island of Texel, known to be moving eastwards by about 100 m each year (Sha 1989). These sandbanks, visible at low tides, are part of a number of much bigger sand ridge complexes; these ridges, formed by the currents from sediments brought by major rivers, provide much texture to the North Sea (Van de Meene 1994; Dyer and Huntley 1999) (Figure 30). Seafarers and navigators will have had knowledge both of the tides and of the temporary and wandering characteristics of these features. The absence of keeled craft in the North Sea until about the ninth century AD (see chapter 7) is undoubtedly due in no small part to the existence of tidal flats, sandbanks, and islands along much of the North Sea coast. When flat-bottomed boats foundered on these islands, all that was required was to wait for the next high tide.

Aside from the tidal islands, which could have been observed and experienced by seafarers directly, islands in general would also have played a role in the social memory. The remarkable finds of two flint axes from Dogger Bank, and two further axes from the Brown Bank, shed a completely new light on the debate surrounding islands in the North Sea after 5000 cal BC. The axes trawled from the Brown Bank are typologically dated to the Michelsberg culture, *c.* 4300–3700 cal BC. The axes trawled from Dogger Bank are only approximately provenanced, and are held in the Craven Museum and Art Gallery in Skipton, Yorkshire (see chapter 3). But these axes too are typologically dated to the early Neolithic. The ground and polished axe, rather than being simply the Neolithic farmer's everyday tool, is understood to have played a part in shaping the social identity of the bearer or community.

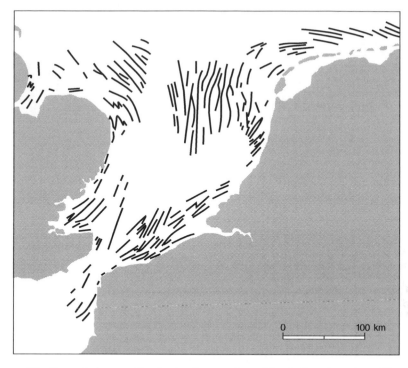

Figure 30. Present-day sandbanks in the southern North Sea (based on Van der Meene 1994)

Ground and polished axes were probably objects of choice in gift exchanges, and the deposition of such axes signifies a deliberate act, rather than accidental loss (Edmonds 1995: 97–114).

The top of the Brown Bank lies currently between 10 and 12 fathoms (18–20 m below the North Sea's surface), and the top of the Dogger Bank between 10 and 20 fathoms (18–36 m). According to the calculated RSL (Shennan et al. 2000b: 310–11), these lands would have been subtidal at least 2,000 years before the start of the Neolithic. Reflecting on the discussion based on geographical modelling of the North Sea's expansion (see chapter 3), the traditional understanding was that the Dogger and Brown banks would have disappeared beneath the surface of the North Sea many centuries before the Neolithic began. If this was indeed the case, than we can agree with Leendert Louwe Kooijmans (1985: 14), when he noted the trawled finds of a polished axe and an axe made of red deer antler from the Brown Bank, and considered these to be not evidence of occupation but objects lost during a Neolithic journey across the North Sea. However, more recently, Vince Gaffney and his colleagues (2009: 145–6) have argued that the Brown Bank may have survived as 'small islands or shallow banks exposed at low tide during the early Neolithic'; possibly the highest parts of Dogger Bank also similarly survived as islands, or else were visible during low tides. This could suggest two alternative explanations for the presence of the polished axes. First, if parts of the Dogger Bank survived well into the Neolithic as islands, it is not inconceivable that people were living here, either permanently or seasonally, in the earliest part of the Neolithic period, as hypothesized by Bryony Coles (1998). Second, the deposition of the polished axes was deliberate and ritually inspired by the social memory of Doggerland, with the islands being attributed special status as the last remnants of the land of the ancestors. In this case, the inundation of the land did not result in a *tabula rasa* of the North Sea, but the memory of the former lands lived on for a considerable period of time. Physically, evidence for past biogenic communities and biogenic action may have survived for long periods after the inundation in a low-energy environment. The lack of detailed information on the context and exact location of these polished axes prevents resolution of this quandary.

CONCLUSIONS

The archaeology of islands in the North Sea has a long history, but this has not produced island archaeologies. Many of the islands that exist presently in the southern half of the North Sea only became detached from the mainland as sea-level rise progressed, and long-term island studies are not possible in these cases; other islands are essentially elevated sand banks that continually 'wander', leading to the destruction of their archaeological heritage. The Shetland and Orkney archipelagos have been, from the early Postglacial onwards, 'real' and stable islands, which explains the focus in this chapter on these islands.

In terms of the isolation and connectedness of islands, Braudel made the observation that 'the Mediterranean has no unity but that created by the movements of men, the relations they imply and the routes they follow' (1972: 276). Similarly, the unity that existed in the North Sea from the late Neolithic onwards was created by select groups of people, notably the elites who had formed networks that extended deep into continental Europe and included Ireland and the British 'mainland'. Later, the elite were joined by others, including missionaries, migrants, pirates, and traders, who sought fame or fortune on the North Sea. However, large parts of the societies who occupied the islands, or the mainlands surrounding the North Sea, were not until relatively recently part of this wider community, and remained largely isolated from the interactions taking place across the North Sea.

Islands have played a major role in the imagination of people throughout the centuries, and a number of the islands in the North Sea have had deviant roles. There were no undisputed 'islands of the dead' in the North Sea, with the possible exception of the imagined islands in the Bohuslän region where the boat carvings on the rocks may have symbolized the existence of water. Islands were selected as refuges, as places for quarantine, or as retreats from the world, especially in the early medieval period when Christian missionaries came to the North Sea to convert the heathens. The small size of islands, and their absence of people, clearly matters, as has been shown in the case of the use of the Farne Islands as a retreat by the monks of Lindisfarne.

In considering the role of islands and archipelagos as 'sailing nurseries', it was noted that such a correlation is evident in the North Sea, and that the earliest logboats can be found in islandscapes in the late Mesolithic and early Neolithic, most notably in the Dutch delta and in the Storebaelt. The centres of boatbuilding innovation in the North Sea can also be linked to islands and archipelagos. Throughout much of prehistory and early history, the Storebaelt appears to have been such an area, with a range of identifiable innovations in boat construction and navigation. The island-rich Wadden Sea in the early medieval period was similarly a region where seafaring skills developed, allowing the Frisians to become the most successful traders in the North Sea.

Finally, the memory of islands drowned by the rising North Sea has been explored. Because of the absence of a clear context, the polished axes from the Dogger and Brown banks cannot be proven to be structural depositions through which the disappearance of the land of the ancestors was remembered. However, the presence of such artefacts at these particular locations illustrates the point that islands, despite their relatively small dimensions, played a significant part in enabling the North Sea to become a knowable place. To paraphrase Cyprian Broodbank (2000: 156), islands played an important role in the shifting of the North Sea from a silent secret world to a space full of voices.

7

Moving across the North Sea

INTRODUCTION

Movements between different lands around the North Sea have always been taking place. While the North Sea was evolving gradually, over the millennia, following the melting of the Devensian ice sheet, close contacts across what remained of the North Sea Plain never ceased, as evidenced by near-parallel developments of the Maglemosian-type tools in southern Scandinavia and Britain (Clark 1936), and by particular practices such as the deliberate deposition of barbed points (see chapter 3). Connections across the North Sea throughout the Mesolithic and the beginning of the Neolithic would have been made easier because of the number of islands surviving within the rising sea. The polished axes from Dogger Bank and Brown Bank either represent human presence on these islands in the early Neolithic or else indicate that the existence of these islands sometime in the pre-Neolithic past was embedded in the social memory of later periods. Both possibilities emphasize the fact that the North Sea was a knowable and visited place.

Movements across the North Sea took various forms: as exchange between elites from different regions of exotic or 'prestige' goods, and possibly of marriage partners; as trade in both luxury and bulk commodities; and in the transfer of people, in some cases as individuals such as pilgrims and missionaries, and in other cases as groups of pirates or as part of larger-scale migrations. Over time, connectedness across the North Sea changed both in nature and in intensity; this was due in no small part to changes in the nature of the craft available. An outline of the movement of goods from the Neolithic through to the end of the Middle Ages illustrates this.

Contacts across the North Sea for the Neolithic and the Bronze Age are demonstrated in the long-distance exchange of exotic objects and artefacts, including Beaker pottery, jewellery, or other adornments of gold, amber, faience, jet, and tin; also copper and bronze weapons and tools, and flint daggers, arrowheads, and wrist guards (e.g. Butler, 1963; O'Connor, 1980; Bradley 1984; Clarke, Cowie, and Foxon 1985). This evidence has formed the basis for extensive discussions among terrestrial archaeologists about the significance of exotic or 'prestige goods' in the emergence of social differentiation in the later Neolithic and early Bronze Age (e.g. Shennan 1982, 1986; Bradley 1984; Barrett 1994; Harding 2000; Needham 2000, 2009). Kristian Kristiansen and Thomas Larsson (2005) have argued that the focus of the Scandinavian elite for the long-distance exchange of exotic goods was southwards via the Baltic Sea, the River Volga, and the Black Sea to the eastern Mediterranean, rather than with the lands around the North Sea. Between *c.* 1500 and 800 cal BC, bronze—and its constituent elements copper and tin—as the most important material exchanged around the North Sea, became more widely available through local smelting and recasting. This decreased the need for long-distance journeys and resulted in more distinctive regional groupings of weapons and tools (Pare 2000).

In the eighth century BC, long-distance material exchange changed from one with a Mediterranean focus (via the coastal regions of France and Iberia), to one focused on central Europe via the River Rhine (e.g. Cunliffe 2005: 446–84; 2009). The presence in the lands around the North Sea of buckets, cauldrons, bronze cart fittings and horse trappings, and Gündlingen-type swords provides the archaeological evidence for this change, which has been linked to the emergence of the Hallstatt C elite (Hawkes and Smith 1957; Cowen 1967). In the northern parts of the region, in Denmark and southern and central Scandinavia, contemporary changes include the transition from a dispersed settlement pattern to a nucleated one, and the first villages comprising groups of farms have been observed for this period. From the burial remains and votive depositions, it is also evident that the previously recognized symbols of status and wealth changed from the possession, use, and occasional deposition of 'cult' objects including axes and drinking cups, to a focus on more everyday possessions (Kaul 1998: 135). Several commentators have argued that around this time of disintegration of the established cosmology—which included the exchange of prestige goods and other movable wealth, such as cattle—the ownership of land became the predominant socioeconomic driver and legitimization of power (e.g. Jensen 1982; Kristiansen 1998; Kaul 1998). It seems probable that, just as happened further south, the collapse in the demand for bronze, copper, and tin, with their restricted natural accessibility, combined with the wider availability of iron ore, produced a collapse of the long-standing exchange systems.

The focus on central Europe for exchange or trade continued until the fourth century BC, but the quantity, frequency, and intensity of these interactions is believed to have been well below that of the Bronze Age. A further decrease in long-distance and cross-North Sea exchange, which caused British communities 'to assume an intensely regional aspect reflecting little of contemporary European developments', is hypothesized for the third century BC onwards (Cunliffe 2005: 484). Only at the beginning of the first century BC are levels of exchange around the North Sea basin noticeably on the increase, with trade links being built with Roman entrepreneurs in southern Gaul.

The Roman period is one of high levels of trade and exchange, and it is not surprising that recent overviews of the Roman economy attribute a key role to seafaring (e.g. Duncan-Jones 1990: 7; Greene 1986: 17), albeit the North Sea takes a rather peripheral role in this. The presence of Roman armies, and later urbanization south of the *limes*, created demands for food which were met in part by the coastal communities around the North Sea (see chapter 6). Market conditions saw the import of Roman 'luxury' goods and coinage into the North Sea basin far north of the *limes* (e.g. Hedeager 1979); in return the region provided the grain, cattle, gold, silver, iron, hides, slaves, and hunting dogs famously described by Strabo in his *Geography* (4.5.2) as the exports from Britain, but representing produce from all the lands around the North Sea.

The collapse of the Roman Empire as a military and administrative entity went hand-in-hand with the collapse of towns and the market economy, and the pursuant large-scale movements of people, at least some of which involved migrations by boat. In the lands around the North Sea there is ample evidence of discontinuity of the larger settlements, and a rapid decline in the exchange of goods. The idea of coinage, however, was not lost. A resurgence of trade and exchange from the sixth century AD is frequently associated with the rise of the Frisians as a major trading force. *Emporia* or 'ports-of-trade' such as Dorestad, Quentovic, Hamwic, London, Ipswich, York, Ribe, and Haithabu were established around the North Sea in the second half of the first millennium BC (Ellmers 1972; Hodges 1982). The theory that *emporia* served primarily as places where the kings controlled prestige goods exchange has now been replaced with the concept that these were places where royal authorities collected tolls from the long-distance-traded finished goods and bulk commodities. Furthermore, alongside these *emporia* many smaller settlements were actively engaged in exchange with communities elsewhere around the North Sea (Loveluck and Tys 2006: 161). The Vikings have been widely credited with causing a decline in North Sea trade in the late eighth, ninth, and tenth centuries, but coastal communities may well have taken advantage of the state of disorder to gain more independence from their terrestrial masters (ibid. 162).

Regionalization in the form of early state formation and urbanization around AD 1000 created new demands for goods such as fish (see chapter 4) and products that were traded around the North Sea basin. With the rise of Lübeck in the 12th century and its alliance with Hamburg in AD 1241, the Hanseatic League of trading towns became a dominant power. While the focus of the Hanse was primarily on the Baltic Sea, it became the most important recognizable trading organization in the North Sea as well, with *Kontors* in Bergen, Bruges, and London (Dollinger 1966).

In short, as this brief overview of the transfer of goods across the North Sea has illustrated, this was not a space that was known and travelled to the same extent at all times and in all areas; sometimes it was perceived as a barrier, and it was precisely the perception of the barrier that made certain connections important. To create connections, or to overcome perceptions of disconnectivity, boats were required. This chapter explores aspects of connectivity and disconnectivity. It is arranged into a consideration of the five broadly defined boatbuilding traditions known in the North Sea basin, in order to bring to the fore the associations between the type of seafaring taking place and the type of connections being made.

HIDE AND SKIN BOATS

Boats made from a sturdy frame covered with animal hide or skin may well have been the most commonly used craft in the waters of the North Sea, especially in the four or five millennia immediately following the glacial retreat. Sean McGrail (e.g. 2001) in particular has argued that the hide or skin boat was probably the most common craft in the early prehistoric period, and that it would also have been used throughout the later prehistoric and early historic eras, especially on smaller rivers and lakes. Such boats would have been relatively light with high freeboard. Seagoing skin boats are well known from the ethnographic record, for example in Greenland, where the *umiak* is used as a whaling boat (Petersen 1986).

Genuine evidence for the existence of hide-covered boats in our early prehistory has, however, eluded archaeologists. It seems very unlikely that the remains of boats where the hull was made of an animal skin will ever be found, at least not in the North Sea or in its main rivers, since the preservation of hides and skins requires acidic soil conditions not present here. The existence of this type of boat, its distribution, and how it was used, remain largely hypothetical. Nevertheless, Detlev Ellmers (1980) has hypothesized that worked reindeer antlers from Husum, Schleswig-Holstein, may have been used as frames for just such a craft. The date of the antlers, around 9500 cal BC, places them in the Ahrensburg, at a time when the North Sea had not yet expanded to the current coast of Schleswig-Holstein. Such craft would have been used on rivers and lakes, and may well have been used to hunt reindeer as they swam across water bodies: the location of mortal wounds on excavated remains of reindeer implies that such an activity was taking place (Tromnau 1987), and this way of hunting reindeer has been ethnographically attested from Anuktuvuk Pass and other locations in Alaska (Jason Rogers, pers. comm.). The skills and technologies needed for making hide boats were undoubtedly present in the earliest Mesolithic. For example, eyed needles used for the sewing or stitching of hides to produce weatherproof clothing were prerequisite technological innovations for the colonization of any Arctic or subarctic climate, and were already being used in Upper Palaeolithic Europe (Soffer 2004).

Despite the absence of contemporary wooden boats regionally, the presence in the archaeological record of very early paddles may potentially be seen as evidence for the existence of hide and skin boats. Such paddles have been found at Star Carr in Yorkshire (*c.* 9000 cal BC), Friesack, Brandenburg (three paddles: 8730–7790 cal BC), and Duvensee, Hamburg (*c.* 8500 cal BC), in regions where no other types of boats are known for this time. Similarly, paddles from Denmark from around 7200 cal BC, Sweden from *c.* 2700 cal BC and from Finland in the second millennium BC all predate by several millennia the earliest boats known for each region, and it seems probable that the craft in which these paddles were used were made with hides (Lanting 1997/8: 644).

In terms of connecting people on the North Sea coasts, the earliest contacts between continental Europe and the emerging British Isles were probably undertaken by hide-covered boats. From the British Isles, no boats predating the Bronze Age are known, and in the absence of other types of craft we must assume that the transport of the first domesticates to the British Isles around 4000 cal BC was undertaken in hide boats. Whereas domesticated seeds could have been straightforwardly brought across the North Sea, the Channel, or the Irish Sea in hide boats, transporting early domesticated cattle in anything but a solid boat, such as a logboat, would make for quite an audacious trip. Recent mitochondrial DNA analysis (Edwards et al. 2007) has shown that the domestic cow in the countries around the North Sea basin, including the British Isles, did not relate to the autochthonous aurochs, which had survived in one or more *refugia* during the final stadial. Rather, the origin of domestic cattle lies in the Near East. Such smaller cattle carrying predominantly T haplotype mitochondrial DNA replaced during the Neolithic and Bronze Age the much larger P haplotype mitochondrial DNA-carrying aurochs, without large-scale introgression.

The journeys that brought the Neolithic polished axes from the Continent to the Dogger and Brown banks (see chapter 6) could have been undertaken either in logboats, which were by this time widely used on the continental side of the North Sea, or in hide boats. Possibly the best evidence for the making of skin boats in Britain before the Bronze Age comes in the form of the techniques used in the building of the first sewn-plank boats: it is highly likely that the 'sewing' of the planks and the construction of the internal frames are techniques that evolved from the construction of larger hide boats (see below; Van de Noort et al. 1999; Roberts 2006).

An alternative debate on the introduction of farming into Britain (and Ireland) focuses on the possible migration of the earliest farmers. Clearly, the complex referred to by its distinctive style of domestic pottery—the linear band ceramic or LBK—never reached the shores of the North Sea; at its furthest extent, in southern Limburg in the Netherlands, LBK came to within just over 100 km of the North Sea coast, around 5300 cal BC. The first Neolithic indicators, around 4000 cal BC, in the archaeological record of the British Isles are unlikely therefore to have originated across the North Sea where forms of hybrid Mesolithic–Neolithic lifestyles survived on the coast. Instead, the source for the British and Irish Neolithic must be sought further south, in western France, where fully agricultural modes of subsistence known as the Michelsberg, Chasseo-Michelsberg and Cheséen du Basin Parisien complexes existed on the coast at around this time (e.g. Louwe Kooijmans 2005/6: 512).

In his recent overview of the prehistory of Britain and Ireland, Richard Bradley (2007: 29–38) concludes that whereas the break between Mesolithic and Neolithic ways of life appears to be clear-cut in Ireland, Scotland, and northern England, the distinction is much less clear for southern England, especially for Wessex. Illustrating this, Alison Sheridan (2003) has connected the megalithic grave site at Achnacreebeag in Argyll, Scotland, to Neolithic remains in Brittany, and believes that this represents a migration from France to Scotland around 3900 cal BC; this idea may be extended to embrace the simple passage tombs in Wales and in Carrowmore, County Sligo, in Ireland. Nevertheless, the date of around 4000 cal BC for the earliest indicators of neolithization appears to apply to the whole of the British Isles and Ireland, and no insular 'spread' has been detected. Bradley (2007: 38) concludes that some of these indicators, such as the earliest domestic cattle, sheep, wheat, and barley, must have been brought across the Channel from the Continent, and that this transfer must have involved the movement of people as well, probably as migrants and settlers. The indigenous population, however, quickly adopted (selected) agricultural elements. In the absence of archaeologically identified boats of this age, a role for the hide-covered boat in this transfer seems likely.

For later periods, the evidence for hide and skin boats is either historical or indirect. For Sweden and Denmark, a number of authors have commented on the boat images in rock carvings and on bronzes, suggesting that these represent hide or skin boats (e.g. Marstrander 1963; Glob 1969; Johnstone 1972, 1980; Malmer 1981; cf. Coles 1993: 27). The Hjortspring boat, however, which bears close resemblance to the boats on the rocks and bronze razors, had a hull made of thin planks of linden wood. But it may be the case that the Hjortspring boat had evolved from hide boats, with its makers adapting existing techniques such as the sewing of the parts that made up the hull, and the construction of an internal frame. Nevertheless, the current emerging consensus is that the boats on the rocks represent plank boats (Kaul 2002, 2004; Kaul and Valbjørn 2003; Crumlin-Pedersen and Trakadas 2003).

The gold model of a ship from Broighter, though lacking any detail of an internal frame, may represent a hide-covered boat. Found in 1896 in a floodplain near Lough Foyle in Northern Ireland, the model has been dated to the first century BC on the basis of the gold torc that was part of this hoard (Praeger 1942). The model is 188 mm long, 80 mm wide, and 48 mm high. It is currently displayed with eight thwarts/benches, but one is missing. Fifteen oars, each 71 mm long, have been preserved, and also a steering oar. Rowlocks are represented as wire rings attached to the side of the boat. The mast goes through the centre seat (Cochrane 1902; Farrell and Penny 1975). This model is often cited as the earliest archaeological evidence that sails were used in north-west Europe at the end of the Iron Age in the North Sea basin (e.g. McGrail 2001).

Several classical authors noted the use of hide and skin in the north-western European boatbuilding tradition, including Caesar in the first-century BC *Bello civili* (1.54) and Pliny the Elder in his first-century AD *Historia naturalis* (4.104), who described British boats as made with a rawhide-covered wicker hull (cf. Cunliffe 2001: 66–7). Where hide boats are studied in ethnographic contexts, their adaptability to a range of environments is frequently mentioned. Thus, hide boats in the form of *umiaks* and *kayaks* are used for hunting in marine environments in the Arctic, but the hide-covered rounded coracles from Ireland are used on small lakes and ponds. The use of hide boats in early medieval Ireland provides an interesting dilemma, in that it appears that hide-covered vessels were the craft of choice for the saints who set out on their long-distance pilgrimages. Thus, in the *Life of Columba*, the monks' boat comes under attack from sea creatures, and the book records that the monks were anxious that the creatures might pierce the leather covering of the ship. In the voyage of St Brendan, the crew of 14 monks set off in a boat that had a hull made of fat-smeared ox hides and oak bark. As already argued (see chapter 6), in the early Christian imagination the sea was a frontier zone between this world and the abyss of Hell. In this sense, it could be suggested that the selection for these journeys of what must have been perceived by the terrestrial-based narrators as light and vulnerable boats was a feature of their hagiographies: such a selection placed the monks' lives, and the success of their *peregrinatio pro amore Dei*, to a greater extent in the hands of their Christian god (Sobecki 2008: 9). But it could also be argued that Irish researchers may have put too much emphasis on the hide-covered coracles or currachs as a craft closely identified with Irish national identity, having discounted the importance of plank-built boats in early medieval Ireland which do not carry such a connotation (O'Sullivan and Breen 2007: 139–42).

LOGBOATS

Logboats, constructed from hollowed-out tree trunks, are the most common type of craft to be found in the North Sea basin and its rivers. They are often referred to as monoxylous craft—that is, made from a single piece of wood—although the use of transom ends has been recorded from as early as the late Mesolithic, for example in the craft from the Ertebølle site of Tybrind Vig (e.g. Andersen 1987). The oldest dated 'Pesse' logboat comes from a small river valley in the province of Drenthe in the Netherlands, and has been dated to 8250–7750 cal BC (Harsema 1992). Previous deliberations questioning wheth-

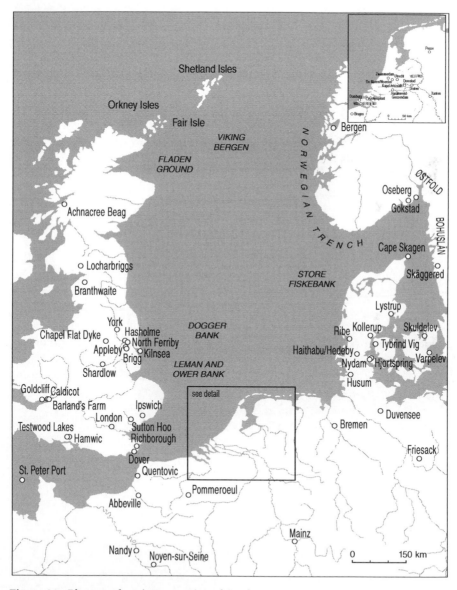

Figure 31. Places and regions mentioned in chapter 7

er the Pesse craft, being so small and crudely made, was indeed a boat at all have been resolved. Close parallels exist in the recent find of three logboats from Noyen-sur-Seine and Nandy in northern France, dated to 7180–6550 cal BC. The Pesse boat is simply too early to have functioned as a trough or as a tree-trunk coffin, and despite its small size could carry a single adult (cf. Lanting 1997/8: 636). The successful testing of replicas made by the Drents Museum in 1999 has swept away any remaining doubts that the Pesse example was anything other than an early logboat (Louwe Kooijmans 2008: 26).

Lanting's (1997/8) analysis of the dates of logboats from Europe has provided some remarkable insights into the origin of these craft around the North Sea. His research into all absolutely dated logboats, organized by country and groupings of country, reveals a number of distinct patterns (Figure 32). Based on several hundred craft, this meta-analysis provides the most robust database currently available for this kind of interpretation. A 'Continental Zone 1', consisting of Denmark, north-west Germany, the Netherlands, Belgium, and north-western France, is identified by Lanting and represented by 116 dated logboats (Figure 33). The earliest logboats in this zone date to before 7500 cal BC; they were in use throughout the Mesolithic, Neolithic, Bronze Age, and Iron Age, and continued into the Roman period and Middle Ages.

Lanting also recognizes a 'Continental Zone 2', represented by 244 dated logboats and comprising the rest of Germany and France, Poland, the Czech Republic, Austria, and Switzerland, and possibly the Baltic States. Within this zone, there are two regions where logboats appear relatively early: the Rhine–Saône–Rhône corridor, with logboats dating from *c.* 4350 cal BC, and the southern shore of the Baltic Sea where logboats date to after *c.* 3800 cal BC. Logboats in Zone 2 are generally significantly later in date than those in Continental Zone 1; within the Zone 2 there are substantial geographical regions where they are distinctly later still, for example Bavaria, where the earliest logboats are of late Bronze Age date. Unsurprisingly for this river-rich part of Europe, logboats continue to appear throughout later prehistory, the Roman period, the Middle Ages, and on into the modern period.

For Ireland and Britain, a different pattern emerges when the 134 dates are reviewed. The earliest dated logboats are late Mesolithic or early Neolithic for Ireland, and for Britain early Bronze Age. The oldest logboat in Ireland is from Carrigdirty, County Limerick (4790–4550 cal BC); Lanting (p. 631) expresses some concerns, however, about this early date, suggesting instead that it is the second oldest example, from Ballygowan in County Armagh (3630–3350 cal BC), that signals the introduction of the logboat into Ireland in the early Neolithic. The British logboats may have developed from Irish precedents. Indeed, the oldest logboats from Britain, such as the Locharbriggs logboat from Dumfries in Scotland (2600–1750 cal BC) and the Branthwaite logboat from Cumbria (2030–1740 cal BC), are to be found on

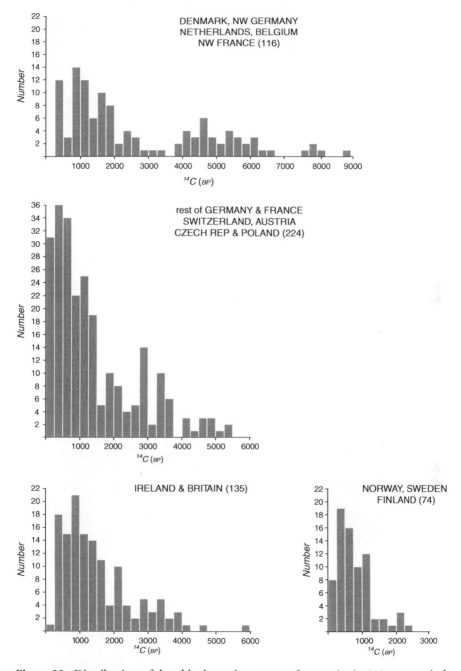

Figure 32. Distribution of dated logboats by groups of countries in 200-year periods (based on Lanting 1997/8)

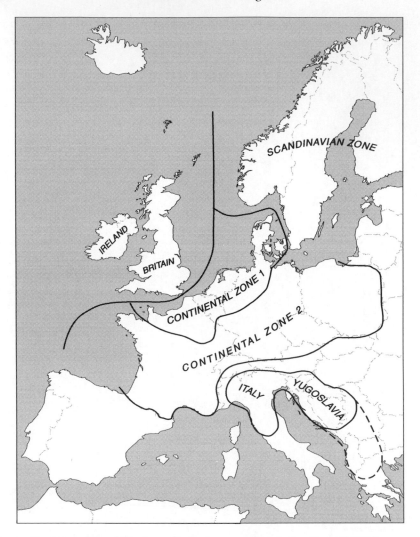

Figure 33. Map of the diffusion of logboats according to Lanting (1997/8)

the Irish Sea side of the British mainland. The oldest British logboats from rivers that drain into the North Sea are the Chapel Flat Dyke logboat from the River Don near Rotherham (2020–1690 cal BC) and the Appleby logboat from the River Ancholme (1500–1300 cal BC).

The Scandinavian database of dated logboats is somewhat small (74 examples), but the results are nevertheless surprising. The oldest logboat in Sweden, from Skäggered, Göteburg, is dated to the late Bronze Age or pre-Roman Iron Age (810–390 cal BC). The southern Swedish region of Bohüslan and the area around Göteburg are relatively well represented for the first millennium BC.

However, the evidence for such an early use of logboats for other parts of Sweden, Norway, and Finland does not exist. On the basis of Lanting's analysis, it appears that this type of craft was introduced into Norway only in the seventh and eighth centuries AD, and after AD 1000 into Finland. Locally, in all these regions, logboats remain in use on lakes and rivers to the present day.

In the title of his paper, 'Dating the origin and diffusion of the European logboat', Lanting expresses a clear predilection for the concept of diffusion to explain cultural change, and links the regions thus: the origin of the European logboat is to be found in Continental Zone 1 in the Mesolithic before 7500 cal BC, with the idea diffusing to Continental Zone 2 at the very end of the Mesolithic or early Neolithic, after 4350 cal BC. The diffusion reached Ireland with the Neolithic, around 3600 cal BC, probably directly from contact with regions in the north-west of France within Continent Zone 1. The first logboats on the British mainland are to be found on the side of the Irish Sea, with Ireland as the likely origin of the British logboat. Finally, the diffusion into southern Scandinavia after *c.* 800 cal BC could have happened either from Continental Zone 1 or 2. While this analysis is highly informative on the presence of this type of craft in the archaeological record, the use of a single concept to explain its use in the past is crude, and even somewhat 'dehumanized' (see also: Maarleveld 2008: 9). The proposed model of origin and diffusion can be criticized in two important respects.

First, it is not impossible that even a meta-analysis has failed to mitigate the impacts of bias in the archaeological record. Postglacial isostatic rebound affected large geographical regions, and northern parts of Scandinavia in particular, and the absence from the record of early craft—not just logboats but craft of any kind—may be due in part to the uplifting of former coastal areas, resulting in a lack of waterlogged archaeological remains from early prehistory. The biases in archaeological traditions, often articulated at national levels, should also not be understated: the varying interest in and treatment of logboats is a case in point.

Second, if we look in greater detail at the design of the logboats, then certain characteristics suggest alternative routes by which particular ideas on how to build these craft were exchanged and adopted. An early example of this concerns the late Mesolithic. It has already been noted that the 5- to 7-m-long, U-shaped, thin-walled, rounded at both stem and stern, logboats from the Swifterbant sites at Hardinxveld-Giessendam in the Netherlands (or Continental Zone 1), appear to have more in common with the Neolithic logboats from Switzerland (in Continental Zone 2) than the transom-end-fitted logboats from Ertebølle sites such as Tybrind Vig and Lystrup (in Continental Zone 1) (Louwe Kooijmans 2001a: 476). For later periods, and indeed well into the post-medieval era, we recognize certain 'traditions' in logboat building that seem to be characteristic of particular river systems, rather than coinciding with the zoning suggested by Lanting. Examples include the use of boats of a certain length and shape, the use of integrated 'ribs', and the fitting of transom ends. Diffusion as the key factor accounting for cultural change appears largely to ignore the role of those people who built the boats and used them. In addition it decontextualizes the logboats from their wider socio-economic and political settings; neither can it explain why certain innovations were adopted and others rejected.

It seems that the most important factors influencing the development and use of logboats were first the availability of other types of craft, such as rafts or hide-covered boats, which are not present in the archaeological record; second, the type of travel that these craft accommodated within the socio-economic and political context; and third the skill and knowledge of the boatbuilder. The latter has been studied in the context of European logboats by Jason Rogers (2009), who has argued that logboat design is determined by three components: a built-in conservatism in logboat design, reflecting the faith held by the boatbuilders in tried and tested craft, as well as a reluctance to experiment with new ideas which might compromise the safety of both crew and cargo; slow 'evolutionary' developments over long periods of time, reflecting socio-economic changes and the availability of material for boat-building; and genuine innovations in logboat construction, which can frequently be traced to particular events or contacts that cross catchments. Rogers notes, for example, how logboat designs in different river systems can remain separate and distinctive for many centuries, until the construction of a canal linking the two rivers results in rapidly changing designs.

In terms of material used for logboats, the earliest examples around the North Sea such as the logboats from Pesse, Noyen-sur-Seine, and Nandy were all made of pine, unsurprisingly as this was the first tree after the Post-glacial to provide trunks of sufficient length and size. In the late Mesolithic lime, alder, and poplar were used, as in the lime logboats found at the Ertebølle site of Tybrind Vig (Andersen 1987) and at the Swifterbant site of Hardinxveld-Giessendam De Bruin (Louwe Kooijmans 2001a). From the Neolithic onwards, logboats were most frequently made of oak, reflecting the widespread application first of polished stone axes and second of metal axe technologies in the fashioning of these 'harder' tree trunks. On all sides of the North Sea, oak remains the most common species for the construction of logboats through to the end of the Middle Ages.

Within this type of boat, significant variations exist in length, bole, shape of stem, stern and hull-form, thickness of the wood, and the use of gauging holes, to name but a few. Some logboats are 'composite' craft, such as the logboats fitted at the stern with transoms, a feature already in use in the Ertebølle logboats; this technique is also used in many craft of later prehistoric date from England. From *c.* 1000 cal BC we see some quite advanced designs, with platforms and seats added, such as is the case with the fourth-century BC Hasholme logboat from the Humber Wetlands (Millett and McGrail 1987). Alongside simpler logboats, craft of the Roman and medieval periods sometimes used a hollowed-out tree trunk as the basis, but with a number of extended side strakes included in the hull, as has been observed for the Zwammerdam-6 Gallo-Roman boat (De Weerd 1988). Logboats are presumed to have been used predominantly on inland lakes, rivers, and in relatively calm estuaries, but their range of operation could have been extended to include coastal waters if they were fitted with outriggers to provide greater stability, or if they were used in pairs, or else were equipped with extended side strakes that would have increased freeboard. No direct evidence for outriggers exists in the archaeological record of the North Sea, nor for the use of paired logboats, but the use of extended strakes is well known for the medieval period. Contentiously, the Utrecht 1 Ship, an expanded logboat extended with side strakes—and several other craft constructed in this fashion, including one from London—is considered by some maritime archaeologists to be an example of a medieval 'hulk', one of the most frequently named craft of around AD 1000 and the type of craft thought to have made the rise of the Frisians as a major trading power possible (Ellmers 1972: 59; Goodburn 2000; Van de Moortel 2009).

Logboats would have been highly suitable for travelling along the North Sea coast and deltas, and among the islands, and for visiting fishweirs, which needed daily emptying. From the late Mesolithic onwards, logboats would have been seen as the 'workhorse' of coastal and riverine communities. For nomadic hunter-gatherer-fishers, the use of the logboat not only provided access to islands in the biodiverse and rich coastal wetlands, but also allowed for an accumulation of possessions to a point unimaginable to hunter-gatherers, who moved through the landscape on foot. Perceptions of the land would have been entirely different. Moving through the watery landscape by boat would be nearly effortless; fishing would be easier, and when hunting, the watering places of larger animals would be more easily identifiable. As suggested earlier (see chapter 4), the long-term survival of an Ertebølle or Swifterbant hunter-gatherer-fisher way of life can possibly be attributed less to the abundance of the resources available to these communities than to the advantages provided by dwelling through the landscape in a boat.

The logboat, being well suited to riverine traffic, most probably played a major role in exchange and trade for much of the prehistoric and early historic past. We can safely assume that for the long-distance exchange of exotic goods, and the shorter-distance movement of bulkier goods, rivers provided the best routes and logboats the most obvious vehicles. Only exceptionally have logboats been found with evidence of their cargos, but where this has been the case, such as the Bronze Age logboat of Shardlow in the River Trent with its sandstone blocks (Pryor 2004) and the Iron Age Hasholme boat containing timbers and joints of beef (Millett and McGrail 1987), the role of logboats at a regional and local level is emphasized. Indirect evidence for early long-distance use of logboats may lie in the similarities in the logboat design at either end of the River Rhine in the early Neolithic. There is no doubting that goods from the Alpine region in the early Neolithic, such as polished jadeite axes, travelled to the Netherlands, Belgium, and Germany, and across the North Sea to England, and it seems at least possible that boatbuilders on the Rhine would have seen craft that travelled along it, and adopted certain similarities in the design of their own logboats.

Logboats before the Bronze Age were quite small, and their carrying capacity suited a family. After *c.* 1200 cal BC, although the majority of logboats still fall within the 'family-sized' category, a small number of larger examples are known. The Brigg logboat from the River Ancholme, dated to 1260–800 cal BC, is nearly 15 m long. The Varpelev logboat from a channel separating the Stevns peninsula from the island of Sjælland, dated to 1250–790 cal BC, has a preserved length of 12.5 m but was originally about 14 m long (Hansen and Nielsen 1979). These longer logboats were less suited to families, and should be considered to have functioned as vessels intended for the transport of bulkier goods; they were probably owned and controlled at a higher social level. However, even the largest logboats were not suited to hostilities, be that in the form of cattle-raiding, piracy or warfare. These craft are too small, too unstable, and too unwieldy for such purposes.

SEWN-PLANK BOATS

The sewn-plank boats from the North Sea date exclusively to the Bronze Age and can be understood as the product of a period during which bronze axe technology enabled the carving or hewing of planks or timbers of oak with intricate detail, at a time when nails or treenails were yet to become widely used in north-western Europe. Thus, the timbers were given bevelled edges to ensure a close and near-watertight fit, but these planks could not be nailed together, and instead were sewn or stitched together with a rope made of yew fibre (Figure 34). The hull was made even more watertight by caulking any gaps between the timbers with moss. This method of construction provided the hull with very little rigidity, and the external pressure of the water would have caused its collapse but for an internal frame system that cleverly used cleats that were integral to the keel and side-strake planks through which transverse timbers were passed. Cross-timbers or thwarts would have contributed to the hull's rigidity, while doubling as seats for the paddlers who provided the propulsion.

A total of ten sewn-plank craft have been discovered to date, all on the British side of the North Sea. These include the Brigg 'raft', discovered in the Ancholme valley in 1888 and re-excavated in the 1970s (McGrail 1981), and the three boats found in the intertidal Humber at North Ferriby. F1 was

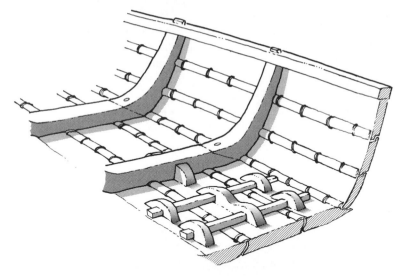

Figure 34. Schematic representation of a sewn-plank boat

discovered in 1937, F2 in 1940, and F3 in 1963 (Wright and Wright 1939; Wright 1990; Wright et al. 2001). From the Welsh side of the Severn estuary come three discoveries, a side strake of one boat (Caldicot 1) and up to three additional fragments of another (Caldicot 2), found during excavations in 1990 (Nayling and Caseldine 1997), as well as two pieces of boat planking from Goldcliff found in 1992 (Bell 1992). The Dover boat was also found in 1992 (Clark 2004). A fragment of a cleat comes from the Testwood Lakes excavations, just north of Southampton in the floodplain of the River Test (Fitzpatrick, Ellis, and Allen 1996; A. Fitzpatrick pers. comm.), and awaits full publication. The most recent boat fragment was a single plank discovered on the beach at Kilnsea in East Yorkshire in 1996 (Van de Noort et al. 1999).

While these remains of craft have been acknowledged as being parts of sewn-plank boats (cf. McGrail 2001), and a number of technological aspects are shared, each boat also has certain unique design characteristics. The shared construction principles include the use of oak planking with bevelled edges, the stitching or sewing of the planks with withies of yew, and an integral system of cleats and transverse timbers that provide rigidity to the hull. But whereas F1 has a single keel plank, F2 has two keel planks joined amidships; the Dover boat's seam was formed by two planks joined by an upstanding longitudinal cleat rail, while the Brigg 'raft' had five bottom-joined planks. These variations suggest that over the 1,000 years during which sewn-plank boats were being constructed, they were built with increasing girths. Not enough remains of the other boats to compare their design in great detail, and it could be that the variations were the consequence of local boatbuilding traditions combined with limited availability of suitable timber. However, one aspect of variability in boat design appears to be more significant. McGrail (e.g. 2001: 190, 2004) has argued for the existence of two subgroups: group A boats, including F1, F2, F3, Caldicot 1, and Dover, are characterized by the use of individual stitches or lashings through relatively big holes to fasten the planks together, while those of group B, including the Brigg 'raft', Caldicot 2, and Goldcliff, have linked stitching through small holes set close together. This subdivision coincides with the age of the boat fragments. The craft in group A are dated to the 20th to 15th centuries cal BC inclusive, and those in group B to the 12th to 8th centuries cal BC. The Kilnsea and Testwood Lakes fragments have not been allocated to either group.

Sewn-plank boats are thought to have been used for seafaring journeys, although it has to be said that discussion of their suitability for such journeys is ongoing, focusing on such aspects as the rocker or the curve of the keel, which defines the boat's ability to ride the waves, and the degree to which these craft were watertight. Nevertheless, the sewn-plank boats were indeed very large boats, up to 18 m in length, with room for a crew of 20 or more, and with a greater freeboard than logboats; overall they are likely to have been capable of successful journeys across the North Sea. The location of the finds of sewn-plank boats, exclusively on the coast or in estuarine situations, strongly supports the argument that this type of craft was used for coastal journeys and sea crossings (Van de Noort 2006).

The introduction of sails is another issue of ongoing debate. It has been shown, experimentally, that sewn-plank boats could have been sailed (Gifford and Gifford 2004). However, the sewn-plank boats were all paddled, and while it is not impossible that these craft were, on occasion and with the wind behind, assisted by sail power, there are no archaeological elements such as mast-steps to suggest that this had been intended at the point of boatbuilding. None of the Bronze or Iron Age rock carvings of boats in Scandinavia depict sails: all these boats on the rocks were paddled.

Inevitably, questions of connections across the North Sea during the period in which the first sewn-plank boats were constructed have been closely linked to the Bell Beaker phenomenon. This phenomenon relates to the presence in the archaeological record, in more or less distinctive regions across Europe, of the type of idiosyncratic pottery known as Bell Beakers. Around the North Sea, these regions are northern Jutland, much of the Low Countries— especially the lower Rhine delta and the Veluwe region south of the Zuiderzee—as well as south-eastern England, Wessex, East Anglia, East York-shire, and the lowlands of Scotland adjacent to the North Sea. Outside the North Sea basin, coastal regions with this distinctive pottery are to be found in Ireland, Normandy, and the Vendée; also in the Basque Country, Galicia, and on the European and African sides of the Strait of Gibraltar, in addition to the southern French coast, northern Italy, Sardinia, and Sicily. Inland regions with Bell Beaker pottery are all to be found in the reaches of the major rivers, such as the Oder, Elbe, Danube, Seine, and Duoro. Clearly, boats seem to have played a key role in the development and maintenance of the contacts between these regions, and for the British Isles and Ireland at the very least, this must have included seagoing craft. The presence of Bell Beaker pottery has been at times attributed to migration of whole populations, the so-called 'Beaker Folk', or of migrations of elite groups (cf. Harrison 1980 for a review); in more recent years, however, the concept of exchange within elite networks across Europe has gained much support (Clarke 1976; Shennan 1976).

The social, political, and economic reasons behind the material-based manifestation of elitism in the early Bronze Age has been discussed by many reputable commentators. There is a degree of consensus on the importance of access to, and control of, exotic or 'prestige goods' in terms of underpinning status and prestige (e.g. Shennan 1982, 1988; Bradley 1984; Barrett 1994; Harding 2000), a concept based initially on structural Marxist and more recently neo-Marxist thinking (e.g. Rowlands 1980). Instead of direct control over land and subsistence as modes of production, in prehistory it was the control of people that was important in becoming powerful. The social transactions involving prestige goods are considered to have played a key role in the reproduction of the socio-political order and organizations or, in other words, in the negotiation, legitimization, and reinforcement of rights over people. There is also some agreement that during the third millennium BC access and control of prestige goods complemented and eventually replaced the social reproductive role of large monuments, such as henges and cursûs (e.g. Barrett, Bradley, and Green 1991). Such a level of agreement does not exist for the debate on whether the significant changes observed in Britain in the late Neolithic should be associated with a new elite (e.g. as advocated by Shennan 1986), or whether they represent a new way in which the status of ruling groups and individuals was defined (e.g. as argued by Barrett 1994).

However, evidence for the local production of Beakers and other artefacts that form part of the 'Beaker package' has reinforced the idea that trade and exchange cannot on its own account for the distribution and near-parallel development of this type of pottery between *c.* 2500 and 1700 cal BC. Most recently, some evidence has been found in central Europe for the movement of people during their own lifetime. This evidence, from skeletal remains associated with Bell Beakers, is based on an analysis of differential strontium isotope ratios (Price, Grupe, and Schröter 1998; Price et al. 2004). However, due to the geological complexity of continental Europe, the evidence has not provided clear markers of the origin of the people concerned. In a recent paper, Marc Vander Linden (2004: 349) concludes that a likely driver underpinning the distinctive distribution of the Beaker package, and the parallel development of the pottery in distinct yet widely separated areas, could be explained by the movement of marriage partners in a generalized exchange mode, even though the reasons for this practice remain unexplained.

In the context of the North Sea, a number of additional observations are relevant. Past research has highlighted the similarities between the Low Countries and Britain in the design of early Beaker pottery (Lanting and Van der Waals 1972; 1976), which indicate close connections across the North Sea from as early as *c.* 2400 cal BC. However, the earliest Beakers in Europe, from Iberia, are now dated to *c.* 2700 cal BC, and the extension of the networks to Britain, around 2400 cal BC for England and around 2200 cal BC for Scotland, suggests that this was a relatively late development within the Beaker phenomenon (cf. Parker Pearson et al. 2007: 634). The oldest Beakers in northern Jutland are also, initially, closely linked in style to the Beakers from the Veluwe region. From a British perspective, Stuart Needham (2005: 209–10) has argued on the basis of detailed analysis of the funerary contexts of the Beakers that we should distinguish three phases in the value attributed to this phenomenon. In the first phase, *c.* 2500–2250 cal BC, the Beaker is 'circumscribed, exclusive culture', and the funerary rites are altogether continental in implementation; such graves are infrequent and presumably reserved for particular individuals. During the second phase, *c.* 2250–1950 cal BC, the Beaker cultural values become the prevailing cultural ethos, and graves containing Beakers become more frequent, losing their exclusiveness. In the third phase, *c.* 1950–1700/1600 cal BC, graves with Beakers are universally poor, and the pots are used as reference to the past.

The debate on whether the onset of the Beaker phenomenon around the North Sea was linked to migrants, be it individuals as marriage partners in a generalized exchange or a religious elite bringing new knowledge and new techniques, or whether the presence in the archaeological record is one of acculturation between elite groups connected in an expanding network, is yet to be resolved. Presently, very few commentators would argue for a large-scale movement of people. What is of interest to the present debate is the nature of the people coming from overseas, either to settle or to exchange. They appear to have had a profound effect on the cultural lives of the indigenous people, partly through the introduction of material culture that was quite alien, such as the first copper axes in England or the very finely crafted lanceolate flint daggers in Jutland, but especially through funerary practices that were adopted relatively quickly from the foreigners. The implication is that the people who introduced the Beaker also introduced new ritual ideas and concepts. Any evidence for missionary zeal is, unsurprisingly, absent from the archaeological record, but the impact of these people was unquestionably significant. The foreignness, both of the people and their ideas, having travelled over great geographical distances, would only have enhanced the values attributed to them.

Returning to the sewn-plank boats, I have argued in previous research (Van de Noort et al. 1999; Van de Noort 2003, 2004b, 2006, 2009), that the sewn-plank boat innovation, occurring at a time when the long-distance exchange of exotic or prestige goods between elite groups in Europe was at its height, or in Needham's words became the prevailing cultural ethos, cannot be considered a coincidence. It seems likely that the sewn-plank boats were the boat-builders' response to increasing demands by their political and religious masters for access to these exotic resources. By building larger, sturdier boats, the number of instances available for sea crossings around the year was extended. The larger sewn-plank boats also provided opportunities for the creation of larger retinues by aspiring leaders, something that will be returned to in the following chapter.

One additional boat must be mentioned here: the Hjortspring boat, from the Danish Island of Als in the Baltic. This *c.* 350 BC craft, found broken up in a small bog, shares with its British counterparts the use of planks sewn or stitched together and an internal frame to provide rigidity to the hull (Rosenberg 1937). However, the Hjortspring boat was made largely from linden, with strakes of a maximum thickness of 3 cm: these had been sewn together, with ten internal frames lashed to the cleats that were integral to the strakes. Each frame had two seats for paddlers, who would have numbered around 20 in all; in addition there would have been an oarsman, and room, possibly, for several other crew. Sea trials in 1999 and 2000 with the reconstructed Hjortspring boat *Tilia Alsie* produced economical speeds of 4 to 5 knots and a top speed of over 7 knots. The trials also proved the boat's ability to navigate in heavy seas, giving it a daily range of around 100 km (Kaul and Valbjørn 2003).

Although the Hjortspring ship remains unique in the archaeological record, its resemblance to the rock-carved depictions from the Østfold and Bohuslän regions has been noted by many. Fleming Kaul, in his detailed analysis of the bronze engravings of ships from Denmark and southern Scandinavia (see chapter 9), found no parallels with the Hjortspring craft. But the Hjortspring type, with its characteristic 'horns' at the stem and stern, is well represented in the rock carvings, suggesting that it post-dates the bronze ships, which have a known end-date of *c.* 500 BC (Kaul 2004). Kaul emphasizes the difference in detail between the Hjortspring boat and earlier Bronze Age representations of boats and ships; the latter have a clear fore and aft aspect, but the Hjortspring boat is symmetrical, enabling it to land on a beach while allowing for a quick retreat without the need to turn the boat around, an ideal situation when raiding. It would appear then that the Hjortspring boat is an advanced type of craft that must have a long tradition in Norse shipbuilding. Its speed and symmetry made it well-suited for surprise attacks and raiding expeditions.

GALLO-ROMAN BOATS

The third group of craft from the North Sea is part of a broader tradition of boatbuilding commonly referred to as 'Gallo-Roman'. This represents an assimilation of Mediterranean and 'Atlantic' boatbuilding traditions, and archaeological excavated examples are known from the second to the fourth centuries AD (Nayling and McGrail 2004: 208–9). The characteristics of this tradition of craftbuilding included a hull made of flush-laid planks, with each plank individually nailed and clenched to a frame timber; the nail was clenched by hammering the protruding point back into the frame timber, but the frame timbers themselves were not connected together (ie. these were half-frames) (Figure 35). Both timbers and nails used were rather big, with planks and frame timbers over 0.3 m thick and the nails 25 mm in diameter.

In the North Sea, this is the first boatbuilding tradition that is represented by two quite different functional types: one for use on rivers and along the coast, and one for seafaring. The first type is known from a number of flat-bottomed 'barges', with the best-known examples coming from the major rivers in the continental parts of the Roman Empire, notably Zwammerdam, De Meern/Woerden, Kapel Avezaath, Druten, Xanten, and Mains, all on the River Rhine; Abbeville on the lower River Seine; Bruges; Pommeroeul, from a tributary of the River Haine in Belgium; and Bevaix, Yverden, and Avenches on or near Lake Morat in Switzerland (De Boe and Hubert 1977; De Weerd 1988; Lehmann 1990; Arnold 1992, 1999; cf. Nayling and McGrail 2004: 170).

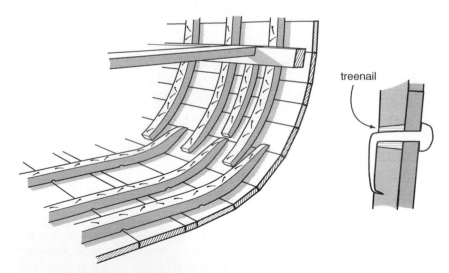

treenail

Figure 35. Schematic representation of the hull construction of a Gallo-Roman boat

In the case of the most recent finds from De Meern, the absence of mast-steps but the presence of large iron rings fastened to the hull hinted that these were barges towed from the riverbank. The second type of craft is known from a number of boats with a full, rounded bilge with a plank-keel, and a mast-step which was characteristically positioned forward of amidships. Examples are the Blackfriars 1 and New Guy's House boats from London, the St Peter Port boat from Guernsey, and the much smaller Barland's Farm boat, from the Severn estuary (Marsden 1994; Rule and Monaghan 1993; Nayling and McGrail 2004). The use of these craft in estuaries and on the open seas is not doubted, as illustrated by the presence of the St Peter Port ship.

The Gallo-Roman tradition is the first in the North Sea basin to incorporate iron nails. This technological innovation allowed for larger ships to be built than had previously been possible, and for the use of timber that was unsuited to the construction of monoxylous logboats. The significance to trade of both the riverine barges and the marine ships in the Roman Empire, in particular with regard to the transport of bulk commodities, is not in doubt. On its last voyage, the Blackfriars ship carried a cargo of blocks of ragstone, a sandy limestone probably from Kent, while an unfinished quern-stone of Millstone Grit, from either the Yorkshire Pennines or the Namur region in Belgium, is thought to represent a remnant of an earlier voyage (Marsden 1990: 71).

The first unequivocal evidence for sailing in the region comes in the form of Julius Caesar's description of the Veneti, who inhabited Armorica, the southern part of Brittany (*Bello Gallico* 3.8–15). In his description of the craft of the Veneti, Caesar includes leather sails among other characteristics, all of which are evident tokens of strength, such as beams a foot [0.3m] in thickness, iron bolts of a thumb's width, and the use of iron anchor chains instead of ropes. It has been argued that the attribution of *virtus* (strength, valour) to the boats rather than to the warriors is a deliberate slur against the Veneti, who preferred to withdraw tactically from the battlefield rather than fight for an unattainable victory; but recent textual analysis has suggested that the ethnographic parts of the text are genuine and accurate (Brice 2002: 609). In his writing, Caesar also pointed out that the Veneti traded with Britain, and it is likely that seamen operating within the North Sea and Channel had knowledge of the use of sails.

Archaeological evidence for sailing is certainly present in the Gallo-Roman finds. Marine craft such as the ships from Blackfriars and County Hall in London, the ship from St Peter Port on Guernsey (Marsden 1994; Rule 1994), and the small boat from Barland's Farm (Nayling and McGrail 2004) all exhibit evidence for masts and for the use of sails as the principal form of propulsion, as do typical river boats such as the barges from Zwammerdam (De Weerd 1988). Nevertheless, there is ample debate as to when the sail was generally adopted, following the departure of the Romans. It is thought by some that the Frisians successfully adopted the sail in the sixth century AD, and the Franks in the seventh, while the Vikings are thought to have become experienced sailors by the eighth or ninth century (Heidinga 1999: 12; Haywood 1991: 17; Westerdahl 1995b).

The material culture from Roman-period sites on both sides of the North Sea, principally but not exclusively south of the *limes*, gives an insight into the diversity and intensity of long-distance trade during the first to the fourth centuries AD. This included wine, olive oil, and fish sauce transported in amphorae from the Mediterranean, exotic building materials such as marble from Italy, and pottery—most notably the Samian ware from Gaul (e.g. Milne 1990: 82; Cunliffe 2001: 417–21). Salt, and its containers, does not appear in a material culture form, but the transport of salt from Britain across the North Sea is illustrated in inscription form on one of a series of altars retrieved from the now eroded sand spit of Colijnsplaat, on the north bank of the Scheldt (or Oosterscheldt) in Zeeland. Here, following successful journeys across the North Sea, salt merchants of British origin fulfilled their promise to the goddess Nehalennia. Other goods mentioned on the Nehalennia altars include fish from Britain, and pottery and wine from Gaul and probably further afield. The altars were placed near a temple which, it has been argued, may have been part of a larger town, possibly named Gantuenta; the inhabitants of the town would have been sailors, merchants, and shipping agents (Bogaers and Gysseling 1971).

One of the consequences of trade with the Romans from the first century BC onwards is the emergence in the North Sea and its hinterland not only of specialist traders, like the salt merchant who set up the altar at Colijnsplaat, but of specialist sailors and boatmen, and a range of associated professions. The existence of the two very different kinds of craft within the Gallo-Roman tradition—for riverine and sea travel—points to the use of transhipment ports where goods were reloaded. The river barges were unsuited to seafaring, while the rounded Blackfriars-type ship was unsuited to the Dutch delta. The likely transhipment ports were Colijnsplaat/Gantuenta and Domburg on the south bank of the River Scheldt, and Richborough in the first century AD, and London and Dover in the second century AD. Problems on the Rhine, where in the third and especially the fourth centuries AD Germanic raiders became increasingly active, led to a southward refocusing of the cross-Channel trade (Milne 1990).

Excavations on the quayside of the River Rhine at Mainz found five craft of a more Mediterranean type. These were military patrol boats, carvel built with mortice-and-tenon joints holding together the thin (20-mm-thick) planks. These fast patrol boats, and a troop transporter, date to the fourth century AD; they were rowed by a crew but carried a small sail as well, and there was ample room for additional soldiers on board (Bockius 2006). There is no archaeological indication that the appearance of these patrol boats on the River Rhine affected the north-west European boatbuilding tradition greatly. Possibly the use of templates or moulds in boatbuilding, which determined the shape of the craft, was simply too far removed from indigenous methods to be adopted by the boatbuilders.

CLINKER-BUILT BOATS

The fourth group of boats concerns the craft built in the clinker tradition. This tradition is characterized by a hull of overlapping planks fastened together with large nails and treenails in a shell-first building technique, with the strakes lashed (rather than nailed) to the frame (Figure 36). The boats were steered using a single side-rudder. The earliest craft representing this boatbuilding type are the fourth-century AD Nydam boats. This 'Nordic type' tradition includes the Sutton Hoo ships (Bruce-Mitford 1975), the Viking boatbuilding tradition as known from the famous Skudelev, Gokstad, and Oseberg ships, and continues into the modern era in the construction of many small boats in the North Sea (Godal 1990; cf. Crumlin-Pedersen 1997: 14). Early representatives of the clinker-type boat were rowed; the oldest known rowlocks in the North Sea region were found on the Nydam boats, with the *c.* 23-m-long oak boat, dated to *c.* AD 310, accommodating 15 pairs of rowers (Engelhardt 1865; Rieck 1994; 1995). Through the centuries, and

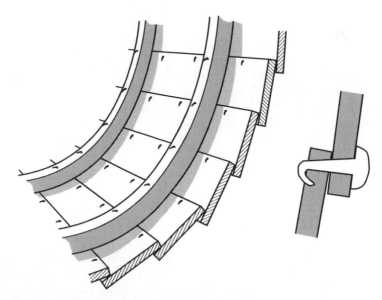

Figure 36. Schematic representation of hull construction using the clinker technique

with an increasingly diverse range of clinker craft, the importance of wind and sail is shown archaeologically in the development of the keel to prevent drift: a fully developed keel emerges towards the end of the first millennium AD, as shown very clearly, for example, in the ninth-century AD Gokstad ship (Nicolaysen 1882).

Clinker-type boats included a range of craft, often differentiated by the length/width aspect ratio. The greater the aspect ratio of length and width, the faster the boat can move through the water as drag is minimized. Furthermore, while the cargo ships relied more on wind, longer boats allowed for a larger number of rowing stations to be deployed: this gave the longships both speed and agility for their expeditions. The Skudelev 5 longboat was 18 m long and only 2.6 m wide (l:w ratio 6.9) but deployed 12 pairs of rowers, whereas the much wider Knarr-type cargo boats such as Skuldelev 1, 16.5 m long and 4.6 m wide (l:w ratio 3.6), accommodated only four pairs of rowers (Olsen and Crumlin-Pedersen 1958, 1968). Rowing such a large craft with four oars would have been useful only when manoeuvring the ship: it clearly relied on its sail for long-distance journeys.

The clinker-type craft, especially those constructed in the Nordic tradition, were particularly strong and suited to seafaring. They were used for trade and exchange, and the ascendancy of the Frisians in the sixth century is attributed to their prowess in sailing such boats in the waters of the North Sea. Piracy in the North Sea, undertaken by the Franks, the Saxons, and later the Vikings, was also dependent on the clinker-type craft with their capacity for speed and surprise (see chapter 8). Additionally, the success of the Hanseatic League in the 13th century has been attributed to the development of the cog, a variant of the clinker-built boat. Without the clinker-type craft, both trade and piracy in the North Sea would not have developed to such an extent.

It seems reasonable to suggest, albeit in the absence of direct evidence, that the migrations of the post-Roman era were only possible due to the existence of reliable seafaring boats, which allowed for the movement of families with their possessions. Through much of the first millennium AD, there were clear links between piracy and migration. For example, the migration of the Saxons to England was preceded by centuries of piracy and raiding. Through the practice of piracy, the Saxons probed the wealth of Roman England and tested the strength of any defence on sea and on land, long before they migrated and settled. Similarly, the Frankish migration southwards into the Roman Empire followed a prolonged period during which the strength of the Roman army across the Rhine and in the North Sea had been tested. The Viking settlements in Scotland, northern England, Ireland, and northern France followed the routes of the raiding parties of earlier decades. The pirates and migrants shared a common perception not only that the lands across the sea were desirable, but that the people living there were sufficiently alien to justify subjugation or enslavement. The wealth across the sea was generally perceived as being 'fair game'.

The migration of Jutes, Saxons, and Angles to Britain—the last giving their name to the new country of England—is the subject of extensive and ongoing debate. The nature of the settlement is all but clear. If we are to believe Gildas, the Saxons came at the invitation of the Britons to help defend against the Picts and Scots, and arrived in only three boats. Bede records that the Jutes settled in Kent by invitation from their king Vortigern. However, the Anglo-Saxon Chronicle describes the Saxons and Angles as bands of seaborne conquerors, idiosyncratically arriving in small fleets of three ships only. Archaeological evidence of early settlement in England exists in the form of fifth-century Germanic cemeteries and settlements such as Spong Hill in Norfolk and Mucking in Essex (Hills 1977). To a degree, the evidence is mirrored along the North Sea coast in southern Jutland and Schleswig-Holstein, where large-scale discontinuity of settlement and cemeteries in the Wadden Sea region, including the abandonment of many terpen has been dated to around AD 450 (Meier 2004: 63).

Migration in the Viking Age is well known from historical sources, but the scale of this has, until recently, been difficult to ascertain. Migration occurred principally in the second half of the ninth century AD, after a prolonged period of piracy and raiding. Over-wintering camps were established in Ireland, England, and Frankia around the middle of the ninth century, creating stepping stones to the establishment of permanent settlements. Norse Vikings undoubtedly settled in the Northern Isles, the Hebrides, northern Scotland, the Isle of Man and Ireland, and parts of north-west England and Wales. The Danish Vikings settled in eastern England and Normandy, and in Frisian territory, where the first settlement of Vikings within the Frankish Empire dates to the mid ninth century, when Lothar granted the island of Walcheren to the Danes Harald and Rorik in return for protection from further Viking attacks (Graham-Campbell 1980: 32). The establishment of the Danelaw in eastern England resulted in a series of land battles with the English, who were forced to pay 'Danegeld' from AD 865.

DNA analysis of Y chromosome haplotypes in samples from modern populations has given a new impetus to the debate on the scale of the migrations. There is no longer any doubt that significant numbers of people living in the British Isles today carry DNA which shows evidence for significant continental introgression. In the case of England, this introgression varied from 50 to 100 per cent (Weale et al. 2002), but was more or less absent in northern Wales. A larger study suggested a continental introgression into Britain of 24.2–72.2 per cent, with the mean at 54.1 per cent (Capelli et al. 2003). Based on an estimated indigenous population in post-Roman Britain of around two million, this would require an immigration of more than half a million people.

The migration from northern and north-western continental Europe across the North Sea into Britain can be attributed to the two phases of historically and archaeologically attested movements of people described above: the migration of Angles, Saxons, Jutes, and possibly Frisians in the fifth and sixth centuries AD, and a migration of Norse and Danish Vikings in the ninth, tenth, and eleventh centuries. Haplotype variants from people living in modern-day Denmark and the area adjacent to the Wadden Sea are abundantly present in eastern England, and this is indicative of a strong introgression from the Continent. It has, to date, not been possible to distinguish between the DNA of the Danish Vikings and that of the people who have been referred to as Angles, Saxon, Jutes, or Frisians. Nevertheless, the survival of the indigenous Y chromosome haplotype variant in southern England, where the Saxons and Jutes settled in the fifth century AD, but the near absence of the indigenous variant in eastern England, suggests that the Danish migration at the end of the first millennium AD was of an order greater that the Anglo-Saxon migration of the Early Middle Ages. This is also true of the Northern Isles, and the northern extremities of Scotland, where the modern-day population shares their haplotype variant with modern Norwegians, reflecting a significant Viking origin in the current population. Perhaps somewhat surprisingly, elsewhere in Scotland and in Ireland the near absence of the Norwegian haplotype variant suggests that the Viking component was concentrated in certain specific regions, rather than present throughout.

A variant of the clinker-type boat, known as the cog, was developed early in the second millennium AD. Already mentioned in historical sources towards the end of the first millennium AD (Ellmers 1972: 70–1), this type of craft is best described as a variant on the Norse-type clinker boat such as the Knarr. It is always single-masted, with a bottom of joined planks connected carvel-style, a straight keel, upright stem- and sternposts, and very high sides. Rejecting the earlier consensus that the cog was based on Frisian prototypes, the German historian Paul Hensius (1956) argued that the cog was a German invention, linked closely to the emerging Hanseatic League. He based this argument on the depictions of cogs on medieval town seals, some of which appear to show the craft having been constructed using a 'reverse clinker' technique, starting from the gunwale downwards. Hensius argued that such a construction could only have been 'frame-first' built, a conceptual departure from 'shell-first' construction of the clinker boats of the Nordic type; he suggested that the first builders of cogs were house-carpenters rather than shipwrights, used to the skeleton-first method of building. Archaeological finds of a number of cogs, including the Bremen Cog of 1380, have now comprehensively refuted these notions, and the 'reverse clinker' technique has never been found on wrecks (Crumlin-Pedersen 2000: 231–2).

The most up-to-date reading of the archaeological evidence is that the cog as the ship with the aforementioned characteristics was first constructed in the 12th century, with the Kollerup ship of *c.* AD 1150 representing the first stages of transformation from Knarr to cog. However, a distinct developmental sequence that includes all ships of this era cannot be assumed (Crumlin-Pedersen 2000, 2003). Ole Crumlin-Pedersen further argues that the impetus for the development of a seaworthy vessel of this type was the closing off of the Limfjord in northern Jutland, as a result of coastal drift. A type of craft was needed that could successfully round Cape Skagen, the tip of northern Jutland, where the North Sea and the Baltic meet (Crumlin-Pedersen 2000: 239). Evidence for such a journey being attempted comes from the cog stranded and sunk at Cape Skagen; this craft dates to around AD 1200, and like the Kollerup cog was built with timber from southern Jutland.

This discussion of the development of the cog serves to emphasize the point that different types of boats operated as merchant ships in the North Sea and the Baltic during the first centuries of the second millennium AD, and that technological innovations were transferred because craft visited foreign harbours where local shipwrights were able to observe and adopt selected concepts as innovations in their own boats. The assumption that ships of the Nordic type could hold only small cargoes compared to the cogs has been disproved, notably with the find of the Big Ship of Bergen, built in AD 1188 in the Nordic style, which was larger than the early cogs (Crumlin-Pedersen 2000: 242–4).

The Bremen cog was lost to the Weser while uncompleted: the deck had yet to be laid, the mast had not been erected and the protective cover of tar had not been applied (Hoffmann 2003: 17). Some structural elements of the wreck are linked to a fore and an aft castle, and this shows that the North Sea was not an uncontested space for the merchants. Fore and aft castles provided extra height and this was essential in the defence of the ship against pirates. It made the boarding of the cog from a much lower Nordic-type craft very difficult, while the defenders could assail the pirates with longbows and other projectiles. Indeed, it has been suggested that the success of the cog has to be sought in its height and its ability to thwart pirates, who used craft of the Nordic type. Similarly, no pirate ship would consider attacking cogs that sailed in pairs (Hoffmann and Schnall 2003: 273).

The development of the large merchant ships at the beginning of the second millennium AD represents a major shift in perceptions of the North Sea. In the second half of the first millennium, trade and exchange were conducted on a relatively small scale, involving 'prestige goods', as well as the produce of the craftsmen in the *emporia* and specialist items such as Ipswich ware pottery and Rhineland quernstones (e.g. Ulmschneider 2000). This marine activity was destabilized by the Viking raids and piracy in the ninth and tenth centuries. After AD 1000, and especially from the 12th century onwards, the movement of bulk goods—in particular agricultural produce such as grain, flax, timber, wool, leather, and wax—came to dominate trade, creating a mercantile North Sea. In the same way as has already been observed in the case of the AD 1000 fish event (see chapter 4), the perception of the North Sea as a mercantile space was closely connected with the growth of towns around this time. This engagement with the North Sea was not led by the terrestrial elite. The landowning classes considered the coast and the sea to be economically marginal, socially inhospitable and ritually 'unholy' places, or a wild(er)ness (see chapter 5; Coates 1998). Engagement with the mercantile sea created opportunities for a new class of professions to gain fortune and fame, including merchants, bankers, shipwrights, sailors, and craftsmen organized into guilds.

CARVEL-BUILT BOATS

Towards the very end of the period considered by this book, carvel-built boats came to the North Sea from the Mediterranean, possibly at first in the shape of the Genoese carracks, which had been in the service of the French king to establish hegemony in the Channel in the early 15th century (Rodger 1997). The carvel-type construction uses flush-laid planks nailed to the frame (Figure 37). The design has the significant advantage of reducing the underwater drag of the craft, and as a rule was more hydro-dynamic. The adoption of the carvel technique may reflect a demise in woodlands and a comparative lack of timbers suited for splitting, or

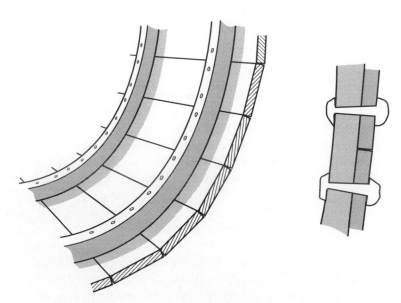

Figure 37. Schematic representation of hull construction using the carvel technique

alternatively a need to build larger boats than could be achieved using the clinker-built method, or a combination of both these factors. The need for larger boats came not only from the merchants, but also from the states who desired to control the seas, including the North Sea, and required ships that could carry more guns. The best-known archaeological example of a carvel ship from north-western Europe is the *Mary Rose*, of early 16th-century date.

Using the carvel technique required a significant conceptual change in the shipwright's skill and ability, shifting from the 'shell-first' technique using split timbers to a 'frame-first' construction method using sawn timbers. Maybe it is unsurprising that even some of the largest warships constructed in the 15th century, such as Henry V's *Grace Dieu*, were still built using the clinker technique (Prynne 1968); it is equally unsurprising that many small boats constructed around the North Sea still use the clinker technique. The introduction of the carvel technique created early modern shipyards. It made it possible to design ships first on paper or as a scale-model, with timbers being sawn to the required lengths. We should remember what a highly significant change this was, as previously 'ships on the slipway grew according to the lines established by the eye of the individual master. This is more the way of sculpture than of engineering' (Westerdahl 2008: 18). The introduction of carvel-built ships seems therefore an appropriate point in time at which to draw to a close an exploration of the changing nature of connections across the North Sea.

CONCLUSIONS

The ways in which people moved across the North Sea have been described in this chapter through a discussion of the main types of craft available through time. The reason for this was to emphasize the point that perceptions of the dangers and opportunities involved in going to sea—whether it be to gain foreign knowledge, to acquire exotic objects or new lands, or to gain wealth from trade or from piracy—depended to a very large extent on the type of craft that determined such an experience. Chronologically ordered, connection across the North Sea can be characterized as follows.

Before the creation of the North Sea, which separated the British Isles from the Continent around 6000 cal BC, it would have been possible to wander across the North Sea Plain, but a number of rivers were present too, and small hide-covered boats may well have been used for movements through and across this landscape. After 6000 cal BC, boats of some sort must have been in use. Hide boats seem the most likely candidates for acts such as the deposition of the polished axe heads on the Dogger and Brown banks, and the transfer of early domesticates—and the first farmers—from the Continent to Britain. Throughout the prehistoric period, logboats were used on the North Sea, but whereas these are known archaeologically from the Mesolithic for Denmark, the Netherlands, and France, the logboat appears to have been used in Britain only from the Bronze Age onwards, and in Scandinavia north of the Bohuslän region only from the first millennium AD. Logboats were ideally suited to riverine transport, and for exploring coastal landscapes and maintaining fishweirs.

The sewn-plank boats of around 2000 cal BC represent an important innovation. Presumably developed from larger hide-covered boats, the sewn-plank craft were reasonably well suited to seafaring. Their role in the long-distance acquisition of exotic or 'prestige' goods as part of the Beaker phenomenon has been hypothesized. At this time, the value of particular goods was greatly enhanced by their journey across the North Sea. Around 1200 cal BC, a number of very large logboats were built, and these are thought to have been used for the transport of exotic items alongside bulky goods. The first millennium BC witnessed a realignment of the main axes of exchange from one focused on the Mediterranean using the Atlantic route, to one focused on central Europe using the River Rhine as the principal conduit. The intensity of exchange appears to have been at a lower level than in the Bronze Age, and a further deterioration in the cross-North Sea exchange, or a disconnection, is hypothesized for the third and second centuries BC.

In the first century BC, the promise of new products and the development of a market economy accompanied Rome's expansion in Gaul. The trade in salt, fish, pottery, wine, olive oil, fish sauce, grain, cattle, gold, silver, iron, hides, slaves, and hunting dogs is archaeologically and historically documented. From the second century AD, a new type craft is introduced in the North Sea: the Gallo-Roman boats, which combine Mediterranean and North Sea features. The use of both seagoing and riverine craft required transhipment ports on both sides of the North Sea, and the presence of specialists engaged in transport and trade.

Following the decline of the Roman Empire and the disappearance of the Gallo-Roman type of craft, the North Sea experienced a period of large-scale migrations and piracy, made possible by a new type of boat constructed using the clinker technique. From the sixth century AD, *emporia* appear around the North Sea, now understood as ports for trade and craft production where royal authorities collected tolls. A lead role has been attributed to the Frisians in the re-emergence of trade and exchange in the North Sea. Viking piracy, also using the clinker-type craft, is widely seen as undermining the further expansion of connectivity across the North Sea through trade activities, but the migration of significant numbers of Danes and Norsemen to England and Scotland can still be detected in the DNA of the present-day population.

In the beginning of the second millennium AD, and in particular from the 12th century, the North Sea becomes once again the place for a dynamic trade system. The importance of the cog in this has, in the past, been overstated, but this new ship design did provide effective protection from pirates still using the clinker-built craft of the Nordic type, and would have offered merchants greater confidence to invest in long-distance trade. The new mercantile North Sea is closely linked to the rise of towns in the region, and the need for the exchange of agricultural produce, for which the cog was ideally suited. By the end of the 15th century, large ships are beginning to adopt the Mediterranean carvel technique of boatbuilding, which allows larger merchant vessels, and also warships, to be built. Only in the construction of small boats is there a survival of the distinctive North Sea boatbuilding tradition using the clinker technique.

8

The daily practice of seafaring: the ship as heterotopia par excellence

INTRODUCTION

The previous chapters explored how communities living around the North Sea were connected, and the roles played by the different types of craft in establishing these connections. This has provided the starting point for developing an understanding of the practice of seafaring. A considerable body of literature exists on the non-functional aspects of seafaring, especially the many practices and rituals that surround the act of putting out to sea. From a historic perspective, Kirby and Hinkkanen (2000: 184–5) recall the numerous rituals that attended the departure of fishing fleets, and how in recent centuries, especially in Catholic regions such as Flanders, such rituals were often sanctioned by, and sometimes integrated within, the practice of the official church. For example, most four-legged animals, especially pigs but not cats, could bring bad luck once on board, and even the names of such animals were taboo. Christer Westerdahl has written extensively on aspects of taboos and *noa*, and the importance of ritualized practices and the role of liminal agents that are meant to ensure successful completion of journeys and fishing expeditions (2005). The survival of these practices in folklore, and in the practice and memories of older fishermen reminds us that the premodern–modern dichotomy so often invoked when interpreting terrestrial archaeology is not always applicable when investigating the sea.

The arguments advanced in this chapter take a somewhat different approach. However, they have developed from the same understanding that to go to sea is a potentially life-threatening activity, unlike most undertakings on land, and something too that is surrounded by peculiar practices and beliefs that transgress the premodern–modern boundary. They aim to place the daily practice of seafaring at the centre of our understanding of socio-political developments through the use of Michel Foucault's concept of the heterotopia (introduced in chapter 2). This chapter takes its title from Foucault's presentation in which he argued that the 'ship is the heterotopia par excellence' (1966), and proposes that whereas the terrestrial sphere has often represented the world of the establishment, the sea has functioned at various points in the past as the space where the conventional is contested and inverted. Obviously, one can think of areas of inaccessible or remote landscape where the same idea can be applied. But throughout much of our history, the sea offered the last place on earth where the authority of organizations was executed effectively; even today, reports of piracy show that the power of nation states is first contested on the sea. These ideas are embodied in the notion of the deviant sea or the Deleuzian Ocean (see chapter 2). However, it is not only the sea itself but also distant islands and coasts that have been seen as the last places of freedom from authority, representing as they do the very margins of the land. This has already been demonstrated in previous chapters. In our own time, the nudist beach functioned as a space where the conventions of the 1950s were challenged and inverted, and it was no coincidence that the very edge of the land seemed an appropriate space for this.

This chapter develops the idea of the heterotopia for ships and seafaring on the North Sea. It focuses on three case studies: the sewn-plank boats of the second millennium BC, the rock-carved Bronze Age boats and their crews from Scandinavia, and the pirates of the Roman and medieval periods. It will argue that the North Sea functioned, to paraphrase Gilles Deleuze, as the realm of the unbound, unconstricted, and free, and that the craft that crossed this space became heterotopias in the sense that the crews simultaneously represented, contested, and inverted the societies bordering the North Sea.

THE BRONZE AGE SEWN-PLANK BOATS

The seafaring craft of the Bronze Age, the sewn-plank boats, have already been introduced (chapter 7). The use of fashioned oak planks, made possible through the introduction of bronze axes, combined with the sewing or stitching of these planks using yew withies—necessary in the absence of nails and tree-nails—produced craft of a size that must have exceeded significantly that of logboats and skin boats that preceded them. Ted Wright, the discoverer of the Ferriby boats, made the point on several occasions that he considered these craft to be 'advanced' and the result of many centuries of development. He referred especially to the ingenious way in which the yew withies were protected from damage when the boats was landed on beaches, and to the use of integral cleats and the transverse timbers, as examples of maritime innovation that could only have developed over time. Obviously, it is by no means impossible that wooden sewn craft older than F3 will be found at some point in the future and this may prove his point. However, it may be that these developments occurred first not in plank boats but in hide-covered boats. Sewing or stitching of skins for a range of uses was something that had been practised for millennia, after all, and may have developed equally on land and water. The use of a woven frame of hazel or willow would have allowed small hide boats to achieve sufficient rigidity, and it seems probable that some form of internal structure to give the hull greater stiffness, better to withstand the pressure of the water, would have been trialled and tested first of all in hide boats.

However, the use of an internal structure limits the size of a boat, and size mattered when it came to building seafaring craft. The size of the boat relative to the size of the waves is an important factor in the boat's safety. Larger boats more easily avoid being foundered (that is, when the waves overtop the gunwale, filling the hull with water) than smaller boats. Larger boats, when fitted with a rounded bilge, are also capable of riding waves much more successfully than smaller boats. It seems probable, therefore, that the hide or skin boats used for coastal travel and for seafaring during the Neolithic and early Bronze Age underwent a progressive development to make them larger and safer, but also that the extent to which this could be achieved was limited by the material used in the construction of these craft. The substitution of hide-covered wicker frames by planks and larger timbers may have been an obvious continuation of this development, underpinned by the unbroken use of the sewing or stitching technique to link the various elements of the craft.

Unfortunately, there is currently no archaeological evidence to prove any of this hypothesized development of the skin boat during the Neolithic and the early Bronze Age. The chance of future discoveries is so fantastically small that it can never be more than an unproven idea. However, the pursuit of larger seafaring craft in the Bronze Age is clearly implied by the changes noted in the sewn-plank boats' design. As Ole Crumlin-Pedersen (pers. comm.) has pointed out, the sewn-plank boats became wider and larger over a period of 1,000 years. The sewn-plank boats from Ferriby, of early second millennium BC date, were all built with single-width keel planks (even though the keel plank of F2 was a composite to make it longer); the mid-second-millennium BC Dover boat had a double base or keel plank, joined amidships by the awkward transverse cleat, while the early-first-millennium BC Brigg 'raft' had a floor of five timbers. If this development was a continuation of what shipbuilders had been trying to achieve from the earliest days of seafaring, then a continuity between the third-millennium BC skin boats and the sewn-plank boats of the second millennium BC has to be a distinct probability.

The size of a boat has implications not only for its safety at sea but also for what could be carried and transported. As already discussed in the previous chapter, the archaeological evidence suggests that the transport of exotic, 'prestige' objects such as gold, amber, jet, and faience jewellery characterized the long-distance movement of goods in the later Neolithic and early part of the Bronze Age, while copper and early bronze tools may have been an important part of the cargo from *c.* 2500 cal BC onwards (Pare 2000). During

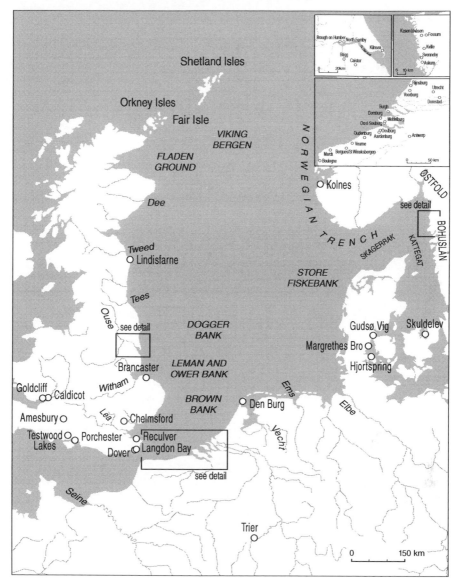

Figure 38. Places and regions mentioned in chapter 8

the Bronze Age, the trade in bronze objects and the elements that make up composite bronze increased, especially in the period after *c.* 1500 cal BC (Northover 1982). Some of the cargoes dated to this period, notably the one found in Langdon Bay off Dover, bear witness to the large-scale transport of bronzes towards the end of the second millennium BC. The changes in the cargoes through time are reflected in the increased size and carrying capacity of sewn-plank boats.

Finally, size is significant in defining the number of crew required to handle the boat, which takes us back to the heterotopia referred to above. Since sewn-plank boats were probably built locally, it seems reasonable to assume that the crew was made up of local people. The concept of the specialist long-distance trader in Neolithic and Bronze Age Europe has been advocated by some (e.g. Chapman 2000 for south-east Europe; Kristiansen and Larsson 2005 for Scandinavia), but the archaeological evidence for such specialists in the North Sea basin is lacking. In the case of the Ferriby boats, the evidence that the boats had been built on the north Ferriby foreshore seems over-whelming, with the remains of F2 and F3 placed on alder roundwoods as if awaiting repair. The presence of woodchips and off-cuts of yew withies, plus some possible shipwright's tools, adds force to the argument that this was a prehistoric shipyard. However, there is nothing in the landscape context or the palaeoenvironmental data of the North Ferriby foreshore to suggest that the people that lived here in the early second millennium BC were anything other than farmers, utilizing the foreshore for seasonal grazing of their cattle, and most likely engaging in the daily business of enabling cross-estuarine traffic. Furthermore, other locations of early Bronze Age sewn-plank boats—notably Kilnsea in the outer Humber estuary and Caldicot 1 in the Severn—relate to pre-existing monuments, implying a close tie to the land and the people who had lived here for centuries. In a similar way, later Bronze Age sewn-plank boat fragments have been found embedded in established struc-tures, such as those at Testwood Lakes, Goldcliff, and Caldicot 2, which again suggests that these boats were not the tools of people who stood somewhat apart from society.

So who were included in the heterotopia of the sewn-plank Bronze Age boat? In a previous study I set out to reconstruct the crew of a sewn-plank craft (Van de Noort 2006), and this work can be summarized here. It has been estimated on the basis of the best-preserved example, Ferriby 1, that such craft had a crew of up to 20 (J. F. Coates, in Wright 1990, 114) (Figure 39). The Dover boat would have required a group of the same size (Marsden 2004; Roberts 2004). I have postulated that the composition of an early Bronze Age seafaring crew could have been some 20 young men who did the physical work, the paddling and bailing, alongside a shipwright, as well as an experienced and older member of the elite group who had made the journey previously, and knew contacts across the North Sea with whom objects were exchanged—and, finally, a young aspiring member of the elite who had to prove himself.

The inclusion of an aspiring young leader may be surprising, but the acquisi-tion and display of exotic objects from distant places was of central importance in the social reproduction of elite groups in this period; it was the essence, after all, of what has been called the 'prestige goods economy' (e.g. Shennan 1993;

Figure 39. A reconstructed Ferriby 1 sewn-plank boat with crew and passengers. Original drawing by John Graig (in Wright 1990: 111 ©Routledge)

Kristiansen 1998). Attributing agency, this could be rephrased by arguing that the 'superordinate' importance of the exotic objects enabled individuals who acquired, possessed, or displayed these objects to become personally associated with privileged access to the other world (cf. Needham 2005, 190). Furthermore, following Mary Helms (1988) and others (e.g. Beck and Shennan 1991; Needham 2000; Kristiansen 2004) in the re-evaluation of foreign knowledge, it is inconceivable that the products of long-distance exchange, the exotic objects, could be separated from the acquisition process. After all, the value attributed to such an object lies precisely in the implied knowledge of the other world held by its bearer. If the person who displays the amber necklace or gold earrings holds no exotic knowledge themselves, the magic will be broken. In this context, the sewn-plank boat on its long-distance journey formed what Foucault would have called a crisis heterotopia, in that it was a place for an individual undergoing some sort of crisis. In this case, the crisis was the growing up of the young member of the elite, who aspired to become—or was destined to become—a future leader of people. As a crisis heterotopia, the seafaring craft would have been a privileged location reserved only for certain individuals. This has two important implications. First, the sewn-plank craft may have been a sacred and forbidden place, and second, the remaining members of the crew were themselves connected with the heterotopia in some way.

The contexts of the early Bronze Age sewn-plank boats indeed seem to support the idea that these boats were in some way sacred and forbidden, and the way in which a number of these were disposed is telling (Figure 40). The Kilnsea boat, for example, came to rest in a landscape that was rich in monuments (Van de Noort 2004a, 2004b). These included the remains of several Neolithic rectangular structures, a Neolithic circular hengiform-type

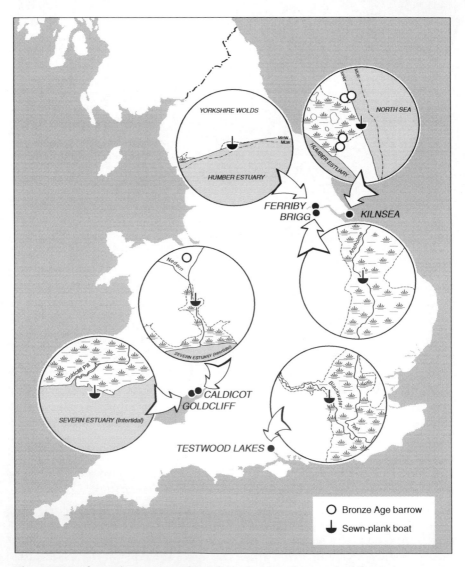

Figure 40. Schematic representation of the context of sewn-plank boats

monument, and several Bronze Age burial mounds, including one with a jet button and another with a Bell Beaker. Such a concentration of prehistoric monuments is exceedingly uncommon in the Humber Wetlands, and the reason for this concentration may have been that the point of departure or return for the journeys across the sea had a close connection to the ancestors. The Caldicot sewn-plank boats had within their landscape context the Neolithic long barrow of Portskewett, which faced towards the Severn estuary rather than towards the land; the site was also one of structured deposition, with material including human remains, the skeleton of a dog, bronze weapons, finely decorated pottery, and an amber bead being placed near a jetty of a bridge across the River Nedern (Nayling and Caseldine 1997, 265–8). The Testwood Lake fragment was found beneath a bridge across the River Test, where a bronze rapier was also discovered (Fitzpatrick, Ellis, and Allen 1996). The Goldcliff fragments had been incorporated into a path on the foreshore; two Bronze Age human skulls had also been deposited in the vicinity (Bell, Caseldine, and Neumann 2000: 82). The Brigg 'raft' had come to rest in the River Ancholme, in a context which included structured depositions such as a late Bronze Age socketed axe, a leaf-shaped spearhead, a polished stone axe-head, and a stone battle-axe, as well as pottery, human and animal bones, and a bronze pin also of late Bronze Age date (Davey 1973; May 1976: 112–14). While these contextual observations do not prove that the sewn-plank boats were considered sacred or forbidden, their deposition contexts differ remarkably from the contexts of Bronze Age logboats, which are unlikely candidates for seafaring journeys, and for which only rarely a ritual or structured deposition can be argued. The absence of the Ferriby boats from this list can be explained by reinforcing the notion that it was not the construction of the boat that was in some way sacred or privileged, so much as the idea that, through seafaring journeys, these craft became sacred.

Returning to the crew, their part in the heterotopia was more specific than has so far been inferred. The presence of an experienced and older relative or promoter can be surmized from the existence of exchange patterns across the North Sea that remained intact for many centuries. While the routes were not fixed, it must have been the case that long-distance journeys were directional travels, undertaken for the purpose of visiting elite groups with whom previous exchange had taken place, and resulting archaeologically, for example, in the distribution on opposite sides of the North Sea of Beaker-type vessels with parallel developments (Lanting and Van der Waals 1972). The existence of long-standing exchange patterns is also inferred from the characteristic distribution of exotic materials; examples include the jet necklaces found along the east coasts of Scotland and England, the distribution of gold, tin, and amber drinking cups in the English Channel (Needham 2009), and the distribution of amber beads and spacer plates in Wessex, southern Germany, and the eastern Aegean (Harding 1984). The older person, experienced in long-distance journeys, would have guided the boat physically as helmsman, possibly with the assistance of a guide such as the *Himmelscheibe* from Nebra (Meller 2002); if seafaring relied on the reading of the stars, the symbolic linkage between geographical distance and the world of the ancestors would undoubtedly have been greatly reinforced.

Intriguingly, the recently discovered 'Amesbury Archer' could be just such an individual. The skeletal remains of this man of about 40 years of age were dated to the final quarter of the third millennium BC (Fitzpatrick 2002). He had travelled a great distance, with the oxygen isotope of his teeth pointing to a central European place of upbringing. Seafaring must have been part of his travels. On these, he had acquired a range of exotic objects such as the golden earrings, copper knives, and a Kimmeridge shale belt ring. He had been buried at a high-status locale, near Stonehenge; his grave had been richly furnished and included five Beaker-type vessels, indicating that elite groups in Wessex knew him and treated him with the respect that they would normally have reserved for one of their own, even though there was no need for a monumental burial mound on this occasion. The excavations also found nearby a second skeleton, less well-endowed with exotic goods and therefore not attracting the same attention. This was of a younger man of about 20 years of age, probably a relative of the Archer as they shared the hereditary calcaneonavicular coalition of the heel bone and the navicular tarsal foot bone. It is tempting to hypothesize that this could have been the younger aspiring member of the elite from somewhere in Europe who had travelled to Wessex under the guidance of the Archer, maybe his uncle, as part of his coming of age.

Alongside the aspirant leader and the promoter, the inclusion in the crew of one or more shipwrights was essential; like most early composite boats, the sewn-plank craft would have required constant maintenance, and during the extended journeys some major repairs are likely to have been necessary. However, if axe ownership and woodworking skills were as ubiquitous as has been inferred from the analysis of the 'Seahenge' wooden mortuary ring in Norfolk, (Brennand and Taylor 2003), a shipwright's status may have been less elevated than previously thought. The absence of any high-status activity in the area around the North Ferriby 'dockyard' would appear to support such a diminished status for the boatbuilders.

Finally, the remainder of the crew would have consisted of paddlers, possibly 18–20 in number, and the shipwright(s) may well have been among them. Paddling in pairs does not require particular skills; physical strength was the principal talent required, and these paddlers would also have had to show endurance and courage. Together, the aspirant leader, the promoter, the shipwright, and the paddlers shared the experience of the journey, the perils of the sea, and the dangers of strange and overseas lands. There can be few ways in which social identity could be formed more effectively than when sharing an extended perilous adventure, and in terms of forming new social structures, the opportunities provided by these Bronze Age journeys was unsurpassed. Within the crisis heterotopia of the sewn-plank boat, and over the length of the journey, the crew developed a distinct social identity which effectively produced a retinue for the aspirant leader.

As with other types of social networks (e.g. kinship, residency, ethnicity, elite networks), identifiable positions and status were ascribed to one's position within the retinue, be it as patron or client (cf. Bazelmans 1991: 121). All social networks require maintenance through continued recreation and confirmation, such as gift-exchange, and the sharing of an extended journey, or an 'adventure', could have created and recreated mutual bonds of loyalty and respect. In premodern societies, where ownership and control of the means of production is not possible or practicable, retinues form effective bases for developing social power (cf. Mann 1986), and it seems likely that retinues would have been a significant factor in the socio-political changes in the later Neolithic and the early Bronze Age. We should not be surprised that the creation of such new social structures took place at sea, on the very margins of 'normal' society. This fits very comfortably with Foucault's thinking about the role of the heterotopia, and about ships as the heterotopia par excellence, as well as with Giles Deleuze's thoughts on the sea as a deviant place.

After *c.* 1500 cal BC, the new order was fully established, the Beaker was no longer an exclusive artefact for the elite (Needham 2005), and the role of the ship as crisis heterotopia for aspiring elites disappeared. This change is manifest archaeologically in the treatment of the sewn-plank boat: we know the sewn-plank boats from this period mainly from fragments that were reused or incorporated in bridges or jetties and possibly used in communal rituals, such as at Testwood Lakes, Caldicot (2) and Goldcliff. The social identity that existed between leader and retinue must have been created and reinforced during this time using one of many alternative mechanisms. Such mechanisms may have been the offering of favours and rewards, sharing of wine and feasting and—possibly the most powerful force of social cohesion between men—warfare and fighting together (e.g. Treherne 1999, Harding 1999).

BOATS ON THE ROCKS

In Norway's Østfold and Sweden's Bohuslän regions are numerous sites with carvings on the rocks of broadly Bronze Age and early Iron Age date, *c.* 1500–300 cal BC. After cup marks, the carvings of boats or ships are the most numerous, and the estimates for the number of such rock carvings in this region lies somewhere between 8000 and 10,000 (Coles 2005: 18). Some-times these boats appear in isolation, but more often carvings of boats were incorporated into composite displays that also included the other main themes in the rock carvings of Østfold and Bohuslän: cup marks, people, discs, animals, animal-drawn vehicles, and feet and footprints. While many of the panels with rock carvings are now in valleys, a reconstruction of the Bronze Age coastline at 13–15 m above the present-day sea-level has revealed that the contemporary setting of most rock-carved scenes was one that overlooked marine inlets (ibid. 100–19). John Coles has argued that the correlation between these marine inlets and the presence of the main concentrations of rock art is no coincidence (ibid. 105), and it may even be the case that some of these panels were meant to be viewed from the water.

Typically, the boats consists of two parallel lines, the lower one interpreted as the keel line, the upper as the gunwale. At stem and stern, the two lines are closed off or joined, and at their terminals the keel line is turned upwards, with sometimes the upward prow distinguishable from an enlarged stabilizer at the stern. The gunwale terminals are frequently turned into S and inverted S-shapes. But beyond this basic description, there are endless variations. Some boats are depicted only by a single line; others have the hull 'filled in', while others again have a distinguishable stem as shown in an upturned keel line at one terminal only. Other depictions show S-shaped gunwale terminals that metamorphose into mythical animal heads. A number of schemes have been devised to categorize these variations; the most extensive of these includes 99 potential variations of the Scandinavian boats on the rocks (Malmer 1981). Much debate has been expended on what types of boat are depicted here. The earlier preference was for the rock carvings to depict hide-covered boats (e.g. Marstrander 1963; Glob 1969; Johnstone 1972; Malmer 1981; cf. Coles 1993: 27). However, in more recent years, the preference has shifted towards the interpretation of these craft as plank boats: the reconstruction of the sewn-plank Hjortspring boat, which in profile resembles closely the boats depicted in rock carvings attributed to the early pre-Roman Iron Age, has compelled many maritime archaeologists to change their minds (Kaul 2002, 2004; Kaul and Valbjørn 2003; Crumlin-Pedersen and Trakadas 2003). Nevertheless, a consensus has not yet been arrived at. Sven Österholm (2002), for example, has recently argued that the boats in Scandinavian rock art show logboats with (multiple) outriggers; he understands these images as so-called 'gatefold illus-trations'—well known from the animal-drawn vehicles depicted in the rock carvings of this region—and, Österholm argues, the bottom line does not show the keel line but the outrigger. Österholm experimentally showed that such a boat could be sailed from Gotland to Öland, and further to Denmark and Germany. However, if the boats on the rocks are indeed logboats, then these would have appeared nearly 1,000 years earlier than proposed by Lanting's evidence, which implies that logboats occurred only towards the end of the

Bronze Age (see chapter 7). Thus, the suggestion that the boats depicted in rock carvings are logboats is not very likely, despite the experimental evidence indicating that the existence of earlier logboats is possible.

In recent years, Flemming Kaul (1998) has made great progress in the dating and interpretation of the meaning of the boats depicted in the rock art. As long as the rock carvings themselves cannot be dated by absolute means, and any relative dating framework remains contested, Kaul uses the incised decoration of boats on bronze artefacts—notably razors, axes, and swords—which have been typologically sorted and dated by their contexts, as a proxy to develop a dating sequence of boats and ships which can be applied to the boats on the rocks as well. Kaul divides the ships into six chronological phases between 1700 and 500 BC, with the plainer versions with stems turned inwards dating generally earlier, and more elaborate variants with stem adornments or outward-turned stems dating to the later phases.

Kaul has also deciphered the cosmological message that was conveyed through the ships on the bronzes. His analysis is based on the direction of the ships, as discernable from the upturned keel at the bow end of the ship and the stabilizer at the stern, and on the presence and absence of the sun in these images. In the northern hemisphere, the sun moves from left to right, and right-sailing boats are often shown carrying the sun; depictions of left-travelling boats, however, never include images of the sun. Thus, the ships on bronzes are shown in various stages of the cyclical movement of the sun, usually represented as a wheel-cross. A number of animals play a significant role, such as the horse that pulls the sun or sun-chariot in the daytime, or the fish and snake that accompany the journey during the sunrise and sunset respectively. Accompanying the ships are people engaged in various ritual activities, such as the playing of lures and the carrying of ceremonial axes. The performance of acrobatics, or acrobatic dances, is depicted on the rocks and razors, as human figures leaping backwards over the ships. In this way, the ship in the Nordic Bronze Age not only represented the cosmology of the sun, but was also a platform for ceremonies and rituals. In other words 'the ship became the paramount symbol of everything powerful, and an important vehicle in all spheres' (Kaul 2004: 132).

The origin of the symbols can be traced back to distant countries: the use of the ship as carrier of the sun may have come from Egypt, the role of the horse as pulling the sun-chariot from the Aegean, and other symbols from further east. Kaul has stressed that the extensive adoption of the boat in the Nordic Bronze Age cosmology—which occurred to a greater extent in this region than in any other region where ritual symbols were adopted—clearly indicates that the boat was already an important vehicle shortly after *c.* 1700 cal BC, the time of its first appearance in the rock art and on bronze artefacts.

In the context of exploring boats and ships as heterotopia, the boats on the rocks in Østfold and Bohuslän are of particular interest because of the presence of the boat or ship's crew in nearly all the carvings. Occasionally, the paddlers are depicted in outline and in some detail, as is the case with one of the boats in the panel of Askum, showing eight figures holding paddles, or at Kalnes where nine boats have their crew outlined in detail. More commonly, however, the crew of paddlers is depicted as dots-and-dashes or upside-down exclamation marks, and the existence of intermediate forms puts beyond doubt that these represent people. A large number of carved boats include, alongside the crew, one or more figures that are much larger than the representations of crew members, and typically are shown with a head, body, arms, and legs (Figure 41). Their male sex is made clear by an exaggerated phallus, and the sheath of a sword. Additional objects carried by these larger figures can include axes (e.g. at Fossum) and shields (e.g. at Upper Svenneby). The crew sometimes includes members holding lures or torches (e.g. at Kasen Lövåsen).

Hypothesizing about these representations of people in boats, we identify three possible aspects of the heterotopia of the boats on the rocks. First, while the overwhelming majority of craft seem to have a crew of a size which seems not unworkable for a Bronze Age context, there are a number of craft with an improbable number of people on board. The largest is at Kville, measuring 4.5 m in length and carrying a crew of 124. Anything above 28 or 30 people on board is simply not realistic, whether these carvings represents hide boats, logboats or Hjortspring-type plank boats. It is by no means improbable that the number of dashes in the boat was a metaphor for, or representation of, the size of the retinue rather than the actual size of the crew. Second, the

Figure 41. Boats on the rocks near Tanum, Bohuslän

prominence given to the leaders on these boats in the form of the larger figures, suggests that what made these journeys important was what happened to these leaders or aspirant leaders, rather than any of the exotic goods that were brought home. Third, the inclusion of lures, torches, and acrobatic dancers within the carvings advocates the notion that these journeys were not undertaken simply to obtain foreign goods, but were reasons for celebration.

As such, the rock carvings in Østfold and Bohuslän could have been created as tributes to or testimonials of the long-distance, dangerous journeys undertaken by aspirant leaders under the guidance of an elder relative. Through contact with distant people the leaders would have acquired foreign knowledge, epitomized through the wearing or display of exotic objects including bronze weapons, while from the members of the crew they would have gained a retinue to provide a real power base for the future. The carvings could well represent accounts of these feats, and may indeed have been altered over time to extend the achievements of particular leaders and their retinues. They could even have functioned as actual props in the storytelling. Evidently, long-distance journeys were not the only means by which leaders could attain and expand their prestige; the carvings offer many hints of other ways in which this could be achieved, most notably fighting. The stories were contextualized cosmologically: reference to the daily journey of the sun made the journey by men more momentous.

In this context, Flemming Kaul—in a language closely resembling the description of the social networks surrounding the British sewn-plank boats, detailed earlier in this chapter—described the social structures that underpinned the use of the Nordic Bronze Age boats as follows: 'the chiefs of warrior (or priest) aristocracies had to organize trading and religious expeditions and to visit political allies, and secure their protection by warrior retinues' (2004: 135). If only for practical reasons, it is only a short step to link this retinue of warriors with the crew of the boats that enabled these expeditions to be undertaken.

PIRACY IN THE DELEUZIAN OCEAN

Pirate ships were very much what Foucault had in mind when thinking about the heterotopia. Before the end of the 15th century, piracy in the North Sea was never a full-time or permanent occupation, and the rules by which the crew lived aboard pirate ships were very different from those in mainstream society. Piracy and raiding provided opportunities for aspiring men to prove themselves in battle, and to gain status, prestige, and wealth. Piracy created retinues through the shared experience of the journeys and of fighting together, opportunities which were not so readily available on land. In this sense, the North Sea was a Deleuzian Ocean. This section recalls the history of piracy in the North Sea, commencing with the fourth century BC Hjortspring boat and taking the story through to the Vikings.

The Hjortspring boat, dated to *c.* 350 BC, provides the first archaeological evidence for piracy and raiding. The boat, along with extensive weapon deposits, was found in a small bog on the island of Als, off the coast of Jutland in the Baltic Sea. Discovered in the 19th century, and excavated in the early 1920s (Rosenberg 1937), the spectacular find has never been out of the archaeologists' limelight, but the recent reconstruction of the boat in the *Tilia Alsie* has resulted in renewed interest and research (e.g. Crumlin-Pedersen and Trakadas 2003; Kaul 2003). The boat itself and the context of its deposition will be discussed later (chapter 9); we are concerned here principally with the nature of the attacking force, as reconstructed by Klaus Randsborg (1995). In his analysis of the weapons accompanying the Hjort-spring boat, Randsborg concludes that this was the armour of an army of some 100 men. The majority of these carried 'standard' equipment, which included both a heavy stabbing spear and a lighter spear for throwing, as well as a round shield for personal protection. A smaller group of some 11 men carried a sword, a bayonet-like spear, and a narrower and lighter shield, and possibly wore chain mail armour. It has been thought that these were the leaders or officers of the standard fighting units, each of which comprised ten men. This would mean that the group attacking the island of Als would have arrived in four boats, assuming that these other boats were of comparable size to the Hjortspring boat.

To date, the attackers have been described as an army (e.g. Randsborg 1995; Kaul 2003: 218). However, the size of the attacking force seems too small for a conquering army. In addition, the bog deposit did not contain tools to support the suggestion that the attackers were engaged in a war of sorts; there was no indication that this army would have been able to repair damage to its weapons or boats, as we might expect if it had come to conquer land, or to defeat an enemy at home. More in keeping with the nature of nautical activity in the northern seas in the first millennia BC and AD would be to consider the possibility that this was a raid, or an act of piracy. In the first millennium AD, when historical sources shed light on the nature of raiding pirates, the size of such groups is often around 100 men in three or four boats (see below). This appears to be a suitably sized fighting machine able to overwhelm unsuspecting villages and local defenders, but not so great that the spoils need to be shared out among too many fighters, or too great for the surprise of attack and rapid retreat to remain unencumbered. Clearly, we cannot be certain that the Hjortspring find can be ascribed to pirates, but if we do so, we need to recognize that something evidently went wrong with this particular surprise attack.

Another source of evidence for coastal dwellers protecting themselves from attack from the sea comes in the form of sea defences from Denmark and Sweden, the oldest of which have been dated to the first and second centuries BC: Gudsø Vig IV (Jørgensen 1997). These barrages are known in various forms, ranging from stakes planted in the water to sunken ships, such as in the Roskilde Fjord at Skuldelev. Sea defences are known from Denmark more or less throughout the first millennium AD, but the majority of barrages date to the period AD 1000–1200. One of the best-known examples is the Margrethes Bro, a barrage comprising upright stakes and roughly hewn 'floating bars', which blocked off the 500-m-wide Haderslev Fjord on the Storebaelt side. The earliest dendrochronological date for this structure is AD 370, and the barrage appears to have been repaired annually for a period of some 50 years. The long-term nature of the defences suggests that they were not intended to repel foreign armies who intended to conquer the south of Jutland, but were designed instead to repel or slow down the progress of raiders who visited Jutland's shores over a considerable period of time.

Raiding across the North Sea and Channel is reported by Julius Caesar as a historical observation, with the Belgae raiding parties turning migrants and settling in southern Britain. Cunliffe dates this activity to around 100 BC (2005: 127). The conquest of Britain was supported by a fleet, the *classis Britannica*, which was based at Boulogne and safeguarded contacts across the Channel with the Roman fort at Dover. Following the conquest, the *classis Brittanica* was maintained through the second and third centuries AD, with a principal role of ensuring that raiders could not attack the Gaulish or southern English towns.

However, in his overview of Roman and early medieval maritime activity on the North Sea, John Haywood (1999) demonstrates convincingly that from as early as the first century AD the *Pax Romana* ruled only intermittently in these northern waters. The first recorded acts of 'piracy', defined as naval acts against the power of the Roman state, date from the first century AD. Even earlier, we are informed of the naval prowess of Germanic tribes through Strabo's *Geography*, from which we know the year of the battle between Drusus' fleet and the naval force of the Bructeri on the River Ems to be 12 BC (ibid. 15). In the centuries that follow, historical sources record many naval feats of the different Germanic tribes. Cassius Dio records the raid by the Chauci, an ancestral tribe of the Saxons, on the coast of Belgica as early as AD 41, and throughout the first and second centuries AD numerous records refer to acts of piracy by this group. Usually, naval power was used for raiding for loot and slaves. But on a number of occasions larger fleets assembled to combat the naval forces of the *classis Germania*, who, stationed at Trier, were responsible for the defence of the Rhine *limes*. An example is the uprising of the Batavians in the lower Rhine delta in AD 69 and 70, as reported by Tacitus. This assembled fleet included 24 Roman galleys seized by mutinying Batavian oarsmen. After initial victorious battles on the North Sea, the Roman fleet eventually overcame the Germanic fleet in AD 70 (ibid. 22–3).

Towards the end of the second century AD, piracy was on the rise again. Attributed mainly to the Chauci, raids on the coasts of *Britannia, Germania Prima*, and *Belgica Secunda* were recorded in historical sources. A number of archaeologically identified 'fire events' in Roman settlements south of the *limes* have been attributed to these raids, and coastal towns were reinforced at the time with earth and timber ramparts. The Aardenburg rampart was constructed in the AD 170s, those at Chelmsford and at Brough-on-Humber *c*. AD 160–175 and AD 170–200 respectively. Defences at Oudenburg and Brancaster were built towards the end of the second century AD; at Caistor and at Voorburg, near The Hague, *c*. AD 200; and finally at Reculver in the lower Thames estuary around AD 220 (ibid. 25–6). Haywood suggests that these ramparts formed the first system of coastal shore forts, predating the defences of the Saxon Shore.

During the third and fourth centuries AD, the Chauci disappear from the historical accounts of naval activity. The Franks from *c*. AD 260 and the Saxons from *c*. AD 280 became the new pirates in the North Sea (Wood 1990). In response, fortifications of coastal settlements on both sides of the North Sea were reinforced between AD 250 and 280. The form that this piracy took was principally one of raids on coastal settlements of the Roman Empire, and the success of these ventures seems to have been made possible by the reduced condition in which the Empire found itself. The Germanic tribes, however, were not the only ones for whom piracy provided opportunities to enrich and empower themselves. The commander of the *classis Britannica*, Carausius, proclaimed himself emperor in AD 286, and with the help of the Franks ruled over Britain and the north-east coast of Gaul. Albeit short-lived, his independence from the Roman Empire was made possible because of the distinct naval nature of his powerbase (Haywood 1999: 59–60). In the Deleuzian Ocean, aspiring leaders from both sides could advance their claims to power.

The poor state of military defence resulted in the settling of some of the Franks as *foederati* within the Roman Empire in AD 358, but it is clear that alongside the land raids, piracy was an important aspect of the Frankish military might in the decades before their pacification. During the fourth century AD, coastal settlements within the Roman Empire were once again being fortified, and around AD 380 the command of the *Comes Litorus Saxonici* included—according to the *Notitia Dignitatum*—ten forts between Brancaster and Porchester on the British side of the North Sea and the Channel, and 13 on the continental side between Marck and Nantes. In AD 367, Britain came under attack from all sides, in what Ammianus Marcellius called the *barbarica conspiratio* (ibid. 65–6). This appears to have involved a concerted attack involving Picts, Scots, Attacotti, Saxons, and Franks, implying that frequent contact between groups north of the Roman Empire across the North Sea and Irish Sea had become well established. The Saxon attack of AD 410 on Britain is understood by Haywood as the final straw for the Britons. The Roman administration was expelled, and the British Isles once again became independent (ibid. 79). The following decades witnessed further raids, but during the second quarter of the fifth century, piracy and raids were replaced with migration and settlement.

Throughout his book, John Haywood emphasizes the nautical skills and naval expertise held by many Germanic tribes throughout the first millennium AD, and in the absence of good archaeological evidence some of the maritime feats are worth repeating. Tacitus' account of the auxiliary cohort of Usipi from the middle Rhine region, who deserted their station in western Britain in AD 83, provides an interesting example. The cohort made their escape by seizing three Liburnian galleys, in which they circumnavigated Scotland and crossed the North Sea only to be captured by Frisians who returned some of the deserters to the Romans as slaves. Tacitus ascribes the failure of the journey to the incompetence of the Usipi. But Haywood argues that their voyage through the uncharted waters of Scotland, and their successful crossing of the North Sea, indicates that it was not lack of expertise in sailing the biremes, or in marine navigation, that caused the failure; rather it was a lack of provisions, leaving the crew undernourished and unable to defend themselves against the Frisians, that caused their capture (Haywood 1999: 16–7). Another example of Germanic seamanship is provided by the remarkable story of the Franks defeated by an army led by emperor Probus in *Gallia* in AD 278, recounted in the *Scriptores historiae Augustae*. The Franks were forcibly resettled in Pontus on the Black Sea, where in AD 279 they seized a fleet of Roman ships and sailed through the Bosporus and the Straits of Gibraltar to return home on the lower Rhine, helping themselves on their way to the riches of Cyrenaica and Syracuse (ibid. 49–50).

In understanding the role of the North Sea in piracy of this period, it is important not to decontextualize it from the terrestrial evidence. After all, the Roman *limes* had never been completely impenetrable, and raids across the River Rhine have been recorded from the first century AD onwards. Raids by North Sea-going ships have much in common with those by riverine boats. Nevertheless, the North Sea offered a space where it was relatively easy to hide from Roman military might, and in which smaller groups, often arriving in fleets of no more than three ships, were able to cause havoc and gain great riches from the Roman Empire. This stands in contrast to the raids across the Rhine, which could only be undertaken by large groups capable of engaging with the regular Roman army. Thus, for much of the Roman period the North Sea was a space where young aspiring leaders could test their combative skills in skirmishes away from the established elite, which, more often than not, had become partly Romanized through collaboration with, or service in, the Roman army. This special place held by the North Sea is shown in the boasting of Frankish ambassadors at the court of Emperor Justinian in Constantinople, who claimed that their king's dominion included Britain and the seas around it, or in the legend of the origin of the Frankish Merovingian royal family who, as late as the seventh century AD, traced their origin to a princess who went bathing with a sea-monster, implying a proud maritime heritage for this Frankish family (Wood 1990: 96).

The year AD 793 is often given as the starting point of the story of the Vikings. In that year, the monastery of St Cuthbert on Lindisfarne off the coast of north-east England was ransacked, heralding a new period of piracy on the North Sea (e.g. Wormald 1991b: 132). But as we have already seen, the Viking activity belongs to an extended period of piracy and raiding in the North Sea which may have gone back as far as the fourth century BC. The Vikings' activity dates from the very late eighth century through to the 11th century, by which time the emerging nation states in Scandinavia had become unified and increasingly controlled under a Christian royal house. Although *viking* is the Old Norse word for pirate or raider, historical and archaeological research has identified a number of phases of activity that often started with raiding but developed, between AD 840 and 855, into the establishment of temporary camps for the pirates to remain in during the winter months; subsequently, permanent settlement took place, involving the migration of whole families. The Danes focused their attention on eastern England, the continental side of the North Sea, and the Atlantic coast, while the Norsemen sailed west to the Northern Isles and from there raided Ireland and northern Scotland (Graham-Campbell 1980: 23).

In the middle of the ninth century transitory camps were being used, allowing the Viking fleets to over-winter in enemy territory and penetrate deeper into the hinterlands, especially in Frankia, and to carry out raids further south along the Atlantic coast. The earliest record of an over-wintering Viking fleet is dated to the winter of AD 841 in Ireland, with such camps being noted in historical records in AD 850/1 for England and AD 852/3 for Frankia (Barrett 2007: 674). It seems a small step from over-wintering camps to the construction of more permanent settlements, and this was most successfully achieved by the Norse in the Northern Isles with the establishment of the Earldom of Orkney, and by the Danes in eastern England.

In what appears to be a parallel development to the piracy and raids of the earlier part of the first millennium AD, the earliest Viking raiding parties comprised a handful of boats, with three ships representing a 'typical' raiding force. During the ninth century, the number of ships in a fleet increased steadily, and by the early 830s could be as many as 30 to 35 ships with over 1,000 fighting men onboard (Haywood 1999: 168). This expansion of the raiding force has been linked directly to the involvement of the Danish King in the raiding expeditions, but it may also be the case that greater fighting forces were required in response to improved defences, such as the ring-wall forts on the Frankish North Sea coast (see below).

So, what drove the Vikings to piracy and raiding? In past research, a number of reasons for the Viking Age have been put forward, and often quickly discarded; these are usefully summarized in a recent paper (Barrett 2008). Thus, the known technological advances of the Nordic clinker-built ship, while enabling successful raids to take place, are unlikely in themselves to have caused piracy and raiding to commence in the first place, since raiding was a long-standing practice in the North Sea before the Viking Age. The beginning of the Medieval Warm Period would have allowed for settlements at more northerly latitudes to flourish, such as those on Iceland and in Green-land, but these settlements are of relatively late date and are unconnected with the early stages of Viking activity in the North Sea. Population pressure in the Scandinavian homeland is also rejected as a potential explanation for the onset of the Viking Age, as the *landnam* commenced only after the middle of the ninth century, some 50 years after the first raids. The idea that the early urbanization of the 'long eighth century', with booming trade centres offering easy targets, is also seen as unlikely, since the earliest attacks were on long-established monasteries and rural sites.

As an alternative hypothesis, James Barrett (2008) brings together three components, all of which have been previously considered in exploring the origins of Viking raids and piracy. The first component is a 'bulge' of young males, possibly the result of selective female infanticide, in need of bride-wealth for a decreasing number of available brides. The second component is a need for wealth in an increasingly competitive socio-political system. The third is a prevailing ideology of the Scandinavians, which recognized the elite status of warriors and the need to prove oneself in battle to preserve one's honour. This combination, possibly inflamed by the influx of silver from the east, appears a likely recipe for the onset of the Viking Age.

In response to the Viking raids, the Franks constructed a series of forts between Flanders and Texel. Haywood argues that Charlemagne's assessment of the situation had been correct, in that defence based at the mouths of major rivers was more likely to be successful than raising a standing fleet of warships to repel attackers (1999: 161–9). After all, if raiding Viking fleets using the benefit of surprise could not be intercepted on their inward route, their escape route could be cut off and the Vikings engaged in battle. This policy appears to have been successful, in that the number of recorded raids for the AD 820s is relatively low, at least much lower than for the 830s when the sons of Louis the Pious fought each other for sovereignty over the Frankish empire, with attacks on Nourmoutier, Rhé, Antwerp, Witla, Utrecht, Frisia (twice), and Dorestad (four times) (ibid: 168). However, improved diplomatic relations between Louis and the Danish King Horic saw a diminishing of pirate activities, and Horic even captured and executed some Viking leaders who had attacked Francia during the late 830s. Towards the end of the ninth century, a series of circular forts was constructed, including: the ringforts of Blokburg, Bergues/St Winoksbergen in the Nord department in France, and Veurne in Flanders; Oostburg, Oost-Souburg, Middleburg, Domburg, and Burgh in Zeeland; and, in Holland, Rijnsburg, and Den Burg. These were not places from where Vikings ships could be intercepted so much as refuges for people and animals, the coastal areas being by this time used mainly for pasture. Archaeological research has found no evidence of occupation on the ground level within these ringforts, which implies that these did not house a population on a permanent basis (Van Heeringen 1995).

The English response was not dissimilar. Fleets were not sufficiently effective to prevent raids, and John Pullen-Appleby (2005: 11) argues that fleets 'were an immeasurably more effective force for attack than defence—fleets of warships offer the opportunity of surprise attacks.' Defence of the realm was nearly always based on land, and from the AD 890s, King Alfred's answer to the Vikings' raids came in the form of defences constructed on land, notably the *burhs* or fortified strongholds, sometimes built as a double *burh* on opposite sides of major rivers, such as on the River Lea, a tributary of the Thames, where the Viking raiders were cut off on their return journey to the North Sea (ibid: 19). This is not to say that the English kings did not employ fleets to fight the Viking attackers. However, the use of partly foreign stipendiary crews, strengthened with ships provided by towns and earls, was a very expensive system to maintain. In addition, loyalty to the Crown was difficult to enforce, and the earls' fleets were frequently turned against royal power (ibid: 39). Only in the 11th century did the kings of England form an effective fleet, but its success lay first and foremost not in repelling attackers, but in its ability to attack others, as shown in Æthelred II's raids on the Isle of Man and Normandy (ibid: 129).

The nautical exploits of the Vikings are too well known to be detailed here, but the adventures of Earl Rognvald of Orkney (1136–58), as recorded in the Orkneyinga Saga, may illustrate some of the most extraordinary feats (Muir 2005: 87–93). Rognvald, a nephew of St Magnus, decided to undertake a pilgrimage to the Holy Land, together with Erling, a Norse chieftain. Having resolved the relative sizes and ornamentation of their ships, which would identify Rognvald's as the most important, their journey took them to Galicia, where they ransacked a castle. The Arab Islamic Iberian coast was raided on numerous occasions, but in Narbonne Rognvald composed poems for the wealthy and beautiful Ermingard. A dromond merchant ship was captured and sunk off the coast of Africa. The Holy Land was visited, where Rognvald swam across the River Jordan. The Vikings over-wintered in Constantinople, where they were received by Emperor Manual, and the return journey went via Rome and back to Denmark and Norway by horse.

From the short history of piracy presented above, it is clear that the North Sea was to many the realm of the unbound, unconstricted, and free, to paraphrase Deleuze (1953), for at least two millennia, and possibly before that as well. The pattern that emerges from the records is one where the North Sea offered opportunities for aspirant leaders, 'warlords', and chieftains as an arena where their limited power, reputation, and wealth could be greatly increased. It was a place where the dreams of certain individuals could become true. The evidence is clearest where the historical record includes the names and status of those engaged in piracy and raiding, and this is in particular the case for the Viking raiders, who appear to be 'leaders without royal associations . . . royal deputies . . . [and] exiled members of royal dynasties' (Barrett 2008: 679). Thus, those instigating piracy and raiding were to be found in regions where state formation had not yet progressed to a point where the hierarchical structures could not be challenged by individuals who had proven their worth in battle. Within early states the situation was, around the turn of the millennium, rather different. Both in England and in Frankia, engagement in war was a royal prerogative, and battles were frequently led by the king in person, or the leadership delegated to appointed generals. While war allowed many to climb up the feudal hierarchy, and victory in battle could bring great riches to the victor, this in itself did not contest the established order nor did it challenge the legitimized position of the king, except when the war was between kings. When the Danes settled in foreign lands, such as the Danelaw in England, and engaged in battles on land, this too became a concern for kings, even though the settlers' status may not always have been recognized back in Scandinavia. James Barrett (2008: 679) aptly summarizes Viking piracy as 'a viable option for contenders in the *realpolitik* of the resulting competition within and between elite Scandinavian dynasties'.

CONCLUSION

This chapter has sought to highlight the role of the North Sea as a space for social dynamics and interactions that were different from those studied by archaeologists on land. Situated somewhere below, or before, the evidence of power becomes archaeologically visible, lie socio-political processes by which the young, ambitious, and aspiring elite have to establish not only their own reputation but also the social networks that ensure their success when back on land. As far back as the Bronze Age, it has been argued, the ship—as evidenced by the craft known to us as sewn-plank boats, and by rock carvings—acted as a heterotopia where such social networks in the shape of leaders and retinues were formed. It has been suggested that for the Bronze

Age, these social dynamics were integrated in broader socio-political and cosmological conventions.

From the late Iron Age onwards, piracy offered opportunities for those who aspired to high office or power that was not otherwise attainable. Piracy works for those who wish to contend establishments. Although we do not have the names and status of the pirate leaders of the Franks and Saxons, their rise to power within the Roman Empire and England respectively had only been made possible through their naval activities. The rise to imperial power by the commander of the *classis Britannica*, Carausius, was also directly related to piracy on the North Sea, and the success of his independence from Rome, albeit only for a short period, was undoubtedly in part the consequence of the separation of Britannia from the rest of the Empire by an expanse of water. For the Vikings, the Icelandic Sagas tell us that piracy and raiding were the means by which contenders' reputations were established, and by which the loyalty of those serving leaders was rewarded. Loyalty was a necessity for small bands of men fighting on foreign soil, and being a pirate under a leader who was victorious not only meant great riches but a greater chance of survival. The creation of strong links between leader and retinue, and a sense of loyalty, were possible on board these ships which were indeed heterotopia par excellence.

9

The cultural biographies of boats

INTRODUCTION

Up to this point, boats and ships have been treated largely as functional objects (Figure 42). The characteristics of these objects enabled people to engage with the sea in many different ways (see chapter 7), while for those who travelled on these craft particular socio-political processes have been observed (see chapter 8). However, the contextualized study of boats suggests that alongside functional properties, craft also had attributed meanings, as implied for example by the deliberate deposition of the Hjortspring boat in a bog on the island of Als, or by the use of boats in burials at Sutton Hoo, Gokstad, Oseberg and at many other locations around the North Sea.

The symbolic significance of ships and boats was the focal point of the 1994 conference 'The Ship as Symbol in Scandinavian Prehistory and Middle Ages', which is recognized as a significant departure from existing debates in maritime archaeology. The ideas in this chapter are to an extent developed from the papers in the published proceedings (Crumlin-Pedersen and Thye 1995). The 1994 conference brought together a range of researchers who considered the other-than-functional and other-than-technical aspects of Scandinavian maritime archaeology. Symbols are understood to be semantically opaque representations producing semiotic systems in society (cf. Kobyliński 1995: 10–1). The use of the ship as a symbol is unsurprising. Much of the early maritime archaeology of Scandinavia is known to us not from wrecks that sank to the sea bed during storms, but from boat burials, and other deliberate depositions of boats in non-maritime contexts such as bogs, as well as from the carved and etched boat images on rocks and bronzes. The contexts of the boats imply that these carried meanings beyond their operational use, functioning therefore as signs and acting as symbols. The role of boats in the Sagas has advanced the notion that ships in the Viking period were more than simply craft to cross the sea with. Kobyliński (ibid. 15) makes the point that the extensive use of boats and ships as symbols in Scandinavia is linked to beliefs that the world of the dead is across the water, be that hell across the Gjoll River or Valhalla across the Thund River. Furthermore, the belief that

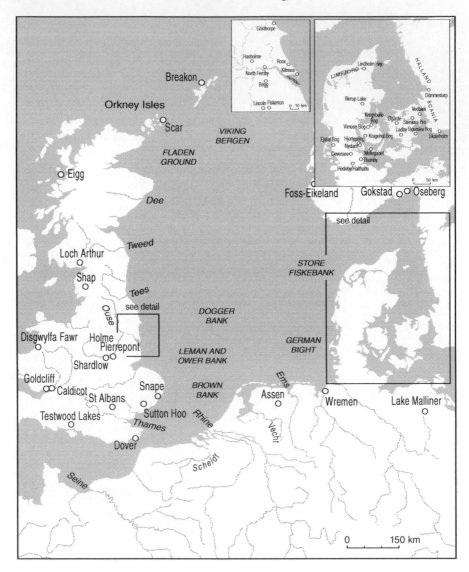

Figure 42. Places and regions mentioned in chapter 9

the daily journey of the sun was, in part, made by boat, creates symbolic links between funerary activities and concepts of renewal.

It is important to recognize that functionality and attributed human meanings are closely related factors (e.g. Westerdahl 1995b, 2008). Studying the cultural biographies of boats brings with it the notion that the functional and operational characteristics of particular craft relate closely to their use as symbols. It is in this sense that this chapter attempts to develop many of the ideas of the 1994 conference further: studying cultural biographies is not merely about the symbolic meaning of boats, but about the social *interactions* between the craft and those that were engaged with them. For the prehistory and early history of the North Sea, this included the attribution of other-than-human agency to boats.

As argued previously (see chapter 2), the archaeological record provides indications that agency was attributed to ships, such as implied by the *oculi* on the logboats of Hasholme, and the early medieval 'dragonheads' from the Scheldt. We can add to these the zoomorphological heads that formed the stem and stern on many of the boats depicted in the picture stones from Gotland (Lindqvist 1941, 1942) and on Viking-period ship graffiti (Christensen 1995), and on the boats used by William the Conqueror in the 11th century as shown on the Bayeux Tapestry (Wilson 1985). We can also add logboats from the North Sea area with *oculi*, notably the Brigg logboat from Lincolnshire, dated to 1260–800 cal BC, and the logboat from Loch Arthur in Scotland, dated to 150 cal BC to cal AD 200 (McGrail 2001: 177). *Oculi* are also present in the Roos Carr model of a zoomorphic boat and eight armed men. This model, found in 1836 in the Holderness district of Yorkshire (Poulson 1840), possibly represents a votive deposition at the edge of the expanding wetlands. It was radiocarbon dated to around 600 cal BC (Coles 1990), but as the models were carved from slow-growing yew wood, and no sapwood was detected on any of the carvings, this date may be too early by several hundred years (Van de Noort 2004a: 98). In a recent paper, Christer Westerdahl (2008: 23) has put forward the notion that boats and ships in the past were attributed animus or other forms of agency. Alongside the pair of male head carvings of the Nydam boat, he refers to rock carvings and ethnographic studies in support of this concept.

This chapter considers the cultural biographies of boats from three perspectives. It will consider, first, the role of boats as liminal agents in funerary activities around the North Sea. Second, the deposition of complete craft in contexts that suggest that these boats were ritually 'killed' will be explored. Third, the use of fragments of boats in a range of contexts will be investigated; focusing on the Bronze Age sewn-plank boats from England and Wales, it will be argued that parts of the boat symbolically represented their whole.

THE BOAT AS LIMINAL AGENT IN FUNERARY PRACTICES

In his overview of the role of the boat of the dead in the Bronze Age, Leslie Grinsell noted: 'In many parts of the world and at many periods the practice has prevailed of depositing boats, or models or other representations of them, with the dead, either as a means of facilitating his supposed voyage to another world, or as a symbol of his maritime activities during his lifetime. That the former is generally the correct explanation of the custom there can be no doubt.' (Grinsell 1940: 360). While the thinking about many aspects of the Bronze Age has fundamentally changed since the 1940s, this statement still holds very much true. The role of boats in burials—usually complete boats, or boat-shaped features or objects within the mortuary rituals—was to facilitate the voyage to the other world. The archaeology of the North Sea has an abundance of examples where boats were used in mortuary rituals. These include real boats that had a long life behind them, as well as boat-shaped log-coffins, stone settings in the shape of boat outlines, and boat models deposited as grave goods. Much has been written on boats in funerary practices, especially relating to the first millennium AD, and this short overview provides little more than a basic background to the subject, before the consideration of the liminal agent in the life of boats is reflected on.

The oldest evidence for boat burials comes from the Baltic islands of Denmark, and dates to the late Mesolithic and early Neolithic. Two cases of close associations of human remains and logboats have been excavated: Møllegabet on Ærø and Øgårde in Sjælland (Skaarup 1995). The Møllegabet boat burial concerns a straight logboat made of lime, dated to 4900–4730 cal BC. On excavation, stakes were found at both ends, understood as an arrangement for mooring the boat. The boat itself had been exposed to fire, and large areas of the wood had been charred. The fragmentary remains of a human skeleton were found, partly inside the boat and partly outside—presumably having been washed out some time after the initial burial of the skeleton. While other graves had been found on the land, this particular boat burial would have been positioned in shallow water along the beach. The Øgårde III burial was found in 1943. It concerns a 7-m-long alder logboat with a rounded stem and a transom end fitted at the stern. This logboat, too, had been held in place by stakes. The boat was dated to *c.* 3360 cal BC. A hearth, containing charcoal and fish remains, was found near the stern. The skeleton of a man was found close to the boat and is thought to have been laid near the prow.

Apart from these two rare cases, where the association of boat with human remains appears beyond discussion, a number of land-based burials have been noted in the Baltic where soil marks suggest logboat-shaped coffins, or where logboats were found without skeletal remains but with a material culture normally associated with burials. Examples include Skateholm and Kiaby in Skåne, Vedbæk, Sigersliv Bog on Sjælland, and somewhat further to the east at Visby on Gotland (Skaarup 1995). I am not convinced that the Neolithic burial near St Albans in Hertforshire involved a logboat burnt *in situ*, as claimed by the excavators (Niblett 2000: 159): there is simply insufficient detail for a positive identification of the burnt wooden vessel as a logboat. Moreover, the charcoal was radiocarbon dated to *c.* 3950 cal BC, some 1,500 years before the first logboats appeared in Britain, according to Lanting's meta-analysis of positively identified and absolutely dated logboats in Europe (Lanting 1997/8: 630).

Boat burials of Bronze Age date from around the North Sea are even more elusive. The most eligible examples concern the burials at Loose Howe and Gristhorpe in Yorkshire, Shap in Cumbria, and Disgwylfa Fawr in Ceredigion, Wales, but as Leslie Grinsell noted (1940: 365), these are not logboats but log-coffins with boat shapes. One of the three wooden vessels found within the burial mound of Loose Howe includes particularly boat-like details, notably a triangular-shaped keel and a stem carved from solid wood (Elgee and Elgee 1949). As Sean McGrail (e.g. 2001: 193) has previously argued, Bronze Age logboats have neither a keel nor a stem, and if the log-coffin was modelled on a known boat, it certainly was not a logboat. In many ways, the use of boat-shaped coffins has similarities with the use of gravestone settings in the shape of boats (see below), where the metaphor of the boat was sufficient for the people who organized the funerary rites. The fact that the four examples of boat-like log-coffins are found away from rivers or lakes, as parts of burials on tops of hills (cf. Harding 2000: 109) only reinforces this notion.

The metaphorical use of boats may also explain the presence of a ceramic model of a surprisingly well-made boat, found in the megalithic monument 'hunebed D-15' near Assen in Drenthe (Bakker 1990). This model has been explained as the probable urn of a sailor or fisherman, but the location of the burial monument far from any major river or body of water negates such an explanation, and a metaphorical use of the boat seems more likely.

Bronze Age 'stone ships', dated to the period 1300–700 cal BC, are known from around the Baltic Sea. These alignments of stones forming boat outlines have been uncovered from beneath some 35 burial mounds. Four examples are dated to the early Bronze Age: Dömmestorp and Serlingsholm on the coast of Halland, and Oeversee and Thumby on the Baltic coast of Schleswig-Holstein (Aner and Kersten 1978; Lundborg 1974; Strömberg 1961; cf. Capelle 1995). The late Bronze Age stone ships come mainly from Gotland (13 sites), Halland (3), Latvia (2), Scania (2), and Småland (1). The stone ships are made of natural erratic block, or limestone on Gotland, with typically the smooth side facing inwards, and with stem and stern accentuated with the highest stones. Different types of craft are represented, and while most present symmetrical outlines, a few have a squared stern, like a transom end-fitted stern on a logboat. Capelle (1995: 74) notes that none of the Bronze Age stone ships has a stone representing a mast step—such as has been observed for a number of Viking-age stone ships (see below)—and the higher stones amidships in some Bronze Age examples arc thought to represent the hole pins of rowed boats. Where rock carvings occur in the stone alignments, these are found on the stone representing the stem, or else on the midship stone. The shapes of the stone settings vary in length from 2 to 16 m, a length that seems 'realistic' for the Bronze Age; two stone ships at Gnisvärd in Gotland, however, were 33 and 45 m in length, and are considered to be 'oversized' (ibid. 71). The Gotlandic stone ship burials differ from their counterparts on the Scandinavian mainland in that they were frequently used for multiple burials, ranging from one to seven, but with an average of four individuals buried within the stone setting (Skoglund 2008: 293–4).

With the first millennium AD, we enter richer waters. Since Michael Müller-Wille's (1970) well-known overview of boat burials in northern Europe, *Bastattung im Boot,* much research has been undertaken that has further extended the temporal and geographical distribution of the boat grave phenomenon. Temporally, the earliest appearance of first-millennium AD boat graves in northern Europe has been put back to the first century. Geographically, boat graves are now also known from Niedersachsen, from Jutland south of the Limfjord, and from Shetland in the north-west, alongside the well-established presence of boat graves in East Anglia, Norway's North Sea coast, and Sweden's and Finland's Baltic coast (e.g. Müller-Wille 1995). The boat graves can be organized into three more or less distinct periods: the Roman period/Roman Iron Age and Migration period (first to the sixth centuries AD), the Merovingian/Vendel period (seventh and eighth centuries AD), and the Viking period (ninth, tenth and first half of the 11th centuries AD). Less than 10 per cent of the known boat graves have been dated to the first period. A somewhat higher percentage can be attributed to the middle period, but over 75 per cent of boat graves are of Viking age (Carver 1995: 112, with data from Müller-Wille 1995 included).

The boat graves and cemeteries of the first period have been phased as follows: to the early Roman Iron Age belong the cemeteries of Slusegaard on Bornholm, and Barkaby in Uppland, both in the Baltic, and Mølen in the Oslofjord, in the Vestfold. The distribution of the 11 or so boat graves and cemeteries dated to the late-Roman Iron Age is largely confined to southern Scandinavia, with 'outliers' at Jangarden in Møre og Romsdal to the north, and Wremen in Niedersachsen to the south. In the Migration period, the distribution represented by five cemeteries extends further, to Skogøy in Nordland in the north and Snape in East Anglia in the west (Müller-Wille 1995: 104).

The Slusegaard boat graves are of particular relevance here, because of the insight they provide into the other-than-functional role of boats. The Slusegaard site was excavated in 1958–64, and recently the interpretation of the cemetery was completed, with the analysis of the boat burials being undertaken by Ole Crumlin-Pedersen (1991, 1995). This nearly completely excavated site of some 1,400 graves included 45 boat graves identifiable as soil marks. The cemetery was in use in the first four centuries AD, with the majority of the boat burials dated *c.* AD 80–160. Boats incorporated in graves included boats of 3 m long, less frequently, boats of 5 m in length. All boats were expanded logboats, and predate the use of clinkers in the region. The boats had been used either as a container of the inhumed body or as a cover for the deceased. Occasionally two boats encased the dead. All the boat graves dated to before AD 160 had been 'robbed' or broken into, with the grave goods partially removed and the inhumation disturbed. Crumlin-Pedersen (1995: 93–5) considers and rejects interpretations that ascribe either a practical or secular role to the boats, or that regards them as ferries to the other world. Instead, he proposes that the occupants of the Slusegaard boat graves were the priests and helpers of a fertility god who was also a shipowner. He suggests that the placing of offerings, in the form of grave goods, represents a belief system of Njord, the father of Freyr. He notes that this would explain the equal presence of men and women, but the absence of children, within the boat graves (1995: 94). Around the middle of the second century AD, he suggests, the hegemony of this priesthood was challenged with the resultant 'robbery' of their ancestors' graves. The extent of the Slusegaard site, and the completeness of its excavation, establishes the simple dictum that while boat burials are known from the Baltic and the North Sea throughout the first millennium AD, they were only ever for selected individuals.

Though the ship burials at Snape in Suffolk belong to the very end of the first boat-burial period, in appearance they resemble Slusegaard closely. Dated to the fifth–seventh centuries AD, the Snape graveyard included originally at least 100 burials, which have been excavated intermittently since 1827 (Filmer-Sankey 1990, 1992). To date, three boats have been found. Snape 2 and Snape 3 surviving only as soil marks, were logboats each of some 3 m long and with a beam of 0.7 m. Snape 2 included two badly preserved (drinking-)horns, while Snape 3 contained a sword, three spears, and a shield-boss—on which basis a date around AD 600 is likely. The first boat was found at Snape in 1862, and while there was no trace of any timbers, the ordered pattern of rivets or clench nails depicted a clinker-built ship of about 14 m long and 3 m in beam, with eight strakes each side (Filmer-Sankey 1990: 126). This ship, which probably had a central burial chamber, had been robbed in antiquity, but nevertheless produced some grave goods demonstrating the high status of the person buried here: a fragment of a claw-beaker and a gold ring with Roman intaglio. On the basis of these finds, Snape 1 is dated to the second half of the sixth century AD. The cemetery of Snape is situated near the River Alde, some 8 km from its mouth at the North Sea.

Nearby Sutton Hoo, explored through two large-scale excavations and several smaller-scale investigations, is undoubtedly the best-known example of a boat burial of the Merovingian/Vendel period. The first large-scale campaign of excavation in 1939 by Basil Brown and colleagues was published by Rupert Bruce-Mitford (1975, 1978, 1983); the second large-scale campaign was undertaken by Martin Carver between 1983 and 1993, and published by him (Carver 2005). The ship burial in Mound 1 formed the focus of the 1939 excavations, with the second campaign broadening the research to take in the surrounding cemetery and landscape. The summary here is principally based on these reports.

A sixth-century AD cemetery at Tranmer House appears to precede the earliest burial at Sutton Hoo, which lies *c.* 700 m to the south, and is thought to be its direct predecessor. The cemetery at Tranmer House comprises a number of furnished cremations and inhumations, some buried beneath small mounds, and with one cremation placed in a bronze hanging bowl. This cemetery remained in use into the early seventh century. The first burials at Sutton Hoo date to the end of the sixth century or early in the seventh century AD. From the outset, this was an elite and restricted cemetery. The oldest burials here (Mounds 5, 6, and 7) are cremations in bronze bowls, with the remains of horses and food animals, and playing pieces, which survived the later barrow robbers. Of early sixth-century date is the burial in a trough or small boat in Mound 3.

The excavations of Mound 1 found the rivets and 'imprint' of a clinker-built boat 27 m long. The boat had been placed in a trench with a burial chamber amidships, and covered by a mound 2–3 m high (Figure 43). The wealth of goods from the burial chamber is well known. These included weapons—sword, helmet, shield, spears, drinking-horns; objects referred to as 'regalia', such as the 'sceptre'—a whetstone topped by a figure of a stag, and the 'standard'—an iron shaft topped by an iron frame, which are thought by some to have had shamanic functions, and a range of other materials, including Merovingian coins, hanging bowls, the Coptic bowl, the so-called 'baptist' spoons, and Byzantine silver. Mound 2 had been partially excavated in 1860, but was fully excavated in the 1983–93 campaign. From the disturbed 500 clench nails, including over 150 rivets with angled shanks, it seems that a clinker-built ship of about 20 m length had been placed over a burial chamber and then covered by a mound. The recovered grave goods included a sword, shield, belt-buckle, bronze bowl, glass jar, silver-mounted cup and box, and five knives. The date for both ship burials is around AD 630.

Following the ship burials, the cemetery remained in use for elite burials into the middle of the seventh century. While none of the burials equalled the extravagance of Mounds 1 and 2, fragments of boats (or otherwise beds, in Burials 12, 15, and 16) suggest an ongoing connection to the concept of boat burials. From the eighth century onwards, the Sutton Hoo site was used for legal killings, with the gallows being removed and set up at a new place in the 12th century.

Much debate has surrounded aspects of the Sutton Hoo ship burials, including the naming of the individuals buried here, which religion(s) were represented in the funerary rituals, and what political allegiances were embodied by the material culture. Martin Carver (2005: 491) describes the burials as poems 'where ideas and allusions are presented together in a rich tableau of theatrical complexity'. Following Frands Herschend (2001), this has

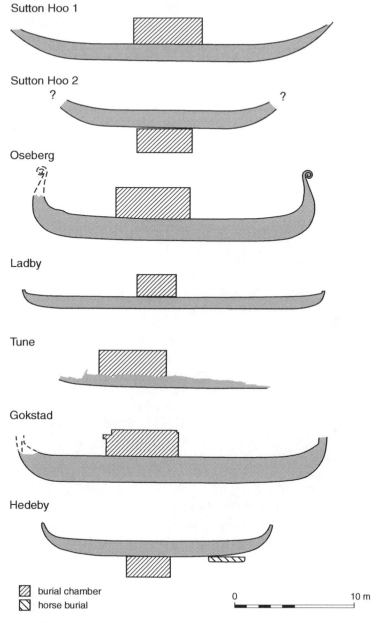

Sutton Hoo 1

Sutton Hoo 2

Oseberg

Ladby

Tune

Gokstad

Hedeby

▨ burial chamber
◩ horse burial

0   10 m

Figure 43. Schematic representation of the position of burial chambers in boat burials of the first millennium AD

to be placed within the context of a time when changing views of cosmology had been brought about by Christian thinking on heaven and hell. Politically, the burial rites at Sutton Hoo align the kin groups of the dead with the maritime polities of the North Sea and the Baltic, and demonstrate an antipathy towards the expanding Christian power bloc of Francia and Kent. The ship burials do not principally imply the emergence of a lordship, kingdom, and early nations; rather they signify the North Sea and the Baltic as a region where there is commonality of ritual practice (Carver 2005: 501). Linking East Anglia with Scandinavia through forms of peer-polity interaction between the emerging kingdoms in the North Sea seems justified, given the existence of the sometimes remarkable parallels in ship burial practices.

The main area of ship burial for the Merovingian/Vendel period is in the Baltic, in the Vendel heartland in Uppland—notably at Valsgårde and Vendel (Arwidsson 1980; Lamm and Nordström 1983). Ship burials in this region started soon after AD 600. Many of the excavated ship burials include grave goods of great wealth, although the use of the term 'princely burial' may be an overstatement, when these burials are compared to the richest graves in northern Europe. The long tradition of boat burials in the Baltic may belong to noble families grown powerful from iron production, linked to the emerging Svear royal dynasty who claimed lineage from Frö/Freyr (Schönbäck 1983: 131). In addition to the use of ships in funerary rites, a direct link between the Vendel and the Sutton Hoo ship burials is retained in the form of the animal ornamentation of the shield from Sutton Hoo Mound 1, which has its origin in east Sweden. The wide variety of grave goods used in both Sweden and East Anglia speaks of a broader, north European, practice of rich graves (e.g. Ambrosiani 1982; Parker Pearson, Van de Noort, and Woolf 1993). Other ship burials dated to this period are also known from Foss-Eikeland in Rogaland, Føre in Vesterålen, and a possible case at Gunnerstad, Småland, where a richly furnished cremation grave may have included a boat (Müller-Wille 1995: 102).

Using data from Müller-Wille's (1970) work, Martin Carver (1995: 112) characterizes the distribution of Viking-age boat graves as being overwhelmingly concentrated in Norway, where inhumation is the norm, with the second largest group coming from Sweden's Baltic coast, where cremation dominates. The best-known examples from this period are the Oseberg and Gokstad ships from Norway's Vestfold, Tune from Østfold, Ladby from the island of Funen, and Hedeby in Schleswig. Apart from these well-known large ship burials, the overwhelming majority of Viking boat burials concern small boats. We know of small boat burials from the Swedish and Norwegian coasts, from northern Denmark, at Scar on Sanday in the Orkney Islands and, beyond the scope of this book, at Ballywillin in Northern Ireland, Île le Groix in Normandy, and at Gnezdova and Plakun near Starajja Ladoga in Russia (Müller-Wille 1995: 102–4). The Scar burial, as an example of a small boat burial, was excavated in 1991 (Owen and Dalland 1999). The boat, traceable by some 300 rivets, was a 6.5 m faering-type rowing boat dating to *c.* AD 900. It had been placed in a stone-filled pit, and contained, somewhat unexpectedly for a small boat, the bodies of three people: a man, with a sword, arrows, a bone comb and a 22-piece gaming set; an old woman with a weaving sword, shears and two spindle whorls, as well as a comb and a sickle; and the body of a child. From this boat burial comes the famous Scar Plaque, a whalebone 'smoothing board' decorated with two dragons or horses.

Most of our understanding of Viking boat burials, however, comes from the larger craft. Possibly the most enigmatic of these, the Oseberg ship, was excavated in 1914. The ship, which had survived remarkably well beneath its earthen mound, was a clinker-built oak ship of 21.85 m length and 5.11 m at the beam. It had a mast-step, a side-rudder and 15 pairs of oar holes, and was found upright on rollers (Christensen, Ingstad, and Myhre 1992). Dendro-chronological analysis of the burial chamber, which had been placed amid-ships, shows that the timber for this structure was cut in AD 834 (Bonde and Christensen 1993: 581). Fifteen decapitated horses had been put in the bow of the ship. The grave had been 'robbed', and the majority of the grave goods removed. What remained were the wooden artefacts such as the cart, sleighs, and chest. The skeletal remains from the burial chamber were those of two women, one significantly older than the other; the older of the two has popularly been associated with Queen Åsa, the grandmother of Norway's first king. Recent research has been able to assign the DNA profile of the younger woman to haplogroup U7, a group largely absent in modern Europeans but common in Iranians (Holck 2006). Probably the most interesting elements of material culture from the ship burial, after the ship itself, are the fragments of textile. A detailed analysis by Anne Stine Ingstad (1995) argues that the scenes depicted on the textile fragments show aspects of the cult of Freya: a procession with the god in a cart drawn by a red horse, sacrifices in a sacred grove, and the use of specific symbols such as swastikas. Ingstad suggests (ibid. 146) that the queen in southern Norway was, around the time of the interment of the Oseberg ship, believed to be the representa-tive and incarnation of Freya herself, and that the burial was meant to keep her in the valley she had served so well. It was 'essential that the ship did not sail away', and it was therefore tied to a large boulder and buried beneath an enormous heap of stones (ibid. 147).

The Gokstad and Tune ship burials share a similar age, their burial cham-bers being dated by dendrochronology to *c.* AD 900 and 910 respectively (Bonde and Christensen 1993: 581). The Tune ship was excavated in 1867—the first time a Viking ship had been seen since the Middle Ages. The ship was clinker-built, from oak (the strakes) and pine (the cross beams and rudder). It measured about 20 m in length and 4.3 m at the beam. Preservation was poor.

The Gokstad ship, excavated in 1880, was a clinker-built oak craft of 23.2 m in length and 5.2 m at the beam (Nicolaysen 1882). It had room for 32 oarsmen. The burial chamber had been robbed in antiquity: the skeleton of an adult male was left with the remains of three smaller boats, a sledge, riding gear, and a tent.

The Hedeby boat burial, excavated in 1908 (Knorr 1911), is of some interest in that it presents an arrangement very similar to that of Sutton Hoo Mound 2. In both cases, the ships were placed *over* the burial chamber. However, the Hedeby boat, which is known only from its 64 rivets, is dated to the middle of the ninth century, about 250 years after the Mound 2 ship was interred at Sutton Hoo. The Hedeby ship was placed over a burial chamber and contained the bodies of three men; three horses were buried in another pit beneath the boat (Crumlin-Pedersen 1997: 252–4). One body, which was separated in the chamber from the others, had as grave goods a sword, a sword-belt with Christian symbols, a horse-harness, arrows, a drinking glass, and a bucket. The two other bodies had swords and a banquet set. Detlev Ellmer's (1980) interpretation that these others were the marshal and cup-bearer of the lord or king, placed separately in the chamber, has been widely accepted (e.g. Wamers 1995: 149). The origin from within the Carolingian Empire of some of the grave goods implies that the lord or king buried here was a retainer of the Carolingian king Louis the Pious, who had been invested with land in Frisia. Citing the parallel placement of the boat over the burial chamber in Mound 2 at Sutton Hoo, Egon Wamers (ibid. 153–4) concludes that this practice was possibly specific to the burial of Scandinavian kings who had been christened but had then reverted, wholly or partly, to the pagan ideas of Valhalla.

The final ship burial discussed here is the Ladby ship burial, on Funen (Thorvildsen 1957; Sørensen 2001). The 1930s excavation found the metal and impression of a warship 21.5 m long and 3 m wide (a length:breadth ratio of just over 7:1), which gave room for 30 or 32 oarsmen. It had been buried under a large mound on the periphery of an existing cemetery. The mound containing the ship had been extensively robbed in antiquity, possibly only a few years after the interment; this is understood to represent the 'desecration' of the burial by new rulers or ruling family in the region. Possibly, the burial and accompanying material was placed in a tent within the ship. Together with the body of a man, the remains of eleven horses and four hounds with their harnesses were uncovered, along with banqueting equipment, a gaming set, and weapons including an axe, shield, and arrows. Assuming that it was part of the funerary dress the presence of a Carolingian silver buckle implies that a sword would have been present at the time of the burial. Intriguingly, the buckle dates to the middle of the ninth century, while the dog-harnesses have been dated to the 'Jelling-style', and the ship burial to the first quarter of the tenth century, all of which suggests that the sword may have been an heirloom (e.g. Wamers 1995: 155).

Stone ship burials are known from various parts of southern Scandinavia (but not Gotland) from between AD 600 and 1000. One possible stone ship is known from Breakon, on the island of Yell in the Shetlands (Fojut 1993: 74). As is the case with the Bronze Age stone boats, the majority of these were small boats, but occasionally larger ships exceeding 40 m in length were represented by the stone settings. The best known of the Viking stone boat burials are those at Lindholm Høje, near Nørresundby, overlooking the Limfjord in northern Jutland (Nielsen 1996) (Figure 44). The burial ground contains some 700 graves, dating from the fifth through to the eighth centuries AD, with some later Viking graves present too. Most of these are cremation graves marked by stone settings in shapes such as squares, triangles, circles, and ovals. There are also many settings shaped unmistakably like small boats. The presence of these boat-shaped cremation patches, some of which included buckles and rivets—one even had its rows of rivets still in place— clearly illustrates that the construction of stone boats and the use of real boats in burials were closely linked practices. Distinguishing between male and female graves at Lindholm Høje, on the basis of their grave goods, leads to the conclusion that female graves were marked by square, oval or round stone settings, and male graves by triangular or ship-shaped stone settings. Further-

Figure 44. A 'stone boat' at Lindholm Høje, Jutland

more, analysis of the relative wealth of the grave goods implies that the richest male graves were those placed within the stone boats. One of these included the main body of a wagon and some tenth-century Kuffic coins. Peter Skoglund (2008) has recently argued—principally on the basis of the changing nature of the Gotlandic picture stones—that after *c.* AD 750 the ship became a metaphor for power and warfare, and that the stone ship burials were originally a manifestation of social inequality. But when the practice of using boat-shaped stone settings began to be adopted by larger groups in society, the metaphorical use of the ship—in stone or otherwise—as an expression of power and warfare was undermined. In this context, Skoglund argues, 'the ship's ritual function is underlined, most likely as a symbol of the dead person's voyage from this world to the world of the dead' (ibid. 399).

In aiming for an understanding of the symbolic significance of the Viking ship burial phenomenon, two historical sources are often quoted: Beowulf and the journal of Ahmad Ibn Fadlan. The Beowulf story is referred to for its description, in the prelude, of the funeral of Beowulf's father, Scyld. Scyld is laid out amidships beside the mast of his ship, with treasure from distant lands and weapons and armour piled up on the ship. His standard and sails are hoisted and the ship and its contents given over to the ocean. Later in the story, Beowulf himself is cremated and buried beneath a barrow which functions as a beacon for sailors for subsequent generations.

Ahmad Ibn Fadlan was a Baghdad diplomat whose travels in the early tenth century AD took him to the Volga-Bulgarians where he observed the funeral of a 'Rus' (Warmind 1995; Parker Pearson 1999: 1–3). Ibn Fadlan states that the size of the ship and the status of the deceased are closely linked. The dead man, a wealthy trader, is put temporarily in a makeshift grave with makeshift grave goods, while the proper funeral is prepared. His ship is placed on 'scaffolding'. The body of the deceased is brought to the ship, where a tent has been set up. Here he is dressed in Byzantine brocade. Grave goods including food and a pandora are also placed here. Animals, including a dog, two horses, two cows, a rooster, and a hen, are killed and the remains placed in the ship as well. A slave-girl of the deceased, who has volunteered for the task and may have been married posthumously to her master to act as a substitute wife, is sacrificed by a woman described as the Angel of Death to accompany her master to the next world, after having had intercourse with her master's kinsmen. The boat is finally set alight by the kinsmen, and the remains are buried beneath a low mound with a post that bears the name of the Rus and his king.

This overview of the use of boats and ships in funerary rites in the North Sea, from the Mesolithic through to the Middle Ages, shows that this was only ever a practice for selected individuals. In every case it reflected the elevated status of the deceased thus honoured, but it was appropriate only in certain contexts, at particular times and in specific places. The message provided by the rites to the participants and observers, and to subsequent generations in the form of any remaining monument, is undoubtedly multilayered; it expresses something of the social identity of the dead and of the mourners— their fears, hopes, and ritual beliefs, as well as the political environment which prevailed. Martin Carver's (2005: 503) description of the Sutton Hoo ship burials as a reified poem which 'draws on the time and space of the imagination, creating not a direct statement but a palimpsest of allusions', seems appropriate in nearly all cases considered here.

That leaves us with the specific role of the boats and ships in these funerals. Even before Leslie Grinsell's (1940) paper on the use of boats in burials, quoted at the beginning of this section, the symbolic or metaphorical function of these craft in facilitating the journey to the next world was recognized as the key to understanding their use in funerary contexts. This short overview has offered many examples of the belief that these craft did not physically facilitate that journey, but symbolized it in the minds of the people we seek to understand: the real boats were either pegged into place (e.g. the Mesolithic Møllegabet boat burial and the Neolithic Øgårde III burial), or buried in the ground or beneath earthen mounds (e.g. Slusegaard, Snape, Sutton Hoo, Oseberg, Gokstad), while the boat-shaped log-coffins and Bronze Age and Scandinavian Iron Age stone boats and ships were evidently regarded as being unable to sail away. If it had been envisaged that these boats would undertake genuine journeys, would the Sutton Hoo Mound 2 and Hedeby ship burials not have held the bodies of the deceased, rather than being placed on top of the grave chambers?

Nevertheless, in spite of this apparent consensus—and in acknowledgement of a few dissenting voices that see boats in burials in the first millennium AD as grave goods or offerings to specific gods, notably Njordr—I would argue that the use of boats and ships in burials cannot be satisfactorily explained by reference to symbolic or metaphorical attributes alone. Beyond the vague phrase of 'facilitating entry into the next world', archaeologists have been at a loss to explain how this was actually perceived by the people we study. However, following Christer Westerdahl's (2005) idea of the use of liminal agents on land and sea, and his recognition of whole boats as liminal agents (2008), it is possible to attribute a more literal function to boats and ships in funerary behaviour.

Approaching the ship burial from a presumed emic perspective, it could be argued that people in the past believed that boats and ships did complete the journey from this world to the next, and did actively facilitate the entry of the person buried with them. In their perception, this was not accomplished by the ships as these were buried beneath mounds, but through the boats and ships operating as liminal agents. If boats and ships could act as liminal agents, then they were attributed forms of agency or other-than-human agency. Forms of agency are linked to forms of personhood and it could be argued that, as was believed to be the case with the human person, the personhood of ships was thought to comprise a body and a 'soul'. It is my supposition that, in the case of boat and ship burials, the other-than-human agency attributed to the ships was believed to disconnect on death from the physical body of the ship, just as the human agency was thought to be able to disconnect from the body of a person on dying. Thus, travelling together, the 'soul' of the ship facilitated the journey of the 'soul' of the human. The stone ships provide a variation on this. Some may have included fragments of the real ship, as has been shown in the case of some graves at Lindholm Høje, or others may have simply been made to look like real boats—although some form of agency must have been attributed to these stone settings too. The stone ships did not merely have some symbolic or metaphorical significance; through their agency they were meant to facilitate the rapid transfer of the deceased to the next world.

Christer Westerdahl (2008: 23) calls this other-than-human agency of boats and ships *animus*. Comparing the agency of boats to the agency of animals is something that may have been familiar to the people around the North Sea in the past: depictions of prows as animal heads on rock carving and bronzes, the Roos Carr model with its *oculi*, and the early medieval dragonheads from the Scheldt, all reflect such an awareness. Using agency and other-than-human agency in this context would also explain the inclusion of animals and human sacrifices in boat and ship burials. Again, the mourners could not have been under the apprehension that the decapitated horses or killed dogs would physically travel with the deceased to the next world. However, if the animals were attributed agency and personhood, and their soul was disconnected from the body on their death, then the sacrifices and burial together would have made sense. For the retainers and slaves who voluntarily or involuntarily became part of the funerary rituals, the same or similar reasoning must have applied.

Returning to the idea of cultural biographies of boats and ships, the use of craft in funerary rites should not be seen as their end-use, limited to their symbolic or metaphorical meanings. Rather, the inclusion of a boat or ship in a funeral presents one aspect of an established and ongoing active social relationship between the craft and those engaged with it. The ship may have been the trustworthy vessel on which the master made his name as a warrior (as was the case for Scyld in Beowulf) or his fortune as a trader (in the case of the Rus described by Ahmad Ibn Fadlan). Alternatively, the ship may have carried with it an extensive experience of sailing across the seas, and predate the burial by several decades, for example the Gokstad ship; or, like the Oseberg ship, it may have been used for ceremonial purposes only. In life and in death, it shared the experience with its master.

KILLING BOATS

From the North Sea and its connected waters come several boats whose contexts suggest that they had been deliberately 'killed'. I use that word consciously as this concerns a select group of boats that experienced an end to their lives distinctive from the symbolic use or reuse of boats—intact or in parts—in other structures or in burials. The selection of boats that appear to have been destroyed in this way is only very small; this, however, is a direct consequence of the frequently unorganized and decontextualized manner in which the boats have entered the 'archaeological record' as explored, for example, by Robert Mowat for the discovery of the Scottish logboats (1996: 116–25). Nevertheless, the few examples available are most instructive.

From the British side of the North Sea come several logboats whose context is of interest in the current discussion. The Holme Pierrepont 1 logboat, from 500 cal BC to cal AD 100, is the only absolutely dated craft of three found in close proximity to one another in the River Trent in Nottinghamshire. The three boats are nearly identical. All three include features such as the three 'steps' that may have been seats, and it seems likely that Holme Pierrepont 2 and 3 are of a similar date to no. 1, that is Iron Age or early Roman. The context of Holme Pierrepont 1 is described as 'trapped by the fork of an oak tree'; significantly, it was lying on top of a twelve-spoked wheel. The context of Holme Pierrepont 2 is described as 'trapped by a fallen oak', and here too we are informed that the logboat itself was on top of an earlier deposit, i.e. 'an ... oak beam with holes at each end' (McGrail 1978: 206–8). The context of the undated Holme Pierrepont 3 was not recorded.

The examples from the River Witham, Lincolnshire, are also relevant. Fiskerton 1 and Fiskerton 2 were discovered in 2001. The excavation, undertaken in advance of flood remediation construction, has not been published formally, but was well publicized in the popular press at the time of excavation. Pending the release of the radiocarbon dates, a provisional fifth- or fourth-century BC date on the basis of the assumed contemporaneity of the logboats with the adjacent timber causeway seems likely. This trackway had been built in 457/6 BC and had been periodically repaired, with an end date for the final repair of around 300 BC (Field and Parker Pearson 2003). Fiskerton 1 was poorly preserved, and little more than its existence was noted. However, Fiskerton 2 was well-preserved. This was a 7.2 m craft with a rounded bow and fitted transom at the squared stern. This craft was destroyed in antiquity, with a piece of timber put through it, pegging it to the ground. The toolmarks on the bottom of this logboat were crisp and clear, as 'fresh as the day they were hewn' (Pryor 2004: 33), and it may be that this craft had barely been used before it was killed. The cultural landscape in which these craft are set is not without significance: the River Witham is famous for some very high quality pieces of metal ritually deposited in it, including the

La Tene shield somewhat further upstream near Lincoln (e.g. May 1976: 130–3). The causeway alongside which the logboats were found had been used for ritual depositions too, and from the riverbed came weapons, bronze fittings, and a complete spear (Field and Parker Pearson 2003).

Francis Pryor (2004: 33) has suggested that other boats too were ritually offered, notably the Bronze Age Shardlow logboat, which had been 'jam-packed with massive boulders', and was sunk on the River Trent in Nottinghamshire near a Flag Fen-style post alignment. The recent find of a second (unexcavated and unpublished) logboat could be understood either as reinforcing this argument, or weakening it if the river was particularly hazardous here.

From the continental side of the North Sea, deliberately deposited boats are known only from Denmark and Norway, and the Hjortspring boat is the earliest of these. Originally excavated in 1921–2 (Rosenberg 1937; cf. Crumlin-Pedersen and Trakadas 2003), this sophisticated warship, dated to 390–210 cal BC and accommodating around 20 paddlers, was found within a small bog on the island of Als, 3.5 km from the nearest coast (Rieck 1995: 127). With the boat were the weapons of an 'army' of some 100 warriors, and the local evidence suggests that this particular bog had already been used for ritual depositions before the boat was broken up and dumped here. The Hjortspring boat is generally interpreted as an invaders' craft, possibly from southern Sweden, which was ritually destroyed after the victory of the inhabitants of Als over the invaders (e.g. Randsborg 1995). I have argued that this craft may have belonged to pirates or raiders, since the number of warriors seems too small for an army setting out to conquer land, and the size of the warring party resembles closely that of pirates and raiders in the early medieval period (chapter 7). The Hjortspring deposit is the oldest known deposition of war booty in wetlands, but it is not the only one of Pre-Roman Iron Age date. Others have been discovered at Lake Malliner in Mecklenburg, Tidavad in Västergötland, Stenløse Bro in Sealand, and Krogsbølle Bog on Funen; and earlier conceptions that the Hjortspring war booty was a chronological outlier of this phenomenon have now been put aside (Kaul 2003: 219–21).

However, the chronological gap to the next war booty deposit to include ships is nearly 500 years. At the Illerup Lake in east Jutland, weapons and warriors' equipment were sacrificed between AD 200 and 500. The origin of the warriors is thought to be Scandinavian. Site Illerup A, dated to c. AD 200, included—alongside Scandinavian spears, lances, and shields, and a few Roman imports of swords and baldric equipment—several logboats. These logboats, which have not been studied in any detail, are thought to have played a role in the deposition of some of the material of Illerup A, as this was found at some distance from the contemporaneous shore (Ilkjær 2003: 47–51; Rieck 1995: 128). One of the logboats from this site, Illerup 3, was radiocarbon dated to cal AD 250–560 (Lanting 1997/8: 633).

The Vimose Bog on Funen has also produced large amounts of military equipment, dating from the end of the first century AD through to the fifth century. The Vimose finds are somewhat different from other war-booty sacrifices from southern Scandinavia. The early depositions here suggest a southern (i.e. from the German/Polish region) origin of the arms, and thus of the attackers, whereas all other bog finds indicate a northern origin (Jensen 2003: 237). Several logboats were recovered from the Vimose Bog in the 19th century, and as was the case in Illerup A, these are thought to have played a role during the sacrificial ceremonies (Rieck 1995: 128).

The best known deposition of boats alongside war booty in a Scandinavian bog is found at Nydam on the Danish–Prussian/German border. The excavations by Conrad Engelhardt (1865), and more recently by the National Museum of Denmark and the Society of Nydam Research (e.g. Jørgensen and Petersen 2003), have been extensively published. The Nydam Bog contains three ships: a fragmented oak boat from the early third century AD, a pine boat from the early fourth century AD and the large oak boat, commonly referred to as the Nydam Boat, dated to *c.* AD 350. After the deposition of the Nydam Boat, weapon sacrifices continued for the next 125 years.

Both the pine boat and the Nydam Boat had been toppled on their sides. Weapons and warriors' equipment were found within, below and outside these craft, but the existence of multiple deposition events has hampered a close determining of the associations between weapons and ships. Alongside spears, lances, bows, and axes, swords and scabbards were uncovered. From the pine boat, a finely decorated commander's scabbard was found with the name of its owner inscribed in runes on the strap hook: Harkila (ibid. 266–7). Among the non-military equipment were found tweezers, bowls, and dishes, various containers, and tools, including working axes, planes and forging equipment. The final deposition in the Nydam Bog, dated to AD 460–475, comprised a heap of over 1,000 items surrounded by a ring of 36 swords and a large decorated lance head (ibid. 281–2). This represents one of the latest ritual depositions of war booty in Denmark.

The next sacrifice of a boat alongside war booty in a bog is the Ejsbøl Bog site, also in East Jutland, where weapons and warriors' equipment, including horse gear, were deposited from the Pre-Roman Iron Age through to *c.* AD 400. From that part of the lake referred to as Ejsbøl D, and dated on the basis of the military equipment to around AD 300, came around 200 large and more than 200 smaller boat rivets, as well as a rowlock. These rivets are thought to have come from a single clinker-built boat, rather than two of different sizes. For both sets of rivets, the rivet plates were still in place, suggesting that the boat had not been broken up, which would have resulted in the plates being twisted off the rivets. Rather, the finds have been interpreted as representing a boat which had been burnt, as were many other offerings here, and the rivets collected afterwards and thrown in the lake as a separate event (Andersen 2003).

From the Kragehul Bog on Funen, a range of weapons and military equipment, including swords and scabbards, lances, spears, bows, arrows, and shield fragments, together with personal equipment such as striking stones, scissors, tweezers, and wooden vessels were recovered. The available evidence is little more than a sample of what can only be understood as a much larger booty, as this former lake had been extensively cut by peat cutters in the 18th century. The 19th-century excavations have never been fully published, but the date range of the equipment recovered suggests a number of sacrifices took place here between AD 150 and 500 (Ilkjær 2003: 47–51). A boat offering is noted in this bog too, but the circumstances are unclear (Westerdahl 2008: 21).

The last boats that appear to have been killed come from the Kvalsund site near Sunnmøre in Norway, some 200 km north of Bergen. Two boats, dated to cal AD 620–890 had been ritually offered here: they had been split into fragments, and placed in a pit dug for this particular purpose. The boats had been covered with branches and twigs from deciduous trees, mostly rowan, which possibly acted as substitutes for weapons; the pit had then been filled with stones and peat and covered up (Shetelig and Johannessen 1929; cf. Rieck 1995: 128; Westerdahl 2005: 21).

All these boats—four from England, possibly 11 from Denmark, and two from Norway—were deliberately deposited. To date, the boat depositions in Denmark have been understood as integral parts of the war booty sacrifices in bogs. However, the presence in this group of a number of boats that do not form part of such war booty sacrifices—that is the logboats from Holme Pierrepont and Kvalsund—or else were unlikely to have belonged to the invaders but were used as part of the ceremony—the Illerup and Vimose logboats, and possibly the Fiskerton and Kragehul craft—suggests otherwise. In effect, only the Hjortspring and Nydam boats appear to fit the description of boats forming part of a war booty sacrificed in natural places with strong ritual connotations.

Effecting ideas from the cultural biography of objects concept, the social interactions existing between boats and their crews would have meant that the Hjortspring and Nydam boats were attributed some of the blame for allowing pirates, raiders or invaders to reach land. The boats, just as the weapons, would not simply have been regarded as objects unencumbered with any human meaning. Rather the reason that boats and weapons were selected as being suitable for sacrifice was exactly that their social interaction with the enemy had given them negative values. Neither HarkilaR nor his sword from the Nydam pine boat could have killed or maimed anybody without interacting with each other; the interaction between owner and sword meant that they shared responsibility for the violence and bloodshed conducted.

It was the same with the boats: the crew/warriors and the boat were inter-dependent in their quest, and both were held responsible. And that is why the Hjortspring and the Nydam boats were killed.

If boats could be held responsible for their actions, and therefore be regarded as suitable candidates for sacrifices, then they must have been attributed other-than-human agency by people in the past. This would also have been the case with the other boats destroyed, but we must seek alternative explanations for the logboats discussed here, because these were unlikely to have been held responsible for bringing over hostile warriors. I propose two complementary explanations. The logboats from Holme Pierrepont and Kvalsund may not have brought warriors but others who, nonetheless, trans-gressed outside their territory and were not welcome. The fate of these boats resembled that of the Hjortspring and Nydam boats. We are reminded that the late Iron Age in Britain was one of 'intense regionalism' (see chapter 7), and one way in which this had come about was that people and their craft were not free to travel the rivers that cut across these regions. As an aside, the contemporary Hasholme logboat had on its stern transom a carved symbol resembling a 'U' (Millett and McGrail 1987). Maybe this was a way in which the tribal or regional home of the craft was signified. The killing of the logboats found at or near the weapon deposits at Illerup and Vimose, and possibly Fiskerton and Kragehul, could be explained by the fact that these craft had taken part in or witnessed ceremonies which should remain secret. To ensure that these secrets were not passed on, the boats had to be killed. Boats of this period, after all, had eyes/*oculi*.

FRAGMENTATION AND *PARS PRO TOTO*

The idea of fragmentation in archaeology was brought to the forefront by John Chapman (2000). Chapman argued that through the practice of frag-mentation of artefacts, in a process he named 'enchainment', the people of prehistoric south-east Europe constructed their social relationships with each other, their ancestors, and with their native soil. In western Europe, fragmen-tation of artefacts has also been observed. Beaker sherds in a grave, for example, are no longer automatically assumed to be incomplete archaeo-logical finds, but objects reflecting contemporary social practice. The idea that boats were fragmented and used in social practices has been tentatively explored by some (e.g. Champion 2004; Pryor 2004; Van de Noort 2006), and the idea of *pars pro toto* ('the part represents the whole') has been invoked on a number of occasions in an attempt to understand the significance of boat fragments (Westerdahl 1995b, 2008). The focus of this section is on the

Bronze Age sewn-plank boats from Britain, but with reference to examples from other places and times.

The oldest boat that may have been deliberately fragmented is the Dover Bronze Age boat, radiocarbon dated to 1575–1520 cal BC (Clark 2004a). The boat consists of four planks, including two bottom- or keel-planks joined together by means of a longitudinal cleat rail, and two ile planks, or transitional strakes (Marsden 2004: 32–3). A transom end and further side strakes had been deliberately removed—there is no debate about this, as the withies that secured these strakes were found to have been cut through, with the remains still in the holes of the ile planks. Wear and tear, and several repairs to the ile planks where these had split in antiquity, both indicate that the Dover boat had seen considerable service. At the point of deposition, the vessel showed signs of leaking but the structure of the boat was 'quite sound' (ibid. 44). With the boat, a considerable amount of flint, debitage, and burnt flint was found, alongside animal bones. These have been interpreted as inwash from a nearby rubbish dump or midden upstream, relating to late Neolithic and Bronze Age habitation (Bown et al. 2004). They also consider a small fragment of Kimmeridge shale from Dorset, found in the boat, to be a leftover of one of its cargoes. The debate on the why and how of the deposition of the boat is ongoing. Unequivocally, the final resting place of the Dover boat was in a 'quiet backwater' in the shallow, freshwater stream of the Dour. However, whether the boat was stripped here 'of anything useful' for reuse and then deserted (e.g. Parfitt 2004: 22; Clark in Bown et al. 2004: 211) or was ritually killed and buried (e.g. Champion 2004; Pryor 2004) remains a topic for debate.

It seems unlikely that any of the earlier sewn-plank boats from England and Wales were fragmented as part of ritualized behaviour. The parts of the three craft found at North Ferriby in the Humber estuary, and the fragment of the older of the two sewn-plank boat finds from Caldicot on the Nedern Brook, a tributary of the Severn estuary, are more likely to be the result of the craft having been taken apart during repairs. The presence of oak woodchips with bronze axe facets on the North Ferriby foreshore, in addition to the off-cuts of yew withies that continue to be retrieved from here, and the placing of the Ferriby 2 and Ferriby 3 fragments on alder roundwood timbers, all suggest that boats were fashioned or repaired at these two locations (Wright 1990; Van de Noort 2006). Several other finds from the Humber estuary, interpreted as shipwrights' tools, support the notion that we are dealing here with a prehistoric boatyard. Such finds include a 'tingle', used for repairing holes and cracks in boats, and a pistol-shaped tool used for stitching the yew withies. The same arguments can be made for the Caldicot 1 fragments consisting of the second or higher side strake of a sewn-plank boat, and a 3.55-m-long plank, both of which had been broken in antiquity (McGrail 2001: 188). The contemporary activity on this site (i.e. Phase III) was described as including 'the deposition of a wide variety of wood including scrub clearance, wood-working debris, and the boat strake' alongside the deposition of some stone and bones of domesticated animals (Nayling and Caseldine 1997: 261–2). It seems unlikely that the sewn-plank boat remains are those of a sunken boat. Rather, both the remains themselves and the associated yew ties have been interpreted as 'discarded material, resulting from the repair of a sewn-plank boat' (ibid. 263). The fragment of a sewn-plank boat from Kilnsea, on the Humber estuary, was found lying on a beach and the context is not precisely known to us (Van de Noort et al. 1999).

The later sewn-plank boats, however, with the exception of the Brigg 'raft', are known to us only as fragments. Caldicot 2, discovered during the same excavations as Caldicot 1, is represented by three oak fragments, including a possible cleat fragment, a 0.3-m-long plank with six holes similar to a bottom plank of the Brigg 'raft', and another plank with what has been described as a possible cleat ridge, similar to the one known from F2 (McGrail 1997: 215–17). By the time of the deposition of Caldicot 2, around 1100–1000 cal BC, the Nedern Brook had become a wide, flat-bottomed channel. At about this time, structure 9014—possibly a fort, hard or weir—was constructed, later to be replaced by a wooden bridge and associated trackway (Nayling and Caseldine 1997: 265–8). From around the bridge and trackway, numerous cultural deposits have been recovered. These include a Wilburton-type chape, fragments of at least two 'finely decorated vessels', decorative bone objects, an amber bead, a near-complete dog skeleton, wooden domestic items, and other artefacts of wood, alongside domestic rubbish such as woodworking debris, substantial timbers, and animal bones (ibid. 266–7). The possibility that at least some of these depositions should be interpreted as 'ritual' or votive was raised by the authors of the Caldicot report (ibid.). Pryor (2004: 33) suggests that Caldicot was associated with ritual depositions, but no differentiation is made between the early Bronze Age Caldicot 1 and the much younger Caldicot 2.

The Testwood Lakes boat fragment of a sewn-plank boat was discovered in 1996 by staff of Wessex Archaeology (Fitzpatrick, Ellis, and Allen 1996). The reservoir was cut into the floodplain of the River Blackwater, just north of its confluence with the River Test, and about 4 km north of the intertidal bay of Southampton Water which offers direct access to the Solent. The Testwood Lakes boat fragment consists of the remains of a single cleat, with dimensions comparable to the cleats used in the other sewn-plank boats. The cleat is provisionally dated to *c.* 1500 cal BC (A. Fitzpatrick pers. comm; *contra* McGrail 2004). It was found near the remains of three bridges (Testwood 1, 2, and 3) which cross the River Blackwater here, the oldest of which has been radiocarbon dated to *c.* 1700 cal BC and the youngest to around 1400 cal BC. The oldest and best surviving structure (Testwood 3) comprises two rows of upstanding timbers, mainly oak, extending for about 26 m, between 1.5 and

2 m apart. Some 15 planks were also found in the former river. Presumably forming the superstructure of the bridge, these planks display a range of carpentry techniques including notches, bevels, and mortise holes, but no cleats or cleat-like features. The cleat itself had been damaged on one side, where it would have been connected to a boat-plank, and the other side was worn. This may be interpreted as evidence that entire boat-planks had been reused for the bridge decking but that the cleat, being something of a potential obstacle, had been removed from the plank in antiquity and thrown into the river. As part of the same excavations, a broadly contemporary bronze Acton 2-type rapier was uncovered from the riverbed. The rapier was not broken, but lacked its handle, and pending further analysis should be broadly dated to the middle of the second millennium BC. The likelihood that this rapier is a votive deposit in the wetlands of the Rivers Blackwater and Test has not been discounted by the excavators.

The remains of the Goldcliff sewn-plank boat consist of two planks of oak, with upstanding cleat ridges through which mortise holes were found to have been cut, as was the case with the cleat ridge of the Dover boat. Closely spaced 'fastening' holes were found along the sides, some still containing plant fibre cord. The excavators initially suggested that the planks had been reused as a platform for hunting, fishing, or fowling within the intertidal zone of the Severn estuary (e.g. Bell 1993: 11); but as a final conclusion, it is now thought that they made up a short trackway crossing a narrow channel within an intertidal context (Bell, Caseldine, and Neumann 2000: 82). For one of the two planks, it has been argued that this was not the first time it had been reused. One of the mortised holes would have had no function in the sewn-plank boat, neither did it serve a function in the platform. Two human skulls of late Bronze Age date link Goldcliff with the practice of the deposition of human crania, which is well documented from wetlands and island contexts in Britain and further afield (e.g. Bradley and Gordon 1988; O'Sullivan 2001; Koch 1998; Pryor 2001; cf. Bell, Caseldine, and Neumann 2000: 72).

The reuse of the fragments of the Caldicot 2, Testwood Lakes, and Goldcliff sewn-plank boats is not coincidental, and cannot be attributed simply to the functional reuse of timber. The context of the three sites clearly shows that these places had been foci for the deliberate or votive deposition of a range of material, including bronze weapons, decorated vessels, human skulls, and a dog skeleton. Moreover, the use of boat fragments in constructions such as bridges, jetties, and trackways is highly significant. Reflecting on the implications of travel in illiterate societies, and the bestowing of foreign knowledge on travellers—as explored by Mary Helms (1988)—it could be inferred that it was not only the crew of the sewn-plank boats who would have gained, alongside any exotic objects they might have acquired, this foreign knowledge. Where boats had agency, some of this knowledge, and in particular the experience of travelling to distant lands over seas, would have been acquired by the boats themselves. Thus the fragmentation of the sewn-plank boats at the end of their lives provided opportunities for social enchainment to the aspirant leaders who had sailed on the boats—leaders whose power on land had perhaps been realized in a material context by this time—through the sharing of the craft that had made it possible for them to gain knowledge and power in the first place. The sewn-plank boats had enabled these leaders to move through a liminal phase in their socio-political ascent. The way in which the boats' fragments were used seems to reflect this: rivers would have formed natural and probably liminal boundaries in the Bronze Age, and the use of agents that had shown themselves capable of transgressing such boundaries was deliberate. Evidence for the role of boats as 'liminal agents' (Westerdahl 2008: 25) is even more extensive in the case of boat burials.

Boat fragmentation has been noted in a number of cases by Christer Westerdahl (1995b, 2008). For example, using the array of material found in Norwegian bogs (cf. Shetelig and Johannessen 1929), Westerdahl suggests that the presence of Iron Age stem pieces was not the result of a boatbuilding practice designed to keep fashioned wooden pieces temporarily wet, but rather that these stem pieces were offerings. The discovery of a Viking-period anchor in one of the bogs indicates that offerings of parts or fragments of ships were definitely being made. Since the stem pieces appear never to have been used in actual boats, they may well have been prepared intentionally for sacrificial purposes (Westerdahl 2008: 20). Two stem pieces found in 1878 in a peat bog on the island of Eigg in the Inner Hebrides are probably a parallel to the Norwegian examples (Graham-Campbell and Batey 1998: 84).

While it is accepted that the stem piece is the easiest element to recognize when found as a fragment, the use of this particular piece in a *pars pro toto* representation of the whole boat is no coincidence. Following James Hornell's (1946: 271) description of the prow of the ship as 'the sanctuary of its tutelary deity', Westerdahl argues that the prow of the Viking-age ship signified 'power, leadership or even the king' (2008: 23–6). The importance of the prow, and sometimes the stern, in this period is also shown in the finely carved stem and stern pieces of the Oseberg ship, and in the elaborate prows of the ships of the picture stones of Gotland (Lindqvist 1941, 1942). In view of the socio-political significance of seafaring in the Bronze Age, the presence of the larger figures in the stem and stern of many boats in rock carvings in Østfold and Bohuslän reinforces this association between power and the place on board ships (chapter 8). The question is raised as to whether the removal of the Dover boat transom piece—probably its stem but possibly its stern—was meant to indicate the removal of the fragment that symbolized the power of the boat, or of its master or crew. Should we expect to find it sacrificed in a non-marine context? Or had the transom end been removed to become part of another boat, thus transferring the achievements of one craft to another? The use of fragments of old boats in newly made ones in the Torres Strait is explained in exactly this way: the new craft crossing these waters is endowed with the experience of the old (Ian McNiven pers. comm.).

CONCLUSIONS

This chapter has explored the cultural biographies of boats and ships in the North Sea through three case studies: the use of boats and ships in burial rites, the deliberate killing of boats, and the secondary use of boat fragments in different structures.

Boats have been used in funerary rites from the Mesolithic through to the Middle Ages. The use of actual boats in the Mesolithic, Neolithic, and Bronze Age is somewhat restricted and known to us from a handful of cases, but a larger body of 'stone ships'—settings of stone in the shape of ships beneath burial mounds—is known from southern Scandinavia, especially in the Baltic Sea. Ship burials are better known from the first millennium AD, ranging from cemeteries such as Slusegaard on Bornholm in the first century AD, to the cemeteries at Snape and Sutton Hoo around AD 600, and the Vendel ship burials which commence around the same date but continue on for several centuries; and finally to the many Viking ship burials, including the high-lighted examples of the Oseberg, Gokstad, Tune, Ladby, and Hedeby ships. Stone ships are also known from the Viking period, and the excavation of the Lindholm Høje cemetery, which overlooks the Limfjord, was presented. In the discussion of the role of ships in funerary rites, it was noted that burials involving ships were indicative of a privileged practice, and expressed either socio-political power, a religious role or wealth. Boats and ships were used in funerals only in certain places and at certain times, and the significance of the boats and ships to the deceased and to the mourners was multilayered. In terms of the role of the boat in the ritual, a merely symbolic or metaphorical use of these vessels as facilitating the journey of the deceased from this world to the next was rejected in favour of understanding ships as liminal agents. To kill the boat released its agency from its body, so that it could accompany its master or owner on the onward journey. In the social interactions between the ship and its master or owner, the ship burial was only one stage in a journey that had its history and its future.

The case study investigating the deliberate killing of boats considered the cases of the logboats from Holme Pierrepont and Fiskerton, the Hjortspring warship and the Nydam boats, along with a number of boat finds from bogs, all but one of which were associated with the sacrifice of war booty: Illerup A, Vimose Bog, Ejsbøl Bog, Kragehul Bog, and Kvalsund. There is little doubt that these boats had been deliberately destroyed, and the case study sought to understand why this had happened. It concluded that the boats had been attributed other-than-human agency, which led in some cases to the apportioning of guilt to the boats for their role in enabling attackers to reach their destination (e.g. for the Hjortspring warship and the Nydam boats), and in others to the perception that because the boats had witnessed the restricted ritual of the sacrifice of war booty, they must be killed.

In the analysis of fragmented boats, the focus was on the secondary use of fragments of sewn-plank boats in Britain in the period 1500–800 cal BC. The reuse of fragments of the Caldicot 2 sewn-plank boat in a bridge or track-way, of the Testwood cleat in a bridge, and of the Goldcliff fragment in a trackway could be understood as the functional reuse of timber, were it not for the fact that at all three sites these fragments were accompanied by structured depositions that included human remains, bronze weapons, and other rare finds such as decorated pottery and an amber bead. This use of boat fragments in structures built to cross water is explained as a case of *pars pro toto*. The parts of the boat represented the whole, so that something of the boat's experience of travelling great distances and across (liminal) boundaries was incorporated into the bridge and trackways. The reuse of fragments was also explained as an example of fragmentation, whereby bits of boats would have been given by the boat owner to others, as an act of social enchainment. The significance of the boat fragments lay in the other-than-human agency they carried with them.

The three case studies have come to the same general conclusion, namely that in a hybrid world, boats and ships formed part of broader social networks involving their masters, owners and crews, and the sea itself. These networks also included people who came across the water in such craft, and those whose lands were attacked. The role of ships and boats was significant because of the agency attributed to them. This chapter has only been able to study the final stages of such social interactions, that is when the boat or ship enters the archaeological record, but it seems probable that boats were considered to have forms of agency and were assigned anthropogenic characteristics—such as trustworthiness and reliability—throughout their operational lives. Indeed, the act of travelling and working on boats and ships produced exactly those social interactions that were to make the craft eligible for partaking in funerary rites, or suitable candidates for deliberate destruction, or acceptable gifts in a process of social enchainment.

10

Conclusions: a maritime biography

INTRODUCTION

The purpose of writing this book was to explore aspects of human behaviour that have been, to varying extents, disregarded, overlooked, or ignored in terrestrial-dominated archaeology to date. Recognizing that the sea 'is good to think', it was envisaged that an exploration of North Sea archaeologies could launch something of a 'maritime turn'. This final chapter considers the broad themes of the human past that have been enlightened through this study, and questions if and how these can be reproduced in land-based research. Five interrelated themes are presented here: the essence of nature–society inter-relationships, the attribution of forms of agency to inanimate objects, deviant spaces, the essence of travelling long distances—including the skills and knowledge required for this—and finally, how the sea contributes to shaping social identities.

NATURE–SOCIETY INTERRELATIONSHIPS

The relationship that people had with their environment, or nature–society interrelationships, is fundamental to archaeological research on land and at sea. Explicitly or implicitly, terrestrial archaeology presents us with something of an irreversible progression towards 'encultured' landscapes—narratives wherein the land becomes increasingly less natural and more cultural (see chapter 2). In much of Europe, the 'enculturation' of the world started back in the Post-glacial. It continued throughout the Mesolithic, with the creation of paths through, and clearances within, otherwise natural landscapes. In the Neolithic, 'enculturation' took place through deforestation, and through the apportioning of symbolic significance to natural features and the construction of monuments relating to these. By the late Neolithic and early Bronze Age, large tracts of land were being accommodated to the needs of humans through the creation of field systems and settlements, producing 'cultural landscapes'.

From the middle Bronze Age onwards, according to accepted land-based archaeological thinking, it would appear that nature played at best a minor role, limited to the impact of climate and weather on the crops being cultivated.

The study of the North Sea has fundamentally challenged the nature–culture dichotomy. The concept of 'enculturation' places *Homo sapiens* centre stage in a changing world, but underestimates the role played by the sea and rivers, as well as animals, trees, and plants, as important co-constructors of landscape. Until relatively recently, people could not physically alter the sea. At sea, there was no perception that nature and culture were separated entities. The sea was indeed socialized, through the construction of structures such as the terpen and dikes around its edges, and through journeys across the sea and maritime myths and stories, but this in itself did not produce an 'encultured' sea. Throughout the preceding chapters, aspects of the sea as a dynamic landscape have been discussed at length, and this dynamic aspect can be seen within the context of different timescales. At the long-term scale, sea-level change drowned extensive landscapes around the North Sea and was responsible for the transgression of coastal and riverine mires; it forced communities to change their way of life, to adopt boatbuilding and seafaring skills, to modify their consumption and production of maritime and terrestrial food, and to construct some of the largest man-made structures in the region, the dikes. At the medium-term scale, the interaction of the sea and sedimentation patterns created, moved, and destroyed islands, saltmarshes, and coasts. While this created opportunities for some, such as the terp dwellers who made the best use of the rich saltmarshes, there were others—such as the urban dwellers who found their ports silting up—whose livelihoods were threatened. At the short-term scale, storms and tides could take land that had been reclaimed from the sea—that had been home for many generations—as well as destroying boats and the lives of seafarers and fishermen, and merchants whose wealth was dependent on the successful completion of the most recent expedition. The dynamic sea produced perceptions and experiences of a part of nature very different from that seen on land. These are visible archaeologically in the deposition of artefacts and human remains on the edges of the sea, in the construction of particular monuments, and in the treatment of seafaring craft. While the sea was at times understood as a bountiful resource, it was never relied on to the same extent as was the faithful land to produce the next crop of grain. The sea was not a trustworthy part of the world. When its storms capsized a boat and drowned fishermen, or when tidal surges breached dikes and submerged reclaimed lands, the sea showed itself as a wild(er)ness, or as the realm of angry gods, ancestors or mythical creatures.

However, the sea was not merely an unchangeable natural force. Christopher Connery has written about the perception of the sea in 'western' beliefs and philosophies, arguing that our Hebrew and Christian heritage bequeaths us with 'particular antagonisms towards the ocean' (2006: 495). However, while the sea is often considered a 'designation of chaos, the realm of the dead, transformation, darkness', in the biblical texts the sea is 'too material, too spatial, too present, to be merely metaphorical' (ibid. 499). In Norse or Scandinavian mythology we note similar mixed understandings of the sea, passed on by way of the Icelandic Sagas and The Poetic Edda. In the Middle Ages, the broadly held beliefs mirror the writings from the Bible closely (e.g. Corbin 1994: 1–18). The sea is probably most evocatively described by the poet W. H. Auden in his famous *The enchafd flood or the romantic iconography of the sea* (1951: 17): 'the sea (. . .) is the state of barbaric vagueness and disorder out of which civilization has emerged and into which, unless it is saved by the effort of gods and men, it is always likely to relapse'. Only in the Romantic period, a time of mercantile expansion and economic growth, did the sea become a positive force (Corbin 1994: 19–53). Modernity at sea only emerges in the second half of the 19th century (Casarino 2002), with the appearance of steam and great ships that gave at least the illusion that the sea had been conquered.

Nature–society interrelationships at sea have retained much of their hybrid nature in the 21st century. Take the example of fish. On the one hand, fish consumption in the countries around the North Sea remains high, and fish reaches inland markets more effectively than at any time in the past. Fish consumption, especially fatty fish such as mackerel, is recognized as having important health benefits, reducing mortality caused by heart disease and certain cancers (e.g. Welch et al. 2002). On the other hand, fishing remains one of the most dangerous jobs in the modern world (e.g. Reilley 1985). Overfishing is the principal cause of the demise of fish populations in the North Sea, as well as being the single greatest contributor to the destruction of marine ecosystems (Gislason 1994). Thus, in the hybrid sea the health of humans and that of fish are closely intertwined.

Another example of the hybrid nature–society interrelationship in the 21st century is carbon emission-induced climate change. As a direct consequence of human activity, global temperatures will increase and the melting of the polar ice and glaciers will result in a higher sea-level. Sea-level is currently predicted by the Intergovernmental Panel on Climate Change to rise by 0.18–0.59 m above current global mean levels by 2100, a pace of change not seen since the Mesolithic. Critically, rising sea-levels will result in waves penetrating closer to the shore, thus exacerbating coastal erosion. A renewed phase of marine transgression and the drowning of low-lying coastal lands should be anticipated, along with the resulting threat to people's lives and livelihoods.

It is evident from the study of the relationship we have with the sea, both in the past as described in the preceding chapters and in the present as illustrated here, that for the people living and working around the North Sea any relationship they may have is a hybrid one. This has implications for land-based archaeological studies, which to date have possibly been too anthropo-centric, too focused on the impact on the land of human activity, and on the creation of cultural landscapes, for a full understanding to be reached of the hybrid interrelationship between society and nature in the co-creation of the worlds we inhabit.

FORMS OF AGENCY

The second theme, attribution of forms of agency to inanimate objects, is closely linked to the first. Agency is a relatively new concept in archaeological research, and has been largely reserved for humans. For example, the 17 papers in the influential edited volume *Agency in archaeology* (Dobres and Robb eds. 2000) are concerned with only human forms of agency. Relatively few terrestrial archaeologists have embraced the attribution of agency to animals and inani-mate objects, but where this has been done it has produced new ways of understanding the relationship between humans and non-human animals, for example in the (re-)interpretation of dog burials in the Mesolithic, or in the destruction of particular objects akin to the burial of humans (e.g. Fowler 2004).

The preceding chapters have extended these discussions through the attri-bution of other-than-human agency to the sea, and to the craft that engaged with the sea. Marine agency, be it exercised directly, or else indirectly through the proxy of deities such as Neptune, the Norse god of the sea Aegir, the Christian God or other creatures such as those noted in the myths recorded by Walter Traill Dennison, was understood in the past as something that was as 'real' as the agency of humans. The deposition on the edge of the sea's visible encroachment on the land of bronze tools and weapons, and human remains, was not just undertaken within particular economical or socio-political frameworks. Rather, these depositions were understood in the Neolithic and Bronze Age to be sacrifices to a living sea, in the same way as sacrifices were made to other deities. It is unsurprising that forms of agency were also attributed to the boats and ships that provided the means to travel across the sea, and this has been explored through the study of the cultural biogra-phies of boats. Boats with identity and agency have been made archaeologically visible through boat and ship burials, through the killing of boats, and in the symbolic reuse of boat fragments in a process of social enchainment. In all three cases, the observed treatment of the craft can only be explained through the attribution of identity and agency to these boats and ships.

In our world, the sea has retained forms of agency for a much longer time than any terrestrial 'scape' or phenomenon. One of the best-known modernist authors of sea narratives, Joseph Conrad, offers an insightful understanding of this in his autobiographic *The mirror of the sea* (1906: 127):

On that exquisite day of gently breathing peace and veiled sunshine perished my romantic love to what men's imagination had proclaimed the most august aspect of Nature. The cynical indifference of the sea to the merits of human suffering and courage, laid bare in this ridiculous, panic-tainted performance extorted from the dire extremity of nine good and honourable seamen, revolted me. I saw the duplicity of the sea's most tender mood. It was so because it could not help itself, but the awed respect of the early days was gone. I felt ready to smile bitterly at its enchanting charm and glare viciously at its furies. In a moment, before we shoved off, I had looked coolly at the life of my choice. Its illusions were gone, but its fascination remained. I had become a seaman at last.

The ascendancy of the steamship in professional seafaring in the 19th century did much to remove forms of agency from ships, especially the larger ones, which were subjected to lesser extents to the moods of the sea. No longer were the seamen dependent on natural forces in completing their journeys in good time. The engineer working in the bowels of the ship, rather than the sailor working on the deck against the wind, had become the key to a successful passage. Nevertheless, ships never seem to have lost all their human-like characteristics. To illustrate this point, we can again turn to Joseph Conrad's autobiography and his description of the essence of the sailing boat and the steamship (1906: 32–3):

> The ... [sailing boat] seems to draw its strength from the very soul of the world, its formidable ally, held to obedience by the frailest bonds, like a fierce ghost captured in a snare of something even finer than spun silk. ... The modern steamship advances upon a still and overshadowed sea with a pulsating tremor of her frame, an occasional clang in her depths, as if she had an iron heart in her iron body; with a thudding rhythm in her progress and the regular beat of her propeller, heard afar in the night with an august and plodding sound as of the march of an inevitable future. But in a gale, the silent machinery of a sailing-ship would catch not only the power, but the wild and exulting voice of the world's soul.

In the modern languages used around the North Sea, the overwhelming perception of the sea is one of a natural entity and a force for good. It is the provider of fish and enabler of trade, and in more recent decades it has been perceived additionally as a somewhat distant place that has contributed greatly to the wealth of western nations, by providing resources such as North Sea oil and North Sea gas. Nevertheless, even today storms and accidents are said to 'claim' or even 'demand' victims, or 'take' lives (Kirby and Hinkkanen 2000: 263). This can be understood as the humanization of natural phenomena, or as the continued attribution of agency to the sea. However, to give the sea attributes that are expressed as human intentions and emotions in our colloquial use of words does not necessarily equate with a salient understanding of the sea as being alive; rather it represents suppressed beliefs in times of mortal danger. Thence, most written works over the past two millennia do not present a singular view of the sea possessed with forms of other-than-human agency, but such agency often forms an undercurrent in these narratives. When the sea behaves unpredictably or badly, it is our emotional rather than our rational reaction that attributes forms of agency to the sea.

Throughout the past, and sometimes in the present, people attributed agency both to the sea and to the craft in which the sea was experienced. The implication of this for the archaeological study of the land is that on land, too, features and phenomena would most likely have been assigned forms of agency to an extent that remains under-represented in archaeological writings. The attribution of agency is highly probable in the case of events such as earthquakes and volcanic eruptions, but the attribution of forms of agency may well have extended to mountains, rivers, landscapes, forests, trees, animals, and plants—for example in the form of healing powers of certain herbs. The seasonal rise and fall of raised mires may have been perceived as the 'breathing' of a living ecosystem that had agency, not unlike the 'breathing' of the sea evidenced by the tides or the waves (Van de Noort and O'Sullivan 2006: 59). And, as an analogy to the boats and ships, carts may have been attributed knowledge and experience in facilitating journeys to distant lands. Their inclusion in graves has been observed in the Hünsruck-Eifel region, in the Middle Rhine, the Ardennes, Champagne, East Yorkshire, from Nijmegen, and from near Edinburgh (e.g. Cahen-Delhaye 1975; 1998; Bloemers 1986; Stead 1991; Carter and Hunter 2003). As with the use of boats in funerary rites, the burial of carts could have been intended as a way of releasing their agency, so that they might accompany the dead to the next world.

DEVIANT SPACES

The third theme concerns the sea as a deviant space. In archaeological research on land, there appears to be very little room for deviant spaces. Indeed, while social sciences have made much of the study of the people who are, or have been, marginalized in modern societies, archaeological research barely touches upon the 'undercurrents' of past societies.

In the preceding chapters the North Sea has been described, on a number of occasions, as a 'Deleuzian Ocean'. This term has been used as shorthand for the ideas developed by Gilles Deleuze concerning the sea as the realm of the unbound, unconstricted, and free. Whereas the land has for millennia been controlled or policed, to greater or lesser extents, by the elite or the establishment, until very recently the sea could not be regulated in the same way, be that by early modern states, medieval kings, or even the Roman *classis*

Britannica—let alone by the elite networks of the late Neolithic and Bronze Age. Examples of how the North Sea has functioned as a Deleuzian Ocean include the arrival of settlers in coastal regions who avoided control from the dominant political forces—such as the freemen in Holland or the terp dwellers in the Wadden Sea, or the early Christian missionaries who founded monasteries on offshore places like the island of Lindisfarne. The deviant nature of the North Sea comes to the fore, in particular, in the study of the ship as heterotopia, a concept from the mind of Michel Foucault. The daily practice of seafaring produced distinct social networks on board ships. In the Neolithic and Bronze Age, these provided aspirant leaders with the mechanisms to become future rulers. The link between the master and the crew on board ships and the patron and his retinue on land, goes some way towards explaining the rise of a social elite in this period. Archaeological evidence in the North Sea for piracy and raiding of coastal settlements goes back to the fourth century BC, in the form of the Hjortspring boat. Such deviant practices offered contenders to the establishment opportunities to gain fame, fortune, and social networks with which they could challenge the terrestrial authorities. For the Franks, the Saxons, and especially the Vikings, piracy and raiding provided fundamental building blocks for their rise to power. Piracy remained a deviant force in the North Sea until the 17th century, with towns such as Dunkirk engaging in state-sponsored piracy or privateering.

During the 20th century, the North Sea was largely stripped of its final remnants of defiance and resistance to the established order. The invention of sonar, radar, and radio, and the growing role of aeroplanes and satellites made the North Sea a much more visible place. The discovery of oil and gas in the North Sea resulted in the creation of exclusive economic sectors, agreed between the nation-states bordering the North Sea in the 1960s, and no part of the North Sea remains 'no man's land'. Similarly, the North Sea fishing industry has been restricted and controlled through the European Commission quota allocations. The construction of oil and gas platforms and their associated infrastructure—such as the pipes that transport the minerals to the land—and, most recently, offshore wind farms, has turned the North Sea into a physically modified landscape.

The archaeological study of the North Sea has shown the importance of deviant spaces in understanding how socio-political change and innovation can come about at the level of societies, and how individuals who aspired to wealth and power used the sea as a place to build fame, prestige, and retinues. On land, similar deviant spaces must have existed, but the archaeological study of these has yet to start in earnest. Here, monuments are all too readily understood as representing aspects of social reproduction. Similarly, material culture as representative of connectivity between, or enchainment of, people—resulting in deviant groups and individuals, practices, and places—tends to be overlooked.

TRAVEL, SKILL AND KNOWLEDGE OF THE SEA

The fourth theme concerns the importance of travel, especially long-distance travel, the skill of seafaring and the knowledge of the sea. Archaeological research on land has taken for granted the ability to travel; moreover, no skill or knowledge was apparently required for this. While archaeologists frequently consider the socio-economical practices behind the exchange of objects, much less attention is paid to the practicalities of the artefacts' journeys, or to the ritual significance of travel.

The preceding chapters have shown something of the varied nature of travel in the North Sea. Temporal and geographical variations were noted, alongside differences in the materials that were moved around, and the different craft that facilitated travel, trade, and exchange. Building on the work of Mary Helms (1988) on the significance of travel in premodern societies, and of a number of archaeologists who have developed her ideas in archaeological contexts, it was argued that travelling on the North Sea was never devoid of meanings that went beyond simply moving from one place to another. Where archaeological evidence was available, it was possible to identify that the use of boats and ships had ritual connotations linked to the contemporary understanding of the cosmos—whether it be the way in which the sun moved around the earth, as surmised from the Bronze Age rock carvings and engravings, or the nature of a cosmos in which gods, ancestors, and creatures gave agency to the sea. It was also noted that travel offered opportunities for those who successfully completed their voyages, for example in the acquisition of foreign knowledge and exotic materials—thus building fame, fortune and retinues—or in the attainment of sainthood. The skills of the boatbuilders and mariners, and the role of the navigator and his knowledge of the sea, were crucial to the successful completion of these journeys. This continued to be the case well into the modern period. For example, detailed local knowledge of the tides and shifting sandbanks continued to be required to navigate the approaches to some of the largest ports around the North Sea. Only in the 19th century did engineering prowess allow for the construction of canals directly to the sea, such as the Noordzee-kanaal, opened in 1824, which linked the port of Amsterdam to the North Sea at IJmuiden. Also, until the middle of the 20th century, fishermen continued to put more faith in their own ability to predict the weather, based on personal and shared experience, than in any 'official' weather forecast, which was considered either too unreliable, or else too general to be of use in real life on the sea (Slager and De Schipper 1990).

The availability of detailed charts, and weather forecasts based on satellite images which are both increasingly accurate and of a high resolution, and the use of GPS—which makes it possible to define the position of a craft accurately with only the slightest of skill and knowledge—have changed the significance of travel, skill, and knowledge in the North Sea. While fishermen and merchantmen still possess relevant skills and knowledge, the ritual of travel has all but disappeared. This changing perception of travel and the sea is also reflected in the emergence in the 20th century of the heritage industry and the transformation of many traditional fishing villages around the North Sea into resorts aimed at attracting tourists. For example, the demise of the traditional fishing fleet at Grimsby in Lincolnshire has been accompanied by the creation of the Fishing Heritage Centre, which boasts the recreation of a 1950s fishing trip 'with authentic aromas and moving deck, and scenes from the street and home life of old Grimsby' (Fishing Heritage Centre website: www.nelincs.gov.uk). Similarly, the Esbjerg Fisheries and Maritime Museum in Jutland includes an open-air exhibition of a harbour from around 1940, removed from Esbjerg when its seaport was built, and reconstructed *ex situ* and without water in the museum grounds (Figure 45). The Grimsby and Esbjerg heritage experiences are replicated elsewhere around the North Sea. For most modern landlubbers, an understanding of the sea comes in the shape of a sanitized experience in a designated place where, if one is lucky, there is a 'stroking' tank and a restaurant with fish on the menu.

From the study of travel, skills, and knowledge of the sea, it is apparent that to go to sea was not simply a matter of practicalities, but was something embedded

Figure 45. Esbjerg Fisheries and Maritime Museum: the old fishing harbour reconstructed

in cosmological frameworks. The skills and knowledge required for the successful completion of journeys were special, restricted, and highly valued. The message emerging from this for the archaeological study of the land is that the cosmological frameworks and restrictions in which travel on land in the prehistoric and early historic past was undertaken have not been fully recognized. To travel across the sea meant to acquire new knowledge and different materials, to meet new people, redefine one's identity and construct new stories. The same may be said for the skills required when travelling great distances over land; this is especially true of the importance, in the absence of maps and travel guides, of owning an understanding of the land and of foreign people. Travelling long distances was not a simple matter of setting off on a walk. It required knowledge, and this knowledge was likely to have been restricted and guarded, just as the navigators guarded their knowledge of the sea.

MARITIME IDENTITIES

The final theme concerns the role of the sea in the construction of social identities. Identifying and comprehending the significance of social identities is a theme well understood and developed in terrestrial archaeology. However, the role of landscape in the construction of social identities, while acknowledged, has not played a significant role in this.

In the preceding chapters, it has been argued that the North Sea was not a deterministic force in the construction of social identities of communities who lived on its edge. Rather, different groups defined their identities to greater or lesser extents by their relationship with the sea. It has been argued, for example, that the consumption of fish was not a defining characteristic of social identity at the Mesolithic–Neolithic transition to the extent that it has previously been made out to be. Nevertheless, the sea was a landscape that shaped the lives of many people, and the archaeological evidence allows for the identification of certain aspects of past material cultures as expressions of social identities for specific groups. For example, fishermen, from the Mesolithic through to the Middle Ages, expressed their social identities through their skills and tools, which included harpoons and leisters, hooks-and-line, nets, fishweirs and, above all, their boats. Their identities would also have been defined by their daily work patterns—emptying fishweirs when the tides were low, for example—rather than by the rhythms of day and night. Through the ages, seafarers of all kinds would have defined their social identities as mariners through their membership of crews, and possibly through special clothing and the ownership of tools such as paddles, and through the use or avoidance of certain words and practices. For other coastal dwellers, such as the inhabitants of the terpen or the people who lived behind the early dikes, the sea was part of their daily lives and shaped much of their daily practice and social identities.

In the present world, this also seems to be the case. The countries or nations around the North Sea define their identity to a certain degree through their relationship with the sea. For the British, this has taken the form of stressing their insularity at times of crises. In this context, Sebastian Sobecki (2008: 1–3) reminds us of Winston Churchill's House of Commons speech on 4th June 1940: 'We shall defend our Island, whatever the cost may be. We shall fight on the beaches, we shall fight on the landing-grounds, we shall fight in the fields and in the streets, we shall fight in the hills; we shall never surrender.' Sobecki notes that the islandness of the English/British as a defining characteristic of identity in times of crisis has a long history and goes back to the Middle Ages. For the Dutch, the fight against the sea itself is a defining aspect of national social identity. The story of Hans Brinker, the boy from Haarlem who prevented a catastrophic flood, has been eagerly embraced by the Dutch, despite Hans himself being a fictional character from the 1865 novel *Hans Brinker or the Silver Skates* by the American author Mary Mapes Dodge.

Intriguingly, in defining national social identities, the archaeology of the sea has played a significant role as well. The adoption of the Vikings within the national identity of Norway can be attributed, to no small extent, to the excavation of the Oseberg and Gokstad ships, which caught the nation's imagination and helped to shift the perception of Vikings as murderers and rapists to one of maritime explorers and achievers. The Danes have followed suit, and the excavation of the Skuldelev boats in the Roskilde Fjord, and the Viking ringforts such as Trelleborg, Aggersborg, and Frykat, have contributed much to the central position held by the Vikings in Danish national identity. At the beginning of the 21st century, the Vikings are used as 'trademarks for present-day Scandinavian industry to symbolize good craftsmanship and a high level of entrepreneur spirit' (Crumlin-Pedersen 1997: 10).

The creation of national social identities, with reference to the North Sea and the past, is an ongoing process, and stories of national identity are told in many of the maritime museums that exist around the North Sea. The story of the Viking North Sea is explored in the Vikingskipshuset in Oslo (Figure 46), and the Vikingeskibsmuseet in Roskilde; the Bremer cog, which takes centre stage at the Deutschen Schiffahrtmuseum, tells the story of the Hansa League; the story of the Dutch Golden Age is told in the Nederlands Scheepvaart-museum in Amsterdam and at the Nationaal Scheepshistorish Centrum Bataviawerf in Lelystad; and the story of Britain's imperial hegemony of the sea is a central theme at the National Maritime Museum in Greenwich. From within the discipline, maritime archaeology has been criticized for its attention to 'highlights' of national pasts (e.g. Cederlund 1997; Maarleveld 2004). The sea is also incorporated into regional and local identities, which tend to be closely linked to the role of fishing and its importance for local economies.

Figure 46. A national symbol: the Oseberg ship in the Vikingskipshuset in Oslo

The story of the small-scale fishing industry in 19th-century Jutland, for example, is told in the Esbjerg Fisheries and Maritime Museum. The Shetland Museum in Lerwick also focuses on fishing, as does the Zuiderzeemuseum, complete with *klederdracht*, in Enkhuizen. In all these examples the museum could be said to act as proxy for social identity.

It is clear, from this maritime study, that the environment played a significant role in the construction of social identities for communities living on and around the North Sea. At sea, the best and the worst aspects of the human past are represented. It is because these aspects speak to the imagination that they are selected for the building of social identities. For the archaeology of the land, a greater recognition of the role of the environment in the construction of social identities may be required.

FINAL THOUGHT

Terrestrial landscapes were and are continually changing, receiving the imprint of human existence. This has produced multiple narratives of trajectories of 'enculturation'. These narratives are understood to represent human socio-political, economical, and religious discourses, frequently conducted by the elite. The focus on the sea in this book confronts this established way of thinking. Until very recently, the sea has remained a physically unmodified part of the world, and while it was socialized through the construction of terpen and dikes on its edges, and through maritime stories and seafaring journeys, it has retained much of its other-than-human agency in the eyes of seafarers, fishermen, and coastal dwellers. By its nature it prolonged the existence of deviant spaces, and continues to be a co-constructor of seascapes and coastal landscapes. Engagement with the sea, either from boats and ships, or from the coastal margins, challenges the notion that nature is merely a human construct that can be 'encultured' by humanity. When nature ceases to be a human construct, and we acknowledge that nature and culture/society are interrelated, new ways of thinking about the hybrid role of humanity in the world are opened up. Thus, the maritime turn in terrestrial archaeological research involves a shift in perception, from an anthropocentric consideration of the 'enculturation' of the land to a recognition of the hybrid socialization of the environment. Because premodern ideas and beliefs that have long since vanished from the land are still present at sea, the North Sea has been good to think.

Bibliography

Abrahamsen, N. (1992). 'Evidence for church orientation by magnetic compass in twelfth-century Denmark'. *Archaeometry* 34: 293–303.

Ambrosiani, B. (1982). 'Background to the boat-graves of the Mälaren valley', in Lamm and H.-Å. Nordström (eds.): 17–22.

Andersen, A. C. H. (2003). 'New investigations in Ejsbøl Bog', in Jørgensen, Storgaard, and Gebauer (eds.): 246–57.

Andersen, S. H. (1987). 'Mesolithic dug-outs and paddles from Tybrind Vig, Denmark'. *Acta Archaeologica* 57: 87–106.

——(1995). 'Coastal adaptation and marine exploitation in Late Mesolithic Denmark—with special emphasis on the Limfjord region', in Fisher (ed.): 41–66.

——(2007). 'Shell middens (*"Køkkenmøddinger"*) in Danish prehistory as a reflection of the marine environment', in Milner, Craig, and Bailey (eds.): 31–45.

Aner, E. and Kersten, K. (1978). *Die Funde der älteren Bronzezeit der Nordischen Kreises in Dänemark, Schleswig-Holstein und Niedersachsen IV.* Neumünster: Wachholz.

Appadurai, A. (1986). 'Introduction: commodities and the politics of value', in Appadurai (ed.): 3–63.

—— (ed.) (1986). *The social life of things; commodities in cultural perspective.* Cambridge: Cambridge University Press.

Armit, I. (2003). *Towers in the North; the brochs of Scotland.* Stroud: Tempus.

Arnold, B. (1992). 'Batellerie gallo-romaine sur le lac de Neuchâtel'. *Archéologie Neuchâteloise* 12/13.

——(1999). 'Some remarks on Romano-Celtic boat construction and Bronze Age wood technology'. *INJA* 28: 34–44.

Arwidsson, G. (1980). *Båtgravarna i Valsgärde.* Borås: Statens historiska museum.

Auden, W. H. (1951). *The enchafed flood: or the romantic iconography of the sea.* London: Random House.

Bailey, G. N. (1978). 'Shell middens as indicators of postglacial economies: a territorial perspective', in P. Mellars (ed.) *The Early Postglacial settlement of northern Europe; an ecological perspective.* Pittsburgh (PA): University of Pittsburgh Press, 37–63.

——and Milner, N. (2002). 'Coastal hunter-gatherers and social evolution: marginal or central?' *Before farming; the archaeology and anthropology of hunter-gatherers* 3–4: 1.

Bakker, J. A. (1990). 'Views on the Stone Age 3: 1848–1931: the impact of the Hilversum finds of 1853 on Dutch prehistoric archaeology'. *BROB* 40: 73–99.

Ballin-Smith, B., Carter, S., Haigh, D., and Neil, N. (1994). *Howe: four millennia of Orkney prehistory, excavations 1978–1982.* Edinburgh: Society of Antiquaries of Scotland (Monograph Series 9).

Barber, J., Duffy, A., and O'Sullivan, J. (1996). 'The excavation of two Bronze Age burial cairns at Bu Farm, Rapness, Westray, Orkney'. *PSAS* 126: 103–20.

——Clark, C., Cressy, M., Crone, A., Hale, A., Henderson, J., Housley, R., Sands, R., and Sheridan, A. (eds.) *Archaeology from the wetlands: recent perspectives. Proceedings of the 11th WARP Conference, Edinburgh.* Edinburgh: Society of Antiquaries of Scotland.

Barrett, J. C. (1994). *Fragment of antiquity; an archaeology of social life in Britain, 2900–1200 BC.* Oxford (UK) and Cambridge (USA): Blackwell.

——Bradley, R., and Green M. (1991). *Landscape, monuments and society; the prehistory of the Cranborne Chase.* Cambridge: Cambridge University Press.

Barrett, J. H. (1997). 'Fish trade in Norse Orkney and Caithness: a zooarchaeological approach'. *Antiquity* 71: 616–38.

——(2007). 'What caused the Viking Age?' *Antiquity* 82: 671–85.

——and Richards, M. P. (2004). 'Identity, gender, religion and economy: new isotope and radiocarbon evidence for marine resource identification in early historic Orkney, Scotland, UK'. *European Journal of Archaeology* 7: 249–71.

——Locker, A. M., and Roberts, C. M. (2004a). ' "Dark Age Economics" revisited: the English fish bone evidence AD 600–1600'. *Antiquity* 78: 618–36.

——Locker, A. M., and Roberts, C. M. (2004b). 'The origins of intensive marine fishing in medieval Europe: the English evidence'. *Proceedings of the Royal Society B* 271: 2417–21.

Barton, N., Roberts, A. J., and Roe, D. A. (eds.) (1991). *The Late Glacial in North-west Europe.* London: CBA (Research Report 77).

Bazelmans, J. (1991). 'Conceptualising early Germanic political structure: a review of the use of the concept of *Gefolgschaft*', in Roymans and Theuws (eds.): 91–129.

——(2009). 'The early-medieval use of ethnic names from classical Antiquity: the case of the Frisians', in T. Derks and N. Roymans (eds.) *Ethnic constructs in Antiquity; the role of power and tradition.* Amsterdam: Amsterdam University Press, 321–38.

——Gerrets, D., and Vos, P. (1998). 'Zoden aan de dijk; kleinschalige dijkbouw in Friesland van de Romeinse tijd'. *Noorderbreedte* 6: 1.

Beck, C. and Shennan, S. (1991). *Amber in prehistoric Britain.* Oxford: Oxbow.

Behre, K.-E. (2003). 'Coastal development, sea-level change and settlement history during the later Holocene in the Clay District of Lower Saxony (Niedersachsen), northern Germany'. *Quaternary International* 112: 37–53.

——(2007). 'A new Holocene sea-level curve for the southern North Sea'. *Boreas* 36: 82–102.

Bell, M. A. (1992). 'Field survey and excavation at Goldcliff, 1992', in Bell (ed.): 15–29.

——(ed.) (1992). *Archaeology in the Severn estuary. Severn Estuary Levels Research Committee Annual Report.* Lampeter: University of Wales.

——(1993). 'Intertidal Archaeology at Goldcliff in the Severn Estuary', in Coles, Fenwick, and Hutchinson (eds.): 9–13.

——(2007). *Prehistoric coastal communities; the Mesolithic in western Britain.* York: CBA (Research Report 149).

——Caseldine, A., and Neumann, H. (2000). *Prehistoric intertidal archaeology in the Welsh Severn Estuary.* York: CBA (Research Report 120).

Beowulf. trans. S. Heaney (2000). New York: W. W. Norton and Company.

Berntsson, A. (2005). *Två män ien båt—om människans relation till havet i bronsåldern.* Lund: University of Lund (Institute of Archaeology Report Series 93).

Besteman, J. C. (1990). 'North Holland AD 400–1200: turning tide or tide turned?', in Besteman, Bos, and Heidinga (eds.): 91–120.

———Bos, J. M., and Heidinga, H. A. (eds.) (1990). *Medieval archaeology in the Netherlands; studies presented to H. H. van Regteren Altena.* Assen/Maastricht: Van Gorcum.

———, ———, Gerrets, D. A., Heidinga, H. A., and De Koning, J. (eds.) (1999). *The excavations at Wijnaldum; reports on Frisia in Roman and medieval times.* Rotterdam: A. A. Balkema.

Bjerck, H. B. (1995). 'The North Sea continent and the pioneer settlement of Norway', in Fisher (ed.): 131–44.

———(2007). 'Mesolithic coastal settlements and shell middens in Norway', in Milner, Craig, and Bailey (eds.): 5–30.

Bloemers, T. (1986). 'A cart burial from a small Middle Iron Age cemetery at Nijmegen', in M. van Bakel, R. Hogesteijn, and P. van de Velde (eds.) *Private politics: a multidisciplinary approach to 'Big Man' systems.* Leiden: E. J. Brill, 76–91.

Bockius, R. (2006). *Die Spätrömischen Schiffswracks aus Mainz.* Mainz: RGZM.

Boersma, J. (2005). 'Woonheuvels in de kustvlakte. Onderzoek van de Friese en Groninger terpen', in Louwe Kooijmans *et al.* (eds.): 557–60.

Bogaers, J. E. A. T. and Gysseling, M. (1971). 'Nehalennia, Gimio en Ganuenta'. *Oudheidkundige Mededeelingen van het Rijksmuseum van Oudheden te Leiden* 52: 86–92.

Bond, E. A. (ed.) (1866). *Chronica Monasterii de Melsa.* Vol. I. London: Roll Series.

Bonde, N. and Christensen, A. E. (1993). 'Dendrochronological dating of the Viking Age ship burials at Oseberg, Gokstad and Tune, Norway'. *Antiquity* 67: 575–83.

Bondevik, S., Mangerud, J., Dawson, S., Dawson, A., and Lohne, Ø. (2005). 'Evidence for three North Sea tsunamis at the Shetland Islands between 8,000 and 1,500 years ago'. *Quaternary Science Reviews* 24: 1757–77.

Boomert, A. and Bright, A. J. (2007). 'Island archaeology: in search of a new horizon'. *Island Studies Journal* 2: 3–26.

Bowen, E. G. (1972). *Britain and the western seaways.* London: Thames and Hudson.

Bown, P,. Bristow, C., Burnett, J., Clark, P., Gibson, A., de Silva, N., Williams, D., Wilson, T., and Young, J. (2004). 'Other artefacts from the site', in Clark (ed.) (2004a): 211–28.

Bradley, R. (1984). *The social foundations of prehistoric Britain.* London: Routledge.

———(1990). *The passage of arms.* Cambridge: Cambridge University Press.

———(1998). 'Ruined buildings, ruined stones: enclosures, tombs and natural places in the Neolithic of south-west England'. *World Archaeology* 30: 13–22.

———(2000). *An archaeology of natural places.* London: Routledge.

———(2007). *The prehistory of Britain and Ireland.* Cambridge: Cambridge University Press.

———and Gordon, K. (1988). 'Human skulls from the river Thames, their dating and significance'. *Antiquity* 62: 503–9.

Braudel, F. (1949/1972). *La Méditerranée et le Monde Méditerranéen à l'Epoque de Philippe II/The Mediterranean and the Mediterranean world in the age of Philip II.* Paris: Armand Colin/London: Collins.

Brennand, M. and Taylor, J. (2003). 'The survey and excavation of a Bronze Age timber circle at Holme-next-the-Sea, Norfolk, 1998–9'. *PPS* 69: 1–84.

Brice, E. (2002). 'Falling masts, rising masters: the ethnography of virtue in Caesar's account of the Veneti'. *The American Journal of Philology* 123: 601–22.

Brinkhuizen, D. (2006). 'Fish', in Louwe Kooijmans and Jongste (eds.): 449–70.

Broodbank, C. (1993). 'Ulysses without sails: trade, distance, knowledge and power in the early Cyclades'. *World Archaeology* 24: 315–31.

——(2000). *An island archaeology of the early Cyclades*. Cambridge: Cambridge University Press.

Bronk Ramsey, C. (2006). *OxCal Program v4.0*. (http://c14.arch.ox.ac.uk/)

Bruce-Mitford, R. (1975). *The Sutton Hoo ship-burial*. Vol 1. London: British Museum.

——(1978). *The Sutton Hoo ship-burial. Vol 2*. London: British Museum.

——(1983). *The Sutton Hoo ship-burial. Vol 3*. London: British Museum.

Brück, J. (1995). 'A place for the dead: the role of human remains in the Late Bronze Age'. *PPS* 61: 245–77.

——(1999). 'Houses, lifecycles and deposition on Middle Bronze Age settlements in southern England'. *PPS* 65: 145–66.

——(2001). 'Body methaphors and technologies of transformation in the English Middle and Late Bronze Age', in J. Brück (ed.) *Bronze Age landscape; tradition and transformation*. Oxford: Oxbow: 149–60.

Butler, J. J. (1963). *Bronze Age connections across the North Sea*. Groningen: Biologisch-Archeologisch Instituut, Rijksuniversiteit Groningen (*Palaeohistoria* 9).

Buurman, J. (1998/9). 'Archaeobotanical investigations of a Middle and Late Bronze Age settlement site at Westwoud (West-Friesland)'. *BROB* 43: 99–140.

Caesar. The *Gallic War*. trans. H. J. Edwards (1917). London: Loeb Classical Library.

Cahen-Delhaye, A. (1975). 'Frülatènezeitliche Wagengräber aus den Ardennen (Belgien)'. *Archäologisches Korrespondenzblatt* 5: 47–58.

——(1998). 'Rites funéraires au sud de l'Ardenne belge'. *Revue archéologique de Picardie* 1–2: 59–70.

Calder, C. S. T. (1950). 'Report on the excavation of a Neolithic temple at Stanydale in the parish of Sandsting, Shetland'. *PSAS* 85: 185–205.

Cameron, T. D. J., Crosby, A., Balson, P. S., Jeffrey, D. H., Lott, G. K., Bulat, J., and Harrison, D. J. (1992). *The geology of the southern North Sea; British Geological Survey United Kingdom offshore regional report*. London: HMSO.

Campbell, J. (ed.) (1991). *The Anglo-Saxons*. London: Penguin

Capelle, T. (1995). 'Bronze-Age stone ships', in Crumlin-Pedersen and Thye (eds.): 71–6.

Capelli, C., Redhead, N., Abernethy, J. K., Gratrix, F., Wilson, J. F., Moen, T., Hervig, T., Richards, M., Stumpf, M. P. H., Underhill, P. A., Bradshaw, P., Shaha, A., Thomas, M. G., Bradman, N., and Goldstein, D. B. (2003). 'A Y-chromosome census of the British Isles'. *Current Biology* 13: 979–84.

Cappers, R. T. J. and Raemaekers, D. C. M. (2008). 'Cereal cultivation at Swifterbant?' *Current Anthropology* 49: 385–402.

Carter, S. and Hunter, F. (2003). 'An Iron Age cart burial from Scotland'. *Antiquity* 59: 531–35.

Carver, M. (1995). 'Boat-burials in Britain: ancient custom or political signal?', in Crumlin-Pedersen and Thye (eds.): 111–24.

——(2004). 'An Iona of the east: the early medieval monastery at Portmahomack, Tarbat Ness'. *Medieval Archaeology* 48: 1–30.

——(2005). *Sutton Hoo; a seventh-century princely burial ground and its context*. London: British Museum.

Casarino, C. (2002). *Modernity at sea; Melville, Marx, Conrad in crisis.* Minneapolis: University of Minnesota Press.

Cederlund, C. O. (1997). *Nationalism eller vetenskap? Svensk marinarkeologi i ideologisk belysning.* Stockholm: University of Stockholm.

Champion, T. (2004). 'The deposition of the boat', in Clark (ed.) (2004a): 276–81.

Chapman, J. (2000). *Fragmentation in archaeology: people, places, and broken objects in the prehistory of south eastern Europe.* London: Routledge.

Christensen, A. E. (1995). 'Ship graffiti', in Crumlin-Pedersen and Thye (eds.): 181–5.

——Ingstad, A. S., and Myhre, B. (1992) *Osebergdronningens grav—vår arkeologiske nasjonalskatt i nytt lys.* Oslo: Chr. Schibstets.

Clark, J. G. D. (1936). *The Mesolithic settlement of northern Europe.* Cambridge: Cambridge University Press.

——(1954). *Excavations at Star Carr.* Cambridge: Cambridge University Press.

——(1961). *World prehistory in perspective.* Cambridge: Cambridge University Press.

Clark, P. (ed.) (2004a). *The Dover Bronze Age Boat.* London: English Heritage.

——(ed.) (2004b). *The Dover Bronze Age Boat in context; society and water transport in prehistoric Europe.* Oxford: Oxbow.

——(ed.) (2009). *Bronze Age connections; cultural contact in prehistoric Europe.* Oxford: Oxbow.

Clarke, C. (2008). 'The allegory of landscape: land reclamation and defence at Glastonbury Abbey', in M. Carr, K. P. Clarke, and M. Nievergelt (eds.) *On allegory: some medieval aspects and approaches from Chaucer to Shakespeare.* Newcastle: Cambridge Scholars Publishing, 87–103.

Clarke, D. (1970). *Beaker pottery of Great Britain and Ireland.* Cambridge: Cambridge University Press.

——(1976). 'The Beaker network—social and economic models', in Lanting and Van der Waals (eds.) *Glockenbecher Symposion Oberreid 1974.* Haarlem: Fibula-Van Dishoeck, 459–77.

Clarke, D. V., Cowie, T. G., and Foxon, A. (1985). *Symbols of power at the time of Stonehenge.* Edinburgh: National Museum of Antiquities of Scotland.

Cloke, P. and Pawson, E. (2008). 'Memorial trees and treescape memories'. *Environment and Planning D: Society and Space* 26, 107–22.

Coates, P. (1988). *Nature—western attitudes since ancient times.* Cambridge: Polity Press.

Cochrane, R. (1902). 'On Broighter, Limavady, Co Derry, and on the find of gold ornaments there in 1896'. *Journal of the Royal Society of Antiquaries of Ireland* 32: 211–24.

Coles, B. J. (1990). 'Anthropomorphic wooden figures from Britain and Ireland'. *PPS* 56: 315–33.

——(1998). 'Doggerland: a speculative survey'. *PPS* 64, 45–82.

——(1999). 'Doggerland's loss and the Neolithic', in Coles, Coles, and Shou Jørgenson (eds.): 51–8.

——Coles, J., and Shou Jørgenson, M. (eds.) (1999). *Bog bodies, sacred sites and wetland Archaeology.* Exeter: WARP.

Coles, J. M. (1993). 'Boats on the rocks', in Coles, Fenwick, and Hutchinson (eds.): 23–31.

——(2000). *Patterns in a rocky land; rock carvings in South-West Uppland, Sweden.* Uppsala: Department of Archaeology and Ancient History.

Coles, J. M. (2005). *Shadows of a northern past; rock carvings of Bohuslän and Østfold.* Oxford: Oxbow.

——Fenwick, V., and Hutchinson, G. (eds.) (1993). *A spirit of enquiry; essays for Ted Wright.* Exeter: WARP, The Nautical Archaeology Society and the National Maritime Museum.

Conneller, C. J. (2003). 'Star Carr recontextualized', in J. Moore and L. Bevan (eds.) *Peopling the Mesolithic in a northern environment.* Oxford: Oxbow, 81–6.

——(2004). 'Becoming deer; corporeal transformations at Star Carr'. *Archaeological Dialogues* 11: 37–56.

——and Schadla-Hall, T. (2003). 'Beyond Star Carr; the Vale of Pickering in the tenth millennium BP'. *PPS* 69: 85–105.

Connery, C. (2006). ' "There was no more sea": the supersession of the ocean, from the bible to cyberspace'. *Journal of Historical Geography* 32: 494–511.

Conrad, J. (1906). *The mirror of the sea.* New York: Harper and Brothers.

Cooney, G. (ed.) (2003). *Seascapes. World Archaeology* 53.

Corbin, A. (1994). *The lure of the sea; the discovery of the seaside in the western world 1750–1840.* London: Polity Press.

Cosgrove, D. E. (1984). *Social formation and symbolic landscape.* Wisconsin: University of Wisconsin.

——and Daniels, S. (eds.) (1988). *The iconography of landscape; essays on the symbolic representation, design and use of past environments.* Cambridge: Cambridge University Press.

Cowen, J. D. (1967). 'The Hallstatt sword of bronze: on the continent and in Britain'. *PPS* 33: 377–454.

Crowson, A., Lane, T, and Reeve, J. (eds.) (2000). *Fenland Management Project excavations 1991-1995.* Sleaford: Heritage Trust for Lincolnshire (Lincolnshire Archaeology and Heritage Reports Series 3).

Crumlin-Pedersen, O. (1991). 'Boat-graves and grave-boats at Slusegård', in S. H. Andersen (ed.) *Slusegårdgravpladsen III.* Aarhus: Jysk Arkæologisk Selskabs Skrifter XIV.

——(1997). *Viking-age ships and shipbuilding in Hedeby/Haithabu and Schleswig.* Schleswig: Archäologisches Landesmuseum der Christian Albrechts Universität, Roskilde: Viking Ship Museum.

——(2000). 'To be or not to be a cog: the Bremen Cog in perspective'. *IJNA* 29: 230–46.

——(2003). 'Die Bremer Kogge—ein Schlüssel zur Geschichte des Schiffbaus in Mittelalter', in Hoffmann and Schnall (eds.): 256–71.

——and Thye, B. M. (eds.) (1995). *The ship as symbol in prehistoric and medieval Scandinavia.* Copenhagen: National Museum of Denmark.

——and Trakadas, A. (2003). *Hjortspring: a pre-Roman Iron-Age warship in context.* Roskilde: Viking Ship Museum.

Cummings, V. and Fowler, C. (eds.) (2004). *The Neolithic of the Irish Sea; materiality and traditions of practice.* Oxford: Oxbow.

Cunliffe, B. (2001). *Facing the ocean; the Atlantic and its people.* Oxford: Oxford University Press.

——(2005). *Iron Age communities in Britain; an account of England, Scotland and Wales from the seventh century* BC *until the Roman conquest.* London: Routledge.

——(2009). 'Looking forward: maritime contacts in the first millennium BC', in Clark (ed.): 80–93.

Davey, P. J. (1973). 'Bronze Age metalwork from Lincolnshire'. *Archaeologia* 104, 51–127.

——and Knowles, G. C. (1972). 'The Appleby hoard'. *Archaeological Journal* 128: 154–61.

Davies, R. W. (1971). 'The Roman military diet'. *Britannia* 2: 122–42.

Dawson, A. G., Smith, D. E., and Long, D. (1990). 'Evidence for a tsunami from a Mesolithic site in Inverness, Scotland'. *JAS*: 17: 509–12.

Day, S. P. and Mellars, P. A. (1994). ' "Absolute" dating of Mesolithic human activity at Star Carr, Yorkshire: new palaeoecological studies and identification of the 9600 BP radiocarbon "plateau"'. *PPS* 60: 417–22.

De Boe, G. and Hubert, F. (1977). 'Une installation portuaire d'époque romaine à Pommeroeul.' *Archaeologia Belgica* 192: 5–57.

De Kraker and Borger, G.J (eds.) (2007). *Veen-Vis-Zout. Landscappelijke dynamiek in de zuidwestelijke delta van de Lage Landen.* Amsterdam: Vrije Universiteit (Geoarchaeological and Bioarchaeological Studies 8).

Deleuze, G. (1953). *Desert islands and other texts 1953–1974.* New York: Semiotext(e).

De Mulder, E. F. J., Geluk, M. C., Ritsema, I., Westerhoff, W. E., and Wong, T. E. (2003). *De ondergrond van Nederland. Geologie van Nederland, deel 7.* Utrecht: Nederlands Instituut voor Toegepaste Geowetenschappen TNO.

De Raaf, H. K. (1957–8). 'De Romeinse nederzetting bij Zwammerdam en het probleem van 'Nigropullo', Zuid-Holland'. *BROB* 8: 31–80.

De Ridder, T. (1999). 'De oudste deltawerken van West-Europa; tweeduizend jaar oude dammen en duikers te Vlaardingen'. *Tijdschrift voor Waterstaatsgeschiedenis* 8: 10–22.

Descola, P. (1994). *In the society of nature; a native ecology in Amazonia.* Cambridge: Cambridge University Press.

——(2005). *Par-delà nature et culture.* Paris: Bibliothèque des Sciences Humaines.

Devoy, R. J. N. (1979). 'Flandrian sea-level changes and vegetational history of the lower Thames estuary'. *Philosophical Transactions of the Royal Society of London. Series B*, 285: 355–407.

De Weerd, M. D. (1988). *Schepen voor Zwammerdam.* Unpublished PhD thesis, University of Amsterdam.

Dinnin, M. and Van de Noort, R. (1999). 'Wetland habitats, their resource potential and exploitation', in Coles, Coles, and Schou Jørgensen (eds.): 69–78.

Dobres, M.-A. and Robb, J. E. (eds.) (2000). *Agency in Archaeology.* London: Routledge.

Dollinger, P. (1966). *Die Hanse.* Stuttgart: Kröner.

Drenth, E. and Lohof, E. (2005). 'Heuvels voor de doden. Begraving en grafritueel in bekertijd, vroege en midden-bronstijd', in Louwe Kooijmans *et al.* (eds.): 433–54.

Duby, G. (1968). *Rural economy and country life in the medieval west.* London: Edward Arnold.

Du Gardin, C. (1993). 'The circulation of amber in prehistoric Europe', in C. Scarre and F. Healy (eds.) *Trade and exchange in prehistoric Europe; proceedings of a conference held at the University of Bristol, April 1992.* Oxford: Oxbow: 131–3.

Duncan-Jones, R. (1990). *Structure and scale in the Roman economy.* Cambridge: Cambridge University Press.

Durnez, J. (2006). 'The provincial Museum of Walraversijde, from archaeological research to a cultural tourism project', in M. Pieters, G. Gevaert, J. Mees, and J. Seys (eds.) *Colloquium: to sea or not to sea—2nd international colloquium on maritime and fluvial archaeology in the southern North Sea area. Brugge (B), 21–3 September 2006.* Oostende: Vlaams Institute voor de Zee (VLIZ Special Publication 32), 103–5.

Dyer, K. R. and Huntley, D. A. (1999). 'The origin, classification and modeling of sand banks and ridges'. *Continental Shelf Research* 19: 1285–1330.

Earle, T. (2002). *Bronze Age economics; the beginning of political economies.* Cambridge (MA): Westview Press.

Edmonds, M. (1995). *Stone tools and society; working stone in Neolithic and Bronze Age Britain.* London: Routledge.

Edwards, C. J., Bollongino, R., Scheu, A., Chamberlain, A., Tresset, A., Vigne, J-D., Baird, J. F., Larson, G., Ho, S. Y. W., Heupink, T. H., Shapiro, B., Freeman, A. R., Thomas, M. G., Arbogast, R-M., Arndt, B., Bartosiewicz, L., Benecke, N., Budja, M., Chaix, L., Choyke, A. M., Coqueugniot, E., Döhle, H-J., Göldner, H., Hartz, S., Helmer, D., Herzig, B., Hongo, H., Mashkour, M., Özdogan, M., Pucher, E., Roth, G., Schade-Lindig, S., Schmölcke, U., Schulting, R. J., Stephan, E., Uerpmann, H-P., Vörös, I., Voytek, B., Bradley, D. J., and Burger, J. (2007). 'Mitochondrial DNA analysis shows a Near Eastern Neolithic origin for domestic cattle and no indication of domestication of European aurochs'. *Proceedings of the Royal Society B* 274: 1377–85.

Elgee, F. and Elgee, H. W. (1949). 'An Early Bronze Age burial in a boat-shaped wooden coffin from north-east Yorkshire'. *PPS* 15: 87–106.

Ellis, S., Fenwick, H., Lillie, M., and Van de Noort, R. (eds.) (2001). *Wetland heritage of the Lincolnshire Marsh.* Hull: Humber Wetlands Project.

Ellmers, D. (1972). *Frühmittelalterliche Handelsschiffahrt in Mittel-und Nordeuropa.* Neuminster: Wachholt.

——(1980). 'Ein Fellboot-Fragment der Ahrensburger Kultur aus Husum, Schleswig-Holstein'. *Offa* 37: 19–24.

——(1995). 'Crew structure on board Scandinavian vessels', in Olsen *et al.* (eds.): 231–40.

Engelhardt, C. (1865). *Nydam mosefund 1859–1863.* Copenhagen: G. E. C. Gad.

Evans, C. and Serjeantson, D. (1988). 'The backwater economy of a fen-edge community in the Iron Age: the Upper Delphs, Haddenham'. *Antiquity* 62: 360–70.

Evans, J. D. (1973). 'Islands as laboratories for the study of cultural process', in A. C. Renfrew (ed.) *The explanation of cultural change; models in prehistory.* London: Duckworth, 517–20.

Farrell, A. W. and Penny, S. (1975). 'The Broighter Boat: a reassessment'. *Irish Archaeological Research Forum* 2: 15–26.

Fenwick, H. (2001). 'Medieval salt-production and landscape development in the Lincolnshire Marsh', in Ellis *et al.* (eds.): 231–41.

——Chapman, H., Fletcher, W., Thomas, G., and Lillie, M. (2001). 'The archaeological survey of the Lincolnshire Marsh', in Ellis *et al.* (eds.): 99–202.

Field, N. and Parker Pearson, M. (2003). *Fiskerton; an Iron Age timber causeway with Iron Age and Roman votive offerings: the 1981 excavations.* Oxford: Oxbow.

Filmer-Sankey, W. (1990). 'A new boat-burial from the Snape Anglo-Saxon cemetery, Suffolk', in McGrail (ed.): 126–34.

——(1992). 'Snape Anglo-Saxon cemetery: the current state of knowledge', in M. O. H. Carver (ed.) *The age of Sutton Hoo.* Woodbridge: Boydell, 83–94.

Fisher, A. (1995). 'An entrance to the Mesolithic world below the ocean. Status of ten years' work on the Danish sea floor', in Fisher (ed.): 371–84.

——(ed.) (1995). *Man and sea in the Mesolithic; coastal settlement above and below present sea-level.* Oxford: Oxbow.

Fitzpatrick, A. P. (2002). ' "The Amesbury Archer": a well-furnished Early Bronze Age burial in southern England'. *Antiquity* 76: 629–30.

——Ellis, C., and Allen, M. J. (1996). 'Bronze Age "jetties" or causeways at Testwood lakes, Hampshire, Great Britain'. *NewsWARP* 20: 19–22.

Fleming, A. (2008). 'Island stories', in Noble *et al.* (eds.): 11–22.

Flemming, B. W. (2002). 'Geographic distribution of muddy coasts', in T. Healy, Y. Wang, and J-A. Healy (eds.) *Muddy coasts of the world: processes, deposits and function.* Amsterdam: Elsevier Science: 99–201.

Flemming, N. C. (ed.) (2004). *Submarine prehistoric archaeology of the North Sea; research priorities and collaboration with industry.* York: CBA (Research Report 141).

Fletcher, W. and Van de Noort, R. (2007). 'The Lake-dwellings in Holderness revisited; new excavations in East Yorkshire', in Barber *et al.* (eds.): 313–22.

Fojut, N. (1993). *A guide to prehistoric and Viking Shetland.* Lerwick: The Shetland Times.

Fokkens, H. (2005). 'Woon-stalhuizen op zwervende erven. Nederzettingen in bekertijd en bronstijd', in Louwe Kooijmans *et al.* (eds.): 407–28.

Foucault, M. (1966). *Les mots et les choses; une archéologie des sciences humaines.* Paris: Gallimard.

——(1970). *The order of things; an archaeology of the human sciences.* London: Pantheon.

Fowler, C. (2004). *The archaeology of personhood; an anthropological approach.* London: Routledge.

Fox, H. (2001). *The evolution of the fishing village; landscape and society along the south Devon coast, 1086–1550.* Oxford: Leopard's Head Press.

Fraser, D. (1983). *Land and society in Neolithic Orkney.* Oxford: BAR (British Series 117).

Frazer, W. O., and Tyrrell, A. (eds.) (2000). *Social identity in early medieval Britian.* Leicester: Leicester University Press.

French, C. A. I. (1999). 'Excavation of the Deeping St Nicholas barrow site 28, Lincolnshire'. *Antiquity* 65: 580–82.

——(2001). 'The development of the prehistoric landscape in the Flag Fen basin', in Pryor (ed.): 400–4.

Gaffney, V., Thomson, K., and Fitch, S. (2007). *Mapping Doggerland; the Mesolithic landscapes of the southern North Sea.* Oxford: Archaeopress.

——Fitch, S., and Smith, D. (2009). *Europe's lost world; the rediscovery of Doggerland.* York: CBA (Research Report 160).

Gardiner, M. (1998). 'The exploitation of sea-mammals in medieval England: bones and their social context'. *Archaeological Journal* 154: 184–95.

Gerrets, D. A. (1999). 'Conclusions', in Besteman *et al.* (eds.): 331–42.

Gerrets, D. A. and De Koning, J. (1999). 'Settlement development on the Wijnaldum-Tjitsma terp', in Besteman *et al.* (eds.): 73–124.

Gibbard, P. L. (1995). 'The formation of the Strait of Dover'. *Geological Society Special Publications* 96: 15–26.

Gifford, E. and Gifford, J. (2004). 'The use of half-scale model ships in archaeological research with particular reference to the Graveney, Sutton Hoo and Ferriby ships', in Clark (ed.) (2004b): 67–81.

Gilman, P. J. (1998). 'Essex fish traps and fisheries. An integrated approach to survey, recording, and management', in K. Bernick (ed.) *Hidden Dimensions; the cultural significance of wetland archaeology.* Vancouver: University of British Columbia Press, 273–89.

Gislason, H. (1994). 'Ecosystem effect of fishing activities in the North Sea'. *Marine Pollution Bulletin* 29: 520–27.

Glimmerveen, J., Mol, D., Post, K., Reumer, J. W. F., Van der Plicht, H., De Vos, J., Van Geel, B., Van Reenen, G., and Pals, J. P. (2004). 'The North Sea project: the first palaeontological, palynological and archaeological results', in Flemming (ed.): 43–52.

——,——, and Van der Plicht, H. (2006). 'The Pleistocene reindeer of the North Sea— initial palaeontological data and archaeological remarks'. *Quaternary International* 142–3: 242–6.

Glob, P. V. (1969). *Helleristninger i Danmark.* Aarhus: Jysk Arkæologisk Selskabs Skrifter VII.

Godal, J. (1990). 'Measurements, figures and formulas for the interpretation of western Norwegian boats and Viking ships'. *Acta Borealis* 20: 56–80.

Godwin, H. and Godwin, M. E. (1933). 'British Maglemose harpoon sites'. *Antiquity* 7: 36–48.

Goodburn, D. (2000). 'New light on the construction of early medieval "Frisian" sea-going vessels', in C. Beltrame (ed.) *Boats, ships and shipyards.* Oxford: Oxbow Books.

Gooder, J. (2007). 'Excavation of a Mesolithic house at East Barns, East Lothian', in Waddington and Pedersen (eds.): 49–59.

Gosden, C. and Lock, G. (1998). 'Prehistoric histories'. *World Archaeology* 30: 2–12.

——and Marshall, Y. (1999). 'The cultural biography of objects'. *World Archaeology* 31: 169–78.

Graham-Campbell, J. (1980). *The Viking World.* New York: Ticknor and Fields.

——and Batey, C. E. (1998). *Vikings in Scotland; an archaeological survey.* Edinburgh: Edinburgh University Press.

Gramsch, B. (1987). 'Ausgrabungen auf dem mesolitischen Moorfundplatz bei Friesack, bezirk Potsdam'. *Veröffentlichen des Museums für Ur- und frühgeschichte Potsdam* 21: 75–100.

——and Kloss, K. (1989). 'Excavations near Freisack: an Early Mesolithic marshland site in the northern plain of Central Europe', in C. Bonsall (ed.) *The Mesolithic in Europe; papers presented at the third International Symposium, Edinburgh, 1985.* Edinburgh: John Donald: 313–24.

Gregory, C. E. (1980). 'Gifts to men and gifts to gods'. *Man* 15: 626–52.

Greene, K. (1986). *The archaeology of the Roman economy.* Berkeley and Los Angeles: University of California Press.

Grinsell, L. V. (1940). 'The boat of the dead in the Bronze Age'. *Antiquity* 14: 360–9.

Groenman-van Waateringe, W. and Van Wijngaarden-Bakker, L. H. (1990). 'Medieval archaeology and environmental research in the Netherlands', in Besteman, Bos, and Heidinga (eds.): 283–97.

Guttmann, E. B. A. (2005). 'Midden cultivation in prehistoric Britain; arable crops in gardens'. *World Archaeology* 37: 224–39.

Haarnagel, W. (1979). *Die Grabung Feddersen Wierde. Methode, Hausbau, Siedlungs- und Wirtshaftsformen sowie Sozialstruktur.* Wiesbaden: Steiner.

Hageneder, F. (2001). *The heritage of trees; history, culture and symbolism.* Edinburgh: Floris Books.

Halbertsma, H. (1963). *Terpen tussen Vlie en Eems; een geographish-historische benadering.* Groningen: Vereniging voor Terpenonderzoek.

Hall, D. and Coles, J. M. (1994). *Fenland survey; an essay in landscape and persistence.* London: English Heritage.

Hallam, H. E. (1965). *Settlement and society: a study of the early agrarian history of South Lincolnshire.* Cambridge: Cambridge University Press.

Halliburton, M. (2002). 'Rethinking anthropological studies of the body: Manas and Bōdham in Kerala'. *American Anthropologist* 104: 1123–34.

Hamilton, J. R. C. (1956). *Excavations at Jarslhof, Shetland.* London: HMSO.

——(1968). *Excavations at Clickhimin, Shetland.* London: HMSO.

Hansen, V. and Nielsen, H. (1979). 'Oldtidens veje og vadesteder, belyst ved nye undersøgelser ved Stevns'. *Aarbøger for Nordisk Oldkyndighed of Historie:* 99–117.

Harding, A. F. (1984). *The Mycenaeans and Europe.* London: Academic Press.

——(1993). 'British amber spacer-plate necklaces and their relatives in gold and stone', in C. W. Beck and J. Bouzek, with D. Dreslerová (eds.) *Amber in archaeology.* Prague: Institute of Archaeology: 53–8.

——(1999). 'Warfare: a defining characteristic of Bronze Age Europe?', in J. Carman and A. F. Harding (eds.) *Ancient warfare; archaeological perspectives.* Stroud: Sutton Publishing, 157–73.

——(2000). *European societies in the Bronze Age.* Cambridge: Cambridge University Press.

Harrison, R. (1980). *The Beaker Folk: Copper Age archaeology in Western Europe.* London: Thames and Hudson.

Harrison, S., Pile, S., and Thrift, N. J. (eds.) (2004). *Patterned ground: entanglements of nature and culture.* London: Reaktion.

Harsema, O. H. (1992). *Geschiedenis in het landschap.* Assen: Drents Museum.

Hassall, M. W. C. and Tomlin, R. S. O. (1984). 'Roman Britain in 1983, II. Inscriptions'. *Britannia* 15: 333–56.

Haswell-Smith, H. (2004). *The Scottish islands; a comprehensive guide to every Scottish island.* Edinburgh: Canongate.

Hau'ofa, E. (1993). 'Our sea of islands', in E. Waddell, V. Naidu, and E. Hau'ofa (eds.) *A new Oceania; rediscovering our sea of islands.* Fiji: University of the South Pacific, 2–16.

Hawkes, C. F. C and Smith, M. A. (1957). 'On some buckets and cauldrons of the Bronze and Early Iron Ages'. *Archaeological Journal* 37: 131–98.

Haywood, J. (1991). *Dark Age naval power; a reassessment of Frankish and Anglo-Saxon seafaring activity.* Hockwold-cum-Wilton: Anglo-Saxon Books.

Haywood, J. (1999). *Dark Age naval power; a reassessment of Frankish and Anglo-Saxon seafaring activity.* 2nd edn. Hockwold-cum-Wilton: Anglo-Saxon Books.

Head, R., Fenwick, H., Van de Noort, R., Dinnin, M., and Lillie, M. (1995). 'The meres and coastal survey', in R. Van de Noort and S. Ellis (eds.) *Wetland heritage of Holderness; an archaeological survey.* Hull: Humber Wetlands Project: 163–239.

Healy, F. (1996). *Fenland Project II. Wissey Embayment; the evidence for pre-Iron Age occupation.* East Anglian Archaeology 78.

Hedeager, L. (1979). 'A quantitative analysis of Roman imports in Europe north of the limes 0–AD 400 and the question of Roman-Germanic exchange', in K. Kristiansen, T. Palluden, and C. Müller (eds.) *New directions in Scandinavian archaeology 1.* Aarhus: University of Aarhus, 191–216.

Hedges, R. E. M. (2004). 'Isotopes and red herrings: comments on Milner *et al.* and Lidén *et al.' Antiquity* 78: 34–7.

Heidinga, H. A. (1999). 'The Wijnaldum excavation: searching for a central place in Dark Age Frisia', in Besteman *et al.* (eds.): 1–16.

Helms, M. W. (1988). *Ulysses' Sail; an ethnographic odyssey of power, knowledge, and geographical distance.* Princeton: Princeton University Press.

——(2009). 'The master(y) of hard materials: thoughts on technology, materiality and ideology occasioned by the Dover boat', in Clark (ed.): 149–58.

Hemmingway, E. (1952). *The old man and the sea.* New York: Charles Scriber's.

Henderson, J. C. (2007). *The Atlantic Iron Age: settlement and identity in the first millennium BC.* London: Routledge.

Hensius, P. (1956). *Das Schiff der hansischen Früzeit.* Weimar: Böhlau.

Herodotus. *The histories.* trans. R. Waterfield (1998). Oxford: Oxford University Press.

Herschend, F. (2001). *Journey of civilisation; the Late Iron Age view of the human world.* Uppsala: University of Uppsala (Opia 24).

Hill, J. D. (1995). *Ritual and rubbish in the Iron Age of Wessex.* Oxford: BAR (British Series 242).

Hills, C. (1977). The Anglo-Saxon cemetery at Spong Hill, North Elmham, Part 1: Catalogue of cremations. Dereham: East Anglian Archaelogy 6.

Hodder, I. (1990). *The domestication of Europe: structure and contingency in Neolithic societies.* Oxford: Blackwell.

Hodges, R. (1982). *Dark Age economics; the origins of towns and trade, AD 600–1000.* London: Duckworth.

Hoffmann, P. (2003). 'Ein Schiff mit vielen Gesichtern', in Hoffmann and Schnall (eds.): 12–17.

——and Schnall, U. (2003). 'Warum wurde die Kogge das erfolgreichste Schiff in 14. Jahrhundert?', in Hoffmann and Schnall (eds.): 272–5.

——, ——, (eds.) (2003). *Die Kogge; Sternstunde der deutschen Schiffsarchäologie.* Bremerhaven: Deutschen Schiffahrtsmuseum.

Hogestijn, W-J. (2005). 'Schelpvissers en veehoeders. Woonplaatsen uit de bekertijd op de West-Friese kwelders', in Louwe Kooijmans *et al.* (eds.): 429–32.

Holck, P. (2006). 'The Oseberg Ship burial, Norway: new thoughts on the skeletons from the grave mound'. *European Journal of Archaeology* 9: 185–210.

Hornell, J. (1946). *Water transport; origins and early evolution.* Cambridge: Cambridge University Press.

Hoskins, W. G. (1955). *The making of the English landscape*. London: Hodder and Stoughton.

Housley, R. (1991). 'AMS dates from the Late Glacial and early Postglacial in north-west Europe: a review', in Barton, Roberts, and Roe (eds.): 25–39.

Hutchins, E. (1995). *Cognition in the wild*. Cambridge (MA): MIT Press.

Hygen, A-S. and Bengtsson, L. (2000). *Rock carvings in the borderlands Bohuslän and Østfold*. Gothenburg: Warne.

IJzereef, G. F. (1981). *Bronze Age animal bones from Bovenkarspel; the excavations at Het Valkje*. Amersfoort: ROB (Nederlandse Oudheden 10).

——Laarman, F. J., and Lauwerier, R. C. G. M. (1989). 'Animal remains from the Late Bronze Age and the Iron Age found in the western Netherlands'. *BROB* 39: 257–66.

Ilkjær, J. (2003). 'Danish war booty sacrifices', in Jørgensen, Storgaard, and Gebauer (eds.): 44–65.

Ingold, T. (1993). 'The temporality of the landscape'. *World Archaeology* 25: 152–74.

——(2000). *Perceptions of the environment. Essays in livelihood, dwelling and skill*. London: Routledge.

Ingstad, A. S. (1995). 'The interpretation of the Oseberg-find', in Crumlin-Pedersen and Thye (eds): 139–48.

Irwin, G. (1992). *The prehistoric exploration and colonisation of the Pacific*. Cambridge: Cambridge University Press.

Jelgersma, S. (1961). 'Holocene sea-level changes in the Netherlands'. *Mededelingen Geologische Stichting* C-VI-7.

——(1979). 'Sea-level changes in the North Sea basin', in E. Oele, R. T. E. Schutten-helm, and A. J. Wiggers (eds.) *The Quaternary history of the North Sea*. Uppsala: University of Uppsala (Acta Universitatis Upsaliensis 2), 233–48.

Jensen, J. (1982). *The prehistory of Denmark*. London: Methuen.

Jensen, X. P. (2003). 'The Vimose find', in Jørgensen, Storgaard, and Gebauer (eds.): 224–39.

Johnstone, P. (1972). 'Bronze Age sea trials'. *Antiquity* 46: 269–74.

——(1980). *The sea-craft of prehistory*. London: Routledge.

Jones, O. W. and Cloke, P. (2002). *Tree cultures; the place of trees and trees in their place*. Oxford: Berg.

Jørgensen, A. N. (1997). 'Sea defences in Denmark AD 200–1300', in A. N. Jørgensen and B. L. Clausen (eds.) *Military aspects of Scandinavian society in a European perspective, AD 1–1300*. Copenhagen: National Museum of Denmark (Studies in Archaeology and History 2), 200–9.

Jørgensen, E. and Petersen, P. V. (2003). 'Nydam Bog—new finds and observations', in Jørgensen, Storgaard, and Gebauer (eds.): 258–85.

Jørgensen, L., Storgaard, B., and Gebauer, L. (eds.) (2003). *The spoils of victory; the North in the shadow of the Roman Empire*. Copenhagen: National Museum of Denmark.

Kars, H. (1982). 'Early-Medieval Dorestad, an archaeo-petrological study part II: the weights and the well; petrology and provenance of the tuff artefacts'. *BROB* 32: 147–68.

Karsten, P. and Knarrström, B. (2003). *The Tågerup Excavations*. Lund: National Heritage Board, Sweden.

Kasteleijn, H. W. (1982). *Archeozoölogische vondsten van de opgraving in Oldeboorn 1980*. Groningen: GIA.

Kaul, F. (1998). *Ships on bronzes; a study in Bronze Age religion and iconography*. Copenhagen: National Museum of Denmark.

——(2002). 'The oldest war-ship sails again', in A Nørgård Jørgensen, J. Pind, L. Jørgensen, and B. Clausen (eds.) *Maritime warfare in Northern Europe. Papers from an International research seminar at the Danish National Museum, Copenhagen, 3–5 May 2000*. Copenhagen: National Museum of Denmark (Studies in Archaeology and History 6): 7–19.

——(2003). 'The Hjortspring find—the oldest of the large Nordic war booty sacrifices', in Jørgensen, Storgaard, and Gebauer (eds.): 212–23.

——(2004). 'Social and religious perceptions of the ship in Bronze Age Europe', in Clark (ed.) (2004b): 122–37.

——and Valbjørn, K. V. (2003). *The Hjortspring find; a Pre-Roman Iron Age warship in context*. Roskilde: Viking Ship Museum (Ships and Boats of the North 6).

Kindgren, H. (1995). 'Hensbacka-Hogen-Hornborgasjön: Early Mesolithic coastal and inland settlement in western Sweden', in Fisher (ed.): 171–84.

Kirby, D. and Hinkkanen, M-L. (2000). *The Baltic and the North Seas*. London: Routledge.

Knorr, F. (1911). 'Bootkammergrab südlich der Oldenburg bei Schleswig'. *Mitteilungen des Anthropologischen Vereins in Schleswig-Holstein* 19: 68–77.

Kobyliński, Z. (1995). 'Ships, society, symbols and archaeologists', in Crumlin-Pedersen and Thye (eds.): 9–19.

Koch, E. (1998). *Neolithic bog pots from Zealand, Møn, Lolland and Falster*. Copenhagen: Kongelige Nordiske Oldskriftselskab.

——(1999). 'Neolithic offerings from the wetlands of eastern Denmark', in Coles, Coles, and Shou Jørgenson (eds.): 125–32.

Kopytoff, I. (1986). 'The cultural biography of things: commoditization as process', in Appadurai (ed.): 64–91.

Kossack, G., Harck, O., Newig, J., Hoffmann, D., Willkomm, H., Averdieck, F-R., and Reichstein, J. (1980). *Archsum auf Sylt Teil 1: Einführung in Forschungsverlauf und Landschaftgeschichte*. Mainz: Philipp von Zabern.

Kristiansen, K. (1987). 'Centre and periphery in Bronze Age Scandinavia', in M. Rowlands, M. Larsen, and K. Kristiansen (eds.) *Centre and periphery in the ancient world*. Cambridge: Cambridge University Press, 74–85.

——(1998). *Europe before history*. Cambridge: Cambridge University Press.

——(2004). 'Seafaring voyages and rock art ships', in Clark (ed.) (2004b): 111–21.

——and Larsson, T. B. (2005). *The rise of Bronze Age society; travels, transmissions and transformations*. Cambridge: Cambridge University Press.

Lambeck, K. (1995). 'Late Devensian and Holocene shorelines of the British Isles and North Sea from models of glacio-hydro-isostatic rebound'. *Journal of the Geological Society* 152: 437–48.

Lambert, A. M. (1971). *The making of the Dutch landscape*. London: Seminar Press.

Lamm, J. P. and Nordström, H.-Å. (eds). (1983). *Vendel Period studies. Transactions of the boat grave symposium in Stockholm, February 2–3, 1981*. Stockholm: Museum of National Antiquities (Studies 2).

Lanting, J. N. (1997/8). 'Dates for origin and diffusion of the European logboat'. *Palaeohistoria* 39/40: 627–50.

——and Van der Waals, J. D. (1972). 'British Beakers as seen from the Continent'. *Helinium* 12: 20–46.

——, —— (1976). 'Beaker culture relations in the Lower Rhine Basin', in Lanting and Van der Waals (eds.): 1–80.

——, —— (eds.) (1976). *Glockenbecher Symposion Oberreid 1974.* Haarlem: Fibula-Van Dishoeck.

Latour, B. (1993). *We have never been modern.* Cambridge (MA): Harvard University Press.

Leary, J. (2009). 'Perceptions of and responses to the Holocene flooding of the North Sea lowlands'. *Oxford Journal of Archaeology* 28: 227–37.

Legge, A. and Rowley-Conwy, P. (1988). *Star Carr revisited.* London: Centre for Extramural studies.

Lehmann, L. Th. (1990). 'The Romano-Celtic boats from Druten and Kapel Avezaath', in McGrail (ed.): 77–81.

Lemaire, T. (1970). *Filosofie van het landschap.* Bilthoven: Ambo.

Lidén, K., Eriksson, G., Nordqvist, B., Götherström, A., and Bendixen, E. (2004). '"The wet and the wild followed by the dry and the tame"—or did they occur at the same time? Diet in Mesolithic-Neolithic southern Sweden'. *Antiquity* 78: 23–33.

Lindqvist, S. (1941). *Gotlands Bildsteine I.* Stockholm: KVHAA.

——(1942). *Gotlands Bildsteine II.* Stockholm: KVHAA.

Long, D., Wickham-Jones, C. R., and Ruckley, N. A. (1986). 'A flint artefact from the North Sea', in D. Roe (ed.) *Studies in the Upper Paleolithic of Britain and northwest Europe.* Oxford: BAR (British Series 296), 55–62.

Lotze, H. K., and Reise, K. (eds.) (2005). *Ecological history of the Wadden Sea.* Helgoland: Helgoland Marine Research.

——, ——, Worm, B., Van Beusekom, J., Busch, M., Ehlers, A., Heinrich, D., Hoffmann, R. C., Holm, P., Jensen, C., Knottnerus, O. S., Langhanki, N., Prummel, W., Vollmer, M., and Wolff, W. J. (2005). 'Human transformations of the Wadden Sea ecosystem through time: a synthesis', in Lotze and Reise (eds.): 84–95.

Louwe Kooijmans, L. P. (1971). 'Mesolithic bone and antler implements from the North Sea and from the Netherlands'. *BROB 20–1*: 27–73.

——(1974). *The Rhine/Meuse Delta; four studies on its prehistoric occupation and Holocene geology.* Leiden: University of Leiden (Analecta Praehistorica Leidensia 7).

——(1985). *Sporen in het land; de Nederlandse delta in de prehistorie.* Amsterdam.

——(1986). 'Het loze vissertje of boerke Naas? Het een en ander over het leven van de steentijdbewoners van het Rijnmondgebied', in M. C. van Trierum and H. E. Enkes (eds.) *Landschap en bewoning rond de monding van de Rijn, Maas en Scheldt.* Rotterdam: Bureau Oudheidkundig Bodemonderzoek Rotterdam (Rotterdam Papers 5), 7–25.

——(1993). 'Wetland exploitation and upland relations of prehistoric communities in the Netherlands', in J. Gardiner (ed.) *Flatlands and wetlands; current themes in East Anglian Archaeology.* East Anglian Archaeology Report 50: 71–116.

Louwe Kooijmans, L. P. (ed.) (2001a). *Hardinxveld-Giessendam De Bruin; een kampplaats uit het Laat-Mesolithicum en het begin van de Swifterbant-cultuur (5500–4450 v.Chr.)*. Amersfoort: ROB (Rapportage Archeologische Monumentenzorg 88).

——(ed.) (2001b). *Hardinxveld-Giessendam Polderweg; een Mesolithisch jachtkamp in het rivierengebied (5500–5000 v.Chr.)*. Amersfoort: ROB (Rapportage Archeologische Monumentenzorg 83).

——(2005). 'Nederland in de prehistorie: een terugblik', in Louwe Kooijmans *et al.* (eds.): 695–719.

——(2005/6). 'Schipluiden: a synthetic view', in Louwe Kooijmans and Jongste (eds.): 485–516.

——(2008). 'Peddelen over de plassen. Over kano's en peddels uit Meso- en Neolithicum in Nederland', in Oosting and Van den Akker (eds.): 26–37.

——and Jongste, P. F. B. (eds.) (2005/6). *Schipluiden. A Neolithic settlement on the Dutch North Sea coast c. 3500 cal BC*. Leiden: Leiden University (Analecta Praehistorica Leidensia 37/38).

——Van den Broeke, P. W., Fokkens, H., and Van Gijn, A. (eds.) (2005) *Nederland in prehistorie*. Amsterdam: Bert Bakker.

Loveluck, C. and Tys, D. (2006). 'Coastal societies, exchange and identity along the Channel and southern North Sea shores of Europe, AD 600–1000'. *Journal of Maritime Archaeology* 1: 140–69.

Lundborg, L. (1974). *Lugnarohögen. Svenska fornminnesplatser 5*. Stockholm.

Maarleveld, T. (1984). *Archeologie in troebel water. Archeologie onder water; 1e onderzoeksrapport*. Amsterdam: Ministerie van Welzijn, Volksgezondheid en Cultuur.

——(2004). 'Finding "new" boats: enhancing our chances in heritage management, a predictive approach', in Clark (ed.) (2004b): 138–47.

——(2008). 'Boten zonder geschiedenis, of wie is er bang voor een boomstamboot?', in Oosting and Van den Akker (eds): 5–25.

MacKie, E. (1998). 'Maeshowe and the winter solstice'. *Antiquity* 71: 338–59.

Malinowski, B. (1922). *Argonauts of the Western Pacific*. London: Routledge.

Malm, T. (1995). 'Excavating submerged Stone Age sites in Denmark; Tybrind Vig', in Fisher (ed.): 385–96.

Malmer, M. P. (1981). *A chronological study of North European rock art*. Stockholm: Almquist and Wiksell.

Manby, T. (1974). *Grooved Ware sites in Yorkshire and the north of England*. Oxford: BAR (British Series 9).

Mann, M. (1986). *The Sources of Social Power*. Cambridge: Cambridge University Press.

Marsden, P. (1990). 'A reassessment of Blackfriars 1', in McGrail (ed.): 66–74.

——(1994). *Ships of the Port of London (vol 1)*. London: English Heritage.

——(2004). 'Description of the boat', in Clark (ed.) (2004a): 32–95.

Marstrander, S. (1963). *Østfolds Jordbruksristninger, Skedbjerg*. Oslo: University of Oslo.

May, J. (1976). *Prehistoric Lincolnshire*. Lincoln: History of Lincolnshire Committee.

McGrail, S. (1978). *Logboats of England and Wales*. Oxford: BAR (British Series 51).

——(1981). *The Brigg 'raft'; and her prehistoric environment*. Oxford: BAR (British Series 89) and Greenwich: National Maritime Museum (Archaeological Series 6).

——(ed.) (1990). *Maritime Celts, Frisians and Saxons*. London: CBA (Research Report 71).

——(1997). 'The boat fragments', in N. Nayling and A. Caseldine (eds.) *Excavations at Caldicot, Gwent: Bronze Age palaeochannels in the Lower Nedern Valley*. York: CBA (Research Report 108), 210–17.

——(2001). *Boats of the world*. Oxford: Oxford University Press.

——(2003). 'The sea and archaeology'. *Historical Research* 76, 1–17.

——(2004). 'North-west European seagoing boats before AD 400', in Clark (ed.) (2004a): 51–66.

McNiven, I. (2003). 'Saltwater people: spiritscapes, maritime rituals and the archaeology of Australian indigenous seascapes'. *World Archaeology* 35: 329–49.

——and Feldman, R. (2003). 'Ritual orchestration of seascapes: hunting magic and dugong bone mounds in Torres Strait, NE Australia'. *Cambridge Archaeological Journal* 13: 169–94.

Meier, D. (2004). 'Man and environment in the marsh area of Schleswig-Holstein from Roman until late medieval times'. *Quaternary International* 112: 55–69.

Meller, H. (2002). 'Die Himmelscheibe von Nebra'. *Archäologie in Sachsen-Anhalt* 1, 7–20.

Mellars, P. (2004). 'Mesolithic Scotland, coastal occupation, and the role of the Oronsay middens', in A. Saville (ed.) *Mesolithic Scotland and its neighbours; the early Holocene prehistory of Scotland, its British and Irish contexts, and some northern European perspectives*. Edinburgh: Society of Antiquaries of Scotland, 167–83.

——and Dark, P. (1998). *Star Carr in context; new archaeological and palaeoecological investigations at the Early Mesolithic site of Star Carr, North Yorkshire*. Cambridge: McDonald Institute for Archaeological Research.

Melton, N. D. (2008). 'West Voe: a Mesolithic-Neolithic transition site in Shetland', in Noble *et al.* (eds.): 23–36.

——and Nickolson, R. A. (2004). 'The Mesolithic in the Northern Isles: the preliminary evaluation of an oyster midden at West Voe, Sumburgh, Shetland, UK'. *Antiquity* 78, no 299 (Project gallery).

Meskell, L. (2001). 'Archaeologies of identity', in I. Hodder (ed.) *Archaeological theory today*. Cambridge: Polity Press: 187–213.

Millett, M. and McGrail, S. (1987). 'The archaeology of the Hasholme logboat'. *Archaeological Journal* 144, 69–155.

Milne, G. (1990). 'Maritime traffic between the Rhine and Roman Britain: a preliminary note', in McGrail (ed): 82–4.

Milner, N., Craig, O. E., and Bailey, G. N. (eds.) (2007). *Shell middens in Atlantic Europe*. Oxford: Oxbow.

——, ——, ——, Pedersen, K., and Andersen, S. H. (2004). 'Something fishy in the Neolithic? A re-evaluation of stable isotope analysis of Mesolithic and Neolithic coastal populations'. *Antiquity* 78, 9–22.

Mitchison, R. (1970). *A history of Scotland*. London: Routledge.

Mithen, S. (2003). *After the Ice Age; a global human history*. London: Weidenfeld and Nicolson.

Mook, W. G. (1986). 'Business meeting: recommendations/resolutions adopted by the Twelfth International Radiocarbon Conference'. *Radiocarbon* 28: 799.

Mowat, R. J. C. (1996). *The logboats of Scotland.* Oxford: Oxbow.

Muckelroy, K. (1978). *Maritime archaeology.* Cambridge: Cambridge University Press.

Müller-Wille, M. (1970). 'Bestattung im Boot; Studien zu einer nordeuropäischen Grabsitte'. *Offa* 25/26: 1–203.

——(1995). 'Boat-graves, old and new views', in Crumlin-Pedersen and Thye (eds.): 101–10.

Muir, R. (1984). *Reading the landscape; a Shell book.* London: Michael Joseph.

Muir, T. (1995). *Orkney folklore and sea legends by Walter Traill Dennison.* Kirkwall: The Orkney Press.

——(2005). *Orkney in the sagas; the story of the Earldom of Orkney as told in the Icelandic Sagas.* Kirkwall: The Orcadian Limited.

Munro, R. (1906). 'Notes on a hoard of eleven stone knives found in Sheltands'. *PSAS* 40: 151–64.

Murphy, P. (1995). 'Anglo-Saxon hurdles and basketry, Collins Creek, Blackwater Estuary, Essex'. *Ancient Monuments Laboratory report 5/95.* London: English Heritage.

——(2005). 'Environment and economy: a summary', in A. Crowson, T. Lane, K. Penn, and D. Trimble (eds.) *Anglo-Saxon settlement on the siltland of eastern England.* Sleaford: Heritage Trust of Lincolnshire (Lincolnshire Archaeology and Heritage Reports Series 7), 260–3.

Nadel-Klein, J. and Davis, D.L. (eds.) (1988). *To work and to weep: women in fishing economies.* St. John's: Institute of Social and Economic Research, Memorial University of Newfoundland.

Nayling, N. and Caseldine, A. (eds.) (1997). *Excavations at Caldicot, Gwent: Bronze Age palaeochannels in the Lower Nedern Valley.* York: CBA (Research Report 108).

Nayling, N. and McGrail, S. (2004). *The Barland's Farm Romano-Celtic Boat.* York: CBA (Research Report 138).

Needham, S. J. (2000). 'Power pulses across a cultural divide: Armorica and Wessex'. *PPS* 66: 151–94.

——(2005). 'Transforming Beaker culture in north-west Europe; processes of fusion and fission'. *PPS* 71: 171–217.

——(2009). 'Encompassing the sea: 'maritories' and Bronze Age maritime interactions', in Clark (ed.): 12–37.

Niblett, R. (2000). 'A Neolithic dugout from a multi-period site near St Albans, Herts, England'. *IJNA* 30: 155–95.

Nicholson, R. A. (1993). 'The fish remains from excavations at Ribchester, Lancashire, 1989–90'. *Ancient Monuments Laboratory report 121/93.* London: English Heritage.

——(1998). 'Fishing in the Northern Isles: a case study based on fish bone assemblages from two multi-period sites on Sanday, Orkney'. *Environmental Archaeology* 2: 15–28.

Nicolaysen N. (1882). *Langskibet fra Gokstad ved Sandefjord. Oslo/A Viking ship discovered at Gokstad in Norway.* Kristiana.

Nielsen, K. H. (1996). 'The burial ground'. *Lindholm Høje. Burial Ground and Village.* Aalborg: Aalborg Historical Society and Aalborg Historical Museum, 27–38.

Nijboer, A. J. and Van Reekum, J. E. (1999). 'Scientific analysis of the gold disc-on-bow brooch', in Besteman *et al.* (eds.): 203–16.

Noble, G. (2006). 'Harnessing the waves: monuments and ceremonial complexes in Orkney and beyond'. *Journal of Maritime Archaeology* 1: 100–17.

——Poller, T., Raven, J., and Verrill, L. (eds.) (2008). *Scottish Odysseys; the archaeology of islands*. Stroud: Tempus.

Northover, J. P. (1982). 'The exploration of the long-distance movement of bronze in Bronze and Early Iron Age Europe'. *Bulletin of the University of London Institute of Archaeology* 19: 45–72.

O'Connor, B. (1980). *Cross-Channel relations in the later Bronze Age; relations between Britain, North-Eastern France and the Low Countries during the later Bronze Age and the Early Iron Age, with particular reference to the metalwok.* Oxford: BAR (British Series 91).

O'Connor, T. P. (1988). 'Bones from the General Accident Site, Tanner Row'. *Archaeology of York* 15/2: 61–136.

Oosting, R. and Van den Akker, J. (eds.) (2008). *Boomstamkano's, overnaadse schepen en tuigage. Inleidingen gehouden tijdens het tiende Glavimans Symposion, Lelystad, 20 april 2006.* Amersfoort: Stichting Glavimans Symposion.

Olsen, O. and Crumlin-Pedersen, O. (1958). 'The Skuldelev Ships'. *Acta Archaeologica* 29: 161–75.

——, ——, (1968). 'The Skuldelev Ships (II)'. *Acta Archaeologica* 38: 73–174.

——Skamby Madsen, J. and Rieck, F. (eds.) (1995). *Shipshape. Essays for Ole Crumlin-Pedersen.* Roskilde: Viking Ship Museum.

Ormeling, F. (2000). 'Sea name categories and their implications', in *Proceedings of the 6th International seminar on the naming of seas: special emphasis concerning the 'East Sea'/Special Session II 29th International Geographical Congress: Geography and Place Names: Political Geography of Sea Names.* East Sea Society, Seoul: 22–32.

Osborne, R. (2004). 'Hoards, votives, offerings; the archaeology of the dedicated object'. *World Archaeology* 36: 1–10.

Österholm, S. (2002). 'Boats in prehistory—report on an archaeological experiment. In. G. Burenhult (ed.) *Remote sensing Vol II; archaeological investigations, remote sensing case studies and osteo-anthropological studies.* Stockholm: Stockholm University theses and papers in North-West European archaeology 13b: 323–42.

O'Sullivan, A. (2001). *Foragers, farmers and fishers in a coastal landscape; an intertidal archaeological survey of the Shannon Estuary.* Dublin: Royal Irish Academy.

——and Breen, C. (2007). *Maritime Ireland; an archaeology of coastal communities.* Stroud: Tempus.

Owen, O. and Dalland, M. (1999). *Scar. A Viking boat burial on Sanday, Orkney.* Edinburgh: Tuckwell Press.

Parfitt, K. (2004). 'Discovery and excavation', in Clark (ed.) (2004a): 9–22. London: English Heritage.

Parker Pearson, M. (1999). *The archaeology of death and burial.* Stroud: Sutton.

——(2000). 'Ancestors, bones, and stones in Neolithic and Early Bronze Age Britain and Ireland', in Ritchie (ed.): 203–14.

——Cleal, R., Marshall, P., Needham, S., Pollard, J., Richards, C., Ruggles, C., Sheridan, A., Thomas, J., Tilley, C., Welham, K., Chamberlain, A., Chenery, C., Evans, J., Knüsel, C., Linford, N., Martin, L., Montgomery, J., Payne, A., and Richards, M. (2007). 'The age of Stonehenge'. *Antiquity* 81: 617–39.

Parker Pearson, M., Van de Noort, R., and Woolf, A. (1993). 'Three men and a boat: Sutton Hoo and the Saxon kingdom'. *Anglo-Saxon England* 22: 27–50.

Pare, C. (2000). 'Bronze and the Bronze Age', in C. Pare (ed.) *Metals make the world go round; the supply and circulation of metals in Bronze Age Europe. Proceedings of a conference held at the University of Birmingham in June 1997.* Oxford: Oxbow: 1–38.

Peacock, D. P. S. (1975). 'Amphorae and the Baetican Fish Industry'. *Antiquaries Journal* 54: 232–4.

Pedersen, L. (1995). '7000 years of fishing: stationary fishing structures in the Mesolithic and afterwards', in Fisher (ed.): 75–86.

Peeters, J. H. M. (2007). *Hoge Vaart-A27 in context; towards a model of Mesolithic-Neolithic land use dynamics as a framework for archaeological heritage management.* Amersfoort: Rijksdienst voor Archeologie, Cultuurlandschap en Monumenten.

——(2009). 'Early Holocene landscape dynamics and forager land use diversity: the example of Hoge Vaart-A27 (Almere, The Netherlands)', in S. McCartan, R. Schulting, G. Warren, and P. Woodman (eds.) *Mesolithic horizons; papers presented at the Seventh International Conference on the Mesolithic in Europe, Belfast 2005.* Oxford: Oxbow, 269–76.

——Makaske, B., Mulder, J., Otte-Klomp, A., Van Smeerdijk, D, Smit, S., and Spek, T. (2002). 'Elements for archaeological heritage management: exploring the archaeological potential of drowned Mesolithic and Early Neolithic landscapes in Zuidelijk Flevoland'. *BROB* 45: 81–123.

——Hogestijn, W-J., and Holleman, T. (2004). *De Swifterbant-cultuur. Een nieuwe kijk op de aanloop naar voedselproductie.* Abcoude: Uniepers.

——Murphy, P., and Flemming, N. (eds.) *North Sea Prehistory Research and Management Framework (NSPRMF) 2009.* Amersfoort: Rijksdienst voor het Cultureel Erfgoed and London: English Heritage.

Petersen, H. C. (1986). *Skin boats of Greenland.* Roskilde: Viking Ship Museum.

Pétrequin, P., Errera, M., Pétrequin, A-M., and Allard, P. (2006). 'The Neolithic quarries of Mont Viso, Piedmont, Italy: initial radiocarbon dates'. *European Journal of Archaeology* 9: 7–30.

Petrie, G. (1862). 'Notice of a barrow at Huntiscarth in the parish of Harray, Orkney, recently opened'. *PSAS* 3: 201–19.

Phillips, T. (2003). 'Seascapes and landscapes in Orkney and northern Scotland'. *World Archaeology* 35: 371–84.

Plini the Elder. *Natural history.* trans. H. Rackham (1940–63). London: Heinemann and Cambridge (MA): Harvard University Press.

Praeg, D. (2003). 'Seismic imaging of Mid-Pleistocene tunnel-valleys in the North Sea Basin'. *Journal of Applied Geophysics* 53: 273–98.

Praeger, R. L. (1942). 'The Broighter gold ornaments'. *Journal of the Royal Society of Antiquaries of Ireland* 72: 29–32.

Price, T. D., Grupe, G., and Schröter, P. (1998). 'Migration in the Bell Beaker period of central Europe'. *Antiquity* 72: 405–11.

——Knipper, C., Grupe, G., and Smrcka, V. (2004). 'Strontium isotopes and prehistoric human migration: the Bell Beaker period in central Europe'. *European Journal of Archaeology* 7: 9–40.

——and Gebauer, A. B. (2005). *Smakkerup Huse; a late Mesolithic coastal site in Northwest Zealand*, Denmark. Aarhus: Aarhus University Press.

Poetic Edda. trans. H. A. Bellows (1936). Princeton: University of Princeton.

Post, K. (2000). 'Everzwijnjagers?'. *Cranium* 17: 13–14.

Poulson, G. (1840). The history of the Seigniory of Holderness, volume 1. Hull.

Prøsch-Danielsen, L. and Høgestøl, M. (1995). 'A coastal Ahrensburgian site found at Galta, Rennedsøy, Southwest Norway', in Fisher (ed.): 123–9.

Prynne, M. W. (1968). 'Henry V's Grace Dieu'. *Mariner's Mirror*, 54, 2.

Pryor, F. (ed.) (2001). *The Flag Fen Basin; archaeology and environment of a Fenland landscape*. Swindon: English Heritage.

——(2004). 'Some thoughts on boats as Bronze Age artefacts', in Clark (ed.) (2004b): 31–4.

Raemaekers, D. C. M. (1999). *The articulation of a 'new Neolithic'; the meaning of the Swifterbant culture for the process of neolithisation in the western part of the North European plain (4900–3400 BC)*. Leiden: University of Leiden (Archaeological Studies Leiden University 3).

Pullen-Appleby, J. (2005). *English sea power c. 871–1100*. Hockwold-cum-Wilton: Anglo-Saxon Books.

Rainbird, P. (2007). *The archaeology of islands*. Cambridge: Cambridge University Press.

Randsborg, K. (1995). *Hjortspring; warfare and sacrifice in early Europe*. Aarhus: Aarhus University Press.

Ransley, J. (2005). 'Boats are for boys; queering maritime archaeology'. *World Archaeology* 37: 621–9.

Reid, C. (1913). *Submerged forests*. Oxford: Cambridge Series of Manuals of Literature and Science.

Reilly, M. S. (1985). 'Mortality from occupational accidents to United Kingdom fishermen 1961–80'. *British Journal of Industrial Medicine* 42: 806–14.

Reinbacher, E. (1956). 'Eine vorgeschichtliche Hirschmaske aus Berlin-Biesdorf'. *Ausgrabungen und Funde* 1, 147–51.

Renfrew, A. C. (1973). 'Social organisation in Neolithic Wessex', in A. C. Renfrew (ed.) *The explanation of cultural change; models in prehistory*. London: Duckworth.

——(2000). 'The auld hoose spaeks: society and life in Stone Age Orkney', in Ritchie (ed.): 1–20.

Richards, M. P. and Hedges, R. E. M. (1999). 'A Neolithic revolution? New evidence of diet in the British Neolithic'. *Antiquity* 73: 891–7.

——and Schulting, R. J. (2006). 'Against the grain? A response to Milner *et al.* (2004)'. *Antiquity* 80: 444–58.

——Schulting, R. J. and Hedges, R. E. M. (2003). 'Sharp shift in diet at onset of Neolithic'. *Nature* 425: 366.

——Price, T. D., and Koch, E. (2003). 'Mesolithic and Neolithic subsistence in Denmark: new stable isotope data'. *Current Anthropology* 4: 288–95.

Rieck, F. (1994). *Jernalderkrigernes skibe. Nye og gamle udgravninger i Nydam Mose*. Roskilde: Viking Ship Museum.

——(1995). 'The Nydam excavation 1995'. *Maritime Archaeology Newsletter from Roskilde, Denmark* 5: 21–2.

Rippon, S. (2000). *The transformation of coastal wetlands; exploitation and manage-ment of marshland landscapes in North West Europe during the Roman and medieval periods.* London: British Academy.

——(2009). ' "Uncommonly rich and fertile" or "not very salubrious"? The percep-tion and value of wetland landscapes'. *Landscapes* 10: 39–60.

Ritchie, A. (ed.) (2000). *Neolithic Orkney in its European context.* Cambridge: McDonald Institute for Archaeological Research.

Rival, L. (ed.) (1998). *The social life of trees; anthropological perspectives on tree symbolism.* Oxford: Berg.

Roberts, O. T. P. (2004). 'Reconstruction and performance', in Clark (ed.) (2004a): 189–210.

——(2006). 'Interpretations of prehistoric boat remains'. *IJNA* 35: 72–8.

Robinson, R. (2000). 'The common North Atlantic pool', in D. J. Starkey, C. Reid, and N. Ashcroft (eds.) *England's sea fisheries; the commercial sea fisheries of England and Wales since 1300.* London: Chatham, 9–17.

Rodger, N. A. M. (1997). *The safeguard of the sea; a naval history of Britain 660–1649.* London: W. W. Norton.

Rogers, J. 2009. *How boats change: explaining morphological variation in European watercraft, based on an investigation of Bohemian and Moravian logboats.* PhD thesis, University of Exeter.

Rosenberg, G. (1937). *Hjortspringfundet.* Copenhagen: Nordiske Fortidsminder III, 1.

Rowe, D. J. (1972). 'A trade union of the North-East coast seamen in 1825'. *The Economic History Review, New Series* 25: 81–98.

Rowlands, M. (1980). 'Kinship, alliance and exchange in the European Bronze Age', in J. Barrett and R. Bradley (eds.) *Settlement and society in the British Later Bronze Age.* Oxford: BAR (British Series 83), 15–55.

Rowley-Conwy, P. (2004). 'How the west was lost. A reconsideration of agricultural origins in Britain, Ireland, and Southern Scandinavia'. *Current Archaeology* 45: 83–113.

Roymans, N. (1991). 'Late Urnfield societies in the Northwest European Plain and the expanding networks of Central European Hallstatt Groups', in Roymans and Theuws (eds.): 9–89.

—— and Theuws, F. (eds.) (1991). *Images of the past; studies on ancient societies in northwestern Europe.* Amsterdam: Instituut voor Prea- and Protohistory.

Rule, M. (1994). 'A Gallo-Roman trading vessel from Guernsey: the excavation and recovery of a third century shipwreck'. *IJNA* 23: 63–72.

—— and Monaghan, J. (1993). *A Gallo-Roman trading vessel from Guernsey.* Guernsey Museum (Monographs 5).

Samson, A. V. N. (2006). 'Off-shore finds from the Bronze Age in North-Western Europe: the shipwreck scenario revisited'. *Oxford Journal of Archaeology* 25: 371–88.

Sauer, A. (2003). 'Segeln mit einem Rahsegel', in Hoffmann and Schnall (eds.): 18–33.

Scarre, C. (2002). 'A pattern of islands: the Neolithic monuments of North-West Brittany'. *European Journal of Archaeology* 5: 24–41.

Schmitt, L. (1995). 'The west Swedish Hensbacka: a maritime adaptation and a seasonal expression of the North-Central European Ahrensburgian?', in Fisher (ed.): 161–70.

Schönbäck, B. (1983). 'The custom of burial in boats', in Lamm and Nordström (eds.): 123–32.

Schoneveld, J. and Zijlstra, J. (1999). 'The Wijnaldum brooch', in Besteman *et al.* (eds.): 191–202.

Schuldt, E. (1961). 'Hohen Viecheln; ein mittelsteinzeitlicher Wohnplatz in Mecklenburg'. *Deutsche Akademie der Wissenschaften zu Berlin, Sektion für Vor- und Frühgeschichte*, Band 10.

Schulting, R. J. and Richards, M. P. (2002). 'The wet, the wild and the domesticated: the Mesolithic-Neolithic transition on the west coast of Scotland'. *European Journal of Archaeology* 5: 147–89.

Sha, L. P. (1989). 'Sand transport patterns in the ebb-tidal delta off Texel inlet, Wadden Sea, The Netherlands'. *Marine Geology* 86: 137–54.

Sharp, N. (2002). *Saltwater People.* Crows Nest: Allan and Unwin.

Sharples, N. and Parker Pearson, M. (1997). 'Why were brochs built? Recent studies in the Iron Age of Atlantic Scotland', in A. Gwilt and C. Haselgrove (eds.) *Reconstructing Iron Age societies.* Oxford: Oxbow, 254–65.

Sheldrick, C., Lowe, J. J., and Reynier, M. J. (1997). 'Palaeolithic barbed point from Gransmoor, East Yorkshire, England'. *PPS* 63: 359–70.

Shennan, I., Lambeck, K., Horton, B. P., Innes, J., Lloyd, J., McArthur, J., and Rutherford, M. (2000a). 'Holocene isostacy and relative sea-level on the east coast of England', in Shennan and Andrews (eds.): 275–98.

——, ——, Flather, R., Horton, B. P., McArthur, J., Innes, J., Lloyd, J., Rutherford, M., and Kingfield, R. (2000b). 'Modelling western North Sea palaeogeographies and tidal changes during the Holocene', in Shennan and Andrews (eds.): 299–319.

——and Andrews, J. E. (eds.) (2000). *Holocene land-ocean interaction and environmental change around the western North Sea.* London: Geological Society (Special Publication 166).

——and Horton, B. (2002). 'Holocene land- and sea-level changes in Great Britain'. *Journal of Quaternary Science* 17: 511–26.

Shennan, S. J. (1976). 'Bell Beakers and their context in central Europe', in Lanting and Van der Waals (eds.): 231–9.

——(1982). 'Ideology, change and the European Early Bronze Age', in I. Hodder (ed.) *Symbolic and structural archaeology.* Cambridge: Cambridge University Press, 155–61.

——(1986). 'Interaction and change in the third millennium BC western and central Europe', in C. Renfrew and J. F. Cherry (eds.) *Peer polity interaction and socio-political change.* Cambridge: Cambridge University Press, 137–48.

——(1993). 'Settlement and social change in central Europe, 3500–1500 BC'. *Journal of World Prehistory* 7: 121–61.

Sheppard, J. A. (1958). *The drainage of the Hull valley.* York: East Yorkshire Local History Society.

——(1966). *The draining of the marshlands of South Holderness and the Vale of York.* PhD thesis, University of Hull.

Sheridan, A. (2003). 'Ireland's earliest "passage tombs": A French connection?', in G. Burenhult and S. Westergaard (eds.) *Stones and bones; formal disposal of the dead in Atlantic Europe during the Mesolithic–Neolithic interface 6000–3000 BC; archaeological conference in honour of the late Professor Michael J. O'Kelly.* Oxford: BAR (International Series 1201), 9–25.

Shetelig, H. and Johannessen, F. (1929). *Kvalsundfundet og andre norske myrfund av fartøyer.* Bergen: Bergen Museum.

Simpson, I. A., Perdikaris, S., Cook, G., Campbell, J. L., and Teesdale, W. J. (2000). 'Cultural sediment analyses and transitions in early fishing activity at Langenesværet, Vesterålen, northern Norway'. *Geoarchaeology* 15: 743–63.

Skaarup, J. (1995). 'Stone-age burials in boats', in Crumlin-Pedersen and Thye (eds.): 51–8.

Skoglund, P. (2008). 'Stone ships: continuity and change in Scandinavian prehistory'. *World Archaeology* 40: 390–406.

Slager, K. and De Schipper, P. (1990). *Vissers verhalen; over hun leven in de delta.* Goes: De Koperen Tuin.

Slicher van Bath, B. H. (1965). 'The economic and social conditions in the Frisian districts from 900 to 1500'. *A. A. G. Bijdragen* 13: 97–133.

Small, A. (1966). 'Excavations at Underhoull, Unst, Shetland'. *PSAS* 98: 225–48.

Smart, D. J. (2003). *Later Mesolithic fishing strategies and practices in Denmark.* Oxford: BAR (International Series 119).

Smith, R. (1911). 'Lake-dwellings in Holderness, Yorkshire'. *Archaeologia* 62: 593–610.

Smits, L. and Louwe Kooijmans, L. (2006). 'Graves and human remains', in Louwe Kooijmans and Jongste (eds.): 91–112.

——and Van der Plicht, H. (2009). 'Mesolithic and Neolithic human remains in the Netherlands: physical anthropological and stable isotope investigations'. *Journal of Archaeology in the Low Countries* 1: 55–85.

Sobecki, S. I. (2008). *The sea and medieval English literature.* Rochester: Boydell and Brewer.

Soffer, O. (2004). 'Recovering perishable technologies through use wear on tools; preliminary evidence for Upper Paleolithic weaving and net making'. *Current Anthropology* 45: 407–12.

Sørensen, A. C. (2001). *Ladby; a Danish ship-grave from the Viking age.* Roskilde: Viking Ship Museum (Ships and Boats of the North Vol. 3).

Stead, I. (1991). *Iron Age cemeteries in East Yorkshire.* London: English Heritage.

Steenhuisen, S. and Fontijn, D. (2006). 'Towards familiar landscapes? On the nature and origin of Middle Bronze Age landscapes in the Netherlands'. *PPS* 72: 289–318.

Steinberg, P. (2001). *The social construction of the ocean.* Cambridge: Cambridge University Press.

Stewart, S. A. and Allen, P. J. (2002). 'A 20-km-diameter multi-ringed impact structure in the North Sea'. *Nature* 418: 520–3.

Stocker, D. and Everson, P. (2003). 'The straight and narrow way: Fenland causeways and the conversion of the landscape in the Witham valley, Lincolnshire', in M. Carver (ed.) *The cross goes north: processes of conversion in Northern Europe AD 300–1300.* York: Woodbridge Medieval Press, 271–88.

Storm, T. (1888). *Der Schimmelreiter.* Berlin: Paetel.

Strabo. *Geography.* trans. H. L. Jones (1924). London: Loeb Classical Library.

Strassburg, J. (2000). *Shamanic shadows; one hundred generations of undead subversion in southern Scandinavia 7000–4000 BC.* Stockholm: University of Stockholm (Stockholm studies in archaeology 20).

Street, M. (1991). 'Bedburg Königshoven. A Pre-Boreal Mesolithic site in the Lower Rhineland, Germany', in Barton, Roberts, and Roe (eds.): 256–70.

Strömberg, M. (1961). *Die bronzezeitlichen Schiffsetzungen im Norden.* Lund: Meddelanden.

Stuiver, M. and Reimer, P. J. (1986). 'A computer program for radiocarbon age calculations'. *Radiocarbon* 28: 1022–30.

Sturt, F. (2006). 'Local knowledge is required: a rhythmanalytical approach to the late Mesolithic and early Neolithic of the East Anglian Fenland, UK'. *Journal of Maritime Archaeology* 1: 119–39.

Tajfel, H. and Turner, J. (1979). 'An integrative theory of intergroup conflict'. in G. W. Austin and S. Worchel (eds.) *The social psychology of intergroup relations.* Wadsworth: Monterey, 33–47.

Taylor-Wilson, R. and Kendall, M. (eds.) (2002). *Excavations at Hunt's House, Guy's Hospital, London Borough of Southwark.* London: Pre-Construct Archaeology Ltd (Monograph 1).

Tauber, H. 1981. ^{13}C evidence for dietary habits of prehistoric man in Denmark'. *Nature* 292: 332–5.

TeBrake, W. H. (2002). 'Taming the waterwolf; hydraulic engineering and water management in the Netherlands during the Middle Ages'. *Technology and Culture* 43: 475–99.

Thomas, J. (1991). *Rethinking the Neolithic.* Cambridge: Cambridge University Press.

——(1999) *Understanding the Neolithic.* London: Routledge.

——(2003). 'Thoughts on the "repacked" Neolithic revolution'. *Antiquity* 77: 67–74.

Thorvildsen, K. (1957). 'Ladby-skibet'. *Nordiske Fortidsminder* VI, 1.

Thrift, N. (2007). *Non-representational theory; space, politics, affect.* London: Taylor and Francis.

Tilley, C. (1994). *A phenomenology of landscape.* Oxford: Berg.

——(2004). *The materiality of stone; explorations in landscape phenomenology.* Oxford: Berg.

Treherne, P. (1999). 'The warrior's beauty: the masculine body and self-identity in Bronze Age Europe'. *Journal of European Archaeology* 3: 105–44.

Tringham, R. (1995). 'Archaeological houses, households, housework and the home', in D. N. Benjamin, D. Stea, and D. Saile (eds) *The home; words, interpretations, meanings, and environments.* Aldershot: Avebury, 79–107.

Tromnau, G. (1987). 'Late Palaeolithic reindeer-hunting and the use of boats', in J. M. Burdukiewicz and M. Kobusiewicz (eds.) *Late Glacial in Central Europe; culture and environment.* Wroclaw: Zaklad Norodowy im. Ossolínskich-Wydawnictwo, 94–104.

Turner, V. (1994). 'The Mail stone: an incised Pictish figure from Mail, Cunningsburgh, Shetland'. *PSAS* 124: 315–25.

Turrell, W. R. (1992). 'New hypotheses concerning the circulation of the northern North Sea and its relation to North Sea fish stock recruitment'. *Journal of Maritime Science* 49: 107–23.

Tys, D. (1997). 'Landscape and settlement: the development of a medieval village along the Flemish coast', in G. de Boe and F. Verhaughe (eds.) *Rural settlement in medieval Europe.* Zellik: I. A. P Rapporten 6, 157–67.

Ulmschneider, K. (2000). 'Settlement, economy and the 'productive' site: middle Anglo-Saxon Lincolnshire AD 650–780'. *Medieval Archaeology* 44: 53–79.

Valentin, H. (1957). 'Glazialmorphologische Untersuchungen in Ostengland', *Abhandlungen der Geographische Institut der Freien Universität Berlin* 4: 1–86.

Van de Meene, J. W. H. (1994). *The shoreface-connected ridges along the central Dutch coast*. Utrecht: Rijksuniversiteit Utrecht (Nederlandse Geographische Studies 174).

Van de Moortel, A. (2009). 'The Utrecht Ship type; an expanded logboat tradition in its historical context', in R. Bockius (ed.) *Between the seas; transfer and exchange in nautical technology*. Mainz: RGZM, 329–36.

Van den Broeke, P. W. (1985). 'Oud zout; prehistorische winning en handel'. *Natuur en techniek*, 53, 410–25.

——and Van Londen, H. (1995). *5000 jaar wonen op veen en klei; archeologisch onderzoek in het reconstructiegebied Midden-Delfland*. Utrecht: Dienst Landinrichting en Beheer Landbouwgronden.

Van de Noort, R. (2003). 'An ancient seascape: the social context of seafaring in the Early Bronze Age'. *World Archaeology* 35: 404–15.

——(2004a). *The Humber wetlands; the archaeology of a dynamic landscape*. Bollington: Windgather Press.

——(2004b). 'The Humber, its sewn-plank boats, their context and the significance of it all', in Clark (ed.) (2004b): 90–8.

——(2006). 'Argonauts of the North Sea—a social maritime archaeology for the 2nd Millennium BC.' *PPS* 72: 267–88.

——(2009). 'Exploring the ritual of travel in prehistoric Europe; the Bronze Age sewn-plank boats in context', in Clark (ed.): 159–75.

——Middleton, R., Foxon, A., and Bayliss, A. (1999). 'The "Kilnsea-boat", and some implications from the discovery of England's oldest plank boat'. *Antiquity* 73, 131–5.

——and O'Sullivan, A. (2006). *Rethinking wetland archaeology*. London: Duckworth.

——, ——, (2007). 'Places, perceptions, boundaries and tasks: rethinking landscapes in wetland archaeology', in Barber *et al.* (eds.): 79–89.

Vander Linden, M. (2004). 'What linked the Bell Beakers in third millennium BC Europe?'. *Antiquity* 81: 343–52.

Van der Vleuten, E. and Disco, C. (2004). 'Water wizards; reshaping wet nature and society'. *History and Technology* 20: 291–309.

Van der Waals, J. D. (1989). 'Excavation of two Beaker domestic sites near Kolhorn: general introduction'. *Palaeohistoria* 31: 44–56.

Van Es, W. A. (1965/6). 'Friesland in Roman Times'. *BROB* 15–16: 37–68.

——(1990). 'Dorestad centred', in Besteman, Bos, and Heidinga (eds.): 151–82.

——Sarfatij, H., and Woltering, P. J. (1988). *Archeologie in Nederland; de rijkdom van het bodemarchief*. Amsterdam: Meulenhoff.

Van Gijn, A. and Bakker, J. A. (2005). 'Hunebedbouwers en steurvissers. Midden-neolithicum B: trechterbekercultuur and Vlaardingen-group', in Louwe Kooijmans *et al.* (eds.): 281–306.

Van Heeringen, R. M. (1995). 'De resultaten van het archeologisch onderzoek van de Zeewse ringwalburgen', in Van Heeringen, Henderikx, and Mars (eds.): 15–39.

——Henderikx, P. A., and Mars, A. (eds.) (1995). *Vroeg-middeleeuwse ringwalburgen in Zeeland*. Goes: De Koperen Tuin, Amersfoort: ROB.

Van Kolfschoten, T. and Van Essen, H. (2004). 'Palaeozoological heritage from the bottom of the North Sea', in Flemming (ed.): 70–80.

Van Neer, W. and Ervynck, A. (2007). 'De zoöarcheologische studie van de ontwikkeling van de exploitatie van de zee: een status quaestionis voor Vlaanderen', in De Kraker and Borger (eds.): 45–54.

Van Wijngaarden-Bakker, L. and Brinkkemper, O. (2005). 'Het veelzijdige boerenbedrijf. De voedselproductie in de metaaltijden', in Louwe Kooijmans *et al.* (eds.): 491–512.

Van Zeist, W. (1974). 'Palaeobotanical studies of settlement sites in the coastal area of the Netherlands'. *Palaeohistoria* 16: 223–371.

Van Zeist, W., Van Hoorn, T. C., Bottema, S., and Woldring, H. (1976). 'An agricultural experiment in the unprotected saltmarsh'. *Palaeohistoria* 18: 111–53.

Veenstra, H. J. (1965). 'Geology of the Dogger Bank area, North Sea'. *Marine Geology* 3, 245–62.

Verhart, L. B. M. (1995). 'Fishing for the Mesolithic; the North Sea: a submerged Mesolithic landscape', in Fisher (ed.): 291–302.

Viveiros de Castro, E. (1998). 'Cosmological deixis and Amerindian perspectivism'. *Journal of the Royal Anthropological Institute* 4: 469–88.

Vos, P. C. (1999). 'The Subatlantic evolution of the coastal area around the Wijnaldum-Tjitsma terp', in Besteman *et al.* (eds.): 33–72.

——and Van Heeringen, R. M. (1997). 'Holocene geology and occupation history of the Province of Zeeland, SW Netherlands'. *Mededelingen Nederlands Instituut voor Toegepaste Geowetenschappen TNO* 59: 5–109.

——and Van Kesteren, W. (2000). 'The long-term evolution of intertidal mudflats in the northern Netherlands during the Holocene: natural and anthropogenic processes'. *Continental Shelf Research* 20: 1687–710.

Waddington, C. (2007). 'Rethinking Mesolithic settlement and a case study from Howick', in Waddington and Pedersen (eds.): 101–13.

——and Pedersen, K. (eds.) (2007). *Mesolithic studies in the North Sea Basin and beyond; proceedings of a conference held at Newcastle in 2003.* Oxford: Oxbow.

——Bailey, G., Bayliss, A., Boomer, I., Milner, N., Pedersen, K., Shiel, R., and Stevenson, T. (2003). 'A Mesolithic settlement site at Howick, Northumberland: a preliminary report'. *Archaeologia Aeliana* 32: 1–12.

Walton, J. K. (1993). *The British seaside: holidays and resorts in the twentieth century.* Manchester: Manchester University Press.

Wamers, E. (1995). 'The symbolic significance of the ship-graves at Haiðaby and Ladby', in Crumlin-Pedersen and Thye (eds.): 149–59.

Warmind, M. L. (1995). 'Ibn Fadlan in the context of his age', in Crumlin-Pedersen and Thye (eds.): 131–8.

Warren, G. (2003). 'An archaeology of the Mesolithic in eastern Scotland: deconstructing culture, constructing identity', in Waddington and Pedersen (eds.): 137–50.

Weale, M. E., Weiss, D. A., Jager, R. F., Bradman N., and Thomas, M. (2002). 'Y-chromosome evidence for Anglo-Saxon mass migration', *Molecular Biology and Evolution* 19: 1008–21.

Weerts, H. J. T., Westerhoff, W. E., Cleveringa, P., Bierkens, M. F. P., Veldkamp, J. G., and Rijsdijk, K. F. (2005). 'Quaternary geological mapping of the lowlands of The Netherlands, a 21st century perspective'. *Quaternary International* 133–4: 159–78.

Welch, A. A., Lund, E., Amiano, P., Dorronsoro, M., Brustad, M., Kumle, M., Rodriguez, M., Lasheras, C., Janzon, L., Jansson, J., Luben, R., Spencer, E. A., Overvad, K., Tjonneland, A., Clavel-Chapelon, F., Linseisen, J., Klipstein-Grobusch, K., Benetou, V., Zavitsanos, X., Tumino, R., Galasso, R., Bueno-De-Mesquita, H. B., Ocke, M. C., Charrondiere, U. R., and Slimani, N. (2002). 'Variability of fish consumption within the 10 European countries participating in the European Investigation into Cancer and Nutrition (EPIC) study'. *Public Health Nutrition* 5: 1273–85.

Weninger, B., Schulting, R., Bradtmöller, M., Clare, L., Colard, M., Edinborough, K., Hilpert, J., Jöris, O., Niekus, M., Rohling, E. J., and Wagner, B. (2008). 'The catastrophic final flooding of Doggerland by the Storegga Slide tsunami'. *Documenta Praehistorica* 35 (Neolithic Studies 15): 1–24.

Westerdahl, C. (1992). 'The maritime cultural landscape'. *IJNA* 21: 5–44.

——(1994). 'Maritime cultures and ship types: brief comments on the significance of maritime archaeology'. *IJNA* 23: 265–70.

——(1995a). 'Traditional zones of transport geography in relation to ship types', in Olsen *et al.* (eds.): 213–30.

——(1995b). 'Society and sail. On symbols as specific social values and ships as catalysts of social units', in Crumlin-Pedersen and Thye (eds.): 41–50.

——(2005). 'Seal on land, elk at sea. Notes on and applications of the ritual landcape at the seaboard'. *IJNA* 34: 2–23.

——(2008). 'Boats apart. Building and equipping an Iron-Age and early-medieval ship in northern Europe'. *INJA* 37: 17–31.

Whatmore, S. (2000). *Hybrid geographies: natures cultures spaces*. London: Sage.

Wheeler, A. (1978). 'Why were there no fish remains at Star Carr?' *JAS* 5: 85–9.

Wickham-Jones, C. (2006). *Between the wind and the water; World Heritage Orkney*. Bollington: Windgather Press.

——(2007). 'Middens in Scottish prehistory: time, space and relativity', in Milner, Craig, and Bailey (eds.): 86–93.

Wiley, J. (2007). *Landscape*. London: Routledge.

Wilson, D. M. (1985). *The Bayeux Tapestry*. London: Thames and Hudson.

Woltering, P. J. (1975). 'Occupation history of Texel, I; the excavations at Den Burgh: preliminary report'. *BROB* 25: 7–36.

——(1979). 'Occupation history of Texel, II; the archaeological survey, preliminary report'. *BROB* 29: 7–114.

——(1996/7). 'Occupation History of Texel, III; the archaeological survey. Palaeogeography and settlement patterns'. *BROB* 42: 209–363.

Wood, I. N. (1990). 'The Channel from the 3rd to the 7th centuries AD', in McGrail (ed.): 93–7.

Wormald, P. (1991a). 'The age of Bede and Aethelbald', in Campbell (ed.): 70–100.

——(1991b). 'The ninth century', in Campbell (ed.): 132–59.

Wright, C. W. and Wright, E. V. (1939). 'Submerged boat at North Ferriby'. *Antiquity*, 13: 349–54.

Wright, E. V. (1990). *The Ferriby boats; seacraft of the Bronze Age*. London: Routledge.

——Hedges, R., Bayliss, A., and Van de Noort, R. (2001). 'New AMS dates for the Ferriby boats; a contribution to the origin of seafaring'. *Antiquity* 75: 726–34.

Wymer, J. (1991). *Mesolithic Britain*. Princes Risborough: Shire.

Yeoman, P. J. (n.d.). *Secrets of Fife's Holy Island; the archaeology of the Isle of May*. Fife.

Zagwijn, W. H. (1986). *Nederland in het Holoceen*. 's-Gravenhage: Geologie van Nederland 1.

Zuther, M., Brockamp, O., and Clauer, N. (2000). 'Composition and origin of clay minerals in Holocene sediments from the south-eastern North Sea'. *Sedimentology* 47: 119–34.

Zvelebil, M. (2003). 'Enculturation of the Mesolithic landscape', in L. Larsson (ed.) *Mesolithic on the move; papers presented at the Sixth International Conference on the Mesolithic in Europe, Stockholm 2000*. Oxford: Oxbow, 65–73.

Zwart, H. (2003). 'Aquaphobia, tulipmania, biophilia: a moral geography of the Dutch landscape'. *Environmental Values* 12: 107–28.

Index

Italic page numbers refer to illustrations.

Index

Printed in Great Britain
by Amazon